TRIBES OF CALIFORNIA

Frontispiece. Klamath River Lodge and Sweat-house. (From a sketch by A. W. Chase.)

STEPHEN POWERS

TRIBES OF CALIFORNIA

With an Introduction and Notes
ROBERT F. HEIZER

UNIVERSITY OF CALIFORNIA PRESS
BERKELEY · LOS ANGELES · LONDON

Reprinted from *Contributions to North American Ethnology*,
Volume III. Department of the Interior, U.S. Geographical and
Geological Survey of the Rocky Mountain Region, J. W. Powell,
in charge (Washington: Government Printing Office, 1877).

UNIVERSITY OF CALIFORNIA PRESS
Berkeley and Los Angeles, California

UNIVERSITY OF CALIFORNIA PRESS, LTD.
London, England

This book is a print-on-demand volume. It is manufactured using toner in place of
ink. Type and images may be less sharp than the same material seen in traditionally
printed University of California Press editions.

The paper used in this publication meets the minimum requirements
of ANSI/NISO Z39.48-1992 (R 1997) (Permanence of Paper).

EDITOR'S INTRODUCTION

Stephen Powers was an unusual man. He was a true adventurer, addicted to what he called "vagabondizing," a writer of some ability, a pioneering anthropologist, newspaper publisher, sheepherder, gold miner, and an expert in the raising of Merino sheep. He was born in Waterford, Ohio, in 1840 and graduated from the University of Michigan in 1863. The Civil War was on, and Powers served as an "army correspondent" for the *Cincinnati Commercial* (now *Enquirer*) until the war's end. In 1866 he went to Europe for fifteen months, supporting himself as a correspondent for various newspapers, principally the *New York Times* and *Nation*. Details of his life can be found elsewhere.[1]

On January 1, 1869, Powers started on a walking trip across the United States by the "southern route." He began at Raleigh, North Carolina, "dressed," as he wrote in his brief autobiography,[2] "in a pair of doeskin trousers, light top boots, with the ends of the trousers inserted therein, a shortish frock coat and a planter's hat." He then proceeded to Charleston, Savannah, Macon, Columbus, Montgomery, Selma, Vicksburg, Shreveport, Athens, El Paso, Tucson, and Los Angeles to San Buenaventura where he reached the Pacific Ocean, and "stooping and dipping my hand into the brine, I said: 'The Sunrise to the Sunset Sea, through a weary footman, Greeting." From there he tramped to San Francisco, where he arrived on November 3, 1869. The entire trip was about 3700 miles and took ten months. Powers in his autobiography says of this excursion, "It was not a remarkable feat in any respect, as the only qualities required were health and persistence; at no time did I accomplish over forty miles a day, generally only twenty or twenty-five." In 1872 Powers published the account of his transcontinental tramp in a book called *Afoot and Alone: a Walk from Sea to Sea.*

[1] S. Park, *The Life of Stephen Powers*, Archaeological Research Facility, Contribution No. 28 (University of California, Berkeley, 1975).

[2] S. Powers, *Autobiographical Sketch*, Archaeological Research Facility, Contribution No. 25 (University of California, Berkeley, 1975), pp. 220-221.

Powers next decided to try his hand at a new writing project—one which would also be based upon his own experiences and observations. He selected the California Indians as his subject, and studied them during the summers of 1871 and 1872. "[I] travelled some thousands of miles on foot and horseback among the California Indians during which time I collected a mass of original material and prepared an elaborate account of the habits, customs, legends, geographical boundaries, religious ideas, etc. of the California Indians of which the principal portion I published serially in the *Overland Monthly*, and one chapter in the *Atlantic*, in the years 1872-1875." Actually Powers wrote more than this in the form of articles, and I append a full list of these at the end of this Introduction. (The complete collection of his articles has recently been reprinted in Contribution No. 25 of the Archaeological Research Facility, Department of Anthropology, University of California, Berkeley.) Powers realized about $600.00 for the articles on Indians published in the *Overland Monthly*. No record has survived to inform us of Powers' itinerary and travel schedule. It seems probable, however, that he wrote the articles soon after his visit with each tribe, beginning with the tribes of the Klamath River (Karok, Yurok, and Hupa) moving south into the Coast Range north of San Francisco Bay to visit the Yuki and Pomo, and from there across the Sacramento Valley to study the Miwok. At the time he owned a 160-acre ranch at Sheridan, Placer County, and the Miwok study could have been done as an independent, local investigation during the period when he was not travelling among tribes. Then follow studies of the Modocs, Yokuts, southern Maidu (Nisenan), Achomawi, Yana, Maidu, Wintun and Patwin—a series of tribes whose locations make it clear their descriptions were not written in the same sequence as they were studied. Powers did not make investigations south of the Tehachapi Pass since he believed the cultures of these tribes had become too much altered in the missions to be worth studying.

In 1874 Powers seems to have decided that the main part of his ethnographic researches were completed, and he got in touch with Major J. W. Powell, then in charge of the Department of Interior's Geographical and Geological Survey of the Rocky Mountain Region. Powell, who was much interested in American Indians, agreed that the collection of articles should be brought out in book form.[3] *Tribes of California* was not a mere reprinting of the earlier published articles. The general order of tribal descriptions was preserved as they were originally presented, but a number of additional tribes were described, and there was much rearrangement, rewriting, and adding of information. So it seems that the sketches appearing in the *Overland Monthly* were exactly that, and that Powers' notes contained additional information secured by him in 1871 and 1872.

In 1875 Powers had left California and was living on the family farm in Ohio. Through his contact with Powell, and at Powell's instigation, came an appointment as Special Commissioner "to make a collection of Indian manufactures, etc., illustrative of Indian life, character, and habits on the eastern slope of the Sierras, and also in California, for the Centennial Exhibition of 1876." To perform this duty, Powers returned to the West, remaining from September, 1875, to late January, 1876, visiting new tribes and revisiting familiar ones. Some of the information he secured on this last trip was incorporated into the book.

Powell apparently objected to certain of Powers' theories. One difference of opinion was regarding Powers' suggestion that the California Indians were descendants of Chinese transpacific voyagers who had first settled at Healdsburg and, as they increased in numbers, expanded out in all directions from this seed colony. Powers had proposed and defended this theory in two articles (1874b, 1874h), but the theory does not appear in *Tribes*. A second point of argument was over what Powell felt was an over-estimation of the number of pre-white Native Californians. Powers had first (1872e) estimated the population at 1,520,000. He later (1875) reduced this to 705,000, and despite Powell's urging, refused to lower it further and insisted that it appear in *Tribes*.

It is obvious, I think, that Powers genuinely liked the California Indians he was visiting and studying in the summers of 1871 and 1872, and was aware of their shattering experience of contact with the Americans from Gold Rush times, some twenty years before. But Powers, as a man of a century ago, could scarcely fail to reflect in his writings (which

[3] R. F. Heizer, ed., *Letters of Stephen Powers to John Wesley Powell Concerning 'Tribes of California,'* Archaeological Research Facility, Contribution No. 28 (University of California, Berkeley, 1975).

we must not forget were directed toward a body of contemporary readers) the low opinion which Americans generally held about all Indians. Powers was no brave champion of the injustices done to the Native Californians. He recognized these injustices, accepted them as facts, deplored them, but made no real attempt to generate corrective measures in his writings. The appeal for federal attention to aid the neglected California Indians came at this time with the Ames[4] and Wetmore reports.[5] Powers apparently saw his job as that of a reporter and not a reformer. And, if Powers often observed the unpleasant realities of Indian life and commented unfavorably on the character of the people themselves, let us remember that these were the broken, dispirited and decimated survivors of a series of independent tribal nations which, until more than two decades before, had never even seen a white man. By 1870, from fifty to seventy thousand Indians were blown away by the well-armed Americans and by starvation and disease. Even the will to live had been destroyed, and this we must remember when we read Powers.

The anthropological value of Powers' century-old observations of the Indian cultures of the northern two-thirds of California is substantial. Powers (perhaps with some help from Powell) drew up the first general linguistic classification for California. It is crude, partly because Powers was not a trained linguist, and partly because he employed the simple method of comparing word lists to decide whether or not two languages were related. But it represented a beginning.

Alexander S. Taylor made the first attempt at drawing up a map showing the locations of Indian tribes in California,[6] but he merely wrote the tribal name in the general area of occupancy—there are no territorial boundaries indicated. Powers' map shows tribal boundaries, which he learned from native informants. The original is a large folded map

[4] J. G. Ames, *Mission Indians of Southern California*, 43rd Congress, 1st Session, Executive Document No. 91 (Washington, D. C., 1874). Idem, "Report of Special Agent John G. Ames in Regard to the Condition of the Mission Indians of California, with Recommendations," *Report of the Commissioner of Indian Affairs of 1873* (Washington, D. C., 1874), Appendix A, pp. 29-40.

[5] C. A. Wetmore, *A Report of Charles A. Wetmore, Special United States Commissioner on the Mission Indians*, GPO (Washington, D. C., 1875).

[6] R. F. Heizer, "Alexander S. Taylor's Map of California Indian Tribes, 1864," *California Historical Society Quarterly* 20(1941):171-180.

printed in colors, and since it is too difficult, as well as too costly, to reproduce it exactly, an abstract is presented here on page 465.

The definitive one-volume coverage of California Indian cultures is Alfred L. Kroeber's *Handbook of the Indians of California* which was published in 1925, a half-century after Powers' *Tribes of California*. Kroeber, the acknowledged master on the subject, had this to say about Powers in the *Handbook*'s Introduction:

I should not close without expressing my sincere appreciation to my one predecessor in this field, the late Stephen Powers, well known for his classic "Tribes of California," one of the most remarkable documents ever printed by any government. Powers was a journalist by profession, and it is true that his ethnology is often the crudest . . . . He possessed . . . an astoundingly quick and vivid sympathy, a power of observation as keen as it was untrained, and an invariably spirited gift of portrayal that rises at times into the realm of the sheerly fascinating. Anthropologically his great service lies in the fact that with all the looseness of his data and method he was able to a greater degree than anyone before or after him to seize and fix the salient qualities of the mentality of the people he described. The ethnologist may therefore by turns writhe and smile as he fingers Powers' pages, but for its values with all their highlights and shadows, he can still do no better than consult the book. With all its flimsy texture and slovenly edges, it will always remain the best introduction to the subject.

Beyond writing this brief Introduction and redrawing Powers' map, I have provided annotations to certain passages in the book. Usually these are corrections or clarifications, and I have tried to keep them as brief and few as possible. The annotations may be found at the end of the text, and they are keyed to the numbers appearing in the outer margin of the book pages. The original illustrations have been condensed into one section at the beginning of the text, and the figure numbers appear in the margins adjacent to the text references.

Annotating this reprint of Powers' book was done at the suggestion of August Frugé, Director of the University of California Press. I thank him for asking me to do this happy task. My own teacher, Alfred Kroeber, would approve of this reprinting, but if he had done the annotations I am certain they would have been far better than mine.

Robert F. Heizer
July 13, 1975

1872a "The Northern California Indians, No. I [the Karok]," *Overland Monthly* 8:325-333.

1872b "The Northern California Indians, No. II [the Karok]," *Overland Monthly* 8:425-435.

1872c "The Northern California Indians, No. III [the Yurok]," *Overland Monthly* 8:531-539.

1872d "The Northern California Indians, No. IV [the Hupa]," *Overland Monthly* 9:155-164.

1872e "The Northern California Indians, No. V [the Yuki]," *Overland Monthly* 9:303-313.

1872f "The Northern California Indians, No. VI [the Pomo]," *Overland Monthly* 9:499-507.

1873a "The Northern California Indians, No. VII [the Meewocs]," *Overland Monthly* 10:323-333.

1873b "The Northern California Indians, No. VIII: The Modocs," *Overland Monthly* 10:535-545.

1873c "The California Indians, No. IX: The Yocuts," *Overland Monthly* 11: 105-116.

1874a "The California Indians, No. X: The Neeshenams," *Overland Monthly* 12:21-31.

1874b "Aborigines of California; an Indo-Chinese Study," *Atlantic Monthly* 33: 313-323.

1874c "A Pony Ride on Pit River," *Overland Monthly* 13:342-351.

1874d "The California Indians, No. XI: Various Tribes [Achumawi, Yana, Sierra Maidu]," *Overland Monthly* 12:412-424.

1874e "The California Indians, No. XII: The Wintoons," *Overland Monthly* 12: 530-540.

1874f "The California Indians, No. XIII: The Patweens," *Overland Monthly* 13: 542-551.

1874g "Aboriginal Botany," *Proceedings of the California Academy of Sciences* 5:373-379.

1874h "The California Aborigines," *Proceedings of the California Academy of Sciences* 5:392-396.

1875 "Californian Indian Characteristics," *Overland Monthly* 14:297-309.

1877a "Centennial Mission to the Indians of Western Nevada and California," *Annual Report of the Smithsonian Institution for 1876:* 449-460.

1877b *Tribes of California*, Contributions of North American Ethnology, Vol. III (Washington, D.C.: United States Department of the Interior, U.S. Geographical and Geological Survey of the Rocky Mountain Region.)

1970 "The Life and Culture of the Washo and Paiutes [in 1875]," D. D. Fowler and C. S. Fowler, eds., *Ethnohistory* 17:117-149

Figure 2. Yu-rok Woman. Figure 3. Yu-rok Woman.

Figure 4. Wooden figure of Victory.

Figure 5. Tolowa man and wife, dressed for White Deer Dance.

Figure 6. Hu-pa Woman.

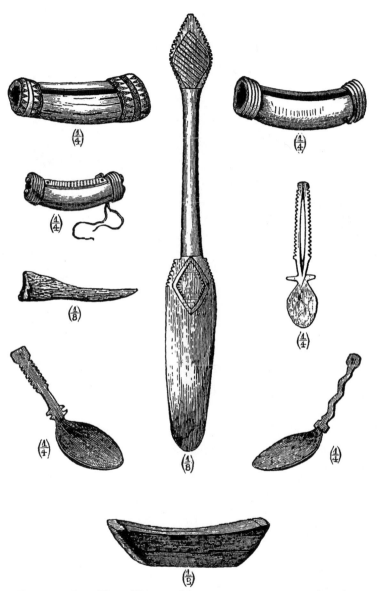

Figure 7. Hu-pa mush-paddle, pillow, and money-purses, spoons and wedge of elkhorn.

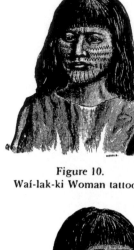

Figure 10.
Waí-lak-ki Woman tattooed.

Figure 11. Yu-ki Tattooing.

Figure 8. Nish-fang.

Figure 12. Huch-nom Tattooing.

Figure 9. Indians at sea.

Figure 13. Huch-nom Tattooing.

Figure 14. Huch-nom Tattooing.

Figure 15. Huch-nom Tattooing.

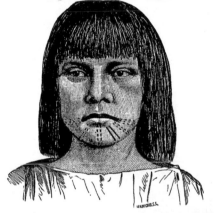

Figure 16. Huch-nom Tattooing.

Figure 17. Huch-nom Tattooing.

Figure 18. Potter Valley Tattooing.

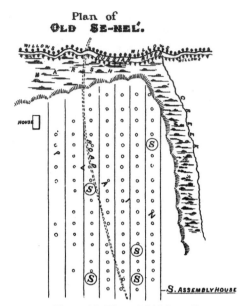

Figure 19. Plan of Old Se-nel'.

Figure 20. Ventura's Lodge.

Figure 21. Earth-lodges of the Sacramento Valley.

Figure 22. Mount Shasta, from the north.

Figure 23. The old Charcoal Artist.

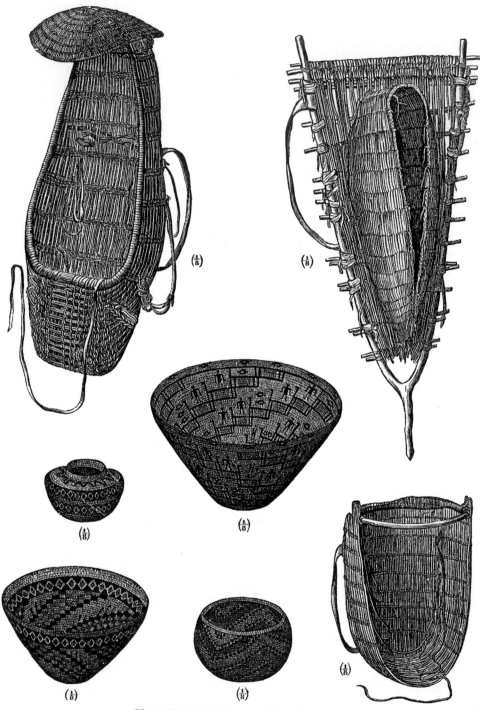

Figure 24. Baby baskets and fancy baskets.

Figure 25. Maí-du Lodge in the high Sierra.

Figure 26. Maí-du Girl, with ornaments. (See page 339.)

Figure 27. Captain John, a Ní-shi-nam Chief.

Figure 28. Captain Tom and wife. (See page 339.)

Figure 29. Captain Tom's Wickiup.

Figure 30. Boy, with ornaments.

Figure 31. Boy, with ornaments.

Figure 32. Acorn granaries.

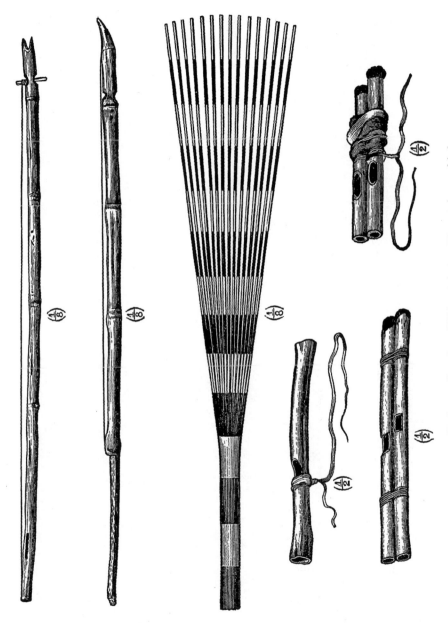

Figure 33. Cornstalk guitars (Yó-kuts), baton (Hu-pa), bone whistles.

Figure 34. A sweat and a cold plunge.

Figure 35. Pu-sí-na-chuk-ha.
(Squirrel and acorn granary).

Figure 36. Cho-ko-nip-o-deh.
(baby-basket).

Figure 37. Yosemite Lodge.

Figure 38. Tis-sé-yak.

Figure 39. Yó-kuts Tule Lodges.

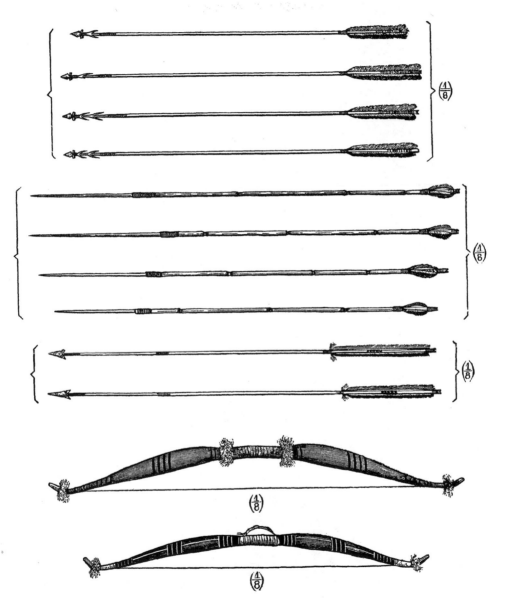

$\left(\frac{4}{8}\right)$

$\left(\frac{4}{8}\right)$

$\left(\frac{4}{8}\right)$

$\left(\frac{4}{8}\right)$

$\left(\frac{4}{8}\right)$

Figure 40. Bows and Arrows.

Figure 41. Baby-basket, acorn-baskets, sifters, &c.

Figure 42. Woman pounding acorns.

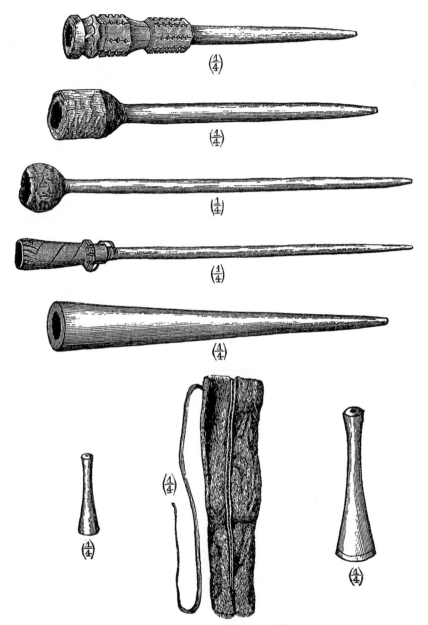

$\left(\frac{4}{4}\right)$

$\left(\frac{4}{4}\right)$

$\left(\frac{4}{4}\right)$

$\left(\frac{4}{4}\right)$

$\left(\frac{4}{4}\right)$

$\left(\frac{4}{4}\right)$

$\left(\frac{4}{4}\right)$

$\left(\frac{4}{4}\right)$

Figure 43. Tobacco pipes and Case.

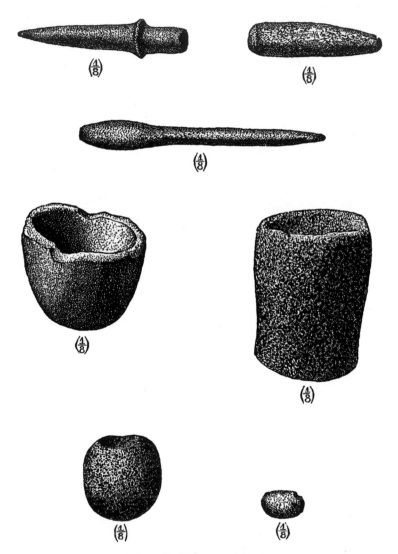

Figure 44. Mortars and Pestles.

Dancing Song of the Karok.

Klamath River.

Hinnowe no-hinno o-hin-no hinnowe o-hin-no nohinno

Hinnowe no-hinno o-hin-no hinnowe o-hin-no nohinno

Konkau Dancing Song.

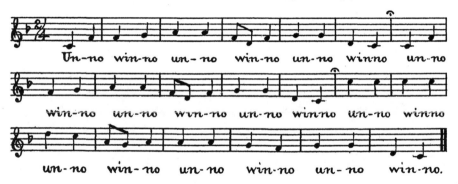

Un-no win-no un-no win-no un-no winno un-no

win-no un-no win-no un-no winno un-no winno

un-no win-no un-no win-no un-no win-no.

Acorn Song (Hūchnōm)

Sung by Ukasuka, a woman.

Ya-a he-le ya-no hi-lo, ya-a he-le ya-no hi-lo,

Ya-a he-le ya-no hi-lo li-mo he-le ya-lo hi-lo

Song of the Hūchnōm

Sung by old Kekhhoal (blind).

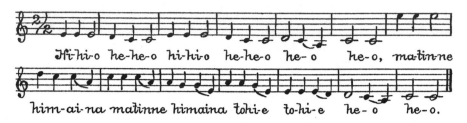

Hi-hi-o he-he-o hi-hi-o he-he-o he-o he-o, matinne

him-ai-na matinne himaina tohi-e to-hi-e he-o he-o.

Religious Song of the Ballo-Kai-Pomo.

Dancing Song of the Ballo-Kai-Pomo.

Potter Valley.

Ho-pil pil-li wela haiyu ha-a-a, hopil pilli wela haiyu ha-a-a.

A-nu-sa a-nu-sa awe killi haiyu hopil pilli wela haiyu ha-a-a.

PREFACE

The word "Pomo" (from *pum, paum, pom,* which signify "earth" in various languages) denotes "earth-people". Though it is the specific name of only one nation on Russian River, it is equally applicable to all the aborigines of California, since they all believe that their first ancestors were created directly from the soil of their respective present dwelling-places.

There are several ideas which the reader who is acquainted only with Atlantic tribes must divest his mind of, in taking up the study of the California Indians. Among them is the idea of the "Great Spirit", for these people are realistic and seek to personify everything; also that of the "Happy Hunting Grounds", for the indolent Californian reared in his balmy clime knows nothing of the fierce joy of the Dakota hunter, but believes in a heaven of Hedonic ease and luxury. The reader must also lay aside the copper-color, the haughty aquiline beak, and the gorgeous, barbaric ornamentation of the person. He must lay aside the gory scalp-lock (for the most part), the torture of the captive at the stake, the red war-paint of terrible import (the Californians used black), the tomahawk, the totem, and the calumet. As the plain and simple "Pomo" is to the more resounding "Algonkin", so is the California aborigine to his Atlantic cousin.

It is a humble and a lowly race which we approach, one of the lowest on earth; but I am greatly mistaken if the history of their lives does not teach more wholesome and salutary lessons—lessons of barbaric providence, plenty, and contentment, of simple pleasures and enjoyments, and of the capacities of unprogressive savagery to fill out the measure of human happiness, and to mass dense populations—than may be learned from the more romantic story of the Algonkins.

Perhaps it is too much to ask any one to believe that there are regions

5

of California which supported more Indians than they ever will of white men. But if those who honor this book with a perusal shall lay it aside with the conviction that the cause of his extinction does *not* "lie within the savage himself", and that the white man does *not* come to "take the place which the savage has practically vacated", I shall be content. Civilization is a great deal better than savagery; but in order to demonstrate that fact it is not necessary to assert, as Wood does in his work, that savagery was accommodatingly destroying itself while yet the white man was afar off. Ranker heresy never was uttered, at least so far as the California Indians are concerned. It is not well to seek to shift upon the shoulders of the Almighty (through the savages whom He made) the burden of the responsibility which attaches to the vices of our own race.

Let it not be thought that this book will attempt to gloze or to conceal anything in the character or conduct of the aborigines. While they had fewer vices than our own race, they committed more frequently the blackest crimes. Revenge, treachery, cruelty, assassination—these are the dark sides of their lives; *but in this category there was nothing ever perpetrated by the California Indians which has not been matched by acts of individual frontiersmen.* As above remarked, the torture of captives was not one of their customs. Infanticide was probably more frequent than among us; and their occasional parricide, done in cold blood, stands perhaps without a parallel.

In order to study their customs I traveled among them the greater part of the summers of 1871 and 1872, and lived many months in sufficient proximity to their villages.

I am indebted to Prof. H. N. Bolander and Mr. R. E. C. Stearns for assistance in the matter of sundry scientific details; and to A. W. Chase, Esq., of the United States Coast Survey, for sketches and photographs.

S. P.

Sheridan, Placer County, California,
August 25, 1874.

TABLE OF CONTENTS

9

CHAPTER XXII.

THE KA-BÍ-NA-PEK.

A Clear Lake tribe—Brave and intelligent—An architectural commission—Lake fish—Language—An interesting query—Sensuality—Sorrow for the dead—Fœticide—Scene of cremation—An Indian revival—An assembling multitude—The proclamation—The dance—Ornaments of the dancers—Indian songs—A midnight spectacle—Infatuation for the dance.

CHAPTER XXIII.

THE MAKH'·EL-CHEL.

An island tribe—Haughty and exclusive—Death to an adulteress—Wigwams, implements, and canoes—Good Indians burned; bad Indians "holed"—A treaty—Medical practices—A story of the lake.

CHAPTER XXIV.

THE PAT-WIN'.

Lack of cohesion—Geographical distribution—Seats of population—Food—Lodges—Chiefship—Clannishness—War—Treatment of children—California Indian physique—Change of skin—Raising the dead—Raising the devil—Widows—Medical art—Bidding the dead adieu—Legends—Origin of Clear Lake—The Great Fire—The Rejos.

CHAPTER XXV.

THE WIN·TUN'.

Characteristics—Distribution of tribes—A metropolitan nation, and a court language—Dress—Fondness for water—Fishing-stations—Manzanita cider—Rotation of foods—Traffic—Puberty dance—Songs—A social race—Scalp dance—Gift dance—Husband and wife—Midwifery—Disposal of the dead—"Spirit-roads"—No religious acts—Trinity Wintūn—Weapons—Specimen of tattooing.

CHAPTER XXVI.

THE SHAS-TÍ-KA.

Difficulty of learning national names—Dominion—Physical aspects—Degenerated—Sweat-ovens—Range of food—Not strictly California Indians—Power of the chief—A treaty with Tolo—Prostitution—Women go to war—Their rights—Old feuds—Strong desire to be buried in native place—Language—Legends—Prehistoric horses.

CHAPTER XXVII.

THE MÓ-DOK.

Origin of name—Habitat—Rugged strength of features—A fierce race—Bloody wars with the settlers—Retaliation—Dealt in slaves—Toughness of vitality—Dwellings stood near water—Dress, canoes, food, fish, etc.—Baby-baskets—Morning chants—Chieftainship—Does civilization improve Indian morals?—Reasons given for polygamy—A new religion—Suicide of Curly-headed Jack—Origin of Modok war—Influence of priests—Their skill and bravery—Lava-bed defenses—Captain Jack—His bad record—Dying speech—John Sconchin—Boston Charley—Why they killed the commissioners—Melancholy history of the Modok—Always a persecuted race, always wronged, and driven to desperation at last.

CHAPTER XXVIII.

THE A-CHO-MÂ'-WI.

Pit River—Physique in Hot Spring Valley—On the South Fork—In Big Valley—Custom of digging pits—Food supply—Position of women—Made slaves of—Social life—One of twins killed—Belief as to spirits of dead—Singular tradition—Legend of creation—Numerals—The Pakamalli.

CHAPTER XXIX.

THE NÓ-ZI, ETC.

A small, fierce, mountain tribe—Their home—Pwiëssy—Aboriginal honesty—Nearly extinct—Tradition of their eastern origin—Mill Creek Indians—A doomed race—Wonderful resistance to civilization—Five Indians against the world—Present home—Summary of customs—Apparently foreign to California—Story of Snowflake.

CHAPTER XXX.

THE MAÍ-DU.

Distribution of tribes—Sites of villages—Guarded against surprise—Hill-stations—Old camps—Description of a village—Daily life—Fowling-snares—Acorn dance—Clover dance—Manzanita dance—Great Spirit dance—Annihilation—Beliefs—An Indian schottish—Legend of the Flood—Wó-lok-ki and Yó-to-wi—The lion and the cat—Legend of Oan-koi'-tu-peh—Sacred songs.

CHAPTER XXXI.

THE NÍ-SHI-NAM.

Classification—Differences in language—Great number of dialects—Boundaries—System of names—Personal names—Villages and geography—Low estate of the tribe—Instances—No payment made for wife—Childless women—Murder of a woman—Nomadic habits—Origin of government—Penalty of crimes—Customs in war—Spears—Collecting debts—Sacrifice of the aged—Indian field-commissary—Captain Sutter's Indians—Not misers—First grass dance—Second grass dance—A gala-day in spring—Spiritualism—Women's dance-house—Medical art—Death scenes—Mourning of widows—Dance for the dead—The "cry"—Story of Captain Tom.

CHAPTER XXXII.

THE NISHINAM—Continued.

Games—Shooting at target—Boys' games—Different kinds of gambling—An athletic game—"Learning the rules"—Jugglery—Shell-money—Wealth of the aborigines—Two kinds of money—Personal ornaments—Mythology—Aí-kutand Yo-tó-to-wi—Origin of incremation—The bear and the deer—Origin of fire—The old man-eater—The road-woman—Insanity—Hermaphrodites.

CHAPTER XXXIII.

THE MÍ-WOK.

A dense aboriginal population—A common language, but no nationality—Greeting—Characteristics—Tribal geography—The Walli—Houses—Food—Shell-money—Chieftainship—Old Sam—Tai-pok'-si—Honeymoons—Kill one of twins—Medicine—Dances—Annual mourning—A legend of the Tu-ol-um-ne—Creation of man—Numerals.

CHAPTER XXXIV.

YOSEMITE.

Meaning of names—Origin of the word—Interpreters—Old Jim—List of names—Translations—Villages in the valley—Legend of Tu-tok-a-nu'-la—Legend of Tis-só-yak—Other legends.

INTRODUCTORY

There is some difficulty in drawing a line sharp between the California Indians and their neighbors. With some exceptions they shade away from tribe to tribe, from valley to valley, so that one can seldom put his finger on a river or a mountain-range and say that here one nation ends and another begins.

There are certain general customs which mark the California Indians, as, for instance the use of the assembly chamber, the non-use of torture on prisoners of war, cremation, and the prevalence of a kind of plutocracy, or if the word is allowable, dorocracy, that is, the rule of the gift-givers. But cremation and the assembly chamber are also used, to a certain extent, by some vicinal tribes that cannot be classed with these; and, on the other hand, cremation is not universal in California.

The term "Digger", vulgarly applied to the race, is opprobious and unjust, equally as much as it would be to designate Chinamen as "Rat-eaters". There are tribes, notably the Apaches, who subsist much more on roots than do the California Indians

Aside from language, the most radical difference between the Californians and the Paiuti or Nevada Indians is, that the latter build their lodges more or less on hill-tops, while the former build theirs near water-courses. As to the Californians and the Siwash, or Oregon Indians, probably the most notable difference is, that the latter have no large assembly chamber proper. Both these points of difference show that the Californians are a more peaceful, effeminate, and sensuous race than their neighbors. They are also more devoted to joyous, social dances and merry-makings.

But the crucial test is that of language. Not only are the California languages distinguished for that affluence of vowel sounds which is more

15

or less characteristic of all tongues spoken in warm climates, but most of them are also remarkable for their special striving after harmony. There are a few languages found in the northern mountains which are harsh and sesquipedalian, and some on the upper coast that are guttural beyond the compass of our American organs of speech; but with these few exceptions the numerous languages of the State are beautiful for their simplicity, the brevity of their words, their melody, and their harmonic sequences.

The Tinné or Athabascan races extend far into California along the coast, reaching to the headwaters of Eel River. The tribes immediately around Humboldt Bay probably do not belong to them, but to the Californians. The former drove the Californians up the Trinity to the mouth of New River. They hold the Smith, the Klamath, Mad, and Eel Rivers entire, except the lower reaches of the last two. They also hold Scott River. Beginning at the head of this river, the line runs across to Mount Shasta; thence to the forks of the Pit; thence up South Fork and down along the Sierra to Honey Lake; thence along the western line of the double crest (the Wá-sho generally hold the summit meadows) to Alpine County. I have not seen the Indians of this county, but they are said to belong to the Paiuti. In Southern California the Paiuti tribes have pushed down King's River and the San Joaquin nearly to the plains, and down the Kern to its mouth, also through Tahichapa Pass, holding nearly the whole Kern Basin. Of the tribes in the Mohave and Colorado Deserts I can say very little.

An accurate distribution of tribes within these limits is a difficult task. In the mountain regions where there are certain natural, well-defined territories, as valleys, etc., there are generally names which may be dignified as tribal; but on the great plains the Indians become scattered and diffused in innumerable little villages or camps, of which it is very seldom the case that even two are bound together by a common name. The chiefs could not hold them together. Hence, on the plains the only useful boundaries are linguistic; and the extent of any given language is generally far greater than in the mountains.

There will be found in these pages no account of the quasi-Christianized Indians of the missions Their aboriginal customs have so faded out, their tribal organizations and languages have become so hopelessly intermingled and confused, that they can no longer be classified. They are known as Diegeños, Migueleños, Rafaeleños, and the like Spanish names, which are formed from the missions to which they respectively belonged; and for purposes of classification it is useless to take down a vocabulary and call it the "San Miguel language", for instance, for the Indians who originally lived there may be all dead, while those who give the vocabulary may be descended from Indians brought by the Spanish missionaries from the San Joaquin Valley, or some other point a hundred miles distant, and which has been forgotten even by the whites.

In this work I have followed the system of orthography recommended in the "Smithsonian Miscellaneous Collections 160", which is substantially the same as the Continental. Occasionally it is found necessary to employ the consonants *ng* to denote the French nasal sound, also the German *umlaut*. *Kh* has the sound of *ch* in the German *Buch*. Indian words are accented and syllabicated the first time they occur; after that they are written solid.

Owing to the great number of dialectic variations in California languages, there is probably not an Indian word in this volume which a person knowing only one dialect could not prove to be wrong.

THE TRIBES OF CALIFORNIA.

BY STEPHEN POWERS.

CHAPTER I.

THE KÁ-ROK.

On the Klamath there live three distinct tribes, called the Yú-rok, Ka'-rok, and Mo'-dok, which names are said to mean, respectively, "down the river", "up the river", and "head of the river". The first two are derived from *yú-ruk, yú-tuk,* meaning "down west", and *ká-ruk,* "up east"; but the third is doubtful. The habitat of the Karok extends from a certain cañon a few miles above Waitspek, along the Klamath, to the foot of Klamath Mountains, and a few miles up Salmon River. They have no recollection of any ancient migration to this region; on the contrary, they have legends of Creation, of the Flood, etc., which are fabled to have occurred on the Klamath.

The Karok are probably the finest tribe in California. Their stature is only a trifle under the American; they have well-sized bodies, erect and strongly knit together, of an almost feminine roundness and smoothness, the legs better developed than the arms; and when a Karok has the weapon to which he is accustomed—a sharp stone gripped in the hand—he will face a white man and give him a handsome fight, though when armed only with a snickersnee or a revolver, in the use of which he does not feel confidence, he flees before him. The Klamath face is a little less broad than that on the Sacramento; in early manhood nearly as oval as the American; cheek-bones large and round-capped, but not too prominent; head brachycephalic;

eyes bright, moderately well sized, and freely opened straight across the face; nose thick-walled and broad, straight as the Grecian, nares ovoid, root not so depressed as in the Sacramento Valley; forehead low and wide, nearly on a perpendicular line with the chin; color ranging from hazel or buff-hazel to old bronze, and almost to black. Many of the young squaws are notable for the fullness of the eyes and the breadth of sclerotic exposed. The women age early, but even at forty or fifty their faces are furrowed with comparatively fine lines, and they very seldom display those odious hanging wrinkles and that simian aspect seen on the Sacramento. All California Indians emit an odor peculiar to themselves, as that of the Chinese or that of the negroes is to them.

With their smooth, hazel skins, nearly oval faces, full and brilliant eyes, some of the young women—barring the tattooed chins—have a piquant and splendid beauty. In those large, voluptuous eyes, so broadly rimmed with white, there is something dangerous, a very unmistakable suggestion of possible *diablerie;* and in truth there are plenty of them every whit as subtle in the arts of coquetry as their white sisters. It is little wonder that so many pioneers, including four county officers and the only editor in Klamath County, have taken them to wives.

The young people of both sexes dress in the American fashion, and I have seen plenty of them appareled in quite correct elegance—the young men in passable broadcloth, spotless shirt-fronts, and neat black cravats; the girls, in chaste, pretty, small-figured stuffs, with sacques, collars, ribboned hats, etc. Some of the young bloods array their Dulcineas for the dance with lavish adornments, hanging on their dresses $30, $40, $50 worth of dimes, quarters, and half-dollars arranged in strings.

The primitive dress of the men is simply a buckskin girdle about the loins; of the women, a chemise of the same material, or of braided grass, reaching from the breast to the knees. The hair is worn in two club-queues, which are pulled forward over the shoulders. The squaws tattoo in blue three narrow fern-leaves perpendicularly on the chin, one falling from each corner of the mouth and one in the middle. For this purpose they are said to employ soot gathered from a stone, and mingled with the juice of a certain plant. In their native state both sexes bathe the entire person every morning in cold water; but in the care of their cabins and the vicinity they are sufficiently filthy.

The Karok is taciturn and indifferent toward, his squaw and parents, but seldom wantonly cruel; easy-going with his children; talkative and merry with his peers; generous to the division of the last crumb; mercenary and smiling to the white man; brave when need is, but cunning always; fond of dancing; extremely curious, inquisitive, and quick to imitate; very amorous; revengeful but avaricious, being always placable with money.

For money they make use of the red scalps of woodpeckers, which rate at $2.50 to $5 apiece; and of the dentalium shell, of which they grind off the tip and string it on strings. The shortest pieces are worth 25 cents, the longest about $2, the value increasing rapidly with the length. The strings are usually about as long as a man's arm. It is called *al'-li-ko-chik* (in Yurok this signifies, literally, "Indian money"), not only on the Klamath, but from Crescent City to Eel River, though the tribes using it speak several different languages. When the Americans first arrived in the country, an Indian would give $40 or $50 gold for a string, but now the abundance of the supply has depreciated its value, and it is principally the old Indians 3 who esteem it.

The Karok are very democratic. They have a headman or captain in each rancheria, though when on the war-path they are in a slight degree subject to the control of one chief. But the authority of all these officers is very slender. The murder of a man's dearest relative may be compounded for by the payment of money, the price of the average Indian's life being *i'-sa pa-só-ra* (one string). If the money is paid without higgling, 4 the slayer and the avenger at once become boon companions. If not, the avenger must have the murderer's blood, and a system of retaliation is initiated which would be without end were it not that it may be arrested any moment by the payment of money.

In war they do not take scalps, but decapitate the slain and bring in the heads as trophies. They do battle with bows and arrows, and in a hand-to-hand encounter, which often occurs, they clutch ragged stones in their hands and maul each other with terrible and deadly effect. They sometimes fight duels with stones in this manner. Though arranged without much formality they are conducted with a considerable degree of fairness, the friends of the respective combatants standing around them and setting them on their pins again when they fall.

There is no process of courtship, but the whole affair of love-making is conducted by the father of the bride and the bridegroom expectant. When a young Philander becomes enamored of some dusky Clorinda, he goes straight to her father, and without any beating of the bush makes him a plump offer of so or so many strings for her. They chaffer and drive bargains, for they are an avaricious race. "My ducats and my daughter", says the old Shylock. A wife is seldom purchased for less than half a string, and when she belongs to an aristocratic family, is pretty, and skillful in making acorn-bread and weaving baskets, she sometimes costs as high as two strings—say $80 or $100. There is no wedding-ceremony, no cake, no wine; but the bride follows her lord to his lodge, and they at once set up their savage Lares and Penates.

No marriage is legal or binding unless preceded by the payment of money, and that family is most aristocratic in which the most money was paid for the wife. For this reason, it stands a young man well in hand to be diligent in accumulating shell-money, and not to be a niggard in bargaining with his father-in-law. So far is this shell-aristocracy carried, that the children of a woman for whom no money was paid are accounted no better than bastards, and the whole family are contemned. Bigamy is not tolerated, even in the chief. A man may own as many women for slaves as he can purchase, but if he cohabits with more than one he brings upon himself obloquy.

Before marriage, virtue is an attribute which can hardly be said to exist in either sex, most of the young women being a common possession; but after marriage, when the dishonor of the woman would involve also that of the husband, they live with tolerable chastity, for savages. Still, no adultery is so flagrant but that the husband can be placated with money, at about the rate that would be paid for murder. Virtue therefore is exceedingly rare as an innate quality, but is simply an enforced condition; and indeed the Karok language, though rich in its vocabulary, is said to possess no equivalent for "virtue".

Notwithstanding this vicious system of intercourse among the young, bastards are universally shunned and despised. They and the children for whose mothers no money was paid—who are illegitimate in fact, according to Karok ideas—constitute a class of social outcasts, Indian Pariahs, who can intermarry only among themselves.

There is an appalling malady which destroys thousands of the civilized, but which was unknown to the Karoks before they became acquainted with white men. Indeed in their simplicity when syphilis first appeared among them they sometimes actually sought it, that they might revenge themselves on their enemies. Their theory of disease is that it is a demoniacal possession; hence they believed that in communicating the contagion to another they would free themselves from it, and the results from this mistake were disastrous in the highest degree.

There prevails in this tribe, as throughout California, a more equitable division of labor than is commonly supposed to have obtained among the Algonkin races. The men build the lodges; kill the game, and generally bring it home; construct the fishing-booths, weirs, and nets; catch the salmon, and generally bring it in and spread it out to dry; cut and bring in all the fuel for the assembly chambers; help to gather acorns, nuts, and berries; make the fish-gigs, bows, and arrows. The women gather and bring in the wood used for secular purposes, that is, for cooking and for heating the common lodges; dig the roots, and carry in most of the vegetable foods; weave their baskets; sometimes bring in and dry the salmon; do all the work of the scullery; make the clothing. It must always be remembered that the men of savage tribes are not obliged to work like the civilized, and everybody knows that when men are at home in a spell of rainy weather, or for some other reason, they do not "help about the house" any more than the Indian does. The Indian woman is eternally puddering about something, because her utensils are so poor; but her husband does nearly as much as the farmer or merchant; that is, he provides the food and brings it home, unless it is some little matter of roots, berries, or the like, and many is the Indian I have seen tending the baby with far more patience and good nature than a civilized father would display. While on a journey the man lays far the greatest burdens on his wife, but in the life at home there is not more in him to complain of than there is in the conduct of thousands of white husbands. Still, the women are regarded as drudges.

The Karok have a conception of a Supreme Being, whom they call Ka-ré-ya. The root of this word is the same as that of "Karok", and probably also Kal'-leh Kal-lé, in the Pomo, signifying "above"; but with the curious accretive capacity of Indian languages, it is expanded to mean "The Old Man Above". Kareya sometimes descends to earth to instruct the prophets or shamans, when he appears as a venerable man clad in a close-fitting tunic, with long white hair flowing down his shoulders, and bearing a medicine-bag. When creating the world, he sat on the Sacred Stool, which is still preserved by the Kareya Indian, and on which he sits on the occasion of the great annual Dance of Propitiation. But as among most tribes in California, the coyote is the most useful and practical deity they have. They also believe in certain spooks or bogeys, which run after people at night in the forest, and leave tracks which when seen in the morning bear a suspicious resemblance to horse-tracks.

The assembly chamber is constructed wholly underground, oblong, about ten by six feet, and high enough for a man to stand in, puncheoned up inside, and covered with a flattish roof level with the earth, and air-tight except for the little hatchway at one side. It is club room, council house, dormitory, sudatory, and medical examination room in one, and is devoted exclusively to masculine occupation. Lafiteau says, among the eastern Indians the man never enters the private wigwam of his wife except under cover of the darkness; but here it is the men's apartment which is *taboo*. No squaw may enter the assembly chamber, on penalty of death, except when undergoing her examination for the degree of M. D. During the rainy season when fires are comfortable, they are kept burning in the assembly chambers day and night; and there are always enough of them in each village to furnish sleeping-room for all the adult males thereof.

In summer the men occupy the common wickiup (this is a word used in California and the Territories, signifying a brushwood booth; it is imported from the Sioux), together with their wives; but in winter they sleep by themselves in the assembly chamber, and I suspect they use the terrors of superstitious interdict to banish the women from them, in order to enjoy the warm and cosy snuggery themselves. But, air tight as they are, and heated perpetually (for once kindled, the fire must not be suffered to go out until spring), the atmosphere in them is simply infernal.

But the Indians are consistent in the matter of the assembly chamber. As they suffer no woman to enter it, so they allow none to gather the wood burned therein. Fuel for the assembly chamber is sacred, and no squaw may touch it. It must be cut green from a standing tree, that tree must be on top of the highest hill overlooking the Klamath, and the branches must be trimmed off in a certain particular manner. The Karok selects a tall and sightly fir or pine, climbs up within about twenty feet of the top, then commences and trims off all the limbs until he reaches the top where he leaves two and a top-knot, resembling a man's head and arms outstretched.

All this time he is weeping and sobbing piteously, shedding real tears, and so he continues to do while he descends, binds the wood in a fagot, takes it upon his back, and goes down to the assembly chamber. While crying and sobbing thus, as he goes along bending under his back load of limbs, no amount of flouting or jeering from a white man will elicit from him anything more than a glance of sorrowful reproach. When asked afterward why he weeps when cutting and bringing in the sacred fuel, if he makes any reply at all, it will be simply, "For luck".

Arrived at the assembly chamber he replenishes the fire making a dense and bitter smudge, while all the occupants lie around with their faces close to the floor to keep themselves from smothering. When they are in a reek of perspiration they clamber up the notched pole at the side, swarming out from the hatchway like rats, and run and heave themselves neck and heels into the river—all "for luck".

The taboo is lifted from the assembly chamber only while a squaw is undergoing the ordeal which admits her to the mysterious realm of therapeutics. This ordeal consists simply in a dance, wherein the woman holding her feet together leaps up and down, and chants in a bald, monotonous sing-song until she falls utterly exhausted. For a man the test is something more rigid. He retires into the forest and remains ten days, partaking of no meat the while, and of just enough acorn-porridge to keep him alive. Then, at the expiration of this rigorous fast, he returns and jumps up and down in the assembly chamber like the woman.

There are two classes of shamans—the root-doctors and the barking doctors—the latter reminding one somewhat of the medieval spagyrics. It is the province of the barking-doctor to diagnose the case, which she (most doctors are women) does by squatting down like a dog on his haunches before the patient, and barking at him like that noble and faithful animal for hours together. After her comes the root-doctor, and with numerous potions, poultices, etc., seeks to medicate the part where the other has discovered the ailment resides. No medicinal simples are of any avail, whatever are their virtues, unless certain powwows and mummeries are performed over them.

It will be perceived that the barking-doctor is the more important functionary of the two. In addition to her diagnostic functions, she takes charge of the "poisoned" cases, which among these superstitious people are very numerous. They believe they frequently fall victims to witches, who cause a snake, frog, lizard, or other noxious reptile to fasten itself to the body and grow through the skin into the viscera. In this case the barking-doctor first discovers, *secundum artem*, in what portion of the body the reptile lurks, then commences sucking the place, and sucks until the skin is broken and blood flows. Then she herself takes an emetic and vomits up a frog or something, which she pretends was drawn from the patient, but which of course she had previously swallowed.

In a case of simple "poisoning", the barking-doctor gives the sufferer an emetic, and causes him to vomit into a small basket. The basket is then covered and held before the patient while he names in succession the various persons whom he suspects of having poisoned him. At each name mentioned the doctor uncovers the basket and looks in. So long as wrong names are mentioned the vomited matter remains; but when the right one is hit upon, presto! it is gone, and when the doctor looks in the basket it is empty.

The Karok hold their medicines personally responsible for the lives of their patients. If one loses a case he must return his fee; more than that, if he receives an offer of a certain sum to attend a person and refuses, and the individual dies, he must pay the relatives from his own substance an amount equivalent to the fee which was tendered him. A shaman who becomes famous is often summoned to go twenty or thirty miles, and receives a proportionately large reward, sometimes a horse, sometimes two, when the invalid is rich.

CHAPTER II.

THE KAROK, CONTINUED.

The first of September brings a red-letter day in the Karok ephemeris, the great Dance of Propitiation, at which all the tribe are present, together with deputations from the Yurok, the Hú-pâ, and others. They call it *sif'-san-di pik-i-á-vish*, (at Happy Camp, *sú-san-ni nik-i-á-vish*), which signifies, literally, "working the earth". The object of it is to propitiate the spirits of the earth and the forest, in order to prevent disastrous landslides, forest fires, earthquakes, drought, and other calamities.

All the villages are then deserted, left unprotected and undefended, for all the women and all the children and the old men must attend the grand anniversary. They come in fleets of canoes up and down the Klamath, or on foot in joyous throngs along the trails beside the river, the squaws bringing in their baskets victuals enough to last their families as long as possible, a fortnight or more. But singular to say, neither on this nor on any other occasion do they have any feasting. Each family partake of their own plain messes, though the greatest generosity prevails, and strangers or persons without families are freely invited to share their simple repasts of dried salmon and acorn-bread or panada.

Some Frenchman has said we have a hundred religions and one gravy. The California Indians have a hundred dances and one acorn-porridge.

In the first place an Indian of a robust frame, able to endure the terrible ordeal of fasting to which he is subjected, goes away into the mountains with an attendant to remain ten days. He is called the Kareya Indian, which may be translated almost literally "God-man"; and their evident belief is that by the keen anguish he undergoes, he propitiates the spirits vicariously in behalf of the whole tribe. During these ten days he partakes of nothing whatever, theoretically, though in case of extreme suffering it is probable that he takes a little acorn-porridge or pinole; but he must abstain from flesh on penalty of death. The attendant is allowed to eat sparingly of acorn-porridge only.

Meantime what is going on in camp? During the long days while they are awaiting the return of the Kareya Indian, the men and squaws amuse themselves with song and lively dance, wherein they join together. Various *Fig. A* games are played; gambling is indulged in. But singing and dancing are the principal amusements, and considerable time is devoted to teaching the boys to dance in imitation of the solemn and momentous ceremonial which is to be observed when the Kareya Indian returns.

Sometimes in a dithyrambic frenzy, men and women mingling together, they wildly leap and dance; now each one chanting a different story, extemporized on the spot in the manner of the Italian *improvisatore*, and yet keeping perfect time, and now all uniting in a chorus. Then again sitting in a solemn circle on the ground, or slowly walking in a ring around the fire, hand joined in hand, while the flames gleam upon their swarthy faces, ripple in the folds of their barbaric paludaments of tasseled deer-skin, and light up their grotesque chaplets and club-queues in nodding shadows, they intone those weird and eldritch chantings, in which blend at once an undertone of infinite pathos and a hoarse, deathly rattle of despair; and which I never yet have learned to listen to without a certain feeling of terror.

And now at last the attendant arrives on the summit of some overlooking mountain, and with warning voice announces the approach of the Kareya Indian. In all haste the people flee in terror, for it is death to behold him. Gaunt and haggard and hollow-eyed, reduced to a perfect skeleton by his terrible sufferings, he staggers feebly into camp, leaning on the shoulder of the attendant, or perhaps borne in the arms of those who have been summoned to bring him in from the mountains; for in such an extreme instance a secular Indian may assist, provided his eyes are bandaged.

Long before he is in sight the people have all disappeared. They take refuge in the deeps of the forest, or enter into their wickiups and cabins, fling themselves down with their faces upon the ground, and cover their eyes with their hands. Some wrap many thicknesses of blankets about their heads. Little children are carefully gathered into the booths, and their faces hidden deep in folds of clothing or blankets, lest they should inadvertently behold that walking skeleton and die the death. All the camp is silent, hushed, and awe-struck as the vicegerent of the great Kareya enters.

Now he approaches the assembly chamber, and is assisted to descend into it. Feeble and trembling with the pangs of hunger, he seats himself upon the sacred stool. Tinder and flint are brought to him. With his last remaining strength he strikes out a spark and nourishes it into a blaze. The sacred smoke arises. As no common creature may look upon the Kareya Indian and live, so also none may behold the sacred smoke with impunity. Let his eyes rest upon it even for one moment, and he is doomed to death. The intercession of the Kareya Indian alone can avert the direful consequences of his inadvertence. If by any mischance one is so unfortunate as to glance at it as it swirls up above the subterranean chamber, seeming to arise out of the ground, he goes down into it, prostrates him before the Kareya Indian sitting on the sacred stool, and proffers him shell-money. The priest demands $20, $30, $40, according to the circumstances. He then lights his pipe, puffs a few whiffs of smoke over the head of the unfortunate man, mumbling certain formularies and incantations, and his transgression is remitted.

After the lapse of a certain time the people return from their hiding-places, and prepare for the last great solemnity—the Dance of Propitiation. They arrange themselves in a long line—the men only, for the women do not participate in this part of the ceremony. They are vestured in all their savage trappings, their jingling beadery, their tasseled robes of peltry, their buckskin bandoleers passing under one shoulder and over the other, and gayly starred with the scarlet scalps of woodpeckers, to the value of $300 or $400 on each. They brandish aloft in their hands their finest bows and arrows, inlaid with sinew and bits of shells, with glinting strings of pink and purple abalones; and if any one can boast of a white or black deer-skin as a trophy of his prowess, he is accounted beloved of the spirits. No Indian can participate in the dance unless he has at least a raccoon's or a deer's head, with the neck stuffed, and the remainder of the skin flowing loose, elevated on a pole within easy eyeshot.

Then two or three singers begin an improvised chant, a kind of invocation to the spirits, and occasionally they all unite in a fixed choral which is meaningless, and repeated over and over *ad libitum.* Both in the recitative where each singer makes an entirely independent invocation, and in the choral, they keep time wonderfully well, and that without beating time. The dancers in the line merely lift and lower one foot, in slow and regular accord. The ceremony continues about two hours, during which profound stillness and decorum prevail among the spectators.

When this dance of religion is ended, all gravity vanishes forthwith; wild and hilarious shouts resound throughout the camp; the gayest dances are resumed, in which both sexes unite, and in the evening there ensues a 11 grossly obscene debauch.

The fire has now been kindled for the rainy season, and once the flame is set going in the several assembly chambers, it must not be suffered to expire during the winter.

In the vernal season, when the winds blow soft from the south, and the salmon begin to run up the Klamath, there is another *dies fastus,* the dance for salmon, of equal moment with the other. They celebrate it to insure a good catch of salmon. The Kareya Indian retires into the mountains and fasts the same length of time as in autumn. On his return the people flee, while he repairs to the river, takes the first salmon of the catch, eats a portion of the same, and with the residue kindles the sacred smoke in the sudatory. No Indian may take a salmon before this dance is held, nor for ten days after it, even if his family are starving.

Before going out on a chase the Karok hunter must abstain three days from touching any woman, else he will miss the quarry. Mr. A. Somes relates an incident which happened to himself when hunting once in company with a venerable Indian. They set out betimes and scoured the mountains with diligence all day, and were like to return home empty-handed, when the old savage declared roundly that the white man was trifling with him, and that he must have touched some woman. No ridicule could shake his belief, so he withdrew a few paces, fell on his knees, turned his face devoutly toward heaven, and prayed fluently and fervently for the space of full twenty minutes. Somes was so much impressed with the old savage's earnestness that he did not disturb him. Although able to speak the language well, he understood nothing the white-haired petitioner uttered.

When he made an end of praying he arose solemnly, saying they would now have success. They started on, and it so fell out that they started up a fine pricket in a few minutes and Somes picked him off, whereupon the old Karok was triumphant in his faith as was ever fire-worshiping Gheber over the rescue of one of his conquerors from the errors of Islam.

Also, the fisherman will take no salmon if the poles of which his spearing-booth are made were gathered on the river-side, where the salmon might have seen them. They must be brought from the top of the highest adjacent mountain. So will they equally labor in vain if they use the poles a second year in booths or weirs, "because the old salmon will have told the young ones about them". It is possible that the latter is only a facetious excuse made to the whites for their indolence in allowing the winter freshet to sweep away their booths every year.

When the salmon are a trifle dilatory in coming up in the spring, it is the good pleasure of the "Big Indians" to believe that some old harridan has bewitched them. In such case they call an indignation meeting, denounce the *suspect* vigorously by name, and send a messenger down to her booth to warn her that unless the spell is released within a certain time, they will descend upon her in a body and put her to instant death. Before sending this warning however, they generally wait until a few days before the time when the salmon are certain to come, or they have private advices that they *are* coming; so their dupes cry out, "Ah! they are terrible fellows after witches"!

In respect of a woman they have a superstition which reminds one of the old Israelitish uses. Every month she is banished without the village to live in a booth by herself, and no man may touch her on penalty of death. She is not permitted to partake of any meat (including fish) for a certain number of days, and only sparingly of acorn-porridge. If a woman at this time touches or even approaches any medicine about to be given to a sick person he will die the death.

The Karok language is said by those acquainted with it to be copious, sonorous, and rich in new combinations. A great many verbs form the tenses from different roots. When spoken by some stalwart, deep-voiced Nestor of the tribe, it sounds more like the Spanish, with its stately procession of periods, than any other Indian language I have heard, and it is far removed from the odious gutturalness of the Yurok. In such words as "Kareya" and "Karok" they trill the "r" in a manner which is quite Spanish, and which an American can scarcely imitate. They are ready and fertile in invention; no new object can be presented to them but they will presently name it in their own language, either by coining a word or by applying the name of some similar object with which they are familiar.

They bury the dead in the posture observed by ourselves, and profess abhorrence for incremation. Neither do they disfigure their countenances with blotches of pitch, as do the Scott River Indians. A widow cuts off her hair close to the head, and so wears it with commendable fidelity to the memory of her dead husband until she remarries, though this latter event may be hastened quite as unseemly as it was by Hamlet's mother. The person's ordinary apparel is buried with him in the grave, but all his gala-robes, his bandoleer, his deer-skins, and his strings of polished bits of abalones, are swung over poles laid across the picket-fence. It is seldom that a grave is seen nowadays which is not inclosed by a neat, white picket fence, copied after the American, for they are very imitative. If it is a squaw, all her large conical baskets are set in a row around the grave, turned bottom side up. 13

They inter the dead close beside their cabins in order that they may religiously watch and protect them from peering intrusion, and insure them tranquil rest in the grave. Near Orleans Bar I passed a village wherein the graves were numerous; every one with its tasty picket-fence and its barbaric treasure of apparel hanging over it. As the long strings of polished shells swayed gently to and fro in the evening breeze, with the purple, and pink, and green brightly glinting to the setting sun, while the streets of the village were silent and peaceful in their Sabbath evening repose, the faint clicking of the shells seemed to me one of the most sad and mournful sounds I ever heard. Each little conical barrow was freshly rounded up with clean earth or sand, on which were strewn snow-white pebbles from the river-bed.

How well and truly the Karok reverence the memory of the dead is shown by the fact that the highest crime one can commit is the *pet-chi-é-ri*, the mere mention of the dead relative's name. It is a deadly insult to the survivors, and can be atoned for only by the same amount of blood-money paid for willful murder. In default of that they will have the villain's blood.

"Macbeth does murder sleep". At the mention of his name the moulder-ing skeleton turns in his grave and groans. They do not like strangers even to inspect the burial-place; and when I was leaning over the pickets, looking at one of them, an aged Indian approached and silently but urgently beckoned me to go away.

They believe that the soul of a good Karok goes to the Happy Western Land beyond the great ocean. That they have a well-grounded assurance of an immortality beyond the grave is proven, if no otherwise, by their beautiful and poetical custom of whispering a message in the ear of the dead. Rosalino Camarena, husband to a Karok woman, and speaking the language well, relates the following incident illustrative of this custom:

One of his children died, and he had decently prepared it for burial, carried it in his own arms and laid it in its lonely grave on the steep mount-ain-side, amid the green and golden ferns, where the spiry pines mournfully soughed in the wind, chanting their sad threnody, while the swamp-stained Klamath roared over the rocks far, far below. He was about to cast the first shovelful of earth down upon it, when an Indian woman, a near rela-tive of the child, descended into the grave, bitterly weeping, knelt down beside the little one, and amid that shuddering and broken sobbing which only women know in their passionate sorrow, murmured in its ear:

"O, darling, my dear one, good-bye! Nevermore shall your little hands softly clasp these old withered cheeks, and your pretty feet shall print the moist earth around my cabin nevermore. You are going on a long journey in the spirit-land, and you must go alone, for none of us can go with you. Listen, then, to the words which I speak to you and heed them well, for I speak the truth. In the spirit-land there are two roads. One of them is a path of roses, and it leads to the Happy Western Land beyond the great water, where you shall see your dear mother. The other is a path strewn with thorns and briers, and leads, I know not whither, to an evil and dark land, full of deadly serpents, where you would wander forever. O, dear child, choose you the path of roses, which leads to the Happy Western Land, a fair and sunny land, beautiful as the morning. And may the great Kareya help you to walk in it to the end, for your little tender feet must walk alone. O, darling, my dear one, good-bye!"

CHAPTER III.

KAROK FABLES.

There are many apologues and fables in vogue among the Karok, which gifted squaws relate to their children on winter evenings and through the weary days of the rainy season, while they are cooped up in their cabins; and some of them are not entirely unworthy of a place in that renowned old book written by one Æsop. A few specimens are given here.

FABLE OF THE ANIMALS.

A great many hundred snows ago, Kareya, sitting on the Sacred Stool, created the world. First, he made the fishes in the big water, then the animals on the green land, and last of all, The Man. But the animals were all alike yet in power, and it was not yet ordained which should be for food to others, and which should be food for The Man. Then Kareya bade them all assemble together in a certain place, that The Man might give each his power and his rank. So the animals all met together, a great many hundred snows ago, on an evening when the sun was set, that they might wait over night for the coming of The Man on the morrow. Now Kareya commanded The Man to make bows and arrows, as many as there were animals, and to give the longest to the one that should have the most power, and the shortest to the one that should have the least. So he did, and after nine sleeps his work was ended, and the bows and arrows which he made were very many.

Now the animals being gathered together in one place, went to sleep, that they might rise on the morrow and go forth to meet The Man. But the coyote was exceedingly cunning, above all the beasts that were, he was so cunning. So he considered within himself how he might get the longest bow, and so have the greatest power, and have all animals for his meat. He determined to stay awake all night, while the others slept, and so go forth first in the morning and get the longest bow. This he devised within his cunning mind, and then he laughed to himself, and stretched out his snout on his fore-paws, and pretended to sleep, like the others. But about midnight he began to get sleepy, and he had to walk around camp and scratch his eyes a considerable time to keep them open. But still he grew more sleepy, and he had to skip and jump about like a good one to keep awake. He made so much noise this way that he woke up some of the other animals, and he had to think of another plan. About the time the morning star came up, he was so sleepy that he couldn't keep his eyes open any longer. Then he took two little sticks and sharpened them at the ends, and propped open his eyelids, whereupon he thought he was safe, and he concluded he would take just a little nap, with his eyes open, watching the morning star. But in a few minutes he was sound asleep, and the sharp sticks pierced through his eyelids, and pinned them fast together.

So the morning star mounted up very swiftly, and then there came a peep of daybreak, and the birds began to sing, and the animals began to rise and stretch themselves, but still the coyote lay fast asleep. At last it was broad daylight, and then the sun rose, and all the animals went forth to meet The Man. He gave the longest bow to the cougar, so he had the greatest power of all; and the second longest to the bear; and so on, giving the next to the last to the poor frog. But he still had the shortest one left, and he cried out, "What animal have I missed?" Then the animals began to look about, and they soon spied the coyote lying fast asleep, with the sharp sticks pinning his eyelids together. Upon that all the animals set up a great laugh, and they jumped on the coyote and danced upon him. Then they led him to The Man—for he could see nothing because of the sticks—and The Man pulled out the sticks, and gave him the shortest bow of all, which would shoot an arrow hardly more than a foot. And all the animals laughed very much.

But The Man took pity on the coyote, because he was now the weakest of all animals, weaker even than the frog, and he prayed to Kareya for him, and Kareya gave him cunning, ten times more than before, so that he was cunning above all the animals of the wood. So the coyote was a friend to The Man and to his children after him, and helped him, and did many things for him, as we shall see hereafter.

In the legendary lore of the Karok the coyote plays the same conspicuous part that Reynard does in ours, and the sagacious tricks that are accredited to him are endless. When one Karok has killed another, he frequently barks like the coyote in the belief that he will thereby be endued with so much of that animal's cunning that he will be able to elude the punishment due to his crime.

ORIGIN OF SALMON.

When Kareya made all things that have breath, he first made the fishes in the big water, then the animals, and last of all The Man. But Kareya did not yet let the fishes come up the Klamath, and thus the Karok had not enough food, and were sore ahungered. There were salmon in the big water, many and very fine to eat, but no Indian could catch them in the big water; and Kareya had made a great fish-dam at the mouth of the Klamath and closed it fast, and given the key to two old hags to keep, so that the salmon could not go up the river. And the hags kept the key that Kareya had given them, and watched it day and night without sleeping, so that no Indian could come near it.

Then the Karok were sore disturbed in those days for lack of food, and many died, and their children cried to them because they had no meat. But the coyote befriended the Karok, and helped them, and took it on himself to bring the salmon up the Klamath. First he went to an alder tree and gnawed off a piece of bark, for the bark of the alder tree after it is taken off presently turns red and looks like salmon. He took the piece of alder-bark in his teeth and journeyed far down the Klamath until he came to the mouth of it at the big water. Then he rapped at the door of the cabin where the old hags lived, and when they opened it he said, "*Ai-yu-kwoi'*", for he was very polite. And they did not wonder to hear the coyote speak, for all the animals could speak in those days. They did not suspect the coyote, and so asked him to come into their cabin and sit by the fire. This he did, and after he had warmed himself a while he commenced nibbling his piece of alder-bark. One of the hags seeing this said to the other, "See, he has some salmon!" So they were deceived and thrown off their guard, and presently one of them rose, took down the key and went to get some salmon to cook for themselves. Thus the coyote saw where the key was kept, but he was not much better off than before for it was too high for him to reach it. The hags cooked some salmon for supper and ate it, but they gave the coyote none.

So he staid in the cabin all night with the hags pretending to sleep, but he was thinking how to get the key. He could think of no plan at all, but in the morning one of the hags took down the key and started to get some salmon again, and then the coyote happened to think of a way as quick as a flash. He jumped up and darted under the hag, which threw her down, and caused her to fling the key a long way off. The coyote quickly seized it in his teeth and ran and opened the fish-dam before the hags could catch him. Thus the salmon were allowed to go up the Klamath, and the Karok had plenty of food.

ORIGIN OF FIRE.

The Karok now had food enough, but they had no fire to cook it with. Far away toward the rising sun, somewhere in a land which no Karok had ever seen, Kareya had made fire and hidden it in a casket, which he gave to two old hags to keep, lest some Karok should steal it. So now the coyote befriended the Karok again, and promised to bring them some fire.

He went out and got together a great company of animals, one of every kind from the lion down to the frog. These he stationed in a line all along the road, from the home of the Karok to the far-distant land where the fire was, the weakest animal nearest home and the strongest near the fire. Then he took an Indian with him and hid him under a hill, and went to the cabin of the hags who kept the casket, and rapped on the door. One of them came out, and he said, "Good evening", and they replied, "Good evening". Then he said, "It's a pretty cold night; can you let me sit by your fire?" And they said, "Yes, come in". So he went in and stretched himself out before the fire, and reached his snout out toward the blaze, and sniffed the heat, and felt very snug and comfortable. Finally he stretched his nose out along his fore-paws, and pretended to go to sleep, though he kept the corner of one eye open watching the old hags. But they never slept, day or night, and he spent the whole night watching and thinking to no purpose.

So next morning he went out and told the Indian whom he had hidden under the hill that he must make an attack on the hags' cabin, as if he were about to steal some fire, while he (the coyote) was in it. He then went back and asked the hags to let him in again, which they did, as they did not think a coyote could steal any fire. He stood close by the casket of fire, and when the Indian made a rush on the cabin, and the hags dashed out after him at one door, the coyote seized a brand in his teeth and ran out at the other door. He almost flew over the ground, but the hags saw the sparks flying and gave chase, and gained on him fast. But by the time he was out of breath he reached the lion, who took the brand and ran with it to the next animal, and so on, each animal barely having time to give it to the next before the hags came up.

The next to the last in the line was the ground-squirrel. He took the brand and ran so fast with it that his tail got afire, and he curled it up over his back, and so burned the black spot we see to this day just behind his fore-shoulders. Last of all was the frog, but he, poor brute! couldn't run at all, so he opened his mouth wide and the squirrel chucked the fire into it, and he swallowed it down with a gulp. Then he turned and gave a great jump, but the hags were so close in pursuit that one of them seized him by the tail (he was a tadpole then) and tweaked it off, and that is the reason why frogs have no tails to this day. He swam under water a long distance, as long as he could hold his breath, then came up and spit out the fire into a log of driftwood, and there it has staid safe ever since, so that when an Indian rubs two pieces of wood together the fire comes forth.

THE COYOTES DANCING WITH THE STARS.

After Kareya gave the coyote so much cunning he became very ambitious, and wanted to do many things which were very much too hard for him, and which Kareya never intended he should do. One of them once got so conceited that he thought he could dance with the stars, and so he asked one of them to fly close to the top of a mountain and take him by the paw, and let him dance once around through the sky. The star only laughed at him and winked its eye, but the next night when it came around, it sailed close to the mountain and took the coyote by the paw, and flew away with him through the sky. But the foolish coyote soon grew tired of dancing this way, and could not wait for the star to come around to the mountain again. He looked down at the earth and it seemed quite near to him, and as the star could not wait or fly low just then, he let go and leaped down. Poor coyote! he was ten whole snows in falling, and when he struck the earth he was smashed as flat as a willow mat.

Another one, not taking warning from this dreadful example, asked a star to let him dance once round through the sky. The star tried to dissuade him from the foolhardy undertaking, but it was of no avail; the silly animal would not be convinced. Every night when the star came around, he would squat on top of a mountain and bark until the star grew tired of his noise. So one night it sailed close down to the mountain and told the coyote to be quick for it could not wait, and up he jumped and caught it with his paw, and went dancing away through the great blue heaven. He, too, soon grew tired, and asked the star to stop and let him rest a little while. But the star told him it could not stop, for Kareya had made it to keep on moving all the while. Then he tried to get on the star and ride, but it was too small. Thus he was compelled to keep on dancing, dangling down from one paw, and one piece of his body after another dropped off until there was only one paw left hanging to the star.

The interpretation of these fables is not difficult. That one about the coyotes dancing with the stars manifestly took its origin from the Indians observing meteors or shooting-stars. A falling star is one which is sailing down to the mountain to take on board the adventurous beast, while the large meteor which bursts in mid-heaven with visible sparks falling from it, is the unlucky æronaut dropping down limb by limb. Probably that one concerning the origin of salmon hints at some ancient obstruction in the mouth of the Klamath, a cataract or something of the sort, which prevented the fish from ascending. The fable respecting the origin of fire, like the eastern Indian story of Michabo, the Great White One, is simply a sun-myth, mingled with a very weak analogue to the Greek fire-myth of Prometheus The bringing of the fire-brand from the east carried by the various animals in succession, is the daily progress of the sun, while the pursuing hags are the darkness which follows after. Of course this poor little story of the Indians is not for a moment to be compared with the majestic tragedy wrought out by the sublime and gorgeous imagination of the Greeks; and it suffers seriously even when set alongside of the ingenious Algonkin myth of Michabo. It falls not a little behind it in imaginative power, albeit there is in it, as in most of the California fables, an element of practical humor and slyness which is lacking in the Atlantic Indian legends. Though the Karok are probably the finest tribe of the State, their imagination is not only feeble but gratuitously filthy. This is shown in their tradition of the flood, which cannot be recited here on account of its obscenity.

STORY OF KLAMATH JIM.

Early in the year 1871, an Indian called Klamath Jim murdered a white man in Orleans Bar, and by due process of law he was tried, condemned, and hanged. In the presence of his doom, even when the fatal hour was hard by, he exhibited the strange and stoical apathy of his race in prospect of dissolution. He might almost have been said, like Daniel Webster, to have coolly anatomized his sensations as he went down to his death. He asked the sheriff curious and many questions on the grim topic, how the hanging was performed, how long it lasted, whether it would give him any pain, whether an Indian could die as quickly when hanging in an erect posture as when lying in his blanket, whether his *spirit* would not also be strangled and rendered unable to fly away to the Happy Western Land, etc.

In going to the gallows he walked with nerve and balance, tranquilly puffing a cigar, and he mounted the scaffold with an unfaltering tread, daintily held out his cigar and filliped off the ashes with his little finger, took a final whiff, then tossed it over his shoulder. He assisted the sheriff in adjusting the noose about his neck, shook that officer's trembling hand without the tremor of a muscle, spoke a few parting words without the least quivering

of voice, and then the drop descended and his soul went suddenly out on
its dark flight.

The Karok had quietly acquiesced in the execution, but they were not
well pleased, and now though they dared not make open insurrection
against the whites, their astute prophets and soothsayers concocted a story
which was intended to encourage their countrymen ultimately to revolt.
They pretended they had a revelation, and that all the Karok who had
14 died since the beginning of time had experienced a resurrection, and were
returning from the land of shadows to wreak a grim vengeance on the
whites and sweep them utterly off the earth. They were somewhere far
toward the rising sun advancing in uncounted armies, and Kareya himself
was at their head leading them on, and with his hands parting the
mountains to right and left, opening a level road for the slow-coming
myriads. The prophets pretended to have been out and seen this great
company that no man could number, and they reported to their willing
dupes that they were pygmies in stature, but like the Indians of to-day in
every other regard. Klamath Jim was with them—the soul and inspiration
of this majestic movement of vengeance, counsellor to Kareya himself.

It is not necessary to follow this cock-and-bull story any further; of
course nothing came of the matter, for the Indians had once tasted the
quality of George Crook's cold lead, and they were very willing to let
these dead-walkers try their hands on the whites first. No doubt they very
earnestly hoped the dead would return and assist them in sweeping the
Americans off the earth, and they did all that lay in human power to bring
them back. They danced for months, sometimes a half day at a time
continuously; and when I passed that way again in 1872, about nine
months afterward, they were dancing still. The old Indians had profound
faith in the prediction, saying that every man who faithfully danced would
liberate some near relative's soul from the bonds of death, and restore him
to earth; but the young Indians, who spoke English, were heretical, and
were a great eyesore to their elders. Pa-chí-ta, a Karok chief at Scott's
Bar, told me that in this dance red paint was used for the first time in their
history as a symbol of war. Two poles were planted in the ground, spirally

painted with red and black streaks, and streamers ("handkerchiefs", the Indians called them) fastened atop; then with their bodies painted in like manner and feathers on their heads, they danced around them in a circle. This excitement raged all over Northern California, especially among the Yurok, Karok, and Shasta, until the Modok war broke out, November, 1872, when it gradually subsided.

CHAPTER IV.

THE YÚ-ROK.

This large tribe inhabit the Klamath, from the junction of the Trinity to the mouth, and the coast from Gold Bluff up to a point about six miles above the mouth of the Klamath. Their name is of Karok origin; they themselves have only names for separate villages, as Rí-kwa, Mí-ta, Pek'-wan, Srí'-gon, Wait'-spek.

Living nearer the coast, they are several shades darker than the Karok, frequently almost black; and they are not so fine a race, having lower foreheads and more projecting chins. On the coast they incline to be pudgy *Figs. 2, 3* in stature, though on the Klamath there are many specimens of splendid savagery. Like all California women, their mohelas (a Spanish word of general use) are rather handsome in their free and untoiling youth, but after twenty-five or thirty they break down under their heavy burdens and become ugly. Both Karok and Yurok plant their feet in walking nearly as broadly as Americans. They have the same tattooing and much the same customs as their up-river neighbors, but a totally different language. They usually learn each other's language, and two of them will sit and patter gossip for hours, each speaking in his own tongue. A white man listening may understand one, but never a word of the other.

The Yurok is notable for its gutturalness, and there are words and syllables which contain no perceptible vowel sounds, as *mrh-prh*, "nose"; *chlek'-chlh*, "earth"; *wrh'-yen-eks*, "child". A Welshman told me he had detected in the language the peculiar Welsh sound of "ll", which is inexpressible in English. In conversation they terminate many words with a 15 strong aspiration, which is imperfectly indicated by the letter "h"—a sort of catching of the sound, immediately followed by a letting out of the residue of the breath with a quick little grunt. This makes their speech

44

harsh and halting; the voice often seems to come to a dead stop in the middle of a sentence.

The following table of numerals will show how entirely different are the languages of the three tribes on the Klamath:

	YUROK.	KAROK.	MODOK.
1	spin'-i-ka.	í-sa.	nos.
2	neh'-ekh.	akh'-uk.	lăf.
3	nakh'-kseh.	kwí-rok.	dūn.
4	tsuh-ú-neh.	pí-si.	ó-nep.
5	mar'-i-roh.	ter-á-oap.	tó-nep.
6	koh'-tseh.	krí-vik.	nats'-ksup.
7	cher'-wer-tseh.	hok-i-rá-vik-y.	lup'-ksup.
8	kneh'-wit-tek.	kwi-ro-ki-ná-vik.	dūn-ksup.
9	krh'-mek.	tro-pi-tit'-i-sha.	ská-gis.
10	wrh'-kler-wer.	ter-aí-hi.	tá-o-nep.

As among the Karok, the functions of the chief are principally advisory Like the pretor of ancient Rome, he can proclaim *do, dico,* but he can scarcely add *addico.* He can state the law or the custom and the facts, and he can give his opinion, but he can hardly pronounce judgment. The office is not hereditary; the head man or captain is generally one of the oldest, and always one of the astutest, men of the village. They also recognize the authority of a head-chief.

Their houses—and the following descriptions will serve also for the Karok—are sometimes constructed on the level earth, but generally they excavate a round cellar, four or five feet deep and twelve or fifteen feet in diameter. Over this they build a square cabin of split poles or puncheons, planted erect in the ground, and covered with a flattish puncheon roof. They eat and sleep in the cellar, (it is only a pit, and it is not covered except by the roof), squatting in a circle around the fire, and store their supplies on the bank above next to the walls of the cabin. For a door they take a puncheon about four feet wide, set it up at one corner of the cabin, and with infinite scraping of flints and elk-horns bore a round hole through it, barely large enough to admit the passage of an Indian on all-fours. The cabin being built entirely of wood and not thatched, accounts partly for the wholesome-looking eyes of the Klamath tribes, compared with the odious purblind optics often seen in the thatched and unventilated wigwams farther south. A space in front of the cabin is kept clean-swept, and is frequently paved with cobbles, with a larger one placed each side of the door-holes; and on this pavement the squaws sit, weaving baskets, and spinning no end of tattle.

Though they have not the American's all-day industry, both these Klamath tribes are job-thrifty, and contrive to have a considerable amount of money by them. For instance, the trading-post at Klamath Bluffs alone sold in 1871, over $3,000 worth of merchandise, though there were only about six miners among their customers. Here is a significant item: The proprietor said he sold over 700 pounds of soap annually to the Yurok alone. I often peeped into their cabins, and seldom failed to see there wheaten bread, coffee, matches, bacon, and a very considerable wardrobe hanging in the smoky attic. They are more generally dressed in complete civilized suits, and more generally ride on horseback, than any others, except the Mission Indians.

How do they get the money to procure these things? They mine a little, drive pack-trains a good deal, transport goods and passengers on the river, make and sell canoes, whipsaw lumber for the miners, fetch and carry about the mining camps, go over to Scott Valley and hire themselves out on the farms in the summer, etc. These Indians are enterprising; they push out from their native valley. You will find them in Crescent City, Trinidad, and Arcata, working in the saw-mills, on the Hupâ reservation, etc. When we remember that they have learned all these things by imitation, having never been on a reservation, it is no little to their credit.

The hills skirting the Klamath are very steep and mountain-high, the north side being open and fern-grown, and most of the villages are on this north side to get the sunshine in winter, planted thick along the bends wherever they can find a little level space. These smoke-blackened hamlets reminded me continually of the villages in Canton Valais, only the Indian cabin has but one story. It is very much like a chalet, and they are every whit as clean, comfortable, and substantial as the *Sennhütten*, wherein is made the world-famous Emmenthaler cheese, for I have been inside of both. And yet, when I saw the swarthy Yurok creeping on all-fours out of their round door-holes, or sticking their shock-pates up through the hatchway of the assembly chamber, just on a level with the earth, I thought of black bears as often as anything.

From willow twigs and pine roots they weave large round mats, for holding acorn flour; various sized, flattish, squash-shaped baskets, water-tight; deep, conical ones, of about a bushel capacity, to be carried on their backs; and others, to be used at pleasure as drinking-cups or skull-caps (for the squaws only, the men wear nothing on their heads), in which latter capacity they fit very neatly. They ornament their baskets with some ingenuity by weaving in black rootlets or bark in squares, diamonds, or zigzag lines, but they never attempt the curve (which seems to mark the transition from barbaric to civilized art), or the imitation of any object in nature.

In carrying her baby, or a quantity of acorns, the squaw fills the deep, conical basket, and suspends it on her back by a strap which passes loosely around it and athwart her forehead. She leans far forward and so relieves her neck; but I have seen the braves carry heavy burdens for miles, walking quite erect, though they showed they were not accustomed to the drudgery, by clasping their hands behind their heads to ease their necks of the terrible strain.

As the redwood grows only along the Lower Klamath, the Yurok have a monopoly of making canoes, and they sell many to the Karok. A canoe on the Klamath is not pointed like the Chippewa canoe, but the width at either end is equal to the tree's diameter. On the great bar across the mouth of the river, and all along the coast for eighty miles there are tens of thousands of mighty redwoods cast up on the strand, having been either floated down by the rivers or grubbed down by the surf. Hence the Indians are not obliged to fell any trees, and have only to burn them into suitable lengths. In making the canoe they spread pitch on whatever place they wish to reduce, and when it has burned deep enough they clap on a piece of raw bark and extinguish the fire. By this means they round them out with wonderful symmetry and elegance, leaving the sides and ends very thin and as smooth as if they had been sandpapered. At the stern they burn and polish out a neat little bracket which serves as a seat for the boatman. They spend an infinity of puddering on these canoes (nowadays they use iron tools and dispatch the work in a few days), two Indians sometimes working on one five or six months, burning, scraping, polishing with stones. When completed, they are sold for various sums, ranging from $10 to $30, or even more. They are not as handsome as the Smith River or the T'sin-ūk canoes, but quite as serviceable. A large one will carry five tons of merchandise, and in early days they used to take many cargoes of fish from the Klamath, shooting the dangerous rapids and surf at the mouth with consummate skill, going boldly to sea in heavy weather, and reaching Crescent City, twenty-two miles distant, whence they returned with merchandise.

When they are not using these canoes, they turn them bottom side up on the sandy beach and bream them, or haul them into damp and shady coves, or cover them thickly with leaves and brushwood, to prevent the thin ends from sun-cracking. When they do become thus cracked, they bore holes through with a buck's horn, and bind the ends together with withes, twisting the same tight with sticks—a kind of rude tourniquet—which closes up the cracks better than calking would.

To make a quiver, the Yurok takes the skin of a raccoon or a marten, turns it wrong-side out, sews it up, and suspends it behind him by a string passed over one shoulder and under the other, while the striped tail flutters gayly in the air at his shoulder. In the animal's head he stuffs a quantity of moss, as a cushion for the arrow-heads to rest in, to prevent breakage.

In catching salmon they employ principally nets woven of fine roots or grass, which are stretched across eddies in the Klamath, always with the mouth down-stream. When there is not a natural eddy they sometimes create one by throwing out a rude wing-dam. They select eddies because it is there the salmon congregate to rest themselves. At the head of the eddy they erect fishing-booths over the water, by planting slender poles in the bottom of the river, and lashing others over them in a light and artistic framework, with a floor a few feet above the water, and regular rafters overhead, on which brushwood is spread for a screen against the sun. In one of these really picturesque booths an Indian sleeps at night, with a string leading up from the net to his fingers, so that when a salmon begins to flounce in it he is awakened. Sometimes the string is attached to an ingenious rattle-trap of sticks or bones (or a bell nowadays), which will ring or clatter, and answer the same purpose.

They also spear salmon from these booths with a fish-gig furnished with movable barbs, which after entering the fish spread open, and prevent the withdrawal of the instrument. Another mode they sometimes employ is to stand on a large bowlder in the main current where the salmon and the little skeggers shoot in to rest in the eddy when ascending the stream, whereupon they scoop them up in dip-nets. Again they construct a weir of willow stakes nearly across the stream at the shallows, leaving only a narrow chute wherein is set a funnel-shaped trap of splints, with a funnel-shaped entrance at the large end. Ascending the stream the bold, resolute salmon shoots into this, and cannot get out. Sometimes the weir reaches clear across, the stakes being fastened to a long string-piece stretching from bank to bank. The building of one of these dams is usually preceded by a grand dance, and followed by a feast of salmon. The greater portion of the catch is dried and smoked for winter consumption.

There are two runs of salmon, one in the spring and one in the fall, of which the former is the better, the fish being then smaller and sweeter. The whites along the river sometimes compel the Indians to leave their weirs open a certain number of days in the week, that they may participate in the catch. Quarrels used to arise between two villages, caused by the lower one making a weir so tight as to obstruct the run, and these occasionally led to bloodshed.

Bread or mush is made from the acorns of the chestnut-oak (*Quercus densiflora*), which are first slightly scorched and then pounded up in stone mortars. The invariable sound that first salutes the ear as one approaches a village is the monotonous thump, thump of the pestles wielded by the patient women. The meal thus prepared is wet up with water, and the mixture poured into little sand-pools scooped in the river beach, around which a fire is made until the stuff is cooked, when the outside sand is brushed

16

off, and the bread is ready to be eaten. They find on the coast a glutinous kind of algæ, which they press into loaves when wet, then dry them in the sun, and eat them raw. They also eat the nuts of the laurel (*Oreodaphne californica*).

On lagoons and shallow reaches of the river they have a way of trapping wild ducks which is ingenious. They sprinkle huckleberries or *salàl*-berries on the bottom, then strètch a coarse net a few inches under the surface of the water. Seeing the tempting decoy, the ducks dive for it, thrust their heads through the meshes of the net, and the feathers prevent their return. Thus they are drowned, and remain quiet with their tails elevated, so that others are not frightened, and an abundant catch sometimes rewards the trapper.

Along the coast they engage largely in smelt fishing. The fisherman takes two long slender poles which he frames together with a cross-piece in the shape of the letter **A**, and across this he stretches a net with small meshes, bagging down considerably. This net he connects by a throat, with a long bag-net floating in the water behind him, and then, provided with a strong staff, he wades out up to his middle. When an unusually heavy billow surges in he plants his staff firmly on the bottom, ducks his head forward, and allows it to boom over him. After each wave he dips with his net and hoists it up, whereupon the smelt slide down to the point and through the throat into the bag-net. When the latter contains a bushel or so he wades ashore and empties it into his squaw's basket.

About sunset appears to be the most favorable time for smelt fishing, and at this time the great bar across the mouth of the Klamath presents a lively and interesting spectacle. Sometimes many scores of swarthy heads may be seen bobbing amid the surf like so many sea-lions. The squaws hurry to and fro across the bar, bowing themselves under their great conical hampers, carrying the smelt back to the canoes in the river, while the pappooses caper around stark naked, whoop, throw up their heels, and playfully insinuate pebbles into each other's ears. After the great copper globe of the sun burns into the ocean, bivouac fires spring up along the sand among the enormous redwood drift-logs, and families hover around them to roast the evening repast. The squaws bustle about the fires while the weary smelt-fishermen, in their nude and savage strength, are grouped together squatting or leaning about, with their smooth, dark, clean-moulded limbs in statuesque attitudes of repose.   Dozens of canoes laden with bushels on bushels of the little silver fishes, shove off and move silently away up the darkling river.   The village of Rikwa perched on the shoulder of the great bluff, amid the lush cool ferns, swashing in the soft sea-breeze, tinkles with the happy cackle of brown babies tumbling on their heads with the puppies; and the fires within the cabins gleam through the round door-holes like so many full-orbed moons heaving out of the breast of the mountain.

Smelt being small the squaws dry them whole by laying them awhile on low wooden kilns, with interstices to allow the smoke to rise up freely, and then finishing the process in the sun.   They eat them uncooked, with sauce of raw *salál*-berries (*Gualtheria shallon*), which are very good in September and October.   Let an Indian be journeying anywhither, and you will always find in his basket some bars of this silver bullion, or flakes of rich orange colored salmon.

When the ocean is tranquil they paddle out in their canoes a mile or more and clamber out on the isolated farralones to gather shell-fish and algæ for food.   It is quite a perilous feat to approach one of these steep, rugged bowlders in the open sea, and leap upon it amid the swish and thudding of the waves.

CHAPTER V.

Weapons of war and the chase are usually made by some old man skilled in knapping stone and in fashioning bows and arrows. Bows are made from the yew (*Taxus brevifolia*), a tough evergreen; the outside is coated with sinew drawn tight, and the string is made of the same material Arrows are made of cedar, and are sometimes furnished with a spiral whorl of feather to give them a rifle motion, and being tipped with flint (or with metal nowadays) they are very powerful and can be driven clear through a man's body. Another weapon made by them is a sword or knife about three feet long, of iron or steel procured from the whites. Of course this is not aboriginal, but is rather a substitute for the large jasper or obsidian knives which they used to make and use, but which nowadays are kept only as ornaments or objects of wealth, to be produced on occasion of a great dance. These may perhaps be called pre-historic, as they seem to have fallen into disuse as weapons before the arrival of the Americans. They occur in numbers in the mounds of Southwestern Oregon. Even common arrow-heads are now manufactured only by old Indians who cling to the traditions of their forefathers. Mr. Chase mentions some very large jasper spear-heads four inches long and two inches wide; but these also are now brought forth only at a dance, to give the owner distinction. Flint or jasper flakes are used to cut and clean salmon, especially the first of the season, as they say that iron or steel is poisonous used for this purpose. In the accompanying sketch are figured two implements which may have been only net-sinkers, but are said by an old pioneer to have been used formerly as *bolas* are in South America, being tied together with rawhide and hurled at the feet of an enemy to entangle him and throw him down. To me it seems more probable that they were used rather like a slung-shot.

The Yurok are not as good hunters as the Karok and are inclined to be timid in the deep forest, but they are bold and skillful watermen. They pretend that when they go into the mountains, devils, shaped like bears, shoot arrows at them, which travel straight until they are about to impinge on them when they suddenly swerve aside.

On the other hand, I could not but admire the dash and coolness of Salmon Billy, whom a bold soldier-boy and myself employed to take us down the river in his canoe. When we were bowling down the rapids where the water curled its green lips as if it would swallow us bodily, and the huge waves now headed her, now pooped her, and now took her amidships, until she was nearly a third full of water, Billy stood up in the stern and his eyes glistened with savage joy while he bowsed away hearty, first on this side, then on that, until we shot down like an Oxford shell on the Thames. He got a little nervous at times, which we could always tell by his commencing to whistle under his breath; and in the roughest rapids he would get to whistling very fast, but his stroke was never steadier than then. In a pinch like this he would bawl out to us to trim the canoe, or to sit still, with an imperiousness that amused me.

I will also relate a little incident, showing the exceeding cunning of this same Salmon Billy. One day I was toiling down the trail along the Klamath in an execrable drizzle of rain, which, together with the labyrinth

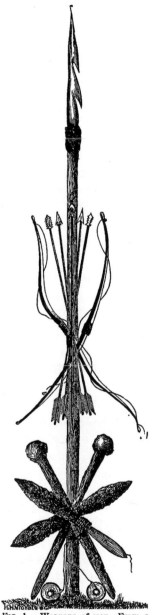

FIG. 1.—Weapons of war. From a sketch by A. W. Chase.

of cattle-trails obscured the path and led me on many a wild-goose chase.
At every village the Indians would swarm out and offer me their canoes
at an extortionate price; but it was only three or four miles to the Klamath
Bluffs trading-post and I determined to push on. I soon discovered that
whenever I left a village an Indian would dash down the bank, leap into
his canoe, shoot swiftly down the river, and put the next one below on the
alert lest I should pass them without being perceived. So it continued for
some time, and each village—they were often less than a quarter of a mile
apart—lowered the price "a bit" or so, though still charging three times too
much. At last I came to fresh tracks in the trail which were evidently
made by American boots and I followed them joyfully; but they soon led
me into a thick jungle dripping with rain where I speedily lost the way
and got saturated from head to foot. In a perfect desperation, I floundered
out somehow and got down on the river-bank determined to take the first
passing canoe at whatever cost. In a few minutes, who of all men in the
world should come paddling quietly around the bend but Salmon Billy !

It is necessary here to go back and mention that Billy had taken note
of me in his village, and instead of going down to warn his neighbors, he
had studied his own advantage, shot down ahead, bowled his canoe ashore,
made the tracks on purpose to decoy me into the jungle, then regained his
canoe by a roundabout way and dashed out of my sight. From his covert
he saw me come down on the bank quite beat out and in a wofully
bedraggled condition; so presently he hove in sight paddling leisurely
around the bend, with the most unconscious and casual air in the world.
In a moment a suspicion of foul play flashed upon me. I was vexed
enough to have thrashed his head off, but there I was. So I gave a shout
at him but he looked the other way. I whooped at him again with a certain elevation of voice. He narrowly scrutinized a woodpecker flying
overhead, then riveted his gaze intently upon a frog singing on a bowlder
ashore. He couldn't hear me, the rascal! until I bawled at him three
times. I paid him his price without a word and got in. The next day he
took me down to the mouth of the river, and when I spoke to him about
the tracks Billy's face remained as placid as a cucumber, but he suddenly
forgot all his stock of English and could understand never a word more!

The Yurok are a very lively, curious, and inquisitive race. One who travels afoot, dressed in the plain garb necessary amid the scraggy thickets of California, will find them making themselves very familiar with him— sometimes to his amusement, often to his great disgust. They had the greatest curiosity respecting myself and my business. They scrutinized every article of my apparel, and men who understood them said they always discussed in detail, and with great minuteness, every stranger's coat, hat, boots, trousers, etc., and tried thus to conjecture his occupation. They wanted to purchase my clothes, they wanted to swap handkerchiefs, they wanted to peep into my traveling-bag. Waxing presently more familiar, they would feel the quality of my cloth, stroke it down, ask what it cost a yard, clasp my arm to test my muscle, and then encourage me with the sententious and comprehensive remark, "Bully for you!" They turned up my boots to inspect the nails and soles of the same; they wanted to try on my coat, and, last and worst of all, the meddlesome rascals wanted to try on my trousers!

Sometimes, when wandering on the great, ferny, wind-swept hills of the coast, keeping a sharp weather-eye out for the trail, I have seen a half-dozen tatterdemalion Yurok, engaged in picking *salàl*-berries, when they saw me, quit their employment with their fingers and lips stained gory-red by the juice, and come rushing down through the bushes with their two club-queues bouncing on their shoulders and laughing with a wild lunatic laugh that made my hair stand on end. But they were never on "butcher deeds" intent, and never made any foray on me more terrible than the insinuating question, "Got any tobac.?"

Filthy as they are they do not neglect the cold morning bath until they have learned to wear complete civilized suits. On the coast I have seen the smooth-skinned, pudgy, shock-pated fellows, on one of those leaden foggy mornings of that region, crawl on all-fours out of their wretched huts which were cobbled up of driftwood, take off the narrow breech-cloths which were their only coverings, and dip up the chilly brine over them with their double-hands letting it trickle all down their swarthy bodies in a manner that made me shiver to see. The sexes bathe apart, and the women do not go into the sea without some garment on.

The Yurok, like their neighbors, are quite acquisitive. Besides the money mentioned among the Karok, they value obsidian knives and ornaments and white deer-skins, the two latter having a superstitious as well as an intrinsic worth. A good white deer-skin, with head and legs intact is worth from $50 to $200 in gold. An Indian possessing even one is accounted rich; at a great dance that was held, a barbaric Astor had four.

They are monogamists, and as among the Karok, marriage is illegal without the prepayment of money. When a young Indian becomes enamored of a maid, and cannot wait to collect the amount of shell-money demanded by her father, he is sometimes allowed to pay half the sum and become what is termed "half-married". Instead of bringing her to his cabin and making her his slave, he goes to live in *her* cabin and becomes *her* slave. This only occurs in the case of soft, uxorious fellows.

Divorce is very easily accomplished at the will of the husband, the only indispensable formality being that he must receive back from his father-in-law the money which he paid for his spouse. For this reason, since the advent of the Americans, the honorable state of matrimony has fallen sadly into disuse among the young braves, because they seldom have shell-money nowadays, and the old Indians prefer that in exchange for their daughters. Besides that, if one paid American money for his wife his father-in-law would squander it (the old generation dislike the white man's, the *wâ-geh* money, but hoard up shell-money like true misers), and thus, in case of divorce he could not recover his gold and silver.

The Yurok are rather a more lively race than the Karok, and observe more social dances. The birth of a child is celebrated with a dance. There is a dance called *ú-me-laik* (salmon dance), which bears a general resemblance to the Propitiation Dance of the Karok. It is held in-doors in early spring, when the first salmon of the season appears. We can well understand with what great joy the villagers engage in this, when after a long and dreary winter of rain during which the wolf has been hardly kept from the door, and the house-father has gone down many a time to peer into the Klamath, if perchance he might see the black-backed finny rovers of the great deep shooting up the river, but in vain, and has then sadly turned on his heel and gone back to his diet of pine-bark and buds—when, at last, as the ferns are greening on the mountain-side and the birds of spring are singing, the joyful cry resounds through the village, *Ne-peg'-wuh! ne-peg'-wuh!* (the salmon! the salmon!) As among the Karok, this dance is generally followed by a licentious debauch. In the fall is celebrated the White Deer 17 Dance (*u-pi-wai-u-gunkhl*), which is held out-doors.

Like the Karok they believe old squaws can by witchcraft prevent the salmon from ascending the river, and in former times they not unfrequently slew with butcherly murder the unfortunate hag so suspected. They do not wish the salmon to be interfered with or be misled in their courses. They even have a pole erected at the mouth of the Klamath to show them the way in—a tall pole on the sand-bar, ornamented with a smallish and rather pretty cross, with two streamers fluttering from it.

The only attempt at carving in imitation of the human figure that I have seen in California was among the Yurok, and was probably connected in some way with the salmon-fishery. It was a figure something like one of the ancient Roman *termini*—a satyr's bust, fashioned in profile from a slab about three inches thick. It was extremely rude, the nose and chin sharp-pointed and the head flattish, the arms rigidly straight and extending *Fig. 4* down at a little distance from the body, and on the rump a curving, devil-ish-looking tail about three feet long. It was arrayed in a United States regulation-coat, with the arms loosely thrust into the sleeves, the body stuffed with grass, and the tail sticking out between the flaps. Perched on a short pole on a lofty fern-grown hill at the mouth of the Klamath, it stood looking out over the ocean—a kind of shabby St. Anthony preaching a silent sermon to the fish. The Indians would not or could not explain its meaning, but I have little doubt that it was intended to assist or direct the salmon in some manner in entering the Klamath River.

In addition to this figure, Mr. A. W. Chase saw and described two others, one on each side of the Klamath at the mouth, one of which he kindly sketched for this work. In a letter to the author he states that both of them commemorate the killing of an enemy in battle. Klamath George of the village of Rikwa, killed a Chillula, and to use his own words, "When I come home, I take board, and cut his picture out, and stick him up". The one on the south bank, which is here figured, and is the more artistic of the two, was made by an old Indian of the Quilshpak Ranch, to celebrate his triumph over a Tolowa.

They trim up trees for assembly-chamber fuel in the same curious way as the Karok, and I have seen hundreds of trees thus fashioned along the Klamath, representing a man's head and arms. The Yurok say they are intended merely as guide-posts for the squaws, to direct them to the villages when they have been out in the mountains berrying; but they have a deeper significance than that.

They also have a curious custom of dropping twigs and boughs at the junction of trails, which sometimes accumulate in heaps several feet high, like the nests of wood-rats. Every Indian who passes deposits a twig on the pile, but without observing any method that a white man can discover. No one will explain the custom, but they laugh the matter off when it is broached; though it is probably observed, like so many other things, merely "for luck".

In saluting each other, the Yurok say *ai-yu-kwoi'* (friendship), without hand-shaking or any further ceremony. With slight variations, this expression prevails among several tribes of Northwestern California who speak entirely different languages.

They bury the dead in a recumbent posture, and observe about the same usages of mourning as the Karok. After a death they keep a fire burning certain nights in the vicinity of the grave. They hold and believe, at least the "Big Indians" do, that the spirits of the departed are compelled to cross an extremely attenuated greased pole, which bridges over the chasm of the "Debatable Land", and that they require the fire to light them on their darksome journey. A righteous soul traverses the pole quicker than a wicked one; hence they regulate the number of nights for burning a light according to the character for goodness or the opposite which the deceased possessed in this world. If this greased pole were perpendicular, like the *Mât de Cocagne* in the frolics of the Champs Élysées, I should account this an Indian parallel to the Teutonic myth of Jack and the Beanstalk. But they appear to think it is horizontal, leading over bridge-wise to the Happy Western Land beyond the ocean, which gives it more resemblance to the Mohammedan fable of Al Sirat.

They fully believe in the transmigration of souls; that they return to earth as birds, squirrels, rabbits, or other feeble animals liable to be harried and devoured. It is more especially the wicked who are subject to this misfortune as a punishment.

A word as to the size of the Yurok tribe. Henry Ormond, chief clerk of the Hupâ reservation told me that in 1870, he descended the Lower Klamath from Waitspek down in a canoe—forty miles—and carefully counted all the Indians living along its banks. He found the number to be 19 2,700, which would be at the rate of 67½ inhabitants to the square mile, along the river. This does not include the Yurok living immediately on the coast. It must be borne in mind that there are no wild oats growing along the Klamath, and few acorns, and that the Yurok are timid and infrequent hunters. Furthermore, before the whites had come among them, bringing their corruptions and their maladies, the Indians were probably twice as numerous as at present, or at the rate of 135 to the riparian square mile.

As to the enormous numbers of salmon which ascended the streams of California before the miners roiled them there can be no doubt. Here one veteran pioneer says he has seen many an Indian lodge containing a ton of dried salmon; another, that he could have walked across the stream and stepped every step on a dead salmon; another, that he has seen them so crowded in the deep and quiet reaches of the river that he could not thrust down a spear without transfixing one or more. From what I have seen on the Upper Sacramento, I believe them all; hence the above figures do not seem extravagant.

THE YUROK SIREN.

There is a certain tract of country on the north side of the river which nothing can induce an Indian to enter. They say that there is a beautiful squaw living there whose fascinations are fatal. When an Indian sees her he straightway falls desperately in love. She decoys him farther and farther into the forest, until at last she climbs a tree and the man follows. She now changes into a panther and kills him; then, resuming her proper form she cuts off his head and places it in a basket. She is now, they say, a thousand years old, and has an Indian's head for every year of her life. It is probable that this legend refers to some poisonous spring or other natural phenomenon. Though game abounds in that locality they carefully avoid it.

For the following I am indebted to Mr. Chase:

THE FOXES AND THE SUN.

The foxes once upon a time gathered together and laid a conspiracy against the sun, from whom they had cause of grievance. Twelve of their number were selected from the bravest to avenge the wrongs of the race. These foxes procured stout ropes of sinew, and watched until the sun in his descent toward the ocean touched the brow of a certain hill. Thereupon they caught him and bound him down with the ropes, and would no doubt have kept him there to this day had not a party of Indians perceived the mischief and killed the foxes with their arrows. They then liberated the sun; but he had in the mean time burned a great hole in the ground. You can see it to this day.

It is quite probable that this story refers to some ancient volcanic eruption or other disturbance. It is the aboriginal way of accounting for a huge rent in the hills near the Klamath, which is surrounded by lava, tufa, etc.

A YUROK'S REVENGE.

A certain Yurok went down to the sea-coast with his family, and in one of his hunting excursions he quarreled with a man of his tribe and shot him unto death. The brother of the murdered man, in accordance with the custom of the tribe, demanded a ransom or blood-money. He asked $60, but he finally offered to compromise the matter upon the receipt of $10 in hand paid. The slayer refused to pay him anything whatever, and after a fierce wrangle he gathered his family about him and returned to his home near Klamath Bluffs saying nothing to any one of the circumstance.

Soon afterward the owner of the Klamath Bluffs trading-post observed a strange Indian prowling about the vicinity in a manner that excited his curiosity. He was always alone, was always fetching quick stealthy glances around him, was never separated one moment from his bow and quiver, and was never visible during daylight hours, coming to the post only after nightfall. The Indians always dawdle around a frontier store in large numbers by day, but soon after the evening dusk comes on they all disappear in their cabins; and it was only when they were all away that this strange Indian would enter cautiously, and glance quickly around to see that no other Indian was present. Then he would go up to the counter, set down his bow within easy clutching distance, and purchase the smallest quantity of crackers the trader would sell, and occasionally also as much more of tobacco, matches, or some other trifling article. After a few half-whispered words, he would slink quietly out and be seen no more until the following evening. He never missed an evening, but always made his appearance in the same manner, went through the same maneuvers, and always bought a half-pound of crackers, never over a pound. The merchant grew uneasy, but he had learned by bitter experience the folly of meddling in Indian feuds, and he said nothing, only watched. Month after month passed away, and still this inscrutable Indian continued to come every evening, slipped softly into the store, carefully closed the door behind him, made his little purchases, then went away. He grew gaunt and haggard, and on his drawn cheeks he could now hardly force a smile as he greeted the trader; but not one word did he ever breathe of his secret purposes.

He was the avenger of his murdered brother, waiting and watching for the life which he had sworn by his god to offer to the horrid Uma. Night after night he was lying beside a certain brook where he awaited the slayer. Week after week, month after month passed on, until five moons had waxed and waned; the shrilling rains and the frosts and the snows of winter came and went, and beat upon his shriveled body; the moaning winds shook his unshortened locks and whistled through his rotting blanket; the great fern-slopes of the mountains faded from green to golden, to wine-color, to russet, to tawny, buried their ugliness under the winding-sheet of the snow, then lived again in the tender green of spring, and still his wasting eyes glared out through the thicket, and still the victim came not. Five months he waited. But at last, one morning in the soft early spring, at daybreak, he beholds him for whom he is waiting. He comes down a winding pathway and descends into the brook to bathe. He lays off his girdle on a ferny bank. He stands erect and supple, stretches up his smooth brown arms above his head, and all his body quivers with the delight of a fresh morning air-bath. Sitting in his blanket, the avenger of blood peers through his leafy screen. A moment ago he was shivering with cold, but all his tremor is suddenly stilled. His stiffened fingers grow suddenly lithe as they grip the arrow. In his eyes, late so faded and rayless, is now the glitter of ferocious hate. Without moving his eyes a moment from the foe, he softly couches the arrow. All the strength wasted through months is now in his arms again. There is no wavering in his aim. The sweet hope of revenge has steadied it to deadly certainty. Twanks the bow and slips the arrow, smooth and swift through the limber air. The blood-guilty one is smitten low. He lies still beside the brook. The long vigil is ended, and savage justice has its rounded dues.

Through the kindness of Mr. H. H. Bancroft, I was allowed to peruse a letter written to himself by Judge J. B. Rosborough, of Yreka, on the Northern California Indians. From it I have copied a legend, which I will here append, merely premising that the Indian words in it are spelled with the English sounds of the vowels.

LEGEND OF WAPPECKQUENOW.

He was a giant, inhabited the country about the mouth of the Klamath (they localize every tradition), and belonged to a race which preceded the Indians. He disobeyed a command of God and was expelled, never to return. Next came the Indians from the Northwest and received those lands for an inheritance, for till then they had a direct care and communication with God. But the Indians in the course of time also violated direct commands of the Almighty, among which were at least two rules of the Decalogue, when God, being angered, withdrew from all care and interposition in Indian affairs and left them a God-forsaken people, to the evil influences of the seven devils, for each of which they have a myth, viz, Omaha, Makalay, Kalicknateck, Wanuswegock, Surgelp, Mapousney, and Nequileh.

In the latter they find a veritable and connecting link, that minor devil being nothing less than a grizzly.

Omaha (Uma?) is ever invisible and ever bent on bringing evil, sickness, and misfortune on them.

Makalay is shaped and moves like a huge kangaroo, has a long horn like the unicorn, moves with the swiftness of the wind, has caused the death of many Indians, is sometimes seen by mortals, but usually destroys the one who sees him.

The third in order is a huge bird that sits on the mountain peak and broods in silence over his thoughts until hungry, when he will swoop down over the ocean and snatch up a large whale and carry it to his mountain throne for a single meal.

Wanuswegock is a comely giant of immense proportions. This is a myth of temptation, beauty, fear at first, then curiosity, then a growing interest, then passion, followed by destruction in the end.

In connection with the story and curse of Wappeckquenow, the Indians relate an incident which occurred when the miners first went over to the Trinity River. The curse upon Wappeckquenow at the time of his expulsion for disobedience, was that neither he nor his descendants should ever return to the happy lands which they had forfeited. On the first appearance of miners, with their long beards, and without women, they excited of course great interest among the Indians, and much speculation about their origin, their fortunes and objects, and their destination. The prevailing opinion was that they were of a fugitive tribe driven away from their native seats, and their women taken away from them; and this opinion was confirmed by the fact that they had no women with them and possessed long beards—a badge of widowhood among the Indians. Finally white women followed the miners; the erection of dwellings, the opening of mines, a manifest readiness to fight which did not comport with timid fugitives, and other evidences of permanent occupation caused further speculations, until finally an old seer of Hoopah Valley solved the question by announcing that there was something wrong with the curse-prophecy, and that the descendants of Wappeckquenow had come to reclaim their inheritance.

The Supreme Being of the Yurok mythology is called Gard; he created all things, and gave them their language, and now lives in the mountains. Any one who will for the space of ten or fifteen days eat only acorn-soup and think only of him, will have good fortune and get rich, and when he goes out hunting will find a white deer—the highest earthly object of desire to the Yurok.

CHAPTER VI.

THE TOL'-O-WA.

In Del Norte County there are three tribes or bands of Indians who speak the same language, and have the same customs, and yet are often arrayed in hostility one against the other. The Hé-nag-gi live along Smith River, the Tol'-o-wa on the Lagoon, and the Ta-ta-ten' around Crescent City. As the Tolowa are the principal band, they may stand for all.

The language of these three tribes is more nearly related to the Hupâ than to any other, as will be shown in a subsequent chapter. Indeed the Tolowa resemble the Hupâ in character, being a bold and masterly race, haughty and aggressive. They have always been a terror to the Yurok of the Lower Klamath, and in old times they often marched down the coast, through the broad belt of redwoods, then over the fern-grown hills, on the slope of which, at the mouth of the Klamath, is the Yurok village of Rikwa, and upon this they would swoop down, sweeping everything before them, and carry away women and children into captivity. The cold blood in which they made these marauding raids merely to raise revenue from the ransom of the captives, is a great stain on their valor, and a remarkable instance of their otherwise notable rapacity.

When I was in Crescent City the Tolowa and the Tataten were at war, in consequence of the latter having perpetrated some wanton outrage on the former. The Tataten, being only a wretched remnant of thirty or forty souls, had fled with terror into Crescent City, and were encamped on the broad beach between the town and the ocean, among the enormous drift-logs, where they had extemporized for themselves some huts to which sea and shore had contributed about equally. By a pleasant fiction of speech, they declared themselves to be "on the war-path", which is to say, Tá-kho-kol'-li, a squalid and tatterdemalion chief, knowing he was perfectly

65

safe under the protection of the whites, would jump up on a huge log, round out his flat breast and beat the same with extreme defiance in sight of one of his enemies.

A few sneaking curs prowled about; a few rows of flags were spread to dry, for the manufacture of mats; a little smoke oozed out through the superabounding crevices of the crazy driftwood huts; while around lay the disorderly and battered riches of the sea—binnacles of shipwrecked vessels, boxes, bits of oakum, cordage, splinters of spars, kelp, seaweed, those beautiful star-marked shells of the Crescent City beach, etc. Within, amid a cluster of baskets, dogs, mats, baskets of *salàl*-berries, and billets of wood, squatted a few broad-faced squaws, of an almost African blackness, with their stiff, harsh hair cut low on their foreheads, blinking in the smoke, and weaving baskets, or shelling acorns, in that quiet, dogged way they have in the presence of an American, without ever deigning him a glance.

The Tolowa are slightly taller than this melancholy remnant about Crescent City, with more sinew and less adipose, their cheeks a little more drawn and longer, and their noses a trifle higher, but they are about as dark as their kinsmen. The Tataten appear to have had their general stature shortened by losing the tallest and finest fellows among them, who were picked off on account of their former rashness in indulging in an occasional brush with the Americans.

These three bands have the coast partitioned off between them, and the boundaries accurately marked by natural objects, such as bowlders, headlands, etc. Each chief or head-man inherits a portion in behalf of his band—for the coast is owned in common, not in severalty—and whatever of jetsam or flotsam is cast upon it by the ocean is his by indefeasible right. Any attempt on the part of a neighboring band to appropriate any part of the treasures yielded them by Neptune and the Nereids, even to a piece of putrescent whale-blubber, is strenuously resisted, and leads to bloody contentions. Curious and many are the stores which they gather from the sea, from a figure-head of a Cleopatra or the spar-deck of a Spanish galleon, to a horse-mussel or a star-fish.

Probably there are no other Indians in California so avaricious as those of Del Norte County. Money makes the chief among them, and he is entitled to that honor who possesses the most *al'-li-ko-chik*. No matter how high may be the intellectual and moral worthiness of the reigning chief, let the lowest vagabond of the tribe win his money from him in a game of "guessing the sticks" (in these days, in a game of cards), and retain the same a certain number of days, and he practically succeeds to the chieftain- 21 ship, such as it is. Even a child is not named for life until it has grown old enough to assert its name-worthiness by winning or otherwise acquiring money. An old Indian often accumulates great store of shell-money, which he hoards up with a miserliness equal to anything recorded of his pale brethren; and when lying on his death-bed he makes a nuncupative will, and solemnly enjoins upon his relatives to see that his riches are divided according to his bequest. Takhokolli, the tatterdemalion chief of the Tataten, refused even to count ten for me in his language unless I paid him money therefor.

There are numerous dances observed among them, chiefly on occasions of rejoicing. For instance, when a whale is stranded on the beach they celebrate the whale dance. No matter how nasty may be the blubber, they collect around the mighty brute and gorge themselves with it; then, joining hands they dance in a circle around the odious carcass, with chantings and glad shouts and lively antics. Pretty much the same is the elk dance, *Fig. 5* which is held when they have been so fortunate as to entrap one of those unwieldy animals, and the white-deer dance. Then there is the salmon dance, which is more especially observed by the Henaggi on Smith River. In a war dance they paint themselves with barbaric gorgeousness, decorate themselves very much after the fashion of the Karok, seize their bows and arrows, chant, whoop, leap, pirouette, and whirl in a curious manner on one foot, brandish their weapons with terrific yells in the direction of their enemies, etc.

Finally, there is the priestess dance, which is celebrated upon the occasion of the consecration of a woman to the priesthood. This is a rigorous ordeal to the candidate for sacerdotal honors. She is first placed on the ground, in the middle of a cabin, and closely covered from view. Then the dancers, men and women, form in a circle around her, decked out in their gala-dress, and dance and chant those hoarse, monotonous rattles of theirs all night, while marching around. This is continued for nine nights in succession, and during all this period she is allowed to partake of nothing except water. During the day-time the dance is intermitted, but the woman is straitly guarded throughout the whole period of the consecration, lest the flesh should prevail over the spirit, and her ravenous hunger should cause her to profane the ceremony and invoke the wrath of the spirits by secretly eating. As they have no tangible forms of worship, this priestess is only really a shaman, corresponding nearly to the female barking-doctor of the Karok. She is supposed to have communication with the devil, and she alone is potent over cases of witchcraft and witch-poisoning.

The Tolowa share in the superstitious reverence for the memory of the dead which is common to the Northern California tribes. When I asked the chief, Takhokolli, to tell me the Indian words for "father", "mother", and certain others similar, he shook his head mournfully and said, "All dead, all dead; no good". They are forbidden to mention the names of the dead, as it is a deadly insult to the relatives; and this poor aboriginal could not distinguish between the proper names and the substantives which denote those relations.

Heaven, according to the Tolowa, is situated just behind the sun. Captain Dick, an old pioneer of Del Norte County, and intimately acquainted with the Indian habits, thinks they worship the sun; but he mentioned no more satisfying proofs of it than the fact that during certain of their dances, incantations over the sick, and various other solemn ceremonials, they frequently cast their eyes toward the sun. This is the happiness in store for the good, while the bad will, in another world, cold and dark, be condemned to be chased by the devil forever and ever.

This belief in the location of heaven just behind the sun is a very natural outgrowth of their climate. Amid those chilling, dank, leaden fogs, which lazily swing and swash all summer on the northern coast, cold as ice, or sullenly brood motionless all day and all night for a week, dimming the sun's eye to a sickly glare, or shutting him out totally, so that the people get not one hour's glimpse of his face, until the very blood and the marrow of the bones are chilled, it is as natural for the Indians to conceive of the highest possible human happiness to be the privilege of basking forever in his warm soft rays as that the tribes in the arid and sweltering valley of the Sacramento should dream of bliss as being far toward the west, hard by the coast, where they might lave and splash in the cool brine.

The Henaggi deserve special mention on account of the handsome canoes which they fashion out of redwood. I saw one on Humboldt Bay, which had been launched by them on Smith River, and which had there-fore demonstrated its sea-worthiness by a voyage of over a hundred miles. It was forty-two feet long and eight feet four inches wide, and capable of carrying twenty-four men or five tons of freight. It was a "thing of beauty", 22 sitting plumb and lightly on the sea, smoothly polished, and so symmetrical that a pound's weight on either side would throw it slightly out of trim. Twenty-four tall, swarthy boatmen, naked except around the loins, stand-ing erect in it, as their habit is, and with their narrow paddles measuring off the blue waters with long, even sweeps, must have been a fine spectacle.

The Del Norte tribes have about the same implements and range of food as the Yurok. In autumn they consume very large quantities of huckleberries, salal-berries, salmon-berries, etc., which grow in abundance on the coast.

In Dana's *American Journal of Science and Arts*, July, 1873, A. W. Chase gives the following account of the origin of the word "Wogie" (pro-nounced "Wâgeh" by the California tribes), as related to him by the Chetkos, of Oregon:

"The Chetkos say that many seasons ago their ancestors came in canoes from the far north, and landed at the river's mouth. They found two tribes in possession, one a warlike race, resembling themselves; these they soon conquered and exterminated. The other was a diminutive people, of an exceedingly mild disposition, and *white*. These called themselves, or were called by the new-comers, 'Wogies'. They were skillful in the manu-facture of baskets, robes, and canoes, and had many methods of taking game and fish unknown to the invaders. Refusing to fight, the Wogies were made slaves of, and kept at work to provide food and shelter and articles of use for the more warlike race, who waxed very fat and lazy. One night, however, after a grand feast, the Wogies packed up and fled, and were never more seen. When the first white men appeared, the

Chetkos supposed that they were the Wogies returned. They soon found out their mistake however, but retained among themselves the appellation for the white men, who are known as Wogies by all the coast tribes in the vicinity."

For the following legend I am indebted to C. J. Barclay. It was related to him at Crescent City, in 1860, by a daughter of the oldest woman then living of the Smith River tribe:

LEGEND OF THE FLOOD.

At one time there came a great rain. It lasted a long time and the water kept rising till all the valleys were submerged, and the Indians (who were very populous at that time) retired to the high land. As the water rose, covering their retreat, they were swept away and drowned. There was one pair however who were more successful. They reached the highest peak in the country and were saved. They subsisted on fish— cooking them by placing them under their arms. They had no fire and could not get any, as everything was water-soaked to such an extent that no fire could be produced. At length the water began to subside and continued to do so till it returned to its former level, and from that forlorn hope are all the Indians of the present day descended, as also all the game, insects, etc. As the Indians died, their spirits took the forms of deer, elk, bear, insects, snakes, etc., as the fancy of the departed prompted. By those means the earth became again peopled by the same kind as formerly existed; but the Indians still had no fire, and they looked with envious eyes on the moon as having fire while they had none. The Spider Indians formed a plan, having secured the co-operation of the Snake Indians, to obtain fire from the moon. In pursuance of their idea the Spiders wove a gossamer balloon, and started on their perilous journey, leaving a rope fastened to the earth paying out as they went. In course of time they reached their destination, but the Moon Indians looked on them with suspicion, divining their errand. The Spiders however succeeded in convincing them that their only object was to gamble. At that the Moon Indians were much pleased, proposing to start the game forthwith. While thus engaged sitting by the fire a Snake Indian arrived, having climbed the rope, and darted through the fire, making good his escape before the Moon Indians had recovered from their surprise. On his arrival on earth it became incumbent on him to travel over every rock, stick, and tree; everything he touched from that time forth contained fire, and the hearts of the Indians were glad. The Spiders were not so fortunate; they were kept as prisoners for a long time, but finally released. They thought the appearance of the world much improved as it again glowed brightly as before the flood, and gave them light. The Spiders returned to the earth expecting to be received as benefactors of their race; but they were doomed to disappointment, for on their arrival they were immediately put to death, for fear the Moon Indians might want revenge (probably as a peace-offering). As the fire has remained constant ever since, the Snake Indians congratulate themselves on their success.

CHAPTER VII.

THE HÚ·PÂ.

Fig. 6 Hoopa Valley, on the Lower Trinity, is the home of this tribe. Next after the Karok they are the finest race in all that region, and they even excel them in their statecraft, and in the singular influence, or perhaps brute force, which they exercise over the vicinal tribes. They are the Romans of Northern California in their valor and their wide-reaching dominions; they are the French in the extended diffusion of their language.

They hold in a state of semi-vassalage (I speak always of aboriginal acts) most of the tribes around them, except their two powerful neighbors on the Klamath, exacting from them annual tribute in the shape of peltry and shell-money, and they compel all their tributaries to this day, to the number of about a half-dozen, to speak Hupâ in communication with them. Although they originally occupied only about twenty miles of the Lower Trinity, their authority was eventually acknowledged about sixty miles along that stream, on South Fork, on New River, on Redwood Creek, on a good portion of Mad River and Van Dusen's Fork; and there is good reason to believe that their name was scarcely less dreaded on Lower Eel River, if they did not actually saddle the tribes of that valley with their idiom.

Although most of their petty tributaries had their own tongues originally, so vigorously were they put to school in the language of their masters that most of their vocabularies were sapped and reduced to bald categories of names. They had the dry bones of substantives, but the flesh and blood of verbs were sucked out of them by the Hupâ. A Mr. White, a pioneer well acquainted with the Chi-mal'-a-kwe, who once had an entirely distinct tongue, told me that before they became extinct they scarcely employed a verb which was not Hupâ. In the Hupâ reservation, in the summer of 1871, the Hupâ constituted not much more than a half of the occupants,

72

yet the Hupâ was not only the French of the reservation, the idiom of diplomacy and of intercourse between tribes, but it was also in general use within each rancheria. I tried in vain to get the numerals of certain obscure remnants of tribes; they persisted in giving me the Hupâ, and in fact they seemed to know no other.

They remind one somewhat of the Mussulmans, who are forbidden by the Koran to learn any foreign tongue except Arabic. As the Sultans for four centuries had no interpreters save the versatile Greeks of the Phanariotic quarter of Constantinople, so among the tribes surrounding the Hupâ I found many Indians speaking three, four, five, or more languages, always including Hupâ, and generally English. Yet I do not think this was due to any particular intellectual superiority or brilliance on the part of the Hupâ, so much as to their physical force.

Notwithstanding the Hupâ were so powerful in their foreign relations, they were divided into many clans or towns, and these were often arrayed in deadly hostility. These clans were named as follows: Hos'-ler, Mi-til'-ti, 23 Tish-tan'-a-tan, Wang'-kat, Chail'-kut-kai-tuh, Mis'-kut, Chan-ta-kó-da, Hún-sa-tung, Wis'-so-man-chuh, Mis-ke-toí-i-tok, Hass-lin'-tung. The Hupâ owned the Trinity from its mouth up to Burnt Ranch, which is a little above the mouth of New River; but that part of it between the mouth of South Fork and Burnt Ranch they occupied only in summer. It is a region rich in acorns and manzanita-berries, and they allowed the Chim-a-rí-ko to gather these products from it after they had helped themselves. Here too on this quasi-neutral ground, they met the latter tribe in summer for barter, and for the annual collection of tribute.

They were not involved in so many wars with the Americans as were some of the brave but foolhardy tribes farther up the river. One reason was that the Americans did not prosecute mining on the Lower Trinity to the same extent that they did on New River and the Middle and Upper Trinity; hence the salmon-fishing of the Hupâ was not so much interrupted by muddy water—a fruitful source of trouble in early days—nor did they themselves come so much in contact with the miners as did those tribes farther up the river.

Their primitive dress, implements, and houses were almost precisely *Fig. 7* like those of the Klamath River Indians. Another style of lodge, very seldom seen, was as follows: A circular cellar three or four feet deep and twelve feet wide was dug, and the side walled up with stone. Around this cellar at a distance of a few feet from the edge of it was erected a stone wall on the surface of the earth. On this wall they leaned up poles, puncheons, and broad sheets of redwood bark, covering the cellar with a conical shaped inclosure. Sometimes this stone wall instead of being on the *inside* of the wigwam supporting the poles, was on the *outside*, around the ends of the poles, and serving to steady them. Shiftless Indians neglected to wall up the cellar with either stone or wood, leaving only a bank of earth. In the center of the cellar is a five-sided fire-pit walled with stone, as in the common square cabin. This cellar is both dining-room and dormitory; a man lying with his head to the wall has his feet in comfortable position for toasting before the fire. Under his head or neck is a wooden pillow, a little rounded out on top, something like that described by travellers among the Japanese.

Politically the Hupâ are fatally democratic, like all their neighbors. There is no head chief even for war. When several villages are met together for a dance there is one in authority over all, who may be called the master of ceremonies. With the California Indians the management of a dance is of more importance than the management of a war.

It is difficult to understand how a war can be conducted without a central chief in command until we remember that their wars were only raids which might be all over in a day, and certainly did not extend beyond a week. Consequently every man fought in such manner as seemed good in his own eyes, taking care only to keep with the main body of the warriors. No scalps were taken; the heads of the slain enemies were cut off and left on the field. Spies were often employed to visit the enemy's camp to ferret out their plans and report the same. They were paid high wages for this dangerous service, sometimes as much as ten strings of *álli-kochik*, equal to $100, which was contributed by the leading men.

They have well-established laws, or rather usages, as to riparian rights, rights to hunting, fishing, and nutting grounds, laws of murder, injury, and insulting words, etc. For instance, if two Hupâ have a quarrel and it is not settled on the spot, they refuse to speak to each other; but if after awhile one desires to open friendly relations, he offers to pay the other man a certain amount of shell-money. If this offer is accepted they exchange moneys, not necessarily in equal amounts, and perfect friendship is restored. These feuds are sometimes of larger dimensions, including whole villages. When I was on the reservation I tried in vain to hire a member of the Hosler village to accompany me to the Tishtanatan village; the two villages were at enmity.

Murder is generally compounded for by the payment of shell-money. Judge Rosborough states that payment is not demanded until the first full moon after the murder. Then the demand is presented by a third party. If the money is paid at once the affair is amicably settled and is never alluded to again.

There is a singular punishment for adultery when committed by a Benedick. One of his eyes is pricked so that the ball gradually wastes away by extravasation. The Hupâ appear to be ashamed of this nowadays, and I never found but one of them who would admit it. All the rest explained the large number of one-eyed men in the tribe by saying that they lost their eyes when children by carelessness in shooting arrows at each other by way of youthful practice. On the testimony of this one Indian and of two or three white men who have lived among them, I have ventured to state the above custom as a fact.

The wife is never punished for adultery except by the husband. The woman seems to be regarded as not responsible for her misdeeds, as the southern slaves used to be.

They have the same shell aristocracy as the Karok, the amount paid for the wife determining her rank in society.

Notwithstanding their gross immorality, the lot of a bastard is a hard one. He is called *kin'-ai-kil*, which the Indians translate "slave", but which might perhaps better be rendered "ward". The unhappy mother of a bastard has not even the consolation left to Hester Prynne, whose child remained her own. As soon as it is old enough it is taken from her, and becomes the property of some one of her male relatives. Though not condemned to absolute slavery, the *kinaikil* has no privileges with the family. All his earnings go to his patrons. He cannot marry any one other than a *kinaikil*. He is subject to abuse and contumely. The only privilege he is entitled to is that he may have his earnings or winnings at play, if he chooses, placed to his credit, and when they amount to $15 or $20 he may go free. Sometimes he has to accumulate $50 before he can go free. He also has the option of remaining a *kinaikil* for life. He may marry a woman of the same condition, and their children will be *kinaikil* after them.

Hupâ *állikochik* is rated a little differently from the Karok. The standard of measurement is a string of five shells. Nearly every man has ten lines tattooed across the inside of his left arm about half way between the wrist and the elbow; and in measuring shell-money he takes the string in his right hand, draws one end over his left thumb-nail, and if the other end reaches to the uppermost of the tattoo-lines, the five shells are worth $25 in gold or $5 a shell. Of course it is only one in ten thousand that is long enough to reach this high value. The longest ones usually seen are worth about $2; that is, $10 to the string. Single shells are also measured on the creases on the inside of the left middle finger, a $5 shell being one which will reach between the two extreme creases. No shell is treated as money at all unless it is long enough to rate at 25 cents. Below that it degenerates into "squaw-money", and goes to form part of a woman's necklace. Real money is ornamented with little scratches or carvings, and with very narrow strips of thin, fine snake-skin wrapped spirally around the shells; and sometimes a tiny tuft of scarlet woodpecker's down is pasted on the base of the shell.

The Hupâ language is worthy of the people who speak it—sonorous and strong in utterance, of a martial terseness and simplicity of construction. Of the copiousness of its vocabulary a single example will suffice, viz, the words denoting some of the stages of human life—*mich-é-i-teh, kil-é-akh-hutch (kil'-la-hutch), ūn-chūl'-chwil (kon-chwil'-chwil), hó-es-teh, hwa-at'-ho-len, ki-ūng-whe-uh (kú-whin)*, which denote, respectively, "baby", "boy-baby", "youth or young man", "man", "married man" (wife-man), "old man". It has the Turanian feature of agglutination; that is, among other things, the pronoun is glued directly to the noun to form a declension. The possessive case is formed by placing the two words in close juxtaposition, the governing word being postpositive. The verb often presents different root-forms in the different tenses.

As the Hupâ may be called the Romans of California, so is their language the Latin of Indian tongues—the idiom of camps—rude, strong, and laconic. Let a grave and decorous Indian declaim it in a set oration, and every word comes out like the thud of a battering-ram. Take the words for "devil" and "death"—words of terrible import—*ki-toan'-chwa* and *chi-chwit*, and note the robust strength with which they can be uttered. What a grand roll of drums in that long word *kon-chwil'-chwil!*

Doubtless the reader has observed that the life-periods above mentioned are not very accurately defined. They take no account of the lapse of time, and consider it a ridiculous superfluity to keep the reckoning of their ages. "Snows", "moons", and "sleeps" answer to years, months, and days. They guess at their ages by consulting their teeth, like a jockey at Tattersall's. A story is told of a superannuated squaw who had buried two or three husbands—*omnes composuit*—and yet was garrulously talking of remarrying. Some of her friends laughed at her immoderately for entertaining such a silly conceit, whereupon the old crone replied stoutly, showing her ivories, and tapping them with her finger, "See, I have good teeth yet!" A grim suggestion, truly, when taken in connection with possible connubial infelicities in the future!

CHAPTER VIII.

THE HUPÂ, CONTINUED.

Among the dances which they observe is the dance of friendship (*hó-na-weh*), which is an act of welcome and hospitality extended to tribes with whom they are on cartel. They, the Karok, the Yurok, and some others, recognize each other as equals, and send deputations to each other's dances. Before this is to be held, two women go up on the mountain to the cairn on the summit which marks the boundary between them and their neighbors, split some fine fagots and make a fire by the cairn, which they keep up all day. At night deputations from the visiting tribes come up, and are met here by the Hupâ, and all dance around the fire; then with torches and singing they march together down into the valley.

The doctor dance (*chilkh'-tal*) is celebrated upon the initiation of a shaman or medicine-man into the mysteries of his art.

Then there is the dance for luck, or the white-deer dance, in autumn, wherein only men participate. It is wonderful what a charm a white or black deer-skin possesses for these Indians, and it seems to be considered just as efficacious and of as happy auspice if bought from a white man as if killed by the Indian himself. They regard the owner of one as especially favored of the spirits, just as some superstitious people believe him very lucky who finds a four-leafed clover, or something of that sort. A chief whom I saw on the reservation had three which had been handed down so long as family heirlooms that he did not know when they were acquired. The possession of them had exalted him to such a pitch that no person crossing the river with him in a canoe could possibly be drowned, and one or two more added to the store would make him "all the same as God"! Whenever a white deer is killed it is skinned with the utmost care, every part is preserved, hoofs, ears, etc.; the head and neck are stuffed, and a narrow strip of red woodpecker's down is sewed on the tips of its long pendulous ears, in a circle around its eyes, and on the lower end of a piece which hangs down four or five inches from the mouth, representing the tongue. In the autumnal dance mentioned above, these are paraded with great pride, rendering their possessors illustrious in the eyes of all men. No Indian will part with a white deer-skin on any consideration. I offered several of them $100 in gold coin for one, but they simply laughed at me. There are other articles paraded and worn in this and other ceremonial dances which they will on no account part with, at least to an American, though they sometimes manufacture them to order for one another. One of these is the flake or knife of obsidian or jasper I have seen several which were fifteen inches or more in length and about two and a half inches wide in the widest part. Pieces as large as these are carried aloft in the hand in the dance, wrapped with skin or cloth to prevent the rough edges from lacerating the hand, but the smaller ones are mounted on wooden handles and glued fast. The large ones cannot be purchased at any price, but I procured some about six inches long at $2.50 apiece. These are not properly "knives", but jewelry for sacred purposes, passing current also as money. Another thing is a ferocious-looking head-band made of the tail of a big gray wolf. Still another is the gorgeous head-dress which is worn in the dance described below. It consists of a piece of almost snow-white buckskin, about three feet long and seven or eight inches wide, blunt-pointed at the ends, richly and brilliantly covered with scarlet woodpecker's down sewed on in broad bands and zig-zag stripes, sometimes intermingled with green down from the same bird. I had almost closed a bargain with an old Indian after much persuasion 26 to pay him $60 gold for an inferior one of these, but in consulting with his family he encountered such determined opposition that he withdrew from his agreement. They held it sacrilegious to sell it.

The greatest Hupâ festival is the dance of peace, the celebration of which, like the closing of the Temple of Janus, signifies that the tribe are at peace with all their neighbors. I will give first the legend on which it 27 is founded, merely premising that it was related to me by a white man, and that the Indians say it is authentic, only the name "Gard" does not properly belong to the Hupâ mythology, being of Yurok origin.

LEGEND OF GARD.

A great many snows ago, according to the traditions of the ancients, there lived a young Hupâ whose name was Gard. Wide as the eagles fly was he known for his love of peace. He loved the paths of honesty and clean was his heart. His words were not crooked or double. He went everywhere teaching the people the excellent beauty of meekness. He said to them: "Love peace, and eschew war and the shedding of blood. Put away from you all wrath and unseemly jangling and bitterness of speech. Dwell together in the singleness of love. Let all your hearts be one heart. So shall ye prosper greatly, and the Great One Above shall build you up like a rock on the mountains. The forests shall yield you abundance of game and of rich nutty seeds and acorns. The red-fleshed salmon shall never fail in the river. Ye shall rest in your wigwams in great joy, and your children shall run in and out like the young rabbits of the field for number". And the fame of Gard went out through all that land. Gray-headed men came many days' journey to sit at his feet.

Now it chanced on a time that the young man Gard was absent from his wigwam many days His brother was grievously distressed on account of him. At first he said to himself: "He is teaching the people, and tarries". But when many days came and went, and still Gard was nowhere seen his heart died within him. He assembled together a great company of braves. He said to them: "Surely a wild beast has devoured him, for no man would lay violent hands on one so gentle". They sallied forth into the forest, sorrowing, to search for Gard. Day after day they beat up and down the mountains. They struggled through the tangled chaparral. They shouted in the gloomy cañons. Holding their hands to their ears they listened with bated breath. No sound came back to them but the lonely echo of their own voices, buffeted, faint, and broken among the mountains. One by one they abandoned the search. They returned to their homes in the valley. But still the brother wandered on, and as he went through the forest he exclaimed aloud: "O, Gard! O, brother! if you are indeed in the land of sprits, then speak to me at least one word with the voice of the wind that I may know it for a certainty, and therewith be content".

As he wandered aimless, at last all his companions forsook him. He roamed alone in the mountains, and his heart was dead.

Then it fell out, on a day, that Gard suddenly appeared to him. He came, as it were, out of the naked hillside, or as if by dropping from the sky, so sudden was the apparition. The brother of Gard stood dumb and still before him. He gazed upon him as upon one risen from the dead, and his heart was frozen. Gard said: "Listen! I have been in the land of spirits. I have beheld the Great Man Above. I have come back to the earth to bring a message to the Hupâ, then I return up to the land of souls. The Great Man has sent me to tell the Hupâ that they must dwell in concord with one another and the neighboring tribes. Put away from you all thoughts of vengeance. Wash your hearts clean. Redden your arrows no more in your brother's blood. Then the Great Man will make you to increase greatly in this land. Ye must not only hold back your arms from warring and your hands from blood-guiltiness, but ye must wash your hearts as with water. When ye hunger no more for blood, and thirst no more for your enemy's soul, when hatred and vengeance lurk no more in your hearts, ye shall observe a great dance. Ye shall keep the dance of peace which the Great Man has appointed. When ye observe it, ye shall know by a sign if ye are clean in your hearts. There shall be a sign of smoke ascending. But if in your hearts there is yet a corner full of hatred, that ye have not washed away, there shall be no sign. If in your secret minds ye still study vengeance, it is only a mockery that ye enact, and there shall be no smoke ascending".

Having uttered these words, Gard was suddenly wrapped in a thick cloud of smoke, and the cloud floated up into the land of spirits.

The reservation agent cherished this as a heathen parallel and corroboration of the story of Christ; but it is a genuine aboriginal legend. At any rate, they celebrate the dance of peace which this Gard authorized. For nearly twenty years it remained in abeyance, because during most of that period their temple of Janus had been open, as they were engaged in many wars, either with the whites or with neighboring tribes. But in the spring of 1871 the old chiefs revived it lest the younger

ones should forget the fashion thereof, there being then profound peace—
the peace of a reservation—*solitudinem faciunt, pacem appellant.* This dance
is performed as follows : First they construct a semicircular wooden railing
or row of palisades, inside of which the performers take their stations.
These consist of two maidens, who seem to be priestesses, and about
twenty-five men, all of them arrayed in all their glory—the maidens in
fur chemises, with strings of glittering shells around their necks and suspended in various ways from their shoulders ; the men in tasseled deer-
skin robes, and broad coronets or headbands of the same material, spangled
with the scarlet scalps of woodpeckers, to the value of scores of dollars
on each headband.   A fire is built on the ground in the center of the semicircle, and the men and maids then take their places, confronted by two,
three, sometimes four or five hundred spectators.   A slow and solemn chant
is begun in that weird monotone peculiar to the Indians, in which all the
performers join.   The exercise is not properly a dance, but rather resembles
the strange maneuvers of the howling dervishes of Turkey.   They stretch
out their arms and brandish them in the air ; they sway their bodies backward and forward ; they drop suddenly almost into a squatting posture,
then as quickly rise again ; and at a certain turn of the ceremony all the
men drop every article of clothing and stand before the audience perfectly
nude.   The maidens however conduct themselves with modesty throughout.   All this time the chant croons on in a solemn monotony, alternating
with brief intervals of profound silence.

By all these multiplied and rapid genuflections, and this strange infec-
tious chanting, they gradually work themselves into a fanatic frenzy, almost
equaling that of the dervishes, and a reeking perspiration, though they
generally keep their places.   This continues a matter of two hours, and is
renewed day by day until they are assured of the favor of the Great One
Above by seeing Gard ascend from the ground in the form of a smoke.

On this occasion the dance was held on the reservation, but an old
man was stationed on the hill-side near the spot where Gard revealed himself to his brother, to watch for the rising of the smoke.   Day after day,
week after week, he took up his vigil on the sacred lookout and watched,
while the weird, wild droning of the incantation came up to him from the

valley below; but still the smoke rose not until four weeks had elapsed. Then one day he saw it curling up at last! Great was the joy of the Hupâ that they had found favor in the eyes of the Great Man; but the dance was prolonged yet two weeks more, such is the patience of their fanaticism and credulity.

This and the dance of propitiation of the Karok are genuine aboriginal customs; and it seems scarcely necessary to remark that they indicate, on the part of the leading Indians at least, a consciousness of a Supreme Being who holds them accountable for their actions, and whom they think to appease by fasting and expiatory dances. No Indian would fast until he is a living skeleton (as Americans testify that the Karok do) merely to dupe the populace and wheedle them out of their money.

The Hupâ bury their dead in a recumbent posture, and mourn for them in the usual savage manner. They have the same superstitious veneration for their memory as the Karok, and the same repugnance toward allowing any one to view their graves. Most of the valuables are buried in the grave with the deceased.

STORY OF NISH-FANG.

Once there was a Hupâ maiden named Nish-Fang, who had left the home of her forefathers and was sojourning with a white family on Mad River. When that mysterious and momentous occurrence first took place which announced her arrival to the estate of womanhood, she earnestly *Fig. 8* yearned to return to her native valley in order that she might be duly ushered into the sisterhood of women by the time-honored and consecrating ritual of the puberty dance. Without this sacred observance she would be an outcast, a pariah dishonored and despised of her tribe. First it was necessary that she should fast for the space of nine days. Three days she fasted therefore, before setting out on her journey, and on the morning of the fourth she started homeward, accompanied by a bevy of her young companions, Hupâ maidens. It was a long and weary journey that lay before them; over two rugged mountain-chains, across deep and precipitous valleys, through wild, lonesome forests.

Already weak and faint from her three days nearly total abstinence,

Nish-Fang set out to ascend the first mountain. No man might behold her countenance during those nine days, and as she journeyed she buried her face in her hands. Wearily she toiled up the great steep, along the rugged and devious trail, often sitting down to rest. When she became so exhausted that she could no longer hold up her arms, her young companions bore them up, lest some man should behold her face and be stricken with sudden death. By slow stages they struggled on among the gigantic redwood roots where the sure-footed mules had trodden out steps knee-deep; through vast, silent forests, where no living thing was visible save the enormous leather-colored trunks of the redwoods, heaving their majestic crowns against the sky, shutting out the sunlight; then down into deep and narrow cañons where the overshadowing foliage turned the daylight into darkness, where the owl gibbered at noonday, and the cougar and the coyote shrieked and coughed through the black, pulseless night. Every night they encamped on the ground, safe under the impenetrable foliage of the redwoods from the immodest scrutiny of the prurient stars. Long pack-trains passed them by day, urged on in their winding trail among the red-woods by the clamorous drivers who looked and wondered if this woman had been stricken blind; but though these were the hereditary enemies of her race and she might have destroyed them by a single glance, she lifted not her hands from her face.

At last they found themselves moiling up the yet steeper and higher slope of the second mountain-chain, through tangled thickets of the huckle-berry, the wild rose, the silvery-leafed manzanita, and the yellowing ferns, with here and there a stalk of dry fennel amid the coarse, rasping grasses, filling the hot mountain air with a faint aroma. Near the summit there is a spring, where the trail turns aside to a camping ground beneath a wide-branching fir-tree that stands solitary on the arid southern slope. Here they rested and drank of the cool waters. Then they rose to descend into the valley. But Nish-Fang could go no farther; she sank in a swoon upon the ground. And yet, with the instinct of her savage superstition ever strong upon her, though insensible, her hands still covered her face. Then her companions lifted her in their arms and bore her down the long descent of the mountain, through the grateful coolness of the fir-trees and the madroños, past many a murmuring spring, down into the sunny valley of the Trinity, straw-colored in its glorious autumn ripeness, and tinted with a mellow lilac haze. There in the home of her fathers, when her nine days were fully accomplished, in the shadow of a grove of little thin-leafed oaks, the Hupâ danced around her and chanted the ancient chorals of the puberty dance. Then the chief lifted her by the hand and the maiden Nish-Fang became a woman of her tribe.

The puberty dance (*kin'-alkh-ta*) above referred to is celebrated in the following manner: For the space of nine days the male relatives of the girl dance all night, but her female relatives do not join in the dancing, only in the singing. The girl eats no meat, and remains apart and· blindfolded all this while. During the tenth night she is in the house, but keeps close in a corner. The finishing stroke of the ceremony is participated in by two old women and two young men, her relatives, the young men having around their heads leather bands thickly set with sea-lions' teeth—a ferocious-looking head-dress consecrated especially to this ceremony. These five persons are in a row, the girl in the center, the two young men standing on either side of her and the two old women squatting on the outside. The girl goes forward a few steps, then backward. She does this ten times, chanting and throwing her hands up to her shoulders. The last time she runs forward, and gives a leap; then the ceremony is ended.

She is now ready for marriage, and she will bring in the market from three to ten strings (about half the valuation of a man); that is, from $15 to $50. If her husband after paying for her is not pleased with his bargain, he can return her to her father and receive back his money. If she has children and the father-in-law takes them he returns all the money; but if the father keeps them he is obliged to content himself with half the money. Sometimes each child she has reared is reckoned at a string in estimating the woman's commercial value. The Indians relate an instance where a man wished to marry his deceased brother's widow. The woman had cost seven strings, and he demanded that she must either marry him or her friends must refund to him the seven strings. The friends were not willing to do this, but they offered, in case the woman did not wish to marry him, to refund the money minus one string for each of her children. Finally, however, the woman married him.

The Hupâ do not compare with the Indians farther south in the number of substances which they employ in their therapeutics. They are poor physicians. Angelica is a panacea with them, and almost the only one. Their great remedy is suction and conjuration.

CHAPTER IX.

TRIBES TRIBUTARY TO THE HUPÂ.

In this chapter I will group together the contiguous tribes that were subject to the Hupâ. Probably not all of them actually paid tribute to that powerful tribe, but they were all so vigorously domineered by them that they eventually lost the distinctiveness of their respective languages and customs, and fell into the ways of their masters. The complete subjugation of these peoples appears to have occupied the Hupâ a long series of years, and in the case of the Chi-mal'-a-kwe at least it was only just completed when the whites arrived.

THE CHIL-LÚ-LA.

This tribe occupied Redwood Creek from the coast up about twenty miles. Very little can be positively stated of their customs, for all that remain of them have been removed to the reservation where the process of absorption into the Hupâ has been completed. Contradictory statements are made as to their original language, some asserting that it was Yurok, and others Hupâ. It was probably a dialect of Yurok, though as usual in this region, most men of the tribe spoke several languages. The name above given them was bestowed by the Yurok. The Hupâ called them Tes'-wan. The greater prevalence of the name "Chillula" goes to show that they were related to the Yurok.

The Chillula bury their dead. Like most of the coast tribes they are very dark-colored, squat in stature, rather fuller-faced than the interior Indians, guttural in their speech, and characterized by hideous and incredible superstitions, and a belief in the almost universal diabolism of nature. They believe in a monstrous and frightful devil, who has horns, wings, and claws; who can fly through the air with inconceivable rapidity; seize and instantly crush to death a human being, or bear him away through the forest. If any one is ever so unfortunate as to behold this fearful hobgoblin he dies upon the spot. Mr. Hempfield related to me a story of a Chillula squaw whom he once found in the forest rigid in the last agonies of death, with blood oozing from the nostrils and ears, and her eyes fixed in a horrid ghastly stare; and who he had no doubt was frightened to death by believing that she had beheld the devil. The Indians told him such was not an uncommon occurrence among the squaws.

Under various forms this superstition is common to the coast tribes of this region. The Chillula multiply terrors to themselves by assigning this one supreme devil legions of assistants, who assume divers forms, as those of bats, hawks, tarantulas, and especially that of the screech-owl; and who make it their business to torment people, bewitch them, poison them, and do other dreadful things. Let a Chillula woman hear the unearthly gibbering of a screech-owl in the dead and pulseless stillness of midnight, and she shudders with unspeakable horror. It is difficult for us to conceive of the speechless terrors which these poor wretches suffer from the screeching of owls, the shrieking of night-hawks, the rustling of the trees, or even the cold-legged and slimy crawling of insects, all of which are only channels of deadly poison wherewith the demons would smite them.

THE WHĪL'-KUT.

This name is said to be derived from the Hupâ verb *hu-al'-kut, whal'-kut*, "to give", from which comes Hó-al-kut-whuh, "the givers", corrupted by the Americans into Whil-kut. Hence these people are "the tributaries". They lived on Upper Redwood Creek, from the territory of the Chillula up to the source. They ranged across southward by the foot of the Bald Hills, which appear to have marked the boundary between them and the Chillula in that direction, and penetrated to Van Dusen's Fork, opposite the Sai'-az and the Las'-sik, with whom they occasionally came in conflict.

Very little can be affirmed of them, for the same reasons which obtain in regard to the Chillula. Mr. Hempfield states that they burned their dead, but this seems somewhat doubtful, seeing they were surrounded on all sides by tribes who regarded cremation as dishonorable. Probably their custom was somewhat varied.

They spoke Hupâ, but were distinguished as a tribe of polyglots, like most tribes of this region.

THE KĒL'-TA.

The south fork of the Trinity is the home of the Kēl'-ta (Khlēl'-ta). I know not if they ever had any tribal name of their own; if they ever had they have allowed it to be supplanted by the one above employed, bestowed on them by the Hupâ.

They formerly had a distinct language, but the Hupâ encroached so much upon it that it now amounts to nothing. They are per force polyglots; and I saw a curious specimen of this class of inter-tribal interpreters, so peculiar to California. He was called "Old One-eye", and had been facetiously dubbed "Mr. Baker", a title which had greatly elevated him in his own opinion. To maintain it with suitable dignity he considered an ancient and badly smashed tile hat and a cast-off regulation-coat with brass buttons, as absolutely indispensable. He had one eye and six languages in his head.

The Kēlta build a conical wigwam, but without a cellar underneath. Their implements, baskets, etc., are about the same as those heretofore described. They have the same curious custom as the Karok of trimming up trees with a head and two outstretched arms, and using the branches for making assembly chamber fires.

A veteran pioneer and "squaw-man" among them informed me that they eat soap-root (*chlorogalum pomeridianum*) when they are hard pushed in the spring. They extract the poisonous quality from it by roasting, which they do by heaping a large quantity of it on the ground, covering it over with green leaves, and building a fire over it. This is allowed to burn many hours until the poison is thoroughly roasted out, when the root is said to be quite sweet and palatable. They also find a root growing in moist places, of which they make much account, and which is probably cammas, and is called the wild potato, which when roasted and peeled is sweetish and toothsome. The great amount of roots in this State which are sweet when roasted, and especially the cammas—the digging of which procured for the California Indians the injurious appellation of "Diggers"—seems to account partly for the sweet-tooth that every one of them has. Let a squaw get together a few dimes by hook or crook, and she will hie her to a trading-post and invest every cent of it in sugar, when she grievously needs a few breadths of calico. They are as fond of the article as the eastern Indians are of whisky, and eat it as they would bread. The large quantity of saccharine matter which the California Indians get in the roots they eat seems to have somewhat to do with their fatness in youth, just as children are always eating candy, and have round cheeks.

They gather also huckleberries and manzanita-berries, which latter are exceptionally large and farinaceous in the Trinity Valley. I have seen thickets of them wherein an acre could be selected that would yield more nutriment to human life, if the berries were all plucked, than the best acre of wheat ever grown in California, after the expenses of cultivation were deducted. The agriculture of the Upper Trinity and South Fork—heaven save the mark!—will never support a population one-fourth as numerous as the Indians were, and I greatly doubt if the placers, even in the halcyon years of their yield, supported as many as lived there in the days of savagery.

Before the miners troubled the waters the salmon crowded up so thick that all the river was darkened by their black-backed myriads, and they sometimes lingered until they perished by hundreds before they could return to salt water and rid themselves of the devouring fresh-water parasites. An old settler says he has often seen them lying so close that he could go across the thin stream in summer-time stepping every step on a dead salmon.

Extreme democracy prevails among the Kēlta, each village having its figure-head of a chief, whom they obey or not, as they list. As among the Hupâ, adultery committed by a married man is punished by the loss of one eye, and murder by ransom.

Like all savages, the Kēlta are inveterate gamblers, either with the game of "guessing the sticks" or with cards; and they have a curious way of punishing or mortifying themselves for failure therein. When one has been unsuccessful in gaming, he frequently scarifies himself with flints or glass on the outside of the leg from the knee down to the ankle, scratching the limb all up criss-cross until it bleeds freely. He does this "for luck", believing that it will appease some bad spirit who is against him.

Their shamans profess to be spiritualists, not merely having visions in dreams, which is common among the California Indians, but pretending to be able to hold converse with spirits in their waking hours by clairvoyance. An incident is related which is about as worthy of credence as the majority of ghost-stories narrated by the *gente de razon*. There was a certain Indian who had murdered Mr. Stockton, the agent of the reservation, besides three other persons at various times, and was then a hunted fugitive. The matter created much excitement and speculation among the tattle-loving Indians, and one day a Kēlta shaman cried out suddenly that he saw the murderer at that moment with his spiritual eyes. He described minutely the place where he was concealed, told how long he had been there, etc. Subsequent events revealed the fact that the shaman was substantially correct, whether he drew on his clairvoyant vision or on knowledge somehow smuggled.

They make a curious and rather subtle metaphysical distinction in the matter of spirits. According to them, there is an evil spirit or devil (*Kitoanchwa*, a Hupâ word) and a good spirit; but the good spirit is nameless. The evil spirit is positive, active, and powerful; but the good spirit is negative and passive. The former is without, and ranges through space on evil errands bent; but the latter is within them; it is their own spirit, their better nature, or conscience. Like Confucius, who calls the conscience the "good heart", they seem to believe that the original nature of man is good, and that he does evil only under temptation from the bad spirit without or external to himself.

When a Kēlta dies, according to their pretty fancy, a little bird flies away with his soul to the spirit-land. If he was a bad Indian, a hawk will catch the little bird and eat him up, soul and feathers; but if he was good, he will reach the spirit-land. Before the Americans came, they used to bury their dead in a squatting posture, which is a Win-tūn custom; but now they follow the Hupâ custom, which is also that of civilization.

THE CHI-MAL'-A-KWE.

The Chi-mal'-a-kwe lived on New River, a tributary of the Trinity, but they are now extinct. When the Americans arrived there were only two families, or about twenty-five persons, on that stream who still spoke Chimalakwe; all the rest of them used Hupâ. On the Trinity itself, from Burnt Ranch up to the mouth of North Fork, there lived a tribe called the Chim-a-rí-ko (evidently the same word as the above), who spoke the same language as the Chimalakwe, and there are perhaps a half dozen of them yet living. The New River Branch were interesting as affording indubitable proof that the Hupâ exacted tribute from certain surrounding tribes, for at the time when the whites arrived the Chimalakwe were paying them yearly a tax of about seventy-five cents *per capita*—that is, an average deer-skin.

An early pioneer among them named White states that they were once nearly as numerous as the Hupâ, but the restless aggression and persistency of that sturdy race crushed them utterly out. The Chimalakwe seem to represent the true California Indians, while the Hupâ belong to the Athabascan races; and we behold here one of the last conquests of this northern invasion, whose steady progress southward was only checked by the advent of the Americans. As above stated, there were two families of Indians speaking more or less Chimalakwe when the whites arrived; but in fifteen years from that time it had dwindled to a mere category of names, though there were not many of the tribe left to speak either Hupâ or Chimalakwe.

They are a melancholy illustration of the rapidity with which the simple tribes of mountaineers have faded away before the white man, while the more pliant and less heroic lowlanders, conserving their strength through sluggishness, have held on for years. When the serpent of civilization came to them, and they found they were naked, like Adam and Eve in the garden, they made for themselves garments or stole them. Then when there came one of those sweltering days of California the savages chafed themselves, and grew hot in their new clothes, and they stripped them off to the last piece. Besides that, they suddenly changed their diet to a semi-civilized fashion. All these things opened a broad door to quick consumption and other maladies, and the poor wretches went off like leaves on a frosty morning in October. It is related that at one time there were not enough able-bodied Indians in the tribe to dig graves for the dead; and the neighboring whites, to their shame be it recorded, refused to assist them, so that many of them became a prey to the birds and the beasts. So they went like a little wisp of fog, no bigger than a man's hand, on the top of a mountain, when the sun comes up in the morning, and they are all gone.

Living so far up the Trinity as they did, toward the great family of Wintūn, on the Sacramento, they showed a trace of Wintūn influence in that they doubled up a corpse into a bunch to bury it. Their doctors were like the Wintūn, too, in sucking the patient for many ailments, especially for snake-bites.

But their panacea was the sweat-house. Mr. White relates that he once ventured an experiment in one of these sweating-dungeons out of curiosity and in despair over a neuralgia, for the healing of which he had suffered many things of many physicians, and had spent all that he had, and was nothing bettered, but rather grew worse. The first time he was well-nigh suffocated by the dense and bitter smudge made by the green wood. For two hours he lay with his face pressed close to the ground, with a wet handkerchief over his nostrils (the Indians purposely build the fire close to the door, so that they cannot escape until it burns down), and it was a wonder to himself that he lived through it. But he was so much benefited that he made a second trial of it, and was quite cured.

We have seen that the branch living on the Trinity are called Chimariko. I have above intimated my belief that these represent the true Californians, while the Hupâ are Athabascan. As far as the Hupâ ascended the river we find the redwood canoe, but no farther. The Chimariko never had the enterprise to get one up over the falls in the cañon at New River Mountain, and no redwoods grow in their own territory. Hence they crossed the river on willow baskets, holding them under their breasts and propelling themselves with their feet and hands.

It is related that their hunters, when they went out to lie in ambush near salt-licks and other springs, were accustomed to smear their bows and arrows with *yerba buena*, to prevent the deer from detecting the human odor, and that when they took this precaution they generally had good success.

The oak mistletoe was occasionally smoked by these Indians in lieu of tobacco.

In the early days, before the mining operations filled up the Trinity, there was a fall five or six feet high at Big Flat, above which the salmon could not pass.   Hence the Wintūn living on the upper reaches of the river were not so well provisioned as their down-river neighbors.   In running up the river the salmon would accumulate in great numbers at this obstruction, and the Chimariko used to allow the Patch'-a-we (Wintūn) living as far up as North Fork and Cañon Creek to come down in the season and catch all they could carry home.

They occupied a long and narrow cañon, which was rich in gold placers and tempting to the *auri sacra fames* of the early miners.   The mining necessarily roiled the river, so that the Indians could not see to spear salmon. As a matter of course they protested.   The miners replied with insults, if nothing worse.   Being deprived of salmon, their staff of life, they stole the miners' pack-mules and ate them.   The miners made bloody reprisals.

The eloquence of Pú-yel-yal-li, of Big Flat, stirred them up to seek revenge, and thus matters went on from bad to worse until the deep cañon of the Trinity was luridly lighted up by the torch of war, and reëchoed to horrid war-whoops and the yells of the wounded and dying.   In 1863–'64 the conflict raged with frightful truculence on either side.   The Indians for the nonce got the upper hand.   For twenty miles along the river there was scarcely a white family or even a miner left; the trading-posts were sacked and burned; the ponderous wheels in the bed of the river lazily flapped in the waters now muddied no longer, silent and untended amid the blackened ruins; and the miners' cabins were very small heaps of ashes.

But the Americans finally rallied and returned, and sternly were the Indians taught that they must not presume to discuss with American miners the question of the proper color for the water in Trinity River.   They were hunted to the death, shot down one by one, massacred in groups, driven over precipices; but in the bloody business of their taking-off they also dragged down to death with them a great share of the original settlers, who alone could have given some information touching their customs.   In the summer of 1871 it was commonly said that there was not an Indian left. The gold was gone too, and the miners for the greater part; and amid the stupendous ripping-up and wreck of the earth which miners leave behind them, in this grim and rock-bound cañon, doubly lonesome now with its deserted villages sagging this way and that on little margins of shores, the stripped and rib-smashed cabins, corrugated gravel-beds, shattered turbine-wheels, and the hollow roaring of the river amid the gray bowlders, as if in a kind of querulous lament over its departed glories—long ago, the dark-skinned fishermen peering keenly down from their leafy booths, with spears ready poised; afterward, the restless, toiling bands of miners—one finds himself indulging in this reflection: "The gold is gone, to return no more; the white man wanted nothing else; the Trinity now has nothing but its salmon to offer; the Indian wanted nothing else; would not a tribe of savages be better than this utter and irreclaimable waste, even if the gold had never been gotten?"

THE PAT'-A-WE (PATCH'-A-WE).

This is the name given by the Chimariko to the Wintūn, consequently they will be treated of elsewhere.   Their habitat extended down the Trinity to the mouth of North Fork.   They were not in any degree subject to the Hupâ.

CHAPTER X.

THE PAT' A-WĂT.

Around Humboldt Bay there is a broad margin of land which is without dispute the most valuable compact body of soil for agricultural purposes in all the northern part of the State—the very jewel of the California coast. The extraordinary exuberance of vegetation in the humid atmosphere of this region makes it look ragged and unhandsome, with flaunting brake and ferns by every roadside, and concealing every fence-row, and affording a lodging-place for great quantities of dust; but the depth and richness of the soil—that is the wonderful thing. And yet this land of almost unparalleled fecundity was the home of some of the most degraded races of Northern California.

The Patawāt live on the lower waters of Mad River, and round Humboldt Bay as far south as Arcata, perhaps originally as far down as Eureka. They are black-skinned; pudgy in stature; well cushioned with adipose tissue; with little berry-like eyes, often bleared; low foreheads; harsh, black, stiff hair; extremely timid and inoffensive; and a prey all their lives long to the most frightful and ghoulish superstitions I have heard anywhere. Living on the richest and goodliest of lands, they were the envy of their poorer neighbors, and were harried from time immemorial by the fierce Mattoal on the south, by the fiercer Sai'-az and Whĭlkut on the east, and by the Chillula on the north. They formerly built either the common conical hut, or the Klamath lodge of puncheons, with a round, shallow cellar, though now most of them imitate the American house; and their implements are about the same as everywhere. The squaws tattoo in blue three narrow, pinnate leaves perpendicularly on their chins, and also

29

lines of small dots on the backs of their hands. They make beautiful robes of hare-skins, and you may any time see a stout brave slumbering on the naked earth with his head pillowed on a convenient billet of wood and his body covered with a wild cat-skin rug that a San Francisco millionaire might envy for an afghan. An Indian will trap and slaughter seventy-five hare for one of these robes, making it double, with fur inside and out; and on one of the dank nights when the sea-wind howls dismally in from Humboldt Bay, or when the fog broods so dense over the land that one can cleave a rift in it with his swung fist, these are very comfortable to lie under. They also make very substantial tule-mats, almost equal to the Chinese manufacture of bamboo.

One day I talked a long while with one Billy, the only son of the last recognized chief, an Indian with a good knowledge of English, and a suit of clothing which was neat and chastened in tone and complete even to the dapper little necktie. He was a man of about five feet two inches in stature; with a pudding-sack face broader than it was long perhaps; his voice was soft; his manner gentle; and his round cheeks easily rippled into a pleasant smile. He said he was fully entitled to the succession and nobody else pretended to be chief; but the tribe was so wasted that he took nothing upon him, and he seemed to grow melancholy when the subject was broached. He appeared to have sufficient acumen to perceive what a mournful farce it would be for him to strut in a little fifteen-man authority.

In my conversation with him I caught a glimpse of what might be called hereditary imbecility—that is, the stunting of intellect which comes of a few families marrying in and in for a long period of years. He said the chief of the I-tok on Eel River (there is no tribe calling themselves that— he probably meant the Ví-ard) had lately died, leaving the succession to his son; but the latter was unfit to rule, being a natural. "White man call him crazy", said Billy in explanation. He also said that himself was not in his sound mind. "Me no want to be chief; me too much like play", he said. Billy was far from being crazy, but he was a fine specimen of that placid and vacuous inutility which we occasionally see illustrated in Europe, among those born in the purple.

The Patawät have reduced the science and practice of law down to a tolerably accurate mechanism in one matter at least—that of mulctuary punishment. The average fine imposed for the murder of a man is ten strings of *állikochik*, each string consisting of ten pieces, and for that of a squaw five strings of equal length. As the pieces of this shell-money generally average, and as it was at first valued in American coin, these fines amount to about $100 and $50, respectively. If any one is curious to have a more determinate Indian standard, I may say that an average Patawät's life is considered worth about six ordinary canoes, each of which occupies two Indians probably three months in the making (that is, of old), or, in all, tantamount to the labor of one man for a period of three years. Many a California homicide has escaped with no more than three years' "hard labor" in the penitentiary.

A wife is always acquired by purchase, and her market value is regulated on a sliding scale, on which the prices range all the way from two up to fifteen strings. Jacob wrought seven years for Rachel; a Patawät may get his spouse for the equivalent of about nine months' labor, such as it is, or she may cost him as much as five years' labor.

The Patawät also have the custom, which prevails among the Yurok, of contracting "half-marriages."

This tribe has a superstition which, if not actually a belief in vampires, is a close approximation thereto. According to my veracious little chief, there are innumerable spooks, in the forms of men and women who are in the habit of digging up dead Indians and carrying them away into the forest. There they extract from these dead bodies, by burning and by some process of infernal alchemy, divers kinds of poisons, which they use in the destruction of other victims. These ghouls have equal power over the dead and the living. In the night they frequently give chase to people in forests, catch them, and rob them with violence of all their *állikochik*. They also have power to turn men and women into dogs, coyotes, ground-squirrels, and other animals; and they often resort to this highly unjustifiable measure. These imps of hell do not appear to be proper vampires, in that they are not dead Indians returned to life, but pre-existing demons assuming the human form.

All these things Billy related to me with the most profound earnestness and good faith, and many other matters he added thereto, the recital of which would make the hair of the human race stand on end. But I have now something to record of him which is greatly more creditable to his intelligence and that of his tribe. One day I strolled leisurely several miles through the Mad River forest with my little *chaperone*, and our conversation turning on the practice of medicine he pointed out to me as we went along every plant or shrub that possessed a healing virtue. He must have called my attention to fifty different kinds of vegetation, all used by the physicians for medicine, and to every one he gave a distinct name. There is not the smallest moss or lichen, not a blossoming shrub or tree or root, not a flower or vine, no forest parasite, bulrush, or unsightly weed growing in the water or out, or any sea-weed or kelp, for which they have not a specific name; and it seemed to me that Billy pointed out as good for one disease or another nearly half of all the herbs or bushes we saw; so copious and carefully defined is the Patawāt *materia medica*. (See chapter on "Aboriginal Botany.")

Among the Patawāt the dead are always buried and their possessions placed in the graves with them. There is evidence to show that this custom long antedates the advent of the Americans. Mr. Hempfield related to me that in the early days of the settlements around Humboldt Bay, he had seen old Indian burying-grounds containing hundreds of graves, each marked with a redwood slab. Though a soft wood, the redwood is noted for its durability; and the size and condition of some of these head-boards rendered it probable that the graves had been made seventy-five or a hundred years.

The Patawāt are like the Viard in almost every respect, and I was able to obtain various supplementary particulars of the latter; so I will only add here the numerals common to both tribes:

1. Koh'-tseh.	5. Weh'-sah.	9. Sri-ró-keh.
2. Dí-teh.	6 Chil-ó-keh.	10. Lo-kel'.
3. Dí-keh.	7. Â-tloh.	
4. Dí-oh.	8. Í-wit.	

The pronunciation of the Patawāt, like that of the Yurok, is quite
guttural. Judge Rosborough states, in the letter above quoted, that one
and the same language extends from Humboldt Bay to Waitspek, and that it
is "not unpleasing to the ear, being free from harsh and guttural sounds."
This does not correspond with my observations. The Patawāt and Viard
are undoubtedly identical with the Koquilth or Kowilth mentioned by
Gibbs. The Yurok does not extend as far south as Humboldt Bay.

FIG. 9.—Indians at sea.

CHAPTER XI.

THE VÍ-ARD OR WÍ-YOT.

The Viard live on lower Humboldt Bay and Eel River as far up as Eagle Prairie. On the north side of Van Dusen's Fork were the Whíl-kut, extending down to the confluence of the streams. The Viard, as above noted, are very nearly identical in customs and language with the Patawāt.

They appear to have constructed both the conical and the Klamath River wigwam of hewn puncheons, in the making of which they displayed some ingenuity. They first took elk-horns and rubbed them on stones to sharpen them into axes and wedges. Then selecting some fallen redwood that was straight and free from knots, with incredible labor they hacked a notch a few inches deep and reaching perhaps a third or more of the way around the tree. Next they brought the elk-horn wedges into play, with stones for beetles, and split off a kind of jacket-slab, long enough for the height of the wigwam, two or three inches in thickness and four or five feet wide. A veteran woodman relates that he has seen them of the enormous width of seven feet. Of course this puncheon observes the curvature of the tree, but on being exposed to the sun for a few days it warps out flat. They then dressed it smooth with elk-horn or flint axes, and it was ready for use. Very much the same process is said to have been employed on the Klamath.

If the lodge was conical they could employ slabs of the huge redwood bark; but only puncheons set in the ground would make a shelter tolerably secure against the tempestuous winds of Humboldt Bay. For a door they take one of these enormous puncheons, and with their elk-horn axes perforate a round hole through it, just large enough to admit the passage of an Indian on all fours ; and on the inside they frequently place a sliding panel, so that the door can be rendered baby-tight on occasion.

Being notably timid and unskillful in hunting the larger animals they depended mainly on snares and traps to supply themselves with game. To catch deer or elk they constructed two long lines of brush-wood fence, so slight as not to arouse the animals' suspicions, or simply tied single strips of bark from tree to tree in a continuous string, the two lines gradually converging until they compelled the elk to pass through a narrow chute. At this point they placed a pole in such a manner that the animal was obliged to let down his horns to pass underneath, and thus he inserted his head into the noose. This was made of grass or fibrous roots, twisted in a rope as large as a man's arm, and was attached to a pole in such a fashion that the elk dragged it down, whereupon it speedily became entangled in the contiguous bushes and anchored him fast.

Sometimes, to their great dismay, they snared "Old Ephraim," instead of an elk or a deer. Among the earliest colonists in the vicinity of Humboldt Bay was Seth Kinman, who relates the following incident: One day an Indian came running to his cabin with all his might, desperately blown after a hard six-mile stretch, and so cut in his wind that he could not divulge the matter of his business for a considerable space of time. Panting and puffing, and in a drip of perspiration as if he had just emerged from the sweat-house, he made out to reveal his errand by pantomime some time before he recovered his wind. Kinman quickly caught down his rifle and they ran back together. Arrived on the spot he found an enormous grizzly bear snared in the noose, frantic with rage, roaring, lunging about, dragging down bushes and saplings with the pole, and throwing himself headlong when suddenly brought up by some tree. The Indian would not venture within rods of him. Kinman slowly approached and waited for the mighty beast to become a little pacified. He waited not long though, lest the rope might chafe off, and presently drew up and sent a bullet singing into his brain. The great brute fell, quivered, then lay quiet. But it was only when Kinman approached and stamped on his head with his heel that the cowardly Indians were assured; and then from all the forest round about there went up a multitudinous shout. From a score of trees they scrambled down in all haste. Not more than a dozen had been in sight when Kinman arrived on the ground, but now scores collected in a few minutes, gazing upon the enormous brute with owl-eyed wonder, not unmixed with terror.

Like all coast tribes the Viard depended largely on fishing for a subsistence, and the lower waters of Eel River yielded them a wonderful
amount of rich and oleaginous eels. To capture these they constructed a
funnel-shaped trap of splints, with a funnel-shaped entrance at the large
end, through which the creature could wriggle, but which closed on him
and detained him inside. Traps of this kind they weighted down so that
they floated mostly below the surface of the water, and then tied them to
stakes planted in the river bottom. Thus they turned about with the
swish of the tide, keeping the large ends always against the current, that
the eels might slip in readily.

The operation of driving these stakes into the river-bed as points of
attachment for eel-traps, illustrates a point of Indian character. Wading
out into the stream the fisherman gripes the top of the stake firmly in one
hand to prevent it from being splintered, and with a stone in the other
softly and carefully beats it into the hard-packed shingle. He works and
saws it about, tapping it gently the while; and in this fashion he labors
sometimes for hours on one pile, but drives it down at last so solid that
nothing can root it out, where a white man, with his impatience and his
sledge-hammer, would have battered it into a hundred slivers and failed
totally. Mr. Dunganne relates that in former times the great number of
these stakes driven into the river-bed in summer made it look like an old,
deserted corn-field.

Besides this they fish for salmon and smelt in all the various methods
practiced by the Yurok. They also drive down little weirs across tide-
water bayous, and by observing the ebb and flow of the waters capture
large quantities of little flat fish resembling the eastern perch, but something different.

The amazing fecundity of both land and water about Humboldt Bay
once sustained a dense Indian population. The populousness of the ancient
grave-yards, above referred to, is one proof thereof; and the concordant
testimony of the oldest settlers—Dunganne, Duncan, Kinman, and others—
as to the multitudes living on the shores of this noble bay when they arrived, is conclusive. But their manner of smelt-fishing in the surf, whereby
their eyes were often filled with brine, and the high, sand-driving winds

which prevail at certain seasons about the estuary of Eel River, occasioned much ophthalmia among them, and eventually a great deal of blindness.

Mighty eaters are the Viard upon occasion. Mr. Robinson relates that he was once hunting in company with four Indians and a white man, when the latter beat up and shot an elk which proved to be not in good condition, and which he consequently abandoned. He gave it to the Indians, and they at once kindled a fire hard by to protect them against the assaults of grizzly bears, made every preparation for a vigorous campaign on the tough and ancient flesh of the animal, and then fell to lively. In twenty-four hours they accomplished the whole matter, and picked the bones clean. Chancing to pass the place again at the expiration of that period of time, he found the Indians lying in a torpid sleep, and nothing left but the skeleton. Now the flesh of the elk is very solid and weighty, like pork, and a fat and full-grown buck on Humboldt Bay not unfrequently weighs 600 or 700 pounds. This one was lean but large-boned, and these four Indians, at a low computation, must have devoured 150 pounds of meat within twenty-four hours. Perhaps their dogs helped.

It was often a source of wonder to me how the delicate arrow-heads used on war-arrows, with their long, thin points, could be made without breaking them to pieces. The Viard proceed in the following manner: Taking a piece of jasper, chert, obsidian, or common flint, which breaks sharp-cornered and with a conchoidal fracture, they heat it in the fire and then cool it slowly, which splits it in flakes. The arrow-maker then takes a flake and gives it an approximate rough shape by striking it with a kind of hammer. He then slips over his left hand a piece of buckskin, with a hole to fit over the thumb (this buckskin is to prevent the hand from being wounded), and in his right hand he takes a pair of buck-horn pincers, tied together at the point with a thong. Holding the piece of flint in his left hand he breaks off from the edge of it a tiny fragment with the pincers by a twisting or wrenching motion. The piece is often reversed in the hand, so that it may be worked away symmetrically. Arrow-head manufacture is a specialty, just as arrow-making, medicine, and other arts.

Paul Schumacher, in a communication to the Smithsonian Institution, gives the following account of a different process in use among the Klamath

River Indians: "*   *   *   A piece of bone is fastened to a wooden shaft one and a half feet in length, the working point of which is crooked and raised to an edge. The motions to be made with this instrument are shown with the two principal angles,   *   *   *   the force employed being all the time solely pushing.   To guide the instrument with a steady hand, the handle is held between the arm and the breast, while the point, with but little play-room, assisted by the thumb, works on the edge of the flake, which again is held for greater safety in a piece of deer-skin.   After the two sides have been worked down to a point, then another instrument is required, with which the barbs and projections are broken out. This is a needle or awl of about three inches length, and by a pushing motion the desired pieces are broken out similar as with the first-mentioned tool".

Judging by this description, the tool here mentioned is made and worked like one I saw among the Washo of Nevada.

Besides the ordinary dances of enjoyment, of friendship, etc., the Viard have an annual thanksgiving dance in autumn.   It is not an extra-foraneous affair like most of the great anniversary dances of the northern tribes, but is held in a large assembly-hall.   A number of men, fifteen or twenty, according to the room, and two or three maidens, constitute the performers, all of whom are arrayed in barbaric splendor, with feather head-dresses, fur robes, strings of abalone shells, beads, etc.   They dance in a circle around the fire, chanting their monotonous and meaningless choruses, as usual, with occasional improvised recitative, as the spirit may move them, but not beating time to their singing.   The observant reader has probably remarked that most of the tribes so far mentioned do not employ the baton to cadence their harmony, although they keep remark-ably good time; but south of Humboldt Bay most of them beat time to their chanting.

But the great feature of the occasion is the ora   n pronounced by some "old man eloquent".   At a certain turn of the c   ration he proceeds to make them a set harangue, in round and sonorous phrasing, wherein he sums up all the bounties and triumphs of the year.   He enumerates all the fat, firm-fleshed elk they have snared or shot, all the cotton-tailed deer they have run down, the cougars, if any, their braves may have killed, the grizzly bears they have snared, the bear, otter, and seal skins they have tanned; dwells with unction on the bushels of rich and oily eels they have captured in their traps, the red-fleshed salmon they have speared, the smelt, the perch, the squaw-fish, the red-fish they have taken in their nets and dried for winter; gives an account of the rich, sweet hazel-nuts, acorns, the scarlet manzanita-berries, and the purple whortleberries they have stored up in the attics of their wigwams; describes with pride the slender, graceful canoes they have launched, the new wigwams that have been built, and the

Fig. 9   fine stock of bows, arrows, nets, baskets, tule-mats, bear-skin rugs, fishgigs, grass ropes, and beads they have accumulated; tells of the births and marriages, but carefully refrains from any naming of the dead; glorifies the victories they have achieved over their enemies, and the heads they have cut off, but patriotically slurs over their defeats, etc.   In short, he combines in this one speech the President's message, Department reports, and the municipal and health officers' statistics, and adds to the whole a brief thanksgiving homily, exhorting them to good behavior, decency—in short, the practice of the whole limited decalogue of Indian virtues.

This oration is received with stolid solemnity and silence, and the conclusion of it is no more disturbed by indecorous applause than a thanksgiving sermon would be in Trinity Church.   But the thanksgiving dinner— that is lacking.   There is no feasting on dainties—nothing but common feeding.   The dance is resumed until the company have their fill, and the winding up at night is celebrated by a carousal, wherein they violate the moral precepts of the chief to the top of their bent.

CHAPTER XII.

THE MAT-TÓAL.

The Mat-tóal have their main habitat on the creek which bears their name (Mattole) and on the still smaller stream dignified with the appellation of Bear River. From the coast they range across to Eel River, and by immemorial Indian usage and prescriptive right they hold the western bank of this river from about Eagle Prairie—where they border upon the Viard—up southward to the mouth of South Fork, where their domain is bounded by that of the Lo-lon'-kūk.

One thing is notable in regard to the Mattoal, and that is that they form the first exception and the termination to the law of supremacy which prevails all along the coast above. The Tolowa, in Del Norte County, have beaten the Yurok on the Lower Klamath time out of mind. The Yurok were always a terror to the Chillula, and the latter to the Patawāt and the Viard on Humboldt Bay; but here the rule is reversed, and a southern tribe masters a northern. Before the whites came to meddle, and for years afterward, the Mattoal harried the feeble folk about the bay; and to this day, excepting the whites alone, there is no other so terrible bugbear to them as the name of the Mattoal. The latter form an exception to this law, because living principally in a valley secluded from the cold, raw ocean fogs, and subsisting more on a strong meat diet, they are fighting men, sufficiently well fed to whip mercilessly the tribes on Humboldt Bay, who subsist on fish, eels, and roots to a greater extent.

And here I would venture most respectfully to suggest that Professor Agassiz's theory of a phosphoric fish-diet being nutritive above all others to the human brain, is not corroborated by the facts prevailing among these races. Not only do the interior tribes almost invariably lord it over the coast tribes by force of arms, but I have found not only the most beautiful legends, but about all there are of any description, at least one or two layers of tribes back from the sea, while these fog-sodden ichthyophagi have the most revolting and incredible superstitions.

As above noted, the Mattoal were ever making predatory raids on the feeble Viard and Patawàt, and after the whites came into the country they enlarged their operations to include them also. For this the unfortunate bay tribes generally had to bear the blame. With that profound disregard of fine-spun distinctions which is characteristic of the sincere but illogical pioneers, they sacrificed whatever Indians came in their way with great impartiality. Their story, as related by a Viard, is touching in its simple pathos: "Mattoal he come steal um, steal hoss, pig, cow, chicken; steal heap; run um off. White man get heap mad; he cuss. He say one Humboldt Bay Injun, 'You steal um.' Injun say, 'No, no; one Mattoal; me no do.' White man say, 'You lie.' Injun he run. White man run after him; he shoot um; kill heap Injun." The Americans forbade the Viard and the Mattoal from quarreling; but when the latter wished to see their hereditary foes suffer, they had only to make a foray and steal some American horses in the Viard territory, and the thing would speedily be done.

The Mattoal language differs from that of Humboldt Bay so much that the two tribes cannot understand each other until they have conversed together some months. Though I have no specimens of it, I am told by the Indians that it is the same as the Wai-lak-ki of Eel River. This being the case, the Mattoal would belong to the Athabascan races who made the great invasion of Northern California, while the Humboldt Bay tribes would seem to be a remnant of the true Californians, still holding their rich lowlands against the invaders surrounding them on all sides but the sea.

Their wigwams, implements, etc., are like those around them everywhere, and there is nothing of special interest to be noted save the glue they manufacture, which is superior to anything made by civilized processes, not excepting Spalding's patent. With it they glue their strips of sinew on their bows, which render them quite infrangible by any ordinary reasonable strain. Bend the bow with the strength of a Ulysses, yet the sinew cleaves

tight, for the glue neither cracks nor scales up until the wood itself is broken. 31
The secret of its composition is not known to the whites.

In another regard, also, the Mattoal differ from other tribes, and that
is that the men tattoo. Their distinctive mark is a round blue spot in the
center of the forehead. The squaws tattoo pretty much all over their faces.

In respect to this matter of tattooing there is a theory entertained
by some old pioneers which may be worth the mention. They hold that
the reason why the women alone tattoo in all other tribes is that in case
they are taken captives, their own people may be able to recognize them
when there comes an opportunity of ransom. There are two facts which
give some color of probability to this reasoning. One is that the California
Indians are rent into such infinitesimal divisions, any one of which may
be arrayed in deadly feud against another at any moment, that the slight
differences in their dialects would not suffice to distinguish the captive
squaws. A second is that the squaws almost never attempt any ornamental
tattooing, but adhere closely to the plain regulation-mark of the tribe.

Besides the coyote stories with which gifted squaws amuse their children,
and which are common throughout all this region, there prevails among the
Mattoal a custom which might almost be dignified with the name of geographical study. In the first place, it is necessary to premise that the boundaries of all the tribes on Humboldt Bay, Eel River, Van Dusen's Fork,
and in fact everywhere, are marked with the greatest precision, being
defined by certain creeks, cañons, bowlders, conspicuous trees, springs, etc.,
each one of which objects has its own individual name. It is perilous for
an Indian to be found outside of his tribal boundaries, wherefore it stands
him well in hand to make himself acquainted with the same early in life.
Accordingly the squaws teach these things to their children in a kind of
sing-song not greatly unlike that which was the national *furore* some time
ago in rural singing-schools, wherein they melodiously chanted such pleasing items of information as this: "California, Sacramento, on the Sacramento River." Over and over, time and again, they rehearse all these
bowlders, etc., describing each minutely and by name, with its surround-
ings. Then when the children are old enough, they take them around to
beat the bounds like Bumble the Beadle; and so wonderful is the Indian

memory naturally, and so faithful has been their instruction, that the little shavers generally recognize the objects from the descriptions of them previously given by their mothers. If an Indian knows but little of this great world more than pertains to boundary bush and bowlder, he knows his own small fighting-ground infinitely better than any topographical engineer can learn it.

It is above remarked that no Indian in war-time can cross his own proper metes and bounds on penalty of death. There is one exception, that of the herald, whose person is inviolable "wide as the *Indian* idiom rings." So far as his dialect is spoken, he can pass with impunity on errands of weighty business, and especially with a declaration of war, protected by the ægis of his sacred function. He simply whispers two mysterious and sacred words as a countersign, which no other Indian may utter even under his breath. What these words are my informant, Mr. Burleigh, did not know; they are *taboo* to the vulgar herd.

The Mattoal burn their dead, thus showing their relationship with the Upper Eel and Russian River races rather than with the northern. They hold that the good depart to a happy region somewhere southward in the great ocean, but the soul of a bad Indian transmigrates into a grizzly bear, which they consider, of all animals, the cousin-german of sin.

Creation, according to this tribe, was accomplished in a very expeditious manner. The Big Man first fashioned the naked ground, without form and void, destitute of animal and vegetable life, with the exception of one solitary Indian. It was a huge, black world, silent and dark and bleak. The one lone aboriginal of humanity roamed over it desolate and cheerless, finding nothing to gladden his eyes or appease his hunger. Then, upon a time, suddenly there came a strong and swift whirlwind, which sucked up from the ground and filled all heaven with drifting sand and dust and smoke, and the Indian fell flat upon his face in an unspeakable terror. When the tempest passed away he arose and looked, and lo! all this pleasant world was finished and perfect as it is to-day—the earth swarded with green, lush grass, and dappled with sweet flowers, the forests already grown and inhabited by beasts, and the great sea teeming with its finny flocks.

The work of creation having been thus consummated all on a sudden, they hold that there is only a certain limited number of spirits existing among the animals. When one departs this life his spirit immediately takes up its abode in some other one just then entering into existence.

Thus they revolve through a never-ending cycle, *qualis ab incepto*, and are of necessity immortal, though the Indians do not carry out the philosophy to these fine conclusions.

They have also a tradition of the flood, and as usual this occurrence took place in their immediate vicinity. Taylor's Peak is the mountain on which the surviving Indians took refuge.

Frogs and white mice are reverenced by the Mattoal, and they never on any account kill or injure one of these sacred animals. Their superstitious regard for frogs is illustrated in the legend following:

LEGEND OF SATTIK.

Many snows ago there came up a white man out of the southland. journeying down Eel River to the country of the Mattoal. He was the first white man who had ever come into that land, and he lost his way and could not find it again. For lack of food through many days he was sore distressed with hunger, and had fallen down faint in the trail, and he came near dying. But there passed that way an Indian who was called Sattik, and he saw the white man fallen in the trail with hunger with his mouth in the dust, and his heart was touched because of him. He took him and lifted him up, and he brought him fresh water to drink in his hands, and from his basket he gave him dried salmon to eat, and he spoke kind words to him. Thus the man was revived, and his soul was cheered within him, but he could not yet walk. Then the heart of Sattik was moved with pity for the white man, and he took him on his back and carried him on the way. They journeyed three sleeps down Eel River, but Sattik carried the white man on his shoulders, and he sat down often to rest. At the end of the third day they came to a large spring wherein were many frogs; and Sattik dipped up water in his hands to drink, as the manner of Indians is, but the white man bowed down on his belly and drank of the waters, and he caught a frog in his hand and eat it, because of the hunger he had. At the sight of this the Indian's heart became as water for terror, and he fled from the wrath of the Big Man, lest, because of this impious thing that was done, he should come down quick out of heaven, and with his red right hand rend a tree to splinters and smite them both dead to the ground. He ran one day and two nights, and turned not his face back to look behind him, neither did he rest. Then he climbed up a redwood tree to the top of it; but the tree was hollow, and he broke through at the top, and fell down on the inside to the bottom and died there.

Like most wild peoples, the Mattoal are exceeding generous upon the spur of the moment—generous with that thriftless disregard of to-morrow characteristic of savages—but they are sometimes heartlessly indifferent to their parents. They will divide the last shred of dried salmon with any casual comer who has not a shadow of claim upon them, except the claim of that exaggerated and supererogatory hospitality that savages use; but when their elders grow too decrepit to contribute anything more to the household stock, and are only a burden on their scant larder, they often turn them adrift. They are made to understand that any assistance which will enable them to shuffle off this mortal coil with dispatch will be cheerfully rendered. Mr. Burleigh, a long time resident among them, says they were sufficiently affectionate toward their parents before the arrival of the whites; but their sadly dwindled resources, and the hard necessities that have griped them since, have stunted their piety.

As an instance of black filial ingratitude, I saw an old squaw who had been abandoned by her children because she was blind, and who was wandering alone in the Eel River Mountains. Day was night and night was eternal to her sightless eyes, and through all hours of the twenty-four alike she groped her way about with a staff in each hand, going everywhere and nowhere, turning her head quickly toward any noise with that piteous, appealing movement so pathetic in the blind, and uttering every few minutes a wild, mournful, and haunting wail, which sounded like the cry of a hare when it is pierced by the fangs of the hounds. It is hardly possible to imagine any spectacle more melancholy than that of this poor blind savage, deserted by all her natural protectors, and left to wander in a darkness which knew no day through those forests and among those wild cañons. By the merest chance she had happened upon the bivouac of a party of men conducting a pack-train, and they gave her what provisions she could take, and volunteered to guide her to the nearest Indian rancheria; but the poor soul could not understand a word they uttered, or if she did, preferred to take her chances of casual whites rather than throw herself again on a people whose hearts a hard and bitter poverty had steeled, or invoke again even that cheap humanity of blood-relationship which years of calamity had destroyed.

THE LO-LON′-KŪK.

The Lo-lon′-kūk live on Bull Creek and the south fork of Eel River, owning the territory between those streams and the Pacific, along which they have a prescriptive right to a certain length of frontage for fishing purposes. They have the same language and customs as the Mattoal, and no separate description of them is required. Their name has been corrupted by the Americans into Flonk′-o, by which they are generally known.

CHAPTER XIII.

THE WAI'-LAK-KI, ETC.

In the Wintūn language *wai* signifies "north," and *lakki* "tongue," hence "people." So these are the North People. But they do not speak a language in any way related to the Wintūn; and are therefore another instance of a California tribe bearing a name given them by a neighbor.

There is a certain mystery attaching to this tribe. They live along the western slope of the Shasta Mountains, from North Eel River (above Round Valley) to Hay Fork; along Eel and Mad Rivers, extending down the latter about to Low Gap; also on Dobbins and Larrabie Creeks. Hence they are not *north* of the Wintūn at all, as their name indicates, but *west* of the Sacramento Wintūn and *south* of the Trinity Wintūn. The Wailakki proper, belonging to the Wintūn nation, and whose name corresponds to their geographical location, live on the Sacramento above Red Bluff.

As remarked, they have a Wintūn name (their own name for themselves is Ken'-es-ti), and there are two names of places, Ketten Chow and Ketten Pum (these should be spelled Hetten), which are drawn from the Wintūn language within their domain. These geographical terms lying within their territory show that they must have displaced the Wintūn at some former time; and their own language being related to the Hupâ shows that they probably came from the north. Is it not possible therefore that they may have received their present name from the Wintūn while they were yet to the *north* of them? This supposition explains the origin of their name, and I see not how else it can be explained.

On linguistic and other grounds I am inclined to believe that the

114

Wailakki are the descendants of a former secession or offshoot from the Hupâ, who migrated up the Trinity many years ago, and acquired their name from the Wintūn while they actually were "North People," though they continued to push on southward, displacing the Lassik (a tribe of Wintūn affinities) within the American period, until they lodged where they now are, and the whites came and arrested all further migration. The whites became acquainted with the Wintūn first, picked up the name "Wailakki" from them, and applied it without any regard to the tribe's own name to the one now bearing it, and it has remained to this day. If the whites call a California tribe by a certain name, no matter what, they soon learn to use that, whether speaking with whites or with one another.

The fact that the Wailakki dwell on small ineligible mountain streams and the head-waters of one or two swift rivers, without having any one really good valley to themselves, shows that they were once interlopers who had to wedge themselves in where they could.

Judge Rosborough, in the letter referred to in a previous chapter, advances the theory that there have been three principal lines of migration from the north—one along the coast, diverging slightly into the interior; a second, up the Willamet River, in Oregon, and over the Kalapuya Mountains into Scott and Shasta Valleys; and a third, down past the Klamath lakes and across the lava regions to Pit River.

I am much inclined to accept this theory, and, indeed, before I had ever seen Judge Rosborough's letter, I had come to a similar conclusion in regard to the line of southward migration along the coast: but I had not at that time any facts in my possession as to the two other migrations, nor even a suspicion that they had ever occurred. I had discovered already that along the supposed track of this coast-line of migration there is a series of tribes, beginning in Del Norte County, and including the Tolowa, the Hupâ, and some of their tributaries (not counting in the Humboldt Bay tribes), and the Wailakki, who speak languages closely related. It is a singular fact that these languages are also closely related to the Navajo, of New Mexico, showing that the Navajo must have removed from the Pacific coast within comparatively recent times. The following table of numerals corroborates this statement. (The Navajo are taken from another work, and probably have the English sound of the vowels).

	TOLOWA.	HUPÂ.	WAILAKKI.	NAVAJO.
1	chlah.	chlah.	klai'-hai.	kli.
2	nakh'-eh.	nakh.	nok'-ah.	nahkee.
3	takh'-eh.	takh.	tok.	tah.
4	tenkh'-eh.	tinkh.	tenkh'-ah.	dteen.
5	swoi'-lahr.	chwó-lah.	tus-kul'-lah.	estlahh.
6	os-tá-neh.	hos-tan'.	kūs'-lak.	hostonn.
7	tsé-teh.	okh'-kit.	kūs'-nak.	susett.
8	la-ní-shi-tná-ta.	ká-nem.	kūs'-tak.	seepee.
9	chlá-ntukh.	no-kos'-tah.	kūs-tenkh'-ah.	nastyy.
10	neh'-sūn.	minkh'-lah.	kwang-en'-ta.	niznahh.

The Wailakki, though so obviously Hupâ in affinity, owing to their nearness to the Wintūn, have adopted some of their customs, as scalping, the scalp dance, the clover dance, and some other things. On the other *Fig. 10* hand they tattoo nearly like the Yuki, so that they are mistaken by some for that singular people. Thus it will be seen that they are a somewhat composite people: Hupâ in speech, Wintūn in name and in several customs, and almost Yuki in tattooing.

They build the common conical wigwam of poles and bark, with a depression slightly scooped out for a floor. One sees among them very pretty strings of shell-money, called *to-kal'-li*, consisting of thin, circular disks about a quarter of an inch in diameter, and resembling somewhat the Catholic rosaries, in having one larger button or "Gloria Patri" to every ten small "Ave Marias". I have seen a Wailakki squaw with ear-drops or pendants carved from the ear-shell (*Haliotis*) in the shape of fish, and exhibiting the glinting tints of that beautiful shell to great advantage. It is the only instance of fancy shell or bone carving, aside from the common shell-money, that I ever remember to have noticed.

In the hot and sweltering interior of the State the Indians generally leave their warm winter lodges as soon as the dry season is well established, and camp for the summer in light, open wickiups of brushwood, which they sometimes abandon two or three times during the summer for convenience in fishing, etc. Immediately on the coast this is scarcely done at all, because not necessary; but the Wailakki generally go higher up the little streams in the heated term, roaming and camping along where the salmon trout (*Salmo Masoni*) and the Coast Range trout (*Salmo iridea*) most abound. They capture those and other minnows in a rather ignominious and un-Waltonian fashion. When the summer heat dries up the streams to stagnant pools they rub the poisonous soap-root in the water until the fish are stupefied, when they easily scoop them up, and the poison will not affect the tough stomach of the aborigines.

In Ketten Chow Valley they used to gather immense quantities of cammas (*Cammasia esculenta*). Then there is a kind of wild potato growing on high and dry places (I saw no specimens of it) which they use to a considerable extent, in addition to roots eaten by all California Indians. In the Wintūn language, "Hetten Chow" denotes "cammas valley," and "Hetten Pum" means "cammas earth".

The Wailakki have also a very unsportsmanlike method of capturing deer. They run them down afoot. This is not so difficult a matter as one might imagine in the case of a very fat buck. Deer have a habit of running pretty much in certain established trails, and the Indians make these trails a study, post relays of men at points where the animal is pretty certain to pass, and so give him continuous chase until he is out of his range, and thereby frequently get him so blown that he either stands at bay or takes to the water. An old hunter tells me he has frequently seen them capture a fine buck in this manner. Then, again, they construct two slight lines of brushwood fence, converging to a point, where a snare is set, and they chase the animal into this snare. Beside deer, they also run down hare and rabbits, and this is still more easily done. A company of Indians get together in a space of meadow or in an open wood, and whoop and beat the cover to flush the quarry. Puss is terrified by the multitude of voices, and runs wild, springs in the air, doubles, tacks, flings somersaults, ducks, leaps square off from a straight run even when nothing moves or makes a noise near it, and so beats itself completely out, or slips into its burrow. This is great sport for the Indians. They whoop, laugh, scurry through the woods, jump, swing their arms, fling clubs, and make a deal of noise. I have seen an Indian boy of fourteen run a rabbit to cover in ten minutes, split a stick fine at one end, thrust it down the hole, twist it into its scut, and pull it out alive. This was easier than it would have been to shoot it, especially if he missed it.

One of their favorite dances is the black-bear dance, which is celebrated when one of the Wailakki braves has been so fortunate as to kill or trap one of these animals of happy omen, or has even succeeded in purchasing a skin of one. They stretch it up on stakes, and then caper and chant around it in a circle, beating the skin with their fists as if they were tanning the same.

Another joyous occasion is the clover dance, which is performed in the season when the burr-clover gets lush and juicy to eat. The squaws deck themselves out in deerskin-robes and strings of pretty shells, which jingle and glint to their hopping, while each man has a circlet or coronal of the soft white down of owls around his head, twisted in a fluffy roll as large as his arm, and another very long one of the same description around his loins, tied behind, with the two ends reaching down to the ground. In short, the men endeavor to make themselves look as much like the great white owl as possible, and the main purpose of their numerous antics appears to be to keep these long tails flopping about. They stand in two circles— the men inside, the women outside; strike up the inevitable droning chant, and the women dance by simply jumping up and down on both feet, while their partners in front of them leap, skip, brandish their arrows, and at a certain turn of the chant they all jump up together, with a loud whoop and shaking of bows and arrows, after which there is a dead silence for a few moments, when they commence chanting again *da capo*. There is no feasting at any time.

Filial piety cannot be said to be a distinguishing quality of the Wailakki, or, in fact, of any Indians. No matter how high may be their station, the aged and decrepit are counted a burden. The old man, hero of a hundred battles, sometime "lord of the lion heart and eagle eye," when his fading eyesight no more can guide the winged arrow as of yore, is ignominiously compelled to accompany his sons into the forest, and bear home on his poor old shoulders the game they have killed. He may be seen tottering feebly in behind them, meek and uncomplaining, even speaking proudly of their skill, while he is almost crushed to earth beneath a burden which their unencumbered strength is greatly more able to support, but they touch it not with so much as one of their fingers. 35

Most people who have traveled in the frontier regions of California, especially if they were on foot, have probably been no little worried and exasperated at the perversity with which the road-makers have run the trails and roads over the summits of the hills. Often have I said to myself in my hot impatience, "If there is one hill in all this land that is higher than another, these engineers and graders are never content until they·have carried the road over the top of it." But the Indians are more responsible for this than our engineers. Time and again I have wondered why the trails so laboriously climb over the highest part of the mountain; but I afterward discovered that the reason is because the Indians needed these elevated points as lookout-stations for observing the movements of their enemies. They run the original trails through the chaparral. The pioneers followed in their footsteps, and widened the path when need was, instead of going vigorously to work and cutting a new one on an easier grade; and in process of time when a wagon-road became necessary they often followed the line of the ancient trail. When the whole face of the country is wooded alike, the old Indian trails will be found along the streams; but when it is somewhat open they invariably run along the ridges, a rod or two below the crest—on the south side of it, if the ridge trends east and west; on the east side, if it trends north and south. This is for the reason, as botanical readers will understand, that the west or north side of a hill is most thickly wooded. The California Indians seek open ground for their trails that they 36 may not be surprised either by their enemies or by cougars and grizzly bears, of which beasts they entertain a lively terror.

The Wailakki are a choleric, vicious, quarrelsome race, like the Yuki of Round Valley, whom they resemble; and these two tribes are the prime rascals of all that country. Naturally, therefore, the tribe has been rapidly fretted away by the white men, and they would have been wholly abolished before this time had they not been gathered on the Round Valley Reservation.

An adventure related by T. G. Robbins, of the California volunteers, shows that the Wailakki are not lacking in bravery. His regiment, the Second Infantry, had been pushing a stiff campaign against them south of Eel River, routed them in a bloody fight, and drove them pell-mell over the river at Big Bend. One of them being a poor swimmer lagged behind, and when Robbins and his comrades emerged on the bank, they saw him resting in the middle of the river, in the eddy of a bowlder. He now struck out again, and the bullets spattered in the water around him like hail. Once across, he perceived it would be death to run up the bank under fire, so he concealed himself again. Robbins stripped to the buff and swam over to tackle him. As he came out of the water the Indian dashed at him with an enormous root in each hand. Both men were stark naked, except that the Wailakki had a shell-button and a dime hanging from each ear. The soldier struck at him, but his rotten billet of driftwood splintered harmlessly over the savage's head. The Indian aimed a mighty blow in return, but the soldier threw up his left arm as in sword practice, and the club broke over it, though the end slammed down on his sconce, causing him to perceive ten or twelve Indians and several hundred stars. The Indian struck with his second club, but Robbins parried again, and the club bounced high in the air. Both men were now disarmed. Instead of closing in and grappling, as he should have done, the Indian made a dive to recover his club. Quick as thought the soldier caught up another, and as the Indian stooped he dealt him a stunning blow on the base of the ear. The savage fell all along on the gravel, and lay quivering in every muscle, while the soldier, as he says, "beat him until there was not a whole bone in his body", and the company on the other side looked on and applauded.

This trifling affair, with its truly Homeric termination, is worth relating only as an instance of a fair, naked fight between men of the two races, armed only with the weapons which nature offered. The upshot shows that the savage was the equal of the other in strength, agility, and courage, but was inferior in fencing.

THE LAS'-SIK.

The Las'-sik formerly dwelt in Mad River Valley, from the head-waters down to Low Gap, or thereabout, where they bordered on the Whilkut. They took their name from their last famous chief. As above narrated, a little before the whites arrived they were driven out of this region by the incursion of the Wailakki, whence they removed to Van Dusen's Fork and Dobbins and Larrabie Creeks. They were of Wintūn affinities, so here again they jostled against the original occupants, the Saiaz and others, and in hard-fought battles were routed again. Thus ousted from every place where they tried to establish homes—crowded, elbowed, super-numerary in a crystallized population, beaten about from pillar to post, with their hearts full of rancorous bitterness and despair—they became a band of gypsies, or rather of thugs, houseless and homeless nomads, whose calling was assassination, and whose subsistence was pillage. Their hand was against every man, and every man's hand against them. All the world was their natural enemy. They roamed over the face of the earth, robbing and murdering. It is said they took no scalps, but cut off a slain enemy's feet and hands. They even penetrated into the distant valley of the Sacramento, where they came in conflict with the newly-arrived white man, and by bloody defeat and fierce pursuit they were hurled back over the mountains whence they came.

After much tough and bitter experience in this adoptive method of life, the Lassik gradually ceased to murder in robbing, but continued to prosecute the latter occupation with undiminished vigor and brilliant success. They would blacken their faces and bodies with charcoal, then go into the forest near some sequestered house, or by the wayside, and squat there for hours together motionless as a stump. So closely would they resemble the latter object that the lynx-eyed backwoodsman and hero of fifty fights would pass them by unaware. When some one came along at last who was seemingly weak, and promised good picking, they would sally forth quickly—strange how these stumps will get up and run!—catch the horse by the bit, and proceed to pluck the rider clean. Day after day, week after week, they would come and squat in this fashion near some lonely house, with that infinite persistence of the Indian, watching the inmates as they came and went, counting them over and over again, until they were certain of their number and quality. Then at last, on some happy day, when all the signs of the zodiac, the sun and moon and planets, were favorable, and no owl screeched, and the spiders were all still, and everybody was gone out of the house except perhaps some old crone or swaddled baby, they would summon courage to make a rush, capture the solitary occupant, pinion him, and plunder the house with neatness and dispatch.

Mr. Robinson related to me an instance where a certain house was plundered by them three Aprils in succession, punctually to a week, and almost to a day. It was the property of a lone wild Irishman, a shepherd, who was necessarily absent day-times with his flock on the mountains, thus leaving his household substance an easy prey to the savages. After being twice robbed in succession, Paddy took unto himself a wife for a bulwark and a defense to his possessions round about. But a third time the Lassik came when he looked not for them, scaled the garden fence, made a sudden irruption into the house, and knowing the propensity of women to talk, caught the Irishman's wife, tied up her mouth tight, and bade her escape for life. This she did, and they then proceeded without interruption to make a choice selection of household goods, which they carried away.

This predatory gypsy life (they subsisted largely this way, not having a right to any fishing-grounds), insured their speedy destruction by the whites. In 1871 it was said there were only three of them left; these had returned to the ancestral valley of Mad River, and were living under protection of the whites.

THE SAI'-AZ.

As nearly as I could ascertain, the Sai'-az· formerly occupied the tongue of land jutting down between Eel River and Van Dusen's Fork. They were all carried away to the Hoopa Valley Reservation, and had been so long dragged about between home, the Smith River Reservation, and this, that they were dwindled away to a most pitiful and miserable remnant, who could give no intelligible account of themselves. The only thing which can be stated with certainty is that they once dwelt somewhere on the east bank of Eel River.

It is the testimony of white men, who had had a taste of their quality, that they were once among the bravest of the California Indians. It was only after a long and heroic resistance that they gave under, and were led away captive to the Smith River Reservation. It was in Hoopa Valley that I saw them, and it was indeed hard to believe then that they had ever done anything manly. They were the most abject of human beings—many of them from living eternally in the smudge, with one or both eyes swollen and horribly protruding; some with their noses half eaten away; all with their coarse black hair drooping over faces pitted and slashed, or purple, blotched, and channel-worn with the dribblings of bleared and sodden eyes. Their naked and unspeakably filthy board cabins stood on a hot *mesa* beside the river, with never a tree or a shrub to dapple their roofs with a sprinkle of shade; the flaming sun made riot in the exhalations staggering up from the fouled earth; bones, chips, skins, festering flesh were strewn about; and in this place of miasma and famine the ghastly beings lay about in their swarming tatters, basking in the sun like muddy-skinned caymans of Louisiana, or drowsily shelling a few acorns, for they received no rations.

Most tribes of California either burn their lodges annually or abandon them frequently to escape from the vermin; but here, condemned to live always on one spot and in the same lodges which they were not taught how to cleanse, they are almost devoured alive. In their native state they always bathe the entire person daily in cold water; but here, huddled together in foul, reeking quarters, what little pride of person they ever had was in a fair way to be crushed out of them.

Judging from the wretched remnants that are left, the Saiaz resemble most Eel River Indians, having rather squatty, adipose bodies, chubby heads, and long simian hands. Like the Kélta they frequently scarify the outside of their legs when they lose a bet in gambling.

They entertain a belief in what, out of contradistinction to Pantheism, may be called Pandemonism. Most tribes living near the coast believe that the devils or evil spirits of the world pervade many forms of animal life, or at least are able to assume those forms at pleasure for the tormenting of men (though all of them have some one or more animals, as a white deer, a white mouse, a frog, a black bear, a black eagle, into which the devil never does enter); but the Saiaz hold that these evil spirits also take possession of the vegetable world for the plaguing of mankind.

For instance, acorns, leaves, or twigs falling from trees on the roofs of their wigwams are all instinct with the devil, replete with demoniac, poisonous influence; and they think that the bad spirits assume these forms to compass their destruction. When the winter wind goes over them with a lonesome, ghostly shriek, and brings the acorns and leaves rattling down on their roofs, they shudder, and the timid squaws scream with terror. One would think that an imagination so lively would involve common sense enough to suggest the building of the lodges in the open ground. And, in fact, most of their villages, as is the case throughout California, are built on open ground, though this is done rather with a view of preventing hostile tribes from ambushing them.

One way the Saiaz and other Eel River Indians sometimes adopt in crossing swift and deep rivers in winter is to hold stones on their heads to weight them down so that they can wade over on the bottom. They will stay under nearly two minutes, and by selecting smooth, gravelly places they can cross streams of some rods in width this way.

My observations have been that the Indians of Eel and Mad Rivers are of a rather short and pudgy stature, especially the Wailakki, and a decidedly inferior physique in general; but the pioneers say that present appearances are deceptive. These tribes have suffered much from wars with the whites, and the remnants of them are the poorest specimens of their race, who took little part in fighting. In an early day they averaged an inch or two taller than the Indians of Sacramento Valley and the Weaverville Basin, and were much finer men. The Wailakki are called by the Yuki "Kak'-wits"; i. e., "North People".

The Wailakki call the Saiaz Noan'-kakhl, and the Mattoal and Lolon-kūk, Tul'-bush. All these tribes here mentioned originally spoke Wailakki.

CHAPTER XIV.

THE YŪ-KI.

To the traveler arriving on the summit between Eden Valley and the Middle Eel River, looking north, there is presented one of the most beautiful and picturesque landscapes in California. The name, "Round Valley", is descriptive of this noble domain, and there it lies, far below and beyond, an ocean of yellow grain and pasture fields, islanded with stately groves of white oak and encompassed on all sides with a coronal of blue, far-sloping mountains, dappled green and golden with wild-oat glades and shredded forest or chaparral. There is something rich and generous, like ripened corn and wine, in the landscapes of the Coast Range in autumn, and over all bends the soft sky of Italy, and pours the wonderful lilac *chiaroscuro* of the atmosphere, which lends an inexpressible charm.

Here in the heart of the lofty Eel River Mountains, which shut it in sixty or seventy miles from all the outer world, was a little Indian cockagne, a pure democracy, fierce and truculent. The inhabitants of this valley, unequaled in its loveliness by all that is said or sung of the Vale of Cashmere—the Yuki—were indisputably the worst tribe among the California Indians.

I had a great deal of trouble in finding this singular people. I heard about "Yuki" over in the Sacramento Valley, at Weaverville, on Hay Fork, on Mad River, on Van Dusen's Fork, and all along Eel River, and always the "Yuki" were to be the next tribe that I would come upon. At last I began to be skeptical of their very existence, and smiled an incredulous smile whenever I heard the name "Yuki" mentioned.

The reason for this is curious. The word *yuki* in the Wintūn language signifies "stranger", and hence, secondarily, "bad Indian" or "thief";

and it was applied by that people to different tribes around them, just as
the ancient Greeks called all the outside world "barbarians". There were
of old many tribes contiguous to them who actually were "bad Indians"
compared with the peaceful Wintūn; but the latter applied the epithet so
indiscriminately that the Americans, not troubling themselves to investigate
the matter, got confused on this subject. Hence the number of tribes
called "Yuki". As a matter of fact, there *are* several tribes whom both
whites and Indians call "Yuki"; but this tribe alone acknowledge the title
and use it.

The unphilosophical and double-seeing Wintūn at Red Bluff described
the "Yuki" to me as terrific fellows, savage giants living in the Coast
Range Mountains, dwelling in caves and dens, horribly tattooed (which
they are), and cannibals.

Their own name for themselves is Ūk-um-nom (meaning "in the valley"), and for those on South Eel River speaking the same language, Hūch'-
nom (meaning "outside the valley"). Those over on the ocean are called
Ūk-hóat-nom ("on the ocean"). It is possible that the word *ukum* was corrupted by the Wintūm into *yuki*, their present name.

Most of them have two names, one given in infancy, the other in later
life; but there is no ceremony in connection with the christening. For
instance, the head-chief of the Yuki, when the Americans became acquainted with them, was Toal-ke-mak' or Wil-osh'. Their present chief,
called on the reservation Captain Mike, is Pam-mem'-mi or Oal'-wal-mi.
When a child does not grow well, or otherwise seem to be prosperous and
lucky under one name, another is frequently given to it. This is previous
to the bestowment of the virile name. I have not often in California found
a name bestowed on account of circumstances in the person's history; but
it is done among the Yuki, though generally a child takes its father's or
grandfather's name. Thus Mil-chói-mil (I talk) was given to a talkative
child; another was called Wo-nun'-nuh (Blue Head); and another Mai-
el-hóat-meh (Big Legs).

The Yuki and the Wailakki are considered of a rather low grade of
intellect, and on the Round Valley Reservation they are the butt of the other
Indians. The common saying regarding these two tribes is that "they do

not want to know anything". They both prefer against each other the charge that, in old times, the dead who had no friends were dragged away into the brush, or hidden in hollow logs, or barely covered with leaves, &c. Hence the Yuki had few friends among their neighbors, except the Wailakki, and they had more intercourse with them than with any others, although they occasionally fought each other with a hearty good-will. They joined territories about half-way between Round Valley and North Eel River, and they intermarried, giving rise to a progeny called Yuki-Wailakki. The Yuki were unrelenting enemies of the Nóam-lak-ki (Wintūn), and often fought them on the summit east of Round Valley. They would climb trees up there and wait for hours for a Nóam-lak-ki to come along, when they would imitate the grouse, the California quail, or some other choice game-bird, and so lure them within arrow-shot. They were also especially bitter against the whites, and seized an early opportunity to kill any of their squaws who went to live with them.

The Yuki have disproportionately large heads, mounted like cannon-balls on smallish, short bodies, with rather protuberant abdomens. Their eyes are a trifle under-sized, but keen and restless, and from the execrable green-wood smudge in which they live in winter they are not unfrequently 39 swollen and horribly protruding. Their noses are stout, short, and straight, the nares expanded; and they have heavy shocks of stiff, bristly hair, cut short, and hence bushy-looking. They are variously complexioned, without any perceptible law, from yellowish-buff to brown and almost black.

They are a truculent, sullen, thievish, revengeful, and every way bad but brave race. Two of them from whom I attempted to get their numerals chose to consider me bent on some devilish errand, and they lied to me so systematically that I did not get a single numeral correct. They have the most desperate persistence in pursuit of revenge. I was told of an instance where a tribe seemed to have decreed that a certain offending pioneer and hunter, formidable with the rifle, must be killed, and more than a dozen of them who were sent to do the work, were one after another slain by him before they accomplished their purpose.

On the reservation at the present day the Yuki quarters are on a low piece of ground which was once occupied as a burying-ground, hence the place is infested with miasmatic exhalations and is unhealthy. The aborigines were better sanitarians when they had the control of these matters; they built their lodges all around the edge of the valley, on the first little bench or series of knolls, and not on the plain at all. Their assembly-hall was of the Sacramento Valley order, dome-shaped, capable of containing from one to two hundred persons, thatched with grass and covered with earth. They had the mountain style of lodge, conical-shaped and built of poles, bark, and puncheons, but often thatched in winter.

Most of the tribes in Northern California use wood almost exclusively in their lodges, especially on the Coast Range, and near the redwood belt; but in the coast valleys and on the great plains of the interior, thatch and earth are used for roofing. As a partial consequence, we find that ophthalmia and blindness prevail in the latter region more than in the former, on account of deficient ventilation.

There have been various estimates of the aboriginal population of Round Valley. I am told that Sam. Kelsey, the first American who ever set foot in the valley, and a man accustomed to Indians, estimated it at 5,000 souls. At this figure there would have been one Indian to every four acres in the valley, or 160 to the square mile! And yet this is not at all improbable, because the Indians lived wholly in the valley (except for brief seasons in the summer), while they had usufructuary possession of a vast circumjacent area of mast-bearing forest, besides many miles of salmon streams. On the same reasoning, the above conjectural rate of population must by no means be applied to the great, naked, arid plains of the Sacramento and San Joaquin.

As the Yuki were so often involved in war, martial matters necessarily engage a great deal of their attention, and occupy a large part of their conversation. Their customs and usages in this direction were quite elaborate. Mrs. Dryden Laycock, one of the pioneer women of Round Valley, described to me a Yuki war-dance, that she once witnessed, which was a fantastic and terrible spectacle. The warriors to the number of several hundred assembled behind a little hill, where they stripped themselves naked (though their aboriginal costume consisted of little else but breech-cloths); then they smeared their bodies with pitch or some other sticky material, and sprinkled on white eagle-down from tip to toe. On their heads they put bushy plumes and coronals of larger feathers. Then, seizing their bows and arrows, and slinging their quivers over their shoulders they rushed over the brow of the hill and down upon the plain in a wild and disorderly throng, uttering unearthly yells and whoops, leaping, and brandishing their weapons above their heads, and chanting their war-songs.

Before a battle takes place the heralds of the two contending parties meet on neutral ground and arrange the time and place of the conflict. The night before going out they dance all night to inflame their courage. If the warrior possesses a wide elk-skin belt he ties it around him to protect his vitals, but otherwise he is quite naked. About three hundred arrows to the warrior is the complement of ammunition for a raid. The Wailakki, on the other hand, wear shields of tanned elk-skin, which are very thick and tough, and proof against most arrows. The body of the skin is stiff, and is left wide enough to shield two or three men. It is worn on the back, so as not to incommode the warrior in battle, and when he sees an arrow coming he turns his back to it, and two or three of his friends, if they choose, screen themselves behind his shield, at the same time shooting over it or around the sides of it. If the shield-bearer sees an arrow coming so low that it may strike him in the legs he ducks. They time their march so as to be at the battle-field at daybreak. If a Yuki stumbles and falls on the march, or 40 is stung by a yellow-jacket, it is a bad omen; he must go home, or he will be killed.

During the battle they simply stand up in masses in the open ground or amid the chaparral, and shoot at each other until they "get enough," as one of them expressed it; then they cry quits and go home. If any dead are left on the field both parties return afterward and carry them away and bury them (they burn only those whom they do not honor, though this rule is not invariable); but a pioneer states that he has seen Yuki dead left on the field, a prey to beasts and birds.

The Yuki say that they never scalped white men, but they take scalps from Indians.

When the men are absent on a war expedition the women do not sleep; they dance without ceasing, in a circle, and chant and wave wands of leaves.   They say their husbands " will not get tired if they dance all the time ".   When they return they join in the dance, in a circle within that of the women.   Each woman is behind her own husband, and she wets him with water, and sprinkles acorn flour over him, to groom and rest him, and waves a wisp of leaves over him to cool him.

When rain falls in autumn enough to give the earth a thorough soaking, and the angle-worms begin to come to the surface, then the Yuki housekeeper turns her mind to a good basket of worm-soup.   Armed with her " woman-stick," the badge of her sex—which is a pole about six feet long and one and a half inches thick, sharpened and fire-hardened at one end—she seeks out a piece of rich, moist soil, and sets to work.   Thrusting the pole into the ground about a foot, she turns it around in every direction, and so agitates the earth that the worms come to the surface in large numbers for a radius of two or three feet around.   She gathers and carries them home, and cooks them into a rich and oily soup, an aboriginal vermicelli, which is much esteemed by the good wife's family.

After this lickerish mess is eaten, perhaps she discovers that the youngest boy's hair needs cutting, and she brings out the scissors.   This consists of a flat piece of stone and a sharp-edged bone ; the stone is held under the hair, while with the bone she haggles it off as best she can.   Then with a coal of fire she evens off the ends around quite nicely.

Tattooing is done with pitch-pine soot and a sharp-pointed bone.   After the designs have been traced on the skin, the soot is rubbed in dry.   In *Fig. 11* another place the reader will find a series of tattoo patterns employed by different tribes.

Candidates for the degree of M. D. pass their competitive examination in the assembly hall—an examination more severe than the contention between Doctor Cherubino and Doctor Serafino in " the great School of Salern ".   It consists simply of a dance, protracted through day and night without cessation, until they all fall utterly exhausted except one, who is then admitted to practice the healing art.

One method of procedure is as follows : The patient is placed on the ground stark naked, face upward, and two doctors take their stations at his feet, one directly behind the other.   Striking up a crooning chant, they commence hopping up and down the unfortunate individual with their legs astride of him, advancing by infinitesimal jumps all the way up to his head, then backward to his feet—both keeping close together and hopping in regular accord.

The "poison doctor" is the most important member of the profession. The office is hereditary; a little child is prepared for holding it by being poisoned and then cured, which in their opinion renders him invulnerable ever afterward. Of course it will be understood that a great part of these supposed cases of poisoning are merely the creation of their superstitious imaginations. They are somewhat homeopathic in their practice; they cure poisoning with poison, expel a cold with cold water, etc. They go by the rule, no cure no pay. Female doctors are not absolutely entitled to a fee, but they expect and generally receive presents. An instance is related where a woman volunteered to extract an arrow-point from the body of a white man who was friendly to the Yuki. Her proposition was accepted, and at the appointed time she arrived followed by a train of about thirty female attendants; she was dressed sumptuously in fringed leggings, a thread petticoat of milkweed fiber, a beautiful wild-cat skin robe tasseled with the tails, and a rich otter-skin bandeau, supporting tall eagle feathers, which were cut in the middle to tremble with her motions. She carried in her hand a wand with a gay feather in the end of it. She was described as a woman of a majestic presence, graceful with that unstudied charm which belongs to the children of the sun. Walking round and round the patient with her attendants, and chanting, she repeatedly applied her wand to the wound and simulated great effort in drawing out the arrow-head. Finally she stooped down and applied her lips to the wound; and after a little while she ejected a flint from her mouth (previously placed there of course), and assured the man he would now speedily recover. For this humbug, so transparent, and yet so insinuatingly and elegantly administered, she expected no less a present than a gayly-figured bandana handkerchief and five pounds of sugar.

When their own friends fall sick they give them sufficient attention; but if an old person has no blood-relations he is generally left to die unattended. Public spirit is a thing unknown.

There is a curious phenomenon among the California Indians called by the Yuki the *i-wa-mūsp* (man-woman), and by the Pomo *dass*. I have heard of them elsewhere, but never saw one except in this tribe. There was a human being in the Yuki village on the reservation who wore a dress and was tattooed (which no man is), but he had a man's (querulous) voice, and an unmistakable though very short and sparse whisker. At my instance the agent exerted his authority and caused this being to be brought to headquarters and submitted to a medical examination. This revealed the fact that he was a human male without malformation, but apparently destitute of desire and virility. He lived with a family, but voluntarily performed all the menial tasks imposed upon a squaw, and shirked all functions appertaining to a man. Agent Burchard informed me that there were at one time four of these singular beings on the Round Valley Reservation, and Charles Eberle, a pioneer, stated that, in his opinion, there were, in an early day, as high as thirty in the Yuki tribe. Why do they do this? *Quien sabe?* When questioned about it the Indians always seek to laugh the matter away; but when pressed for an explanation they generally reply that they do it because they wish to do it; or else with that mystifying circumlocution peculiar to the Indian, they answer with a long rigmarole, of which the plain interpretation is, that, as a Quaker would say, the spirit moves them to do it, or, as an Indian would say, that he feels a burning in his heart which tells him to do it. There are several theories advanced by the whites to account for this phenomenon: one, that they are forced to dress like women as a penalty for cowardice in battle; another, that it is done as a punishment for self-abuse; still another, that they are set apart as a kind of order of priests or teachers. This last theory has some appearance of confirmation in the fact that one of these men-women once went down from Pit River to Sonoma County and "preached" to the Mission Indians in Spanish. Others among the Yuki have been known to devote themselves to the instruction of the young by the narration of legends and moral tales. They have been known to shut themselves up in the assembly-hall for the space of a month, with a few brief intermissions, living the life of a hermit, and spending the whole time in rehearsing the tribal history in a sing-song monotone to all who chose to listen.

Nevertheless, I consider the Indian explanation the best, because the simplest—namely, that all this folly is voluntary; that these men choose this unnatural life merely to escape from the duties and responsibilities of manhood; and that the whole phenomenon is to be regarded as another illustration of that strange capacity which the California Indians develop for doing morbid and abnormal things.

The Pit River Indians have a regular ceremony for consecrating these men-women to their chosen life. When an Indian shows a desire to shirk his manly duties they make him take his position in a circle of fire, then a bow and a "woman-stick" are offered to him, and he is solemnly enjoined in the presence of the witnesses assembled to choose which he will, and ever afterward to abide by his choice.

From the outrageous character of this tribe, white men know very little about their religious beliefs and ideas. Tai-kó-mo is the name of the Great Man of the Yuki mythology; he created the world and was himself the first man in it. But this has probably been ingrafted from the Christian story.

The Yuki bury their dead in a sitting posture. They dig a hole six feet deep sometimes, and at the bottom of it "coyote" under, making a little recess in which the corpse is deposited.

There is an anniversary dance observed by them called the green-corn dance, though this manifestly dates only from the period when the Spaniards taught them to cultivate corn. The performers are of both sexes; the men being dressed with a breech-cloth and a mantle of the black tail-feathers of eagles, reaching from under the shoulders down to the thighs, but not encumbering the arms; while the squaws wear their finest fur robes, strings of shells, etc., and hold gay-colored handkerchiefs in their hands. The men hop to the music of a chant, a chorister keeping time with a split stick; but the squaws, standing behind their respective partners in an outside circle, simply sway themselves backward and forward, and swing their handkerchiefs in a lackadaisical manner.

Thievery is a virtue with them, as it was with the Spartans, provided the thief is sly enough not to get caught. Turbulent and choleric, they often treat their women and children with cruelty, whereas most California

Indians are notable for their leniency. They were frequently involved in deadly feuds among themselves, and were seldom off the war-path in former times, the pacific and domestic Pomo being their constant victims.

A veteran woodman related to me a small circumstance which illustrates the remarkable memory of savages. One time he had occasion to perform a piece of labor in a certain wood where water was very scarce, and where he was grievously tormented with thirst. He remembered to have seen a little spring somewhere in that vicinity, and he considered it worth his while under the circumstances to search for it two days, but without success, when there came along a Yuki woman, to whom he made mention of the matter. Although she had not been near that place for six years, and, like himself, probably had never seen the spring but once, yet without a moment's hesitation or uncertainty she led him straight to the spot. Probably there is no other thing in this country, so arid through the long summer months, of which the Indians have better recollection than of the whereabouts of springs.

THE YUKI DEVIL.

On the reservation there once lived an Indian who was so thoroughly bad in every respect that he was generally known by the sobriquet of The Yuki Devil. He committed all the seven deadly sins and a good many more, if not every day of his life, at least as often as he could. One time he wandered off a considerable distance from the reservation, accompanied by two of his tribal brethren, and the three fell upon and wantonly murdered three squaws. They were pursued by a detachment of the garrison, overtaken, captured, carried back, manacled hand and foot, and consigned to the guard-house. In some inexplicable manner the Devil contrived to break his fetters asunder, and then he tied them on again with twine in such fashion that when the turnkey came along on a tour of inspection he perceived nothing amiss. Being taken out for some purpose or other soon afterward, he seized the opportunity to wrench off his manacles and escape. He was speedily overtaken and brought down with a bullet, which wounded him slightly, taken back to the guard-house, heavily ironed, and cast into a dungeon. Here he feigned death. For four days he never swallowed a crumb of nutriment, tasted no water, breathed no breath that could be discovered, and lay with every muscle relaxed like a corpse. To all human perception he was dead, except that his body did not become rigid or cold. At last a vessel of water was placed on a table hard by, information of that fact was casually imparted to him in his native tongue, all the attendants withdrew, the dungeon relapsed into silence, and he was secretly watched. After a long time, when profound stillness prevailed, and when the watchers had begun to believe he was in a trance at least, he cautiously lifted up his head, gazed stealthily all around him, scrutinized every cranny and crevice of light, then softly crawled on all-fours to the table, taking care not to clank his chains the while, took down the pitcher and drank deep and long. They rushed in upon him, but upon the instant— so fatuous was the obstinacy of the savage—he dropped as if he had been shot, and again simulated death. But he was now informed that this sub- terfuge was quite too thin for any further purposes, and as soon as the gal- lows could be put in order the executioners entered and told him plainly that the preparations were fully completed for his taking-off. He made no sign. Then, half dragging, half carrying the miserable wretch, they con- duct him forth to the scaffold. All limp and flaccid and nerveless as he is, they lift him upon the platform; but still he makes not the least motion, and exhibits no consciousness of all these stern and grim preparations. He is supported in an upright position between two soldiers, hanging a lifeless burden on their shoulders; his head is lifted up from his breast where it droops in heavy helplessness; the new-bought rope, cold and hard and prickly is coiled about his neck, and the huge knot properly adjusted at the side; the merciful cap which shuts off these heart-sickening preparations from the eyes of the faint and shuddering criminal is dispensed with, and everything is in perfect readiness. The solemn stillness befitting the awful spectacle about to be enacted falls upon the few spectators; the fatal signal is given; the drop swiftly descends; the supporting soldiers sink with it, as if about to vanish into the earth and hide their eyes from the tragedy; with a dead, dull thud the tightened rope wrenches the savage from their upbear- ing shoulders into pitiless mid-air, and the Yuki Devil, hanging there·with- out a twitch or a shiver quickly passes from simulated to unequivocal and unmistakable death.

THE CHU-MAI'-A.

In the Pomo language *chu-mai'-a* signifies "stranger", hence "enemy". Some writer has finely remarked that it is a good commentary on our civilization that, in frontier parlance, "stranger" is synonymous with "friend"; but in the Indian tongues it seems to be generally tantamount to "enemy".

The Chu-mai'-a are simply Yuki; the more southerly bands of them, in Eden Valley and on the Middle Eel, south of Round Valley, are sometimes called the Spanish Yuki, because their range was southward and this brought them in contact with the Spaniards from whom they acquired some words and customs.

They and the Yuki were ever on the war-path against the peaceful and inoffensive Pomo, and the brunt of their irruptions generally fell on the Potter Valley Pomo, because the mountains here interposed slighter obstacles to their passage. At the head of Potter Valley the watershed is very low and the pass is easy, so easy that it could readily be traversed by heavy masses of civilized troops. On the summit, a rod or two from a never-failing spring, there is to this day a conspicuous cairn, which was heaped up by the Indians to mark the boundary; and if a member of either tribe in war-time was caught beyond it he suffered death. When the Chumaia wished to challenge the Pomo to battle, they took three little sticks, cut notches around their ends and in the middle, tied them in a fagot, and deposited the same on this cairn. If the Pomo took up the gauntlet, they tied a string around the middle notches and returned the fagot to its place. Then the heralds of both tribes met together in the neutral territory of the Tatu, a little tribe living at the foot of the pass, and arranged the time and place of the battle, which took place accordingly. William Potter, the first settler in Potter Valley, says they fought with conspicuous bravery, employing bows and arrows and spears at long range, and spears or casual clubs when they came to a square stand-up fight in the open field. They frequently surged upon each other in heavy, irregular masses.

The following almost incredible occurrence was related to me by a responsible citizen of Potter Valley, and corroborated by another, both of whose names could be given if necessary:

STORY OF BLOODY ROCK.

After the whites became so numerous in the land that the Indians began to perceive they were destined to be their greatest foes, the Chumaia abandoned their ancient hostility to the Pomo, and sought to enlist them in a common crusade against the newly-come and more formidable enemy. At one time a band of them passed the boundary-line in the defile, came over to the Pomo of Potter Valley, and with presents and many fair words and promises of eternal friendship, and with speeches of flaming, barbarian eloquence and fierce denunciation of the bloody-minded intruders who sacrificed everything to their sordid hankering for gold, tried to kindle these "tame villatic fowl" to the pitch of battle. But the Pomo held their peace, and after the Chumaia were gone their ways they hastened to the whites and divulged the matter, telling them all that the Chumaia were hoping and plotting. So the Americans resolved to nip the sprouting mischief in the bud, and fitting out a company of choice fighters went over on Eel River, fell upon the Chumaia, and hunted them over mountains and through cañons with sore destruction. The battle everywhere went against the savages, though they fought heroically, falling back from village to village, from gloomy gorge to gorge, disputing all the soil with their traditional valor, and sealing with ruddy drops of blood the possessory title-deeds to it they had received from nature.

But of course they could not stand against the scientific weapons, the fierce and unresting energy, and the dauntless bravery of the whites, and with sad and bitter hearts they saw themselves falling one by one, by dozens, by scores, fast going out of existence, all their bravest dropping around them. The smoke of burning villages and forests blackened the sky at noon-day, and at night the flames snapped their yellow tongues in the face of the moon, while the wails of dying women and helpless babes, brained against a tree, burdened the air.

At last a band of thirty or forty—that was as near the number as my informant could state—became separated from their comrades, and found themselves fiercely pursued. Hemmed in on one side, headed off on another, half-crazed by sleepless nights and days of terror, the fleeing savages did a thing which was little short of madness. They escaped up what is now called Bloody Rock, an isolated bowlder standing grandly out scores of feet on the face of the mountain, and only accessible by a rugged, narrow cleft in the rear, which one man could defend against a nation. Once mounted upon the summit the savages discovered they had committed a deplorable mistake and must prepare for death, since the rifles in the hands of the Californians could knock them off in detail. A truce was proclaimed by the whites, and a parley was called. Some one able to confer with the Indians advanced to the foot of the majestic rock, and told them they were wholly in the power of their pursuers, and that it was worse than useless to resist. He proffered them their choice of three alternatives: Either to continue to fight, and be picked off one after another, to continue the truce and perish from hunger, or to lock hands and leap down from the bowlder. The Indians were not long in choosing; they did not falter, or cry out, or whimper. They resolved to die like men. After consulting a little while they replied that they would lock hands and leap down from the rock.

A little time was granted them wherein to make themselves ready. They advanced in a line to the brow of the mighty bowlder, joined their hands together, then commenced chanting their death-song, and the hoarse, deathly rattle floated far down to the ears of the waiting listeners. For the last time they were looking upon their beloved valley of Eel River which lay far beneath them in the lilac distance, and upon those golden, oat-covered and oak-dappled hills, where they had chased the deer in happy days forever gone. For the last time they beheld the sweet light of the sun shine down on the beautiful world, and for the last time the wail of his hapless children ascended up to the ear of the Great One in heaven. As they ceased, and the weird, unearthly tones of the dirge were heard no more, there fell upon the little band of whites a breathless silence, for even the stout hearts of those hardy pioneers were appalled at the thing which was about to be done. The Indians hesitated only a moment. With one sharp cry of strong and grim human suffering—of the last bitter agony—which rang out strangely and sadly wild over the echoing mountains, they leaped down to their death.

CHAPTER XV.

THE TÁ-TU.

The Tá-tu are known in their own language as Hūchnom and on the reservation as "Redwoods"; the title here given them is that applied to them by the Pomo of Potter Valley. The Hūchnom live along South Eel River, but that part of them included in the above name live in the extreme upper end of Potter Valley. They constitute a mere village, a little Indian Monaco, wedged in between two powerful families, the Yuki and the Pomo, yet allowed to retain their neutrality and independence most of the time. *Figs. 12-17* 44

As I once before intimated, the Pomo were a harmless and inoffensive race, yet they had the fondness of most savages for martial trophies and displays, though lacking the courage to procure them. So they sometimes employed the Hūchnom to make war for them against the Yuki and bring them scalps, for which they paid at the rate of about $20 a scalp. And frightful scalps they took! They skinned the whole bust, including the shoulders, but omitted from the scalp that part of the face within a triangle, whose angles are the root of the nose and the extremities of the lower jawbone. This is a mercenary transaction quite germane to the character of the Northern California Indians.

The Tatu wigwams do not differ essentially from those of the vicinal tribes; they are constructed of stout willow wicker-work, dome-shaped, and thatched with grass. Sometimes they are very large and oblong, with sleeping-room for thirty or forty persons. The assembly-hall is made with heavier timbers to support the thick layer of earth necessary to render it air-tight. Having only very contracted holes at the side for ingress and egress, these wigwams maintain within a most execrable and everlasting acrid smudge which makes bloodshot and protruding eyes horribly common among the aged.

At the head of Potter Valley there is a singular knoll of red earth which the Tatu believe to have furnished the material for the creation of the original coyote-man. They mix this red earth into their acorn bread, and employ it for painting their bodies on divers mystic occasions. I supposed at first that the mixing of this red earth in their bread was a ceremonial performance, but seeing it afterward done by other tribes I came to the conclusion that the Indians spoke truthfully in saying that they did it merely to make the bread sweet, and make it go further. They have quarried out immense quantities of it from the knoll for these purposes. I visited it myself, and found that my worthy host spoke truly in saying that they have
45 taken out "hundreds of tons". At any rate, I will venture the suggestion that they must have been living in the valley a thousand years, in order to have quarried out this quantity of earth for yeast and cosmetics alone.

They are remarkable for their timidity. My host, Mr. Carner, related how a full-grown, vigorous Tatu in his employ was once frightened to death in broad daylight by a belligerent turkey-cock. The poor fellow had never seen that species of fowl before, when one day as he was walking through the yard the gobbler, being greatly blown out and enlarged in appearance, made a furious dash at him, and so frightened him that he straightway took to his bed and expired in two days. Another one of the same tribe unwittingly trod in a bear-trap when hunting one day with a companion, whereupon he dropped all in a heap upon the ground, helpless and lifeless, with unspeakable terror, and died in his tracks in half an hour, though a subsequent examination revealed the fact that the steel trap had inflicted no mortal injury on him, and that he undoubtedly perished from fright. His comrade, instead of unclamping the trap, fled for his dear life, believing it was the devil they had encountered.

Mr. Carner, himself a Christian who had labored zealously for their conversion, said he had often seen them engage in wordy quarrels, bickering, and jangling, and jabbering strange, voluble oaths, until almost the whole village was involved, and until his own patience was entirely gone, but never once advance to blows. His Saxon blood once got the better of his religion, his indignation waxed hot, and he offered them clubs, and told them either to fight or be silent, but they did neither the one nor the other.

A secret society exists among the Tatu something similar to that described in the Pomo chapter, the members of which, in conversation with their white acquaintances, make no secret of the fact that it is designed simply to keep the women in due subjection. To accomplish this highly laudable purpose they profess to be able to hold communication with the devil. The Pōm Pomo also do this in the secrecy of the lodge, but the Tatu go further; they boldly usher him forth into the outer world, and reveal his corporeal presence to the terrified squaws. In the private lodge occupied by the society, which is the assembly-hall, they prepare one of their number to personate that terrific being. First, they strip him naked, and paint his body with alternate stripes of red and black, spirally, from head to foot. Then they place on his head a chaplet of green leaves, and in his hand a sprig of poison-oak. With the leaves of the chaplet drooping over his face to prevent the squaws from recognizing him, all naked and hideously painted as he is, he rushes forth with pranks, and lively capers, and dreadful whoops, while the assembly-hall he has just left resounds with diabolical yells. Dipping his wisp of poison-oak in water he sprinkles it upon the faces of the squaws as he gambols and pirouettes around them, whereat they scream with uncontrollable terror, fall prostrate upon the earth, and hide their faces.

Probably the water from the poison-oak blisters their faces slightly, and as these things are commonly done in the evening when they cannot perceive the poison-oak, the victimized squaws are confirmed in their belief of his satanic attributes. They are forbidden to discuss the matter among themselves, for if one ever sees a spook and mentions it he dies! It is wonderful that these thin tricks can be maintained for years and centuries perhaps, unchanged until they are worn down threadbare, and still continue to work out terror and fainting of heart to the women as before. Yet the savages are not Pyrrhonists, and these simple souls least of all.

Many varieties of medical practice are in vogue. For instance, Tep, a great shamin of the Tatu, will sit for hours beside a patient, chanting in that interminable, monotonous way of the Indians, and beating his knee with a bunch of rabbit-bladders filled with pebbles, ending finally with a grand flourish of the bladders in the air, and a whirring chatter of the voice, to exorcise the evil spirit.

Another and more sensible mode is as follows: A hole is dug in the ground large enough to admit the sick person, partly filled with stones painted with red and black stripes; then a fire is kindled in it and continued until the ground is thoroughly heated. The fire and stones are then removed, and a quantity of rushes with their joints painted with the sacred red earth is thrown in, followed by a wisp of damp hay or grass, for the purpose of creating a steam. First, the practitioner himself lies down on the hay and wallows his breast and back in it, probably to round it into shape; then the patient is laid on it, thickly covered with hay or blankets, and allowed to perspire freely.

Still another method is, to place the patient on his back, naked, stretch out his arms and legs wide asunder, plant four springy twigs in the ground at a distance, bend them over, and tie each to a hand or foot with a string. Then the physician, spirally painted like the devil above described, approaches with a coal of fire on a fragment of bark, and burns the strings in two, allowing the twigs to spring up one after another, whereupon the patient screams. The notion appears to be that the evil spirits lurking in the several limbs are somehow twitched out or burned.

Mr. Carner described to me an interesting operation which he once witnessed, whereby a squaw whose nervous system had received a severe shock from fright was restored by what might be likened to the Swedish movement-cure. Dr. Tep, the renowned Tatu shaman, officiated on the occasion, and it seems to have been his exceptional good sense and ingenuity which devised the remedy. The woman had been frightened simply by a pebble falling into the brook where she was drinking; but, however trivial was the producing cause, there could be no doubt as to the genuineness and intensity of her suffering. The disease appeared to have assumed, finally, the form of an inflammatory rheumatism, and had baffled the skill of all their physicians.

At last Dr. Tep assembled nearly the whole village together, placed the woman in the center on the ground, caused the company to lock hands in a circle, and then they commenced a dance around her, accompanied by a chant. The singing was slow and mournful at first, corresponding to the movement of the dance, and the sick woman gave no response to it except her continual groaning and cry of *"ahwe! ahwe!"* The tone of the chanting was full of sadness and commiseration, as if the dancers were deeply moved with pity for the sufferer, but slowly it quickened, and the dance gradually became more lively. Still she seemed not to be aware of their presence, and only continued to cry out piteously, *"ahwe! ahwe!"* Faster and faster droned the chant, and still more gaily capered the dance, first round one way, then the other, while animation began to beam on their countenances. At last the woman seemed to be awakening to the contagious enthusiasm. She could not resist the old familiar frenzy of the dithyrambic dance. Still swifter and swifter circled the dancers. Her eyes began to brighten. Strain now followed strain, instead of the first monotony. She was plainly catching the infection. That wild and wizard *verve* of savage fanatics was taking possession of her senses. Her wailing *"ahwe! ahwe!"* began to follow the ever-quickening time of the chant. But still she was unable to rise. Then the swift circle of dancers swerved suddenly in their mad enthusiasm, swooped upon her with shouts, she was caught up in strong arms, and half-carried, half-dragged around the ring, while her *"ahwe! ahwe!"* gradually changed into the general voice of the chanting, and melted out of hearing, and step by step, feebly at first, but carried irresistibly away at last by the rapture of the hour, she joined in the dizzy whirl until perspiration had done its perfect work.

Mr. Carner added that two or three days afterward he saw the woman again, and she was perfectly cured.

The Tatu observe the acorn dance or thanksgiving dance, which is common among the Pomo, and under one name or another common in all these parts. Both sexes participate in it, the squaws having as their principal ornament plumes of tall feathers in their hair, while the Indians are *Fig. B* decorated with cowls or garlands of white owl's down, and mantles of eagles', buzzards', or hawks' tail feathers. This white garland of down is a feature peculiar to the Yuki and Wailakki, but the mantle is universal in this region. The extensive use of feathers made by the Eel and Russian River tribes is attributable to their fetichism, as they believe that various birds, especially the great white owl, are devils, and their feathers are worn as a propitiation.

This dance is performed in the evening, soon after the acorns are ripe, outdoors, and within a circle of fires. A chorister beats time on his hand with a split stick, and sometimes a trumpeter blows a monotonous blast on a whistle fashioned from the leg-bone of some animal. At the proper time the chief delivers an oration, of which the one great burden is an exhortation to the squaws to lead virtuous and industrious lives.

Transmigration of souls is an article of their *credo;* that is, they believe that bad Indians' spirits take up their abode in various animals, especially the screech-owl and the coyote, while the souls of the good are wafted up to heaven in the smoke of the funeral pyre. To one who has ever heard the eldritch and blood-curdling midnight gibbering of the screech-owl, it is little wonder that the California Indians so generally assign to him the souls of the ungodly dead, or even those of the hobgoblins; but inasmuch as the coyote was the original of the human kind, it is something exceptional that he should afterward become the embodiment of the wicked only. Herein is a crude idea of Italic progression: first, coyote; second, man; third, the good become beatific in heaven, and the bad return to coyotes.

Thunder, according to the Tatu, is caused by the flight of some Indian's many-winged spirit up to heaven, flapping its pinions loudly as it ascends.

Snakes are an object of superstitious belief and of unfeigned terror, inasmuch as they consider them to be vivified by the souls of the impious dead, dispatched as special emissaries of the devil to work them evil. They have a legend of one that lived on Mill Creek, which was a hundred feet long, with a single horn on its forehead, and which it required over a hundred Indians to destroy. Another one they tell of was so long that it reached around a mountain, bit its own tail, and died, and whosoever crosses the line of its bones to this day straightway gives up the ghost.

They also relate a legend of the coyote which is something different from that of the Pomo.

LEGEND OF THE COYOTE.

Many hundred snows ago while mankind were yet in the form and flesh of the coyote, there dwelt in Eel River Valley a famous coyote with his two sons. In those days there came a terrible drought in that region, 46 which was followed by a plague of grasshoppers, and this by a fire which destroyed every living thing on the face of the earth except the grasshoppers. Then the coyote and his two sons eat very many grasshoppers, for that all flesh and all grass were consumed by the fire in the mountains; and they had thirst, and there was no water in all that land; but in Clear Lake there was water. So they started toward Clear Lake, these three coyotes, and on the mountain pass, as you go over into Potter Valley, one of the sons died of thirst, and his father buried him and heaped over him a cairn of stones. Then they went on to the lower end of that valley, and as they passed over the mountain, going to Clear Lake the other son died, and him likewise the father buried and heaped stones above him. After that he journeyed on alone to Clear Lake and came into it and drank of the waters, so much as never was drunk before, until he drained the lake dry. Then he lay down and fell into a deep sleep. As he slept there came up a man out of the south country and pricked him with his spear, so that the waters flowed forth from him and returned into the lake until it was full again, and the grasshoppers which he had eaten became fishes in the water, and thus the lake was filled with them.

As to the legends of the huge snakes above mentioned, it is possible that they refer to some lingering member of a species of gigantic saurian now extinct. If so, the Indians must have been here many hundreds of years.

The Tatu (Hūchnom) bury the dead with their heads to the north and their faces to the east, but not invariably.

CHAPTER XVI.

THE PÓMO.

Under this name are included a great number of tribes or little bands—sometimes one in a valley, sometimes more—clustered in the region where the head-waters of the Eel and Russian Rivers interlace, along the latter and around the estuaries of the coast. Below Calpello they do not call themselves Pomo, but their languages include them in this large family. There are many dialectic variations as one goes along. An Indian may start from Potter Valley, which may be considered the nucleus and starting-point of the family, and go over a low range of mountains, ten miles or so, and find himself greatly at fault in attempting to converse; ten miles farther, and he would find himself still more at sea, so rapidly does the language shade away from valley to valley, from dialect to dialect. Yet the vocabularies printed in the appendix show that they spring from one language, as do English and Italian from Sanskrit; and in fact any Indian living on Russian River can learn to speak any dialect spoken anywhere along its banks much sooner than an American can learn to speak Italian, although, in proportion to his whole vocabulary, he may have to learn outright more words of a totally different root than the American would.

In disposition the Pomo are much different from the Yuki and their congeners, being simple, friendly, peaceable, and inoffensive. They are also much less cunning and avaricious, and less quickly imitative of the whites than the lively tribes on the Klamath, to whom they are inferior in intellect. As to their physique, there prevails on Russian River essentially the same type as that seen in the Sacramento Valley, which will be described elsewhere.

Like all California tribes, they have a certain conception of a Supreme Being, whom they call the Great Man or the Great Chief; but I am satisfied that this is chiefly a modern graft on the stock of their mythology. The coyote exercised supreme functions in the genesis of all things. It is singular how great is the admiration of the California Indians for this tricksy and dishonest beast. He was not only the progenitor, but he has been the constant benefactor of mankind.

Nearly all their acts of worship are held in honor of beasts, reptiles, or birds. One of the tribes on the lower reaches of Russian River is named for a snake, but on the upper waters nearly all the tribal names are formed from some characteristic or prominent object of the valley where they dwell. They all believe too that their coyote ancestors were molded directly from the soil; hence their family designation "Pomo," though it now signifies "people", originally, I think, meant "earth" or "earth-people", being evidently related to the Wintūn *pum, paum*, which denotes "earth".

As the Pomo are less warlike, less cunning and more simple-hearted than the northern tribes, so they are more devoted to amusement. The tribes hitherto described engage with passionate eagerness in gambling, and have certain austere and solemn dances of religion; but the Pomo add to these a kind of ball-playing, and down about Healdsburg they also have a curious sort of pantomime or rude theatrical performance.

The broadest and most obvious division of the Pomo family is into Eel River and Russian River Pomo. There are two tribes on Eel River, between it and South Fork, who call themselves Pomo (Kas'-tel Po-mo and Kai Po-mo), though it is an assumed name, because they belong to the Wailakki family, and prefer their company. It was mentioned heretofore that the Wailakki were rather despised by their neighbors; hence when any member of these two tribes intermarried with a true Pomo, he or she went to live with that nation and learned their language; hence also the fact that nearly every man of the Kai Pomo understands both Pomo and Wailakki. Nevertheless, because of their name and their claims, I have included them here.

THE KAS'-TEL PO-MO.

Concerning both this tribe and the next I know very little, for in the ferocious and destructive wars which their audacity badgered the whites into waging upon them, both they and many of the old pioneers went down

together. Men now living on South Fork could impart to me little save
bald stories of butchery and bloody reprisal. The Kastel Pomo dwelt
between the forks of the river, extending as far south as Big Chamise and
Blue Rock, and as above mentioned spoke the Wailakki language. They
tattooed the face and nose very much in the fashion of that people and the
Yuki. Mr. Burleigh related to me a curious instance which he once saw
among them of tattooing by a brave, which is exceedingly rare. An old
warrior whom he once found upon the battle-field on South Fork was tattooed all over his breast and arms, and on the under side of one arm was
a very correct and well-executed picture of a sea-otter, with its bushy tail.

Women of this and other tribes of the Coast Range frequently tattoo a
rude representation of a tree or other object, covering nearly the whole
abdomen and breast.

Their lodges, implements, etc., require no description, being made in
the common Eel River fashion with inconsiderable variations. They formerly burned their dead, wherein they showed that they were Pomo; but
what of them now remain have generally adopted the civilized custom,
except when one dies at such a distance that the body cannot readily be
conveyed home, when they reduce it to ashes for convenience in transportation. They generally desire, like the Chinese, to be buried in the ancestral
soil of their tribe.

THE KAI PO-MO.

The Kai Po-mo (Valley tribe or People) dwell on the extreme head-
waters of the South Fork, ranging eastward to Eel River, westward to the
ocean, and northward to the territory of the Kastel Pomo. With these latter
they were ever jangling, and from the manner in which Indian trails are
constructed, their wars generally raged on the hill-tops. On the vast wind-
swept and almost naked hog-back between the two forks of Eel River,
some thirty miles or more north of Cahto, looming largely up from the
broad, grassy back of the mountain, is the majestic, rugged, isolated bowlder
called Blue Rock. A few miles still farther north there is an enormous
section of this mountain-chain almost entirely covered with evergreen bush,
whence its name Big Chamise. Between these two points, and more especially about the base of Blue Rock, is one of the most famous ancient bat-

tle-grounds in California, where Indian blood has been poured out like
water, and where the ground is yet strewn with flint arrow-heads and spear-
points.   But the bones of the warriors slain on this fatal field are no longer
visible, having been doubtless consumed on the funeral pyre and sacredly
carried home for interment.

The Kai Pomo are the same in all respects as the Kastel Pomo, which
is to say, about the same as the Wailakki.   One matter is notable among
these Eel River Indians—I observed it more especially among the Kai
Pomo—and that is the extreme youthfulness of both sexes when they arrive
at the age of puberty.   In the warm and sheltered valley of South Fork
(however bleak the naked mountain-tops may be in winter), it was a thing
not at all uncommon, in the days of the Indians' prosperity, to see a woman
become a mother at twelve or fourteen.   An instance was related to me
where a girl had borne her firstborn at ten, as nearly as her years could be
ascertained, her husband, a white man, being then sixty-odd.   For this
reason, or some other, the half-breeds on Eel River are generally sickly,
puny, short-lived, and slightly esteemed by the fathers, who not unfrequently bestow them as presents on any one willing to burden himself with
their nurture.

There is another noteworthy phenomenon in regard to California half-
breeds which I have observed, and which, when mentioned to others they
have seldom failed to corroborate, and that is the girls generally predomi-
nate.   Often I have seen whole families of half-breed girls, but never one
composed entirely of boys, and seldom one wherein they were more
numerous.

I wish to call attention here to what may be denominated the peculiar
stratification of the tribes in this vicinity.   On the northern rivers, which
debouch into the ocean nearly at right angles, each tribe occupies a certain
length of the stream on both sides; but on Eel River, South Fork, and
Van Dusen's Fork, which flow almost parallel with the coast, every tribe
owns only one bank of a river, unless it chances to dwell between two
waters.   It should seem that the influence of the ocean has distributed the
Indians in certain parallel climatic belts, those living nearest the coast
being darker, more obese, more squat in stature, and more fetichistic; while,

as you go toward the interior, both the physique and the intelligence gradually improve.   This kind of stratification does not obtain on Russian
River, but fetichism increases as you go down approaching the ocean.

We now commence with the true Pomo. The Ká-to Pomo (Lake People)
were so called from a little lake which formerly existed in the valley now
known by their name (Cahto).   They do not speak Pomo entirely pure,
but employ a mixture of that and Wailakki.   Like the Kai Pomo, their
northern neighbors, they forbid their squaws from studying languages—
which is about the only accomplishment possible to them save that of dancing—principally, it is believed, in order to prevent them from gadding
about and forming acquaintances in neighboring valleys, for there is small
virtue among the unmarried of either sex.   But the men pay considerable
attention to linguistic studies, and there is seldom one who cannot speak
most of the Pomo dialects within a day's journey of his ancestral valley.
The chiefs especially devote no little care to the training of their sons as
polyglot diplomatists; and Robert White affirms that they frequently send
them to reside several months with the chiefs of contiguous valleys to acquire the dialects there in vogue.

They construct lodges in the Russian River manner, and do not differ-
entiate their costumes or utensils to any important extent.   In appetite they
are not at all epicurean, and in the range of their comestibles they are quite
cosmopolitan, not objecting even to horse-steak, which they accept without
instituting any squeamish inquiries as to the manner in which it departed
this life.   They consume tar-weed seed, wild oats, California chestnuts,
acorns, various kinds of roots, ground-squirrels and moles, rabbits, buckeyes,
kelp, yellow-pine bark (in a pinch), clams, salmon, different sorts of berries, etc.   Buckeyes are poison, but they extract the toxical principle from
them by steaming them two or three days underground.   They first excavate
a large hole, pack it water-tight around the sides, burn a fire therein for
some space of time, then put in the buckeyes, together with water and
heated stones, and cover the whole with a layer of earth.   When they go
over to the ocean to fish and dig clams they collect quantities of kelp and

chew the same. It is as tough as whitleather, and a young fellow with good teeth will masticate a piece of it a whole day. Kelp tastes a little like a spoiled pickle, and the Indians relish it for its salty quality, and probably also extract some small nutriment of juice therefrom.

There is a game of tennis played by the Pomo of which I have heard nothing among the northern tribes. A ball is rounded out of an oak-knot about as large as those generally used by school-boys, and it is propelled 51 by a racket which is constructed of a long, slender stick, bent double and bound together, leaving a circular hoop at the extremity, across which is woven a coarse meshwork of strings. Such an implement is not strong enough for batting the ball, neither do they bat it, but simply shove or thrust it along on the ground.

The game is played in the following manner: They first separate themselves into two equal parties, and each party contributes an equal amount to a stake to be played for, as they seldom consider it worth while to play without betting. Then they select an open space of ground, and establish two parallel base-lines a certain number of paces apart, with a starting-line between, equidistant from both. Two champions, one for each party, stand on opposite sides of the starting-point with their rackets, a squaw tosses the ball into the air, and as it descends the two champions strike at it, and one or the other gets the advantage, hurling it toward his antagonist's base-line. Then there ensues a universal rush, pell-mell, higgledy-piggledy, men and squaws crushing and bumping—for the squaws participate equally with the sterner sex—each party striving to propel the ball across the enemy's base-line.

They enjoy this sport immensely, laugh and vociferate until they are "out of all whooping"; some tumble down and get their heads batted, and much diversion is created, for they are very good-natured and free from jangling in their amusements One party must drive the ball a certain number of times over the other's base-line before the game is concluded, and this not unfrequently occupies them a half-day or more, during which they expend more strenuous endeavor than they would in a day of honest labor in a squash-field.

Schoolcraft says in his "Oneóta" that the chiefs and graver men of the tribes in the West, however much they encourage the younger men in ball-playing, do not lend their countenance to games of hazard. This is not true of the California Indians, for here old and young engage with infatuation and recklessness in all games where betting is involved, though, of course, the very decrepit cannot personally participate in the rude hustle of ball-playing. The aged and middle-aged, squaws, men, and half-grown children stake on this, as well as on true games of hazard, all they possess—clothing, baskets, beads, fancy bows and arrows, etc.

There is another fashion of gambling, with little sticks or bones rolled in pellets of grass, which is universal throughout Northern California; but as I had an excellent opportunity of observing a great game of it elsewhere among the Pomo it will be described there.

Among the upper tribes, especially on the Klamath, many women are honored as shamins and prophetesses; but here none at all are admitted to the medical profession. It is only the masculine sex who receive a "call"; there are none but braves whom "the spirit moves", for it is thus that the elect are assured of their divine mission to undertake the healing of men. The methods of practice, vary with the varying hour, every physician being governed in his therapeutics by the inspiration of the spirit of the moment; and if he fails in effecting a cure, the obloquy of the failure recurs upon his familiar spirit. For instance, a shamin will stretch his patient out by a fire, and walk patiently all the livelong day around the fire, chanting to exorcise the demon that is in him. Thus the *modi operandi* are as numerous as the whimseys of this mysterious medical spirit. Besides these, they have in their pharmacopœia divers roots, poultices, and decoctions, and often scarify their breasts with flint. When the patient delays dying, if he is old and burdensome he is generally carried forth and cast into the forest to die alone and unattended; but the mere removal from the loathsome smudge and stench of the lodge, and the exposure to the clean, sweet air of heaven sometimes bring him round, and he returns smiling to his friends who are nowise pleased.

Formerly all the dead were disposed of by incremation, but in later times under the influence of the white men a mixed custom prevails. An intelligent Indian told me that, in case of burial, the corpse was always placed with the head pointing southward. Most of the Indians thus far mentioned believe the Happy Land is in the west or southwest, but their notions are evidently confused. A young man who was born and bred among the Pomo told me that they nowadays burn only those killed or hanged by the whites, and bury the others. I know not if there is any special significance in their discrimination.

Robert White affirms that he has frequently seen an aged Indian or woman, living in hourly expectation of his demise, go dig his own burial-place, and then repair thither daily for months together, and eat his poor repast sitting in the mouth of his grave. The same strange, morbid idiosyncrasy prevails among the Wintūn, in the Sacramento Valley.

Before the irruption of the white men had reduced them to their present abject misery, the Kato Pomo treated their parents with a certain consideration, that is, they would always divide the last morsel of dried salmon with genuine savage thriftlessness; but as for any active, nurturing tenderness, it did not exist, or only very seldom. They were only too glad to shuffle off their shoulders the burden of their maintenance. On the other hand they gave their children unlimited free play. Men who have lived familiarly amidst them for years tell me they never yet have seen an Indian parent chastise his offspring, or correct them any otherwise than with berating words in a frenzy of passion, which also is extremely seldom.

They have an absurd habit of hospitality, which reminds one of the Bedouin Arabs. Let a perfect stranger enter a wigwam and offer the lodge-father a string of beads for any object that takes his fancy—merely pointing to it, but uttering no word—and the owner holds himself bound in savage honor to make the exchange, whether it is a fair one or not. The next day he may thrust the stranger through with his spear, or crush his forehead with a pebble from his sling, and the bystanders will look upon it as only the rectification of a bad bargain.

It is wonderful how these Indians have all the forest and plain mapped out on the tablet of their memory. There is scarcely a bowlder, gulch, prominent tree, spring, knoll, glade, clump of bushes, cave, or bit of prairie within a radius of ten miles which is not perfectly familiar to the savage, even if it does not bear its own distinctive name. Yet he cannot give any satisfactory description of this forest or this plain to a white man in English, or even to a brother Indian in his vernacular. He prefers to go and lead you to the spot, and if he once can be persuaded to attempt this he will not fail, he will conduct you to the desired place with the absolute infallibility of the sun's rays in finding out the hidden corners of the earth.

55   There is occasionally a Pomo who is named for some animal, snake, or bird, in accordance with some whim, or fancied resemblance in the child's actions or babyish pipings, as chi-kok'-a-we (quail), mi-sal'-la (snake), etc.

The Kato Pomo believe in a terrible and fearful ogre called Shil'-la-ba Shil'-toats. He is described as being of gigantic stature, wearing a high, sugar-loaf head-dress, clothed in hideous tatters, striding over a mountain or valley at a step, and like the Scandinavian Trolls, a cannibal, having an appreciative appetite for small boys. He is very useful to the Indian in the regulation and administration of his household affairs, and especially in the " taming of a shrew ", as he has only to rush into the wigwam with his eyes judiciously dilated, and his hair somewhat toused, and vociferate, " Shillaba Shiltoats ! Shillaba Shiltoats !" when his squaw will scream with terror, fall flat upon the ground, cover her face with her hands—for that squaw dies who ever looks upon this ogre—and she will remain very tractable for several days thereafter. The children will also be profoundly impressed.

This and the other branches of the Pomo living nearest the ocean have a conception of a sort of Hedonic heaven, which is quite characteristic. They believe that in some far, sunny island of the Pacific—an island of fadeless verdure; of cool and shining trees, looped with clinging vines; of bubbling fountains; of flowery and fragrant savannas, rimmed with lilac shadows, where the purple and wine-stained waves shiver in a spume of gold across the reefs, shot through and through by the level sunbeams of the morning—they will dwell forever in an atmosphere like that around the Castle of Indolence; for the deer and the antelope will joyously come and offer themselves for food, and the red-fleshed salmon will affectionately rub their sides against them, and softly wriggle into their reluctant hands. It is not by any means a place like the Happy Hunting Grounds of the lordly and eagle-eyed Dakotas, where they are "drinking delight of battle" with their peers, or running in the noble frenzy of the chase; but a soft and a forgetting land, a sweet, oblivious sleep, awaking only to feast and then to sleep again.

As for the bad Indians, they will be obliged to content themselves with a palingenesis in the bodies of grizzly bears, cougars, snakes, etc.

Among other noted ceremonials the Kato Pomo observe an autumnal acorn dance in which the performers wear the mantles and head-dresses of eagles' or buzzards' tail-feathers customary in this region, and which appears to be much like the thanksgiving dance of the Humboldt Bay Indians, being accompanied, like that, by the oration of plenty. It is not strictly an anniversary dance, but rather a "movable festival" in the Indian *fasti dies*, celebrated when the crop of acorns has proven generous, but otherwise omitted.

Besides the Kato Pomo, there are many other little bands in divers valleys, of whom the most important are here mentioned. In Potter Valley, taken as a whole, are the Bal-ló Kai Pó-mo (Oat Valley People); in Sherwood Valley, the Ku·lá Kai Pó-mo (*kula* is the name of a kind of fruit, like little pumpkins, growing on water, as the Indians describe it); in Redwood Cañon, the Dá-pi-shūl Pó-mo (*dapishūl* means "high sun"; that is, a cold place, because of the depth of the cañon); at Calpello, the Choam Cha-dí-la Pó-mo (Pitch Pine People); at Ukiah City, the Yo-kai′-a Pó-mo (Lower Valley People); in Coyote Valley, the Shó-do Kai Pó-mo; on the coast, and along Usal Creek, the Yú-sâl Pó-mo or Kam′-a-lel Pó-mo (Ocean People); at Little Lake, the Mi-toam′ Kai Pó·mo (Wooded Valley People); on the Rio Grande, or Big River, the Bul′-dam Pó-mo. At Clear Lake, about Lakeport, is a branch of this family called the Eastern People (I do not know the Indian word). The Ku-lá Kai Pó-mo are also called by the Kato tribe, Shi-bal′-ni Pó-mo (Neighbor People).

Fig. C

Fig. 18

56

CHAPTER XVII.

THE POMO, CONTINUED.

I have already intimated my belief that the word "Pomo" is allied to the Wintūn *pum*, meaning "earth". William Potter, one of the pioneers of Potter Valley, and a man well acquainted with the Pomo language, informed me that there was a word, *poam*, in it signifying the same thing, from which *pomo* is derived. I questioned the Indians concerning the existence of such a word, and none of them had ever heard it. They were young Indians however, and it is possible that this word is an archaism, and beyond the range of their knowledge. At any rate, it was given by Mr. Potter as the basis of a tribal name, Poam Pomo, which is equivalent in extent to Ballo Kai Pomo. And there is a great deal of probability in this theory, because they believe, as did the Greeks respecting the fabled autochthones, that their ancestors, the coyote-men, were created directly from the soil, from the knoll of red earth mentioned in a previous chapter.

THE POAM POMO.

I shall therefore assume this name as equivalent to Ballo Kai Pomo, which we have seen denotes "Oat Valley People". Some readers may raise an objection to this name on another score. Many Californians hold that wild oats are not a native crop, but an acclimated product, having spread from early scatterings left by the Spaniards; but the Indians of this valley declare they have been growing in California so long that they know nothing of their origin. Indeed the mere fact that the valley bears the name of this cereal indicates for the latter an existence therein coeval with the Indian occupation.

In regard to government the Pomo are perhaps a little less ochlocratic

57

than the upper tribes. The chieftainship is hereditary to a certain extent, and dual, which is to say, there are two chiefs, who might be compared, as to their functions, to the Japanese Tycoon and Mikado, in that one administers more particularly the secular affairs, and the other the spiritual. But the Indians designate them as the war-chief (arrow-man) and peace-chief (shell-man), the war-chief becoming the peace-chief when he grows too decrepit to conduct them to battle. The peace-chief is a kind of *censor morum*, adjusts disputes, delivers moral homilies on certain anniversary occasions, performs the marriage ceremonies, so far as they extend, and watches over the conduct of his people, and especially over that of the wanton young squaws. Even the war-chief is obedient to him at home, and in fact that functionary is of secondary importance, since the Pomo are eminently a peaceable people.

There is rather more formality in the marriage ceremony than prevails among most California Indians. The bridegroom can hardly be said to purchase his bride, yet he is expected to make generous presents to her father, and unless these were forthcoming probably the marriage would not be permitted. The peace-chief causes the parties to enter into a simple covenant in presence of their parents and friends, after which there is dancing and merry-making for a considerable space of time, together with eating and drinking, but not in such measure or quality as to constitute feasting.

As is true of California Indians generally, there is scarcely such an attribute known as virtue or chastity in either sex before marriage. Up to the time when they enter matrimony most of the young women are a kind of *femmes incomprises*, the common property of the tribe; and after they have once taken on themselves the marriage covenant, simple as it is, they are guarded with a Turkish jealousy, for even the married women are not such models as Mrs. Ford. Indeed the wantonness of their women is the one great eyesore of the Pomo Indians, and it seems to be almost the sole object of government to preserve them in proper subjection and obedience. The one great burden of the harangues delivered by the venerable peace-chief on solemn occasions is the necessity and the excellence of female virtue; all the terrors of superstitious sanction and the direst threats of the great prophet are leveled at unchastity, and all the most dreadful calamities and pains of a future state are hung suspended over the heads of those who are persistently lascivious. All the devices that savage cunning can invent, all the mysterious and masquerading horrors of devil-raising, all the secret sorceries, the frightful apparitions and bugbears, which can be supposed effectual in terrifying the women into virtue and preventing smock-treason, are resorted to by the Pomo leaders.

William Potter, a high authority on Indian matters and master of most of the Pomo dialects described to me as far as he was able a secret society which exists among the Poam Pomo, and which has branch chapters at Clear Lake, Calpello, Redwood Cañon and several other places, whose simple purpose is to conjure up infernal terrors and render each other assistance in keeping their women in subjection.

Their meetings are held in an assembly-house erected especially for the purpose, constructed of peeled pine poles. It is painted red, black, and white (wood color) on the inside in spiral stripes reaching from the apex to the ground. Outside it is thatched and covered with earth. When they are assembled in it there is a door-keeper at the entrance who suffers no one to enter unless he is a regular member, pledged to secrecy. Even Mr. Potter, though a man held in high honor by them was not allowed to enter, though they offered to initiate him, if he desired. They do not scruple to avow to Americans who are well acquainted with them, and in whose discretion they have confidence, that their object is simply to "raise the devil", as they express it, with whom they pretend to hold communication; and to carry on other demoniacal doings, accompanied by frightful whooping and yelling, in order to work on the imaginations of the erring squaws, no whit more guilty than themselves.

Once in seven years these secret woman-tamers hold a grand devil-dance (*cha'-du-el-keh*), which is looked forward to by the women of the tribe with fear and trembling, as the scourging visit of the dreadful Yu-ku-ku'-la (the devil). As this society has its ramifications among many Pomo tribes, this great dance is held one septennium in one valley, another in another, and so on through the circuit of the branch societies.

Every seven years, therefore, witnesses the construction of an immense assembly-house, which is used for this special occasion only. I have seen the ruins of one which was reared in Potter Valley somewhere about the year 1860. The pit or cellar which made a part of it was circular, 63 feet in diameter, and about 6 feet deep, and all the enormous mass of earth excavated from it was gouged up with small fire-hardened sticks and carried away in baskets by both men and women, chiefly men. It was about 18 feet high in the center, and the roof was supported on five posts, one a center-pole and four others standing around it, equidistant from it and the perimeter of the pit. Timbers from six to nine inches in diameter were laid from the edge of the pit to the middle posts, and from these to the center-pole. Over these were placed grass and brush, and the whole was heavily covered with earth. Allowing four square feet of space to each person, such 61 a structure would contain upward of 700 people. In their palmy days hundreds and even thousands of Indians attended one of these grand dances.

When the dance is held, twenty or thirty men array themselves in harlequin rig and barbaric paint, and put vessels of pitch on their heads; then they secretly go out into the surrounding mountains. These are to personify the devils. A herald goes up to the top of the assembly-house, and makes a speech to the multitude. At a signal agreed upon in the evening the masqueraders come in from the mountains, with the vessels of pitch flaming on their heads, and with all the frightful accessories of noise, motion, and costume which the savage mind can devise in representation of demons. The terrified women and children flee for life, the men huddle them inside a circle, and, on the principle of fighting the devil with fire, they swing blazing firebrands in the air, yell, whoop, and make frantic dashes at the marauding and blood-thirsty devils, so creating a terrific spectacle, and striking great fear into the hearts of the assembled hundreds of women, who are screaming and fainting and clinging to their valorous protectors. Finally the devils succeed in getting into the assembly-house, and the bravest of the men enter and hold a parley with them. As a conclusion of the whole farce, the men summon courage, the devils are expelled from the assembly-house, and with a prodigious row and racket of sham fighting are chased away into the mountains.

After all these terrible doings have exercised their due effect upon the wanton feminine mind, another stage of the proceedings is entered upon.

A rattlesnake was captured some days beforehand, its fangs were plucked out, and it was handled, stroked, fed, and tamed, so that it could be displayed with safety. The venerable, white-haired peace-chief now takes his station before the multitude, within the great assembly-house, with the rattlesnake before him as the visible incarnation of the dreadful Yukukula. Slowly and sonorously he begins, speaking to them of morality and feminine obedience. Then warming with his subject, and brandishing the horrid reptile in his hand full in the faces and over the heads of his shuddering auditors, with solemn and awful voice he warns them to beware, and threatens them with the dire wrath of Yukukula if they do not live lives of chastity, industry, and obedience, until some of the terrified squaws shriek aloud and fall swooning upon the ground.

Having such a pother as they do with their own women to keep them in a proper mood of humbleness, the Pomo make it a special point to slaughter those of their enemies when the chances of battle give them an opportunity. They do this because, as they argue with the greatest sincerity, one woman destroyed is tantamount to five men killed. How different this from the treatment of their women by the old German barbarians, as described by Tacitus.

In another direction however, the women exercise some authority. When an Indian becomes too infirm to serve any longer as a warrior or hunter, he is thenceforth condemned to the life of a menial and a scullion. He is compelled to assist the squaws in all their labors—in picking acorns and berries, in threshing out seeds and wild oats, making bread, drying salmon, etc. As the women have entire control of these matters without interference from their lords, these superannuated warriors come entirely under their authority as much as children, and are obliged to obey their commands implicitly. We may well imagine that the squaws, in revenge for the ignoble and terrorizing surveillance to which they are subjected by the braves, not unfrequently domineer over these poor old nonagenarians with hardness, and make them feel their humiliation keenly.

Cronise, in his "Natural Wealth of California", makes mention of an ancient tradition to the effect that when the Spaniards first arrived in California, they found a tribe in what is now Mendocino county, in which the squaws were Amazons and exercised a gyneocracy. I am inclined to think the fable was not without some foundation. When we consider the infinite trouble which these Pomo find it necessary to give themselves in order to keep the women in subjection, and also that the latter actually bear despotic rule over childhood and senility—that is, over the beginning and the ending of human life—we can easily perceive that these Pomo wives are stronger than the common run of Indian women. At least, by diligent inquiry, I never found any other trace of such a race of Amazons.

The Poam Pomo believe that lightning was the origin of fire; that the primordial bolt which fell from heaven deposited the spark in the wood, so that it now comes forth when two pieces are rubbed together. As to the lightning itself, they believed it to be hurled by the Great Man Above, as it was by Jupiter Tonans.

There is no doubt that they believe in a Supreme Being, but as usual among the California Indians he is quite a negative being, possessing few, if any, active attributes. His name is Cha-kal-lé. The syllable *cha* denotes "man" (though the usual word meaning an ordinary mortal is *atabunya*), and *kallé* signifies "above", being apparently derived from the same root as *kálleh* in the Gallinomero language. Hence the name denotes "The Man Above", or "The Great One Above". But as before remarked, he is a being of no manner of consequence in their cosmogony, for the Platonic Eon, the active principle, has always resided in the coyote. He it 62 was who created the world and mankind, or rather he deigned to take on himself the human form divine.

Their happy land is in the heavens above us, to which, like the Buddhists, they believe they will ascend by a ladder. The souls of the wicked will fall off the ladder in the ascent and descend into negative and nondescript limbo, where they will be neither happy nor tormented, but rove vacantly and idly about forevermore; while others, in punishment for greater wickedness, transmigrate into grizzly bears, or into rattlesnakes 63 condemned to crawl over burning sand, or into other animals condemned to hunger and thirst; to a California Indian, a place where he is hungry is hell. They believe that every grizzly bear existing is some old savage Indian thus returned to this world to be punished for his wickedness.

LEGEND OF THE COYOTE.

Once upon a time there lived a man among the Yuki of the Black Chief's tribe, fierce and terrible, with two sons like to himself, bloody-minded and evil men. For their great wickedness he and his two sons were turned into coyotes. Then they started from Rice's Fork and journeyed southward, biting and slaying all the beasts they came upon. As they passed over the defile to come into Potter Valley, one of the coyote's sons drank so much water from the spring near the summit that he died, and his father buried him, and heaped over him a cairn of stones, and wept for his son. Then they journeyed on through Potter Valley and went down to Clear Lake, and there the other son drank so much water that he died also, and his father buried him and wept sore. Then the father turned back and went on alone to a place called White Buttes, and came unto it, and discovered there much red alabaster, of which the Pomo make beads to this day, which, among them, are to the shell-beads as gold to silver. And when he had discovered the red alabaster at White Buttes his hair and his tail dropped off his body, he stood up on his hind legs and became a man again.

In this silly fable I can discern no other significance than the superstitious belief of its inventors, that for an evil action a human being may be punished by transmutation into a beast, and that for a good one he may be restored.

CHAPTER XVIII.

This name has been corrupted by the Americans into "Ukiah", and applied to the town around which these Indians live. The word *yo* means "down below" or "lower", and *kaia* is a dialectic variation of the Pomo *kai*, "valley". Sometimes they were called by the Pomo, Yokaia Pomo, and sometimes Yo-kai'-a-mah.

They occupied the fertile and picturesque valley of Russian River from a point a little below Calpello down to about seven miles below Ukiah. They were once very numerous. In Coyote Valley, near by, Mr. Christy states that there were between three hundred and four hundred when he arrived, while now eight American families in the same valley think themselves crowded.

Their style of lodge is the same which prevails generally along Russian River—a huge framework of willow poles covered with thatch, and resembling a large, flattish haystack. Though still preserving the same style and materials, since they have adopted from the Americans the use of boards they have learned to construct all around the wall of the wigwam a series of little state-rooms, if I may so call them, which are snugly boarded up and furnished with bunks inside. This enables every family in these immense patriarchal lodges to disrobe and retire with some regard to decency, which could not be done in the one common room of the old-style wigwam.

I paid a visit to their camp four miles below Ukiah, and finding there a unique kind of assembly-house desired to enter and examine it, but was not allowed to do so until I had gained the confidence of the old sexton by a few friendly words and the tender of a silver half-dollar. The pit of it was about fifty feet in diameter and four or five feet deep, and it was so heavily roofed with earth that the interior was damp and somber as a tomb. It looked like a low tumulus, and was provided with a tunnel-like entrance about ten feet long and four feet high, and leading down to a level with the floor of the pit. The mouth of the tunnel was closed with brush, and the venerable sexton would not remove it until he had slowly and devoutly paced several times to and fro before the entrance. Passing in I found the massive roof supported by a number of peeled poles painted white and ringed with black, and ornamented with rude devices. The floor was covered thick and green with sprouting wheat which had been scattered to feed the spirit of the captain of the tribe lately deceased.

Not long afterward a deputation of the Se-nel' came up to condole with the Yokaia on the loss of their chief, and a dance, or series of dances was held which lasted three days. During this time of course the Senel were the guests of the Yokaia, and the latter were subjected to a considerable expense. I was prevented by other engagements from being present and shall be obliged to depend on the description of an eye-witness, Mr. John Tenney, whose account is here given with a few changes:

There are four officials connected with the building, who are probably chosen to preserve order, and to allow no intruders. They are the assistants of the chief. The invitation to attend was from one of them, and admission was given by the same. These four wore black vests trimmed with red flannel and shell ornaments. The chief made no special display on the occasion. In addition to these four, who were officers of the assembly-chamber, there was an old man and a young woman who seemed to be priest and priestess. The young woman was dressed differently from any other, the rest dressing in plain calico dresses. Her dress was white, covered with spots of red flannel, cut in neat figures, ornamented with shells. It looked gorgeous, and denoted some office, the name of which I could not ascertain.

Before the visitors were ready to enter, the older men of the tribe were reclining around the fire smoking and chatting. As the ceremonies were about to commence, the old man and young woman were summoned, and standing at the end opposite the entrance they inaugurated the exercises by a brief service, which seemed to be a dedication of the house to the exercises about to commence. Each of them spoke a few words, joined in a brief chant, and the house was thrown open for their visitors. They staid at their post until the visitors entered and were seated on one side of the room. After the visitors, then others were seated, making about two hundred in all, though there was plenty of room in the center for the dancing. Before the dance commenced the chief of the visiting tribe made a brief speech, in which he no doubt referred to the death of the chief of the Yokaia, and offered the sympathy of his tribe in this loss. As he spoke some of the women scarcely refrained from crying out, and with difficulty they suppressed their sobs. I presume that he proposed a few moments of mourning, for when he stopped the whole assemblage burst forth into a bitter wailing, some screaming as if in agony. The whole thing created such a din that I was compelled to stop my ears. The air was rent and pierced with their cries. This wailing and shedding of tears lasted about three or five minutes, though it seemed to last a half hour. At a given signal they ceased, wiped their eyes, and quieted down.

Then preparations were made for the dance. One end of the room was set aside for the dressing-room.

The chief actors were five men, who were muscular and agile. They were profusely decorated with paint and feathers, while white and dark stripes covered their bodies. They were girt about the middle with cloth of bright colors—sometimes with variegated shawls. A feather mantle hung from the shoulder, reaching below the knee, strings of shell ornamented the neck, while their heads were covered with a crown of eagle-feathers. They had whistles in their mouths as they danced, swaying their heads, bending and whirling their bodies; every muscle seemed to be exercised, and the feather ornaments quivered with life. They were agile and graceful as they bounded about in the sinuous course of the dance.

The five men were assisted by a semicircle of twenty women, who only marked time by stepping up and down with short step; they always took their places first and disappeared first; the men making their exit gracefully one by one.

The dresses of the women were suitable for the occasion. They wore white dresses trimmed heavily with black velvet. The stripes were about three inches wide, some plain and others edged like saw-teeth. This was an indication of their mourning for the dead chief in whose honor they had prepared that style of dancing. Strings of *Haliotis* and *Pachydesma* shell-beads encircled their necks, and around their waists were belts heavily loaded with the same material. Their head-dresses were more showy than those of the men. The head was encircled with a bandeau of otters' or beavers' fur, to which were attached short wires standing out in all directions, with glass and shell beads strung on them, and at the tips little feather flags and quail plumes. Surmounting all was a pyramidal plume of feathers, black, gray, and scarlet, the top generally being a bright scarlet bunch, waving and tossing very beautifully. All these combined gave their heads a very brilliant and spangled appearance.

The first day the dance was slow and funereal, in honor of the Yokaia chief who died a short time before. The music was mournful and simple, being a monotonous chant, in which only two tones were used, accompanied with a rattling of split sticks and stamping on a hollow slab.

The second day the dance was more lively on the part of the men, the music was better, employing airs which had a greater range of tone, and the women generally joined in the chorus. The dress of the women was not so beautiful, as they appeared in ordinary calico.

The third day, if observed in accordance with Indian custom, the dancing was still more lively and the proceedings more gay, just as the coming home from a Christian funeral is apt to be much more jolly than the going out.

A Yokaia widow's style of mourning is peculiar. In addition to the usual evidences of grief she mingles the ashes of her dead husband with pitch, making a white tar or unguent with which she smears a band about two inches wide all around the edge of the hair (which is previously cut off close to the head), so that at a little distance she appears to be wearing a white chaplet.

It is their custom to "feed the spirits of the dead" for the space of one year by going daily to places which they were accustomed to frequent while living, where they sprinkle pinole upon the ground. A Yokaia mother who has lost her babe goes every day for a year to some place where her little one played while alive, or to the spot where its body was burned, and milks her breasts into the air. This is accompanied by plaintive mourning and weeping, and piteous calling upon her little one to return, and sometimes she sings a hoarse and melancholy chant, and dances with a wild, ecstatic swaying of her body.

The one great charm and panacea of the Yokaia physician or powwow is a stuffed lizard, while his Æsculapian robes are a mantle of black eagle's tail-feathers and a gaudy plume of the same. Equipped with the one and panoplied in the others, he pirouettes, curvets and prances around the patient, brandishing the lizard aloft, with many wild and lunatic whoops and crooning chants; now dancing swiftly up to him, then backward away from him, to draw out the evil spirits. Then he stoops down and waves the lizard over him with countless motions, gradually advancing from the body to the extremities of the limbs as if thus driving out the devil at his fingers' ends.

In Coyote Valley I saw some of this tribe *motu proprio* cultivating a little garden of corn which belonged to themselves. They employ neither plow nor hoe, but the squaws sit sheer down on the ground beside the hills, and work probably fifteen minutes at each one, digging up the earth deep and rubbing it all up fine in the hands. By this means they can till only an extremely small crop, but they do it excellently well and get a greater yield than Americans would.

Following is a table of numerals, showing how the Pomo language changes as one comes down Russian River. The first column was taken at Cahto, the second at Ukiah, the third at Sanel, the fourth at Healdsburg:

1	cha.	tá-ro	tá-to.	chah.
2	ko.	kâ.	ko.	á-ko.
3	sib'-bo.	sib'-bo.	sib'-bu.	mi-sib'-bo.
4	tak.	dú-hâ.	dú-ko.	mí-tah.
5	shal.	ná-twi.	ná-to.	tú-shuh.
6	fá-deh.	tsá-deh.	tsá-deh.	lan'-kah.
7	kó-pa.	hoi'-nait.	kó-i-naz	lat'-ko.
8	kó-wal.	kó-go-dol.	kó-go-dol.	ko-mí-tah.
9	shal'-shal.	nem'-go-shun.	nú-mo-shun.	chá-ko.
10	sá-la.	nem'-po-tek.	ná-va-ko-tek.	cha-sú-to.

THE SE-NEL'.

The Se-nel', together with three other petty tribes, mere villages, occupy that broad expansion of Russian River Valley, on one side of which now stands the American village of Sanel. Among them we find unmistakably developed that patriarchal system which appears to prevail all along Russian River. They construct immense dome-shaped or oblong lodges of willow poles an inch or two in diameter, woven in square lattice-work, securely lashed and thatched. In each one of these live several families, sometimes twenty or thirty persons, including all who are blood relations. Each wigwam therefore is a *pueblo*, a law unto itself. And yet these lodges are grouped in villages, some of which formerly contained hundreds of inhabitants, and one of which will presently be described.

During the dry season they abandon these huge wigwams entirely, and live in booths close by the river side, in the cool shadows of the willows, where they can almost dip up the salmon-trout and the skeggers, as they lie on their leafy couches. Here in the damp silt they have nowadays patches of maize, with a few squashes, beans, and melons, where they can sling water over them from the shrunken river with their hands or baskets, if there is need of irrigation. But, like little children, they generally eat the melons prematurely, and the squashes unwholesomely green, the latter being roasted whole. When the rainy season sets in they return to the wigwams, though they generally burn the old ones to destroy the vermin, and construct new ones.

Just opposite the American village of Sanel, on the east side of the river, are the ruins of an old Indian town which was once probably more populous than its civilized successor will ever become. I wandered over it one day, traced out its streets and the sites of its barbaric temples (assembly-*Fig. 19* houses), sketched it, and endeavored to form some estimate of its ancient population. The streets were quite straight, and each wigwam formed a block, the sites of them being plainly discernible by the hollows which were rounded out. Owing to their custom of burning old wigwams occasionally, it is not easy to determine what the population was, since the largest limits of the town may never have been occupied at once, part being built upon and part being in ashes. The assembly-houses are the best standard of measurement, because most permanent. There were five of them, each of which would contain a hundred persons; and as they were intended for men chiefly it is safe to estimate that the town once numbered 64 1,500 souls. Mr. March states that in 1847 it still contained between 300 and 400 people.

When a Senel woman is sterile she and her husband go on a long journey into the mountains, where they take upon themselves certain vows, make certain offerings, and perform rites, none of which are proper sub- 65 jects for description. All this they do in hope of having offspring.

Their ceremonial dances are much the same as those of the Pomo, both in the manner, objects, and accouterments worn.

According to the Senel, the sun and moon are active, potent, and malignant spirits, the same as the innumerable other devils in whom they believe. Hence if one has the headache or sunstroke he thinks he is tormented by one or the other of these evil luminaries—sun-poisoned or moon-poisoned. As a means of relief he sometimes thumps his head unmercifully, causing his nose to bleed. They torture their bodies too, not only for themselves, but also for their friends when afflicted. They believe that by lacerating themselves they help to placate the wrath of the evil one, and thereby alleviate the distress of their relatives.

The dead are mostly burned. Mr. Willard described to me a scene of incremation that he once witnessed which was frightful for its exhibitions of fanatic frenzy and infatuation. The corpse was that of a wealthy chieftain, and as he lay upon the funeral pyre they placed in his mouth two gold twenties, and other smaller coins in his ears and hands, on his breast etc., besides all his finery, his feather mantles, plumes, clothing, shell-money, his fancy bows, painted arrows, etc. When the torch was applied they set up a mournful ululation, chanting and dancing about him, gradually working themselves into a wild and ecstatic raving—which seemed almost a demoniacal possession—leaping, howling, lacerating their flesh. Many seemed to lose all self-control. The younger, English-speaking Indians generally lend themselves charily to such superstitious work, especially if American spectators are present; but even they were carried away by the old con-

tagious frenzy of their race.   One stripped off a broadcloth coat, quite new
and fine, and ran frantically yelling and cast it upon the blazing pile.
Another rushed up and was about to throw on a pair of California blankets,
when a white man, to test his sincerity, offered him $16 for them, jingling
the bright coins before his eyes; but the savage (for such he had become
again for the moment), otherwise so avaricious, hurled him away with a
yell of execration and ran and threw his offering into the flames.   Squaws,
even more frenzied, wildly flung upon the pyre all they had in the world—
their dearest ornaments, their gaudiest dresses, their strings of glittering
shells.   Screaming, wailing, tearing their hair, beating their breasts in their
mad and insensate infatuation, some of them would have cast themselves
bodily into the flaming ruins and perished with the chief had they not been
restrained by their companions.   Thus the swift, bright flames with their
hot tongues licked this "cold obstruction" into chemic change, and the once
"delighted spirit" of the savage was borne up—

> " To be imprisoned in the viewless winds,
> And blown with restless violence round about
> The pendent world ".

It seems as if the savage shared in Shakspeare's shudder at the thought
of rotting in the dismal grave, for it is the one passion of his superstition to think of the soul of his departed friend set free and purified by
the swift, purging heat of the flames, not dragged down to be clogged and
bound in the moldering body, but borne up in the soft, warm chariots of
the smoke toward the beautiful sun, to bask in his warmth and light, and
then to fly away to the Happy Western Land.   What wonder if the Indian
shrinks with unspeakable horror from the thought of *burying his friend's
soul!* of pressing and ramming down with pitiless clods that inner something
which once took such delight in the sweet light of the sun !   What wonder
if it takes years to persuade him to do otherwise, and follow our custom !
What wonder if even then he does it with sad fears and misgivings !   Why
not let him keep his custom ?   In the gorgeous landscapes and balmy climate
of California and India incremation is as natural to the savage as it is for
him to love the beauty of the sun.   Let the vile Esquimaux and the frozen

Siberian bury their dead if they will; it matters little; the earth is the same above as below; or to them the bosom of the earth may seem even the better; but in California, do not blame the savage if he recoils at the thought of going under ground! This soft, pale halo of the lilac hills—ah, let him console himself if he will with the belief that his lost friend enjoys it still.

The narrator concluded by saying that they destroyed full $500 worth of property. "The blankets," said he, with a fine Californian scorn of such absurd insensibility to a good bargain, "the blankets that the American offered him $16 for were not worth half the money."

After death the Senel hold that bad Indians return into coyotes. Others fall off a bridge which all souls must traverse, or are hooked off by a raging bull at the further end, while the good escape across.

Like the Yokaia and the Konkau, they believe it necessary to nourish the spirits of the departed for the space of a year. This is generally done by a squaw, who takes pinole in her basket, repairs to the scene of the incremation or to places hallowed by the memory of the dead, where she scatters it over the ground, meantime rocking her body violently to and fro in a dance, and chanting the following chorus:

" Hel-lel-li-ly
Hel-lel-lo,
Hel-lel-lu ".

This refrain is repeated over and over indefinitely, but the words have no meaning whatever.

Their "Big Indians" profess to believe that the whole world was once a globe of fire, whence that element passed up into the trees, and now comes out whenever two pieces of wood are rubbed together. So, also, they hold the world will finally be consumed by fire. They may have acquired these notions from the Spaniards, but I think not, for the California Indians while accepting our outward customs cling tenaciously to their ancient beliefs. Nearly all the Wintūn tribes entertain the same notion, and the earthquakes of California are sufficient to account for it.

Clear Lake was created by a coyote which drank too much brine from the ocean, and fell sick before he traveled far, whereupon he vomited up this lake.

Besides the Senel, there live in this vicinity the So-kó-a, the Lá-ma, and the Sí-a-ko, very small tribes or villages.

THE KO-MÁ-CHO.

These Indians live in Rancheria and Anderson Valleys, and are a branch of the great Pomo family, although more nearly related to the Senel than to the Pomo proper. Their name is derived from their present chief, whose authority extends over both valleys.

One custom is observed by the Komacho, which I have not heard of among the Pomo or any other Indians in the State. It is the levying of a kind of free-will tax on the people for the support of the chief. Every autumn, on the occasion of the great annual gathering which prevails quite generally throughout California upon the ripening of the acorns, they bring up their voluntary contributions to himself and to the members of his family as regularly as the medieval Englishman paid his Rome-scot on Lammas-day. Dried salmon, acorn-bread, fine buckskins, baskets ornamental and baskets useful, strings of shells; all these are acceptable. Also, when one of the chief's family dies all the tribe assemble at his wigwam to condole with him, and each brings an offering according to his several ability, for himself or some member of his family.

Their principal anniversary dance is the watermelon dance. It is celebrated with the same sacred costumes of feathers, and with very much the same manner of chanting and dancing as have been described in the chapters on the Pomo. They stand around the fire in two circles, the women outside, and the men dance or rather stamp with one foot only, while the women simply sway themselves to and fro and swing their handkerchiefs.

Like the Senel, they frequently torture themselves in behalf of their sick relatives. When any one dear to them is lying at the point of death the squaws are stricken with the wildest frenzy of grief, and fling into the air handful after handful of their most valuable shell-money. Then they suddenly fall to the earth as if in a trance, where they lie motionless and lifeless for hours, like those smitten by the "power" in a negro revival.

They do this with the hope of creating a diversion, to induce the tormenting spirits to quit their relatives and assault themselves. They believe that by distracting or dividing their attention they can overpower and expel them.

When dancing around the funeral pyre they show the same passionate and frenzied sorrow and make the same fanatic manifestations as do the Senel. Everything belonging to the deceased, even to his horse, is sacrificed.

CHAPTER XIX.

THE GAL-LI-NO-MÉ-RO.

In Russian River Valley, from Cloverdale down to the redwood belt and south to Santa Rosa Creek, and also in Dry Creek Valley, live the remnants of a tribe whom the Spaniards called the Gal-li-no-me'-ro nation The Gallinoméro proper occupy only Dry Creek and Russian River, below Healdsburg, within the limits above named; while above Healdsburg, principally between Geyserville and Cloverdale, are the Mi-sal'-la Ma-gūn', or Mu-sal-la-kūn', and the Kai-mé. This nation may be considered a branch of the great family of the Pomo, whose *habitat* is co-extensive with Russian River Valley, covers the lowlands on the northwest of Clear Lake, and includes all the habitable coast from Usal Creek down to Bodega.

What their vernacular name was neither the chief, Ventura, nor his Cardinal Woolsey, Andres, though both are quite intelligent, can now recollect if they ever knew. It is a good instance of that moral feebleness and abdication of the California Indians which accepts without question any name the pale-face bestows, and adopts it instead of their own. Their mountainous neighbors, the Ashochimi, have a rather more honorable reason for accepting from the Spaniards *their* name (Wappos), for it was given to them by the latter when smarting under the terrible whippings which they used to suffer at the hands of that valorous tribe. From the fetichism prevailing in Russian River Valley generally, I am inclined to think the Gallinoméro were named after some species of birds, owls or hawks, to which they paid a kind of worship, as to devils who were to be feared and propitiated. At any rate, the early Spaniards named one of their great chiefs Gallina (a cock), from whom the tribe derives its present title.

As with most of the aborigines in that valley, their social and governmental organization is patriarchal and the chiefship hereditary, though the

67

174

functions of that office are nebulous. The remnant of them now living a little way below Healdsburg occupy one great wigwam, Ventura with his subjects, twenty or thirty together, on the most democratic equality. This *Fig. 20* wigwam is in the shape of the capital letter L, made up of slats leaned up to a ridge-pole, and heavily thatched. All along the middle of it the different 68 families or generations have their fires, while they sleep next the walls, lying on the ground underneath rabbit-skin and other less elegant robes, and amid a filthy clutter of baskets, dogs, large conical-shaped baskets of acorns stacked one upon the other, and all the wretched trumpery dear to the aboriginal heart. There are three narrow holes for doors, one at either end and one at the elbow.

They are nearly black, Ventura being the blackest of all; and on a warm, sunny day in February when he is chopping wood briskly his cuticle shines like that of a Louisiana field-hand. The nose is moderately high, straight and emphatic, with thick walls, and ovoid or nearly round nares; lips rather thick and sensual; forehead low, but nearly perpendicular with the chin; face rounder and flatter than in the Atlantic Indian; eyes well-sized and freely opened straight across the face, with a sluggish but foxy expression; color varying from old bronze or brown almost to black, though an occasional freckled face and sparse whisker betray a touch of Castilian blood in the veins. They live on the land of a good-natured farmer, and do occasional small services in the field in return for casual flitches of dubious bacon, baskets of specked apples, cast-off clothing, and the like. These and the contributions of the neighbors eke out their stock of salmon and acorns and enable them to live in considerable affluence. In the matter of providing for the casual necessities of the patriarchal household, Ventura is worth all the dozen or so of his male subjects; and he demonstrates daily his right to the chiefship by chopping wood, breaking mustangs, fishing, and otherwise playing an altogether manly part.

Their small dogs are fat and churlish, and they themselves look well fed, their black-brown faces shining out oleaginous amid their tatters. Whisky is interdicted by a wise and humane statute which is generally obeyed, and they appear to dwell together in great tranquillity, dozing 69 away their vacuous lives from day to day in the sun and calmly brushing off the flies. The California Indian has a negro's fondness for the sunshine.

But the men provide all the wood needed in the scullery and bring it in. Neither are they sluggards in this matter at all. I have seen Ventura and two or three of his right-hand men chopping lustily on a warm day in February until the perspiration rolled in great drops down their grave, dark, furrowed faces. Sometimes they have two or three cords of wood neatly stacked in ricks about the wigwam. Yet even then, with the heartless cruelty of the race, they will dispatch an old man to the distant forest with an ax, and you may see him returning, with his white head painfully bowed under a back-load of knaggy limbs, and his bare bronzed bow-legs moving on with that cat-like softness and evenness of the Indian, but so slowly that the poor old creature scarcely seems to get on.

Strange mingling of cruelty and generosity ! Give the chief a handful of buns on Christmas or a bottle of Bourbon, of which they are most covetous and stingy, yet will he distribute to all a portion, making his own no larger than any other.

These Indians walk more pigeon-toed than do those on the Klamath, at least in old age, and they emit an odor which is a trifle more offensive. An Indian scarcely ever totters in his walk, no matter how old. All his life long he has put down his feet with so even and steady a motion that, if he can get on his legs at all, he moves forward with balance.

They have the avarice common to the California Indians amusingly developed. One day I offered Ventura half a dollar if he would tell me what traditions he knew. He refused because he had been at the trouble of learning Spanish. He said it was worth more than half a dollar to learn Spanish, and if I wanted the traditions cheaper I must learn Indian. I did learn some Indian during the winter, and discovered that the sly old man *had* no traditions to speak of.

When a strange Indian arrives in a camp of the Gallinomero some one says to him, " *á-mi-ka*" (is that you) ? To this he replies, "*hi-o*", (yes) The stranger then advances into the circle or enters the wigwam, as the case may chance, and squats down without ceremony and without a word. A squaw brings him some food in a small basket, of which he partakes in silence, neither does any one address him so much as a word until he has finished his repast. Then he is gradually drawn into conversation and is expected to give some account of himself. In primitive times these Indians frequently lay flat on their bellies in eating.

When a young Gallinomero loses his parents and older brothers he can bind himself to others by a sort of apprenticeship. That is to say, with a certain amount of shell-money he can purchase parents and brothers for himself who are bound to guarantee him the same protection that they would if they were blood relations. If he possesses the requisite amount of money to pay them for this service he does not become more beholden to them than before the contract; but in default of it he becomes an apprentice or slave to his adopted parents.

In like manner a refugee or exile from another tribe can find among the Gallinomero a kind of Alsatia, and entitle himself to citizenship and protection by buying parents and brothers. Joseph Fitch related an instance of a squaw who came from some tribe in Sacramento Valley, purchased parents and brothers, and by thus becoming naturalized and owing allegiance to the tribe could not be taken away by her own people. From this one would infer that extradition treaties were unknown.

No crime is known for which the malefactor cannot atone with money. It seems to be the law however, that in case of murder the avenger of blood has his option between money and the murderer's life. But he does not seem to be allowed to wreak on him a personal and irresponsible vengeance. The chief takes the criminal and ties him to a tree, and then a number of persons shoot arrows into him at their leisure, thus putting him to death by slow torture.

According to their own confession, and the statements of the early settlers, they were addicted to infanticide. They do not seem to have limited themselves to twins, or to have made any distinction of sex, but cut off boys and girls alike, especially if deformed. When resorted to the act was immediate; it was done by pressing the knees on the infant's stomach. If allowed to live three days its life was thenceforth secure. They did not call it a "relation" until they had decided to spare its life. When remonstrated with for this abominable practice, they plead "not guilty"; they

say they do not kill it, but "God kills it". It seems to have been that mere
70 heartless and stolid butchery which comes of over-population, and of that
hard and grim penury which stamps out of the human heart its natural
affections. They are grossly licentious, like all California Indians, but this
horrible crime did not result from the shame of dishonest motherhood.
Neither was it caused, as in later years, by that deep and despairing melancholy which came over the hapless race when they saw themselves perishing
so hopelessly and so miserably before the face of the American.

If in regard of their treatment of infants they resemble the Chinese,
in their bearing toward the aged they are as far removed from them as light
from darkness. While the Chinaman sometimes slays his helpless babe
that he may the better support his equally helpless parents, the Gallinomero
reverses the practice. He puts his decrepit father or mother to death.
When the former can no longer feebly creep to the forest to gather his
back-load of fuel or a basket of acorns, and is only a burden to his sons,
the poor old wretch is not unfrequently thrown down on his back and
securely held while a stick is placed across his throat, and two of them seat
themselves on the ends of it until he ceases to breathe. I could hardly
have believed this horrible thing, and I record it only on the testimony of
two trustworthy men, Joseph Fitch and Louis Piña, both veteran pioneers
who had lived among them many years.

A young Gallinomero buys his wife, in accordance with the usual custom, without any preceding courtship, but the parents must give their consent to the marriage. If dissatisfied with her, and he can strike a bargain
with another man, he sells her to him for a few strings of shell-money.
They very seldom beat their wives, but if they do not like them they
quietly abandon them, so that in case of separation or divorce the wife
always retains the children.

Being eminently a peaceable people they have no war-dances, and
take no scalps when they do go to battle. Among themselves there was
never anything that could be dignified with the name of a battle, hardly
even a fisticuff, but they were sometimes compelled to fight with the war-
71 like Wappos. So timid were they that when the Spaniards first made their
appearance among them on horseback they fled with the greatest terror

and secreted themselves in the bushes. To this day they do not eat the flesh of a horse, though they will ride that noble animal even unto death if they can possess themselves of one. There are many old Indians, however, especially squaws, whom the younger ones will never succeed to the day of their death in inducing to bestride a horse. They will lug all the baggage they can possibly go under, and fall far behind in the march, coming into camp only after nightfall, or perhaps not arriving until the mounted party are ready to start on next morning, rather than mount the animal which caused them such a precious fright thirty or forty years ago.

There is one very curious exhibition—a kind of pantomime or rude theatrical performance—which deserves a somewhat minute description, as it does not generally prevail among the California Indians. They give it no other name but *kó-ha*, which signifies simply "dance", although they translate it into Spanish by "fandango"; but I will call it by way of distinction, the spear dance. It might also be called the coward's dance, for it seems to be intended as a kind of take-off on the greatest coward in the tribe, much on the same principle that a wooden spoon is presented to the ugliest man in Yale.

First they all unite, men and squaws together, in a pleasant dance, accompanied by a chant, while a chorister keeps time by beating on his hand with a split stick. In addition to their finest deer-skin chemises and strings of beads, the squaws wear large puffs of yellow-hammers' down over their eyes. The men have mantles of buzzards', hawks', or eagles' tail-feathers, reaching from the arm-pits down to the thighs, and circular head-dresses of the same material, besides their usual breech-clouts of rawhide, and are painted in front with terrific splendor. They dance in two circles, the squaws in the outside one; the men leaping up and down as usual, and the squaws simply swaying their bodies and waving their handkerchiefs in a lackadaisical manner. Occasionally an Indian will shoot away through the interior of the circle, and caper like a harlequin for a considerable space of time, but he always returns to his place in front of his partner.

After this is over, the coward or clown is provided with a long, sharp stick, and he and his prompter take their places in the ring ready for performances. A woman as nearly nude as barbaric modesty will permit is placed in the center, squatting on the ground.   Then some Indian intones a chant, which he sings alone, and the sport, such as it is, begins.   At the bidding of the prompter the coward makes a furious sally in one direction, and with his spear stabs the empty air.   Then he dashes back in the opposite direction and slashes into the air again.   Next he runs some other way and stabs again.   Now perhaps he makes a feint to pierce the woman.   Thus the prompter keeps him chasing backward and forward, spearing the thin air toward every point of the compass, or making passes at the woman, until nearly tired out, and the patience of the American spectators is exhausted, and they begin to think the whole affair will terminate in "mere dumb show".   But finally at a word from the prompter, the spearman makes a tremendous run at the woman, and stabs her in the umbilicus.   She falls over on the ground quivering in every limb and the blood jets forth in a purple stream.   The Indians all rush around her quickly and hustle her away to another place where they commence laying her out for the funeral pyre, but huddle around her so thickly all the while that the Americans cannot approach to see what is done.   Thus they mystify matters, and hold some powwow over her for a considerable space of time, when she somehow mysteriously revives, recovers her feet, goes away to her wigwam, encircled by a bevy of her companions, dons her robe, and reappears in the circle as well as ever, despite that terrible spear-thrust.

Men who have witnessed this performance tell me the first time they saw it they would have taken their oaths that the woman was stabbed unto death, so perfect was the illusion.   Although this travesty of gladiatorial combat is intended merely for amusement, yet all the Indians, these stoics of the woods, gaze upon it with profound and passionless gravity.   If they laugh at all it is only after it is all over, and at the mystification of the Americans.

As an evidence of their peaceful disposition, it may be mentioned that Joaquin Carrillo, a cousin of the celebrated Pio Pico, established himself on the Santa Rosa Plains as early as 1838, and lived alone far from any garrison in perfect security.   He was surrounded by hundreds of them, and he gathered around him a baronial following, as the custom of the early

Spaniards was. Señor Carrillo mentions that in 1838, there were no wild oats growing on the plains, though they were found in patches on the 73 mountains, and that they subsequently took root on the plains from seed scattered by the Indians.

In autumn is held the wild-oat dance. Not only is there no feasting on the part of anybody, but none who participate in the dance are allowed to partake of any meat. One of the most singular circumstances touching the California Indians is the number of occasions when they are required to abstain from flesh. One is constantly reminded of the ancient Israelites.

In their medical practice they make use of several conjurations, one of which is to place the patient in a pole pen which is ornamented with owls', hawks', buzzards', and eagles' feathers as a propitiation to those diabolical birds. Then they chant and caper around the pen in a circle. Sometimes the shamin scarifies the person, sucks out some blood, gargles his mouth with the same, then ejects it in a hole dug in the ground, and buries it out of sight, thinking he has thus eliminated from the body the *materia peccans*. The physician must abstain rigidly from food while performing his conjurations over a patient, and they sometimes continue a good part of a day.

As soon as life is extinct they lay the body decently on the funeral pyre, and the torch is applied. The weird and hideous scenes which ensue, the screams, the blood-curdling ululations, the self-lacerations they perform during the burning are too terrible to be described. Joseph Fitch says he has seen an Indian become so frenzied that he would rush up to the blazing pyre, snatch from the body a handful of burning flesh and devour it. To augment the horror of these frightful orgies, the horse or dog belonging to the deceased is led up to the spot, and cut off with butcherly slaughter. When the fire is burned down they scoop up the ashes in their hands and scatter them high into the air. They believe that they thus give the disembodied spirit wings, and that it mounts up to hover forever in the upper regions, westward by the sea, happy in the boundless voids of heaven, yet ever near enough still to delight itself with the pleasant visions of earth. But different Indians hold different views, and the totality of them believe in a greater number of heavens than the Shakers. Some of them believe that they go to the Happy Western Land beyond the sea; others, that they ascend up indefinitely. The bad return into coyotes, or sink immeasurably deep into the bowels of the earth.

There is one very curious conceit which they entertain concerning that region, which is not to be mentioned to ears polite. They say it is an island in the bitter, salt sea, an island naked, barren, and desolate, covered only with brine-spattered stones, and with glistening salt, which crunches under the tread, and swept with cursed winds and blinding acrid sea-spray. On this abhorred island bad Indians are condemned to live forever, spending an eternity in breaking stones one upon another, with no food but the broken stones and no drink but the choking brine. They are forced to this unending toil by a task-master who is the most hideous of conceivable beings. Though created in the human form, he is scarcely recognizable; one shoulder is higher than the other; his face is horribly contorted and drawn to one side; one eye is protruded and ten times its natural size, while the other is shrunken, bleared, and infernal; one arm is twice as long as the other; one of his legs is wrenched forward, and the other backward; they are of uneven length, etc.

The dead are mourned for a year. Every morning and evening for about two hours, during that length of time, the relatives seat themselves in a circle on the ground, and set up their mournful wails and chants, while they beat themselves and tear their hair. Lifting their eyes to heaven, they cry out, "*Wa, toch-i-dé! Wa, toch-i-dé!*" (O, my mother!) or whatever may be the relation. During the remainder of the day they go about their several employments with their ordinary composure.

They have a vague notion of a great ruling power somewhere in the heavens, whom they call Kal-li-top'-ti, which means "The Chief Above". But the coyote performed all the work of creation. They do not pretend to explain the origin of the world, but they believe that astute animal to be the author of man himself, of fire, of the luminaries of heaven, etc. Fire he created by rubbing two pieces of wood together in his paws, and the sacred spark he has preserved in the tree-trunks to this day.

ORIGIN OF LIGHT.

In the early days of the world all the face of the earth was wrapped in darkness, thick and profound. All the animals ran to and fro in dire confusion; the birds of the air flew wildly aloft, then dashed themselves with violence upon the ground, not knowing whither to steer their course. By an accident of this kind the coyote and the hawk happened to thrust their noses together one day, and they took counsel how they might remedy this sore evil. The coyote groped his way into a swamp and gathered a quantity of dry tules which he rolled into a large ball. This he gave to the hawk, with some flints, and sent him up into heaven with it, where he touched it off and sent it whirling around the earth. This was the sun. The moon was made the same way, only the tules happened to be damp and did not burn so well.

THE MI-SAL'-LA MA-GUN'.

This branch of the nation was named after a famous chief they once had. A Gallinomero told me the name was a corruption of *mi-sal'-la-a'-ko*, which denotes "long snake". Another form for the name is Mu-sal-la-kūn'.

Resembling the Gallinomero so closely, they require only a few paragraphs. They and the Kai-me' occupy both banks of Russian River from Cloverdale down to the territory of the Rincons (Wappos), about Geyserville.

Like all California Indians they are very hospitable and sociable, and are continually inventing pretexts for one of their simple dances. When their friends of a neighboring village come to visit them, straightway they must have a dance of welcome. Men and women form in two circles, the women on the outside. The chorister climbs up in a tree or mounts a rude kind of rostrum, with a crooked twig in his hand for a baton. Perhaps two or three others get up with him, each with two or three or four wooden whistles in his mouth, on which they blow intensely monotonous blasts, while the dancers leap up and down and chant lively as a grig.

The Misalla Magūn occasionally commit infanticide to this day, for they say they do not wish to rear any more children among the whites. There seems to have fallen on them a great and bitter despair, so far as their natures are capable of entertaining any profound emotion; they see themselves slowly and surely throttled by the white man with his busy engines, his vast enterprises, his thundering locomotives; all their fine broad valleys wrenched from them with bloody violence; themselves jostled, elbowed back, crushed to earth; all their rich nut-bearing forests filled with the swarming flocks and herds of the avaricious and never resting American, consuming the acorns which are their subsistence, and for presuming to gather which off lands which were their own from time immemorial, and for which they have never received the compensation of one poor dollar, they have been sometimes pursued and shot unto death like jackals. They see themselves swiftly dwindling, dwindling, melting away before some mysterious and pathless power, which they can neither comprehend nor resist; they foresee that they can leave to their degraded and unhappy off-spring nothing but a heritage of contempt, isolation, and discontent; and in the voiceless and unreasoning bitterness of their "small-knowing souls", in mere sullen "dumb despair", they resolve to cut them off in unconscious infancy from a fate so miserable and so sad.

To me the prevalence of infanticide among the Indians of California (for other tribes also confess it) is an eloquent testimonial to their great antiquity as a race, for we see it likewise among the Chinese, confessedly one of the oldest races on the globe, and in many things, especially in their dark and abominable cruelties, closely resembling the Indians of this vicinity; and it testifies not alone to their antiquity, but also to the dense masses of population who must have existed here before the advent of either Spaniard or American.

LITTLE HARVEY BELL.

For many months during the year 1871 the stage-road between Healds-burg and Cloverdale was so infested by robbers that many and valuable packages were frequently sent through hidden deep in the capacious bodies of lumber-wagons. The bandits were commanded by one Houx, and among them was a little Indian boy, called Harvey Bell, who was supposed to be about fourteen years old. At last all of the band were arrested except little Harvey, who it appears was not suspected. Being left alone he could not at once abandon his calling, but like that chicken-thief mentioned by the Chinese philosopher Mencius he could break off only by degrees. So on Christmas day, in the soft gloaming which was rendering all things dim, he equipped himself with a redwood picket, advanced boldly upon the stage which just then came rattling and teetering along, near Geyserville, and, presenting his stick ordered the driver to halt. The driver obeyed and asked what was wanted. Little Harvey swelled his voice out big and gruff and commanded him to throw out the express-box (the usual summons of California robbers). The driver quietly obeyed. This little matter of business having thus passed off pleasantly without any ill-feeling and with true Californian nonchalance and gentlemanliness, the boy ordered the driver to proceed. A third time he obeyed, and was presently out of sight in the darkness, while the boy proceeded to break open the box.

The California Indians are so often charged with the most arrant cowardice that it gives me much pleasure to record the above circumstance.

CHAPTER XX.

THE GUA-LÁ LA.

This tribe is closely related to the Gallinomero, both belonging to the great Pomo family, and they understand each other with very little difficulty. They are separated, however, by the low coast-mountains, a range about twenty-five miles in width, as the Gualala live on the creek called by their name, which empties into the Pacific in the northwest corner of Sonoma County. Fort Ross, on the coast, is the seat of the old Russian Mission and colony for the supply of Sitka; and here to-day within the line of the stockade is the quaint old Greek chapel with its bell-tower from which on Sunday rang out the imperious summons to prayers, for stern was the rule of the Russian commandant. It is pretty well summed up in the saying, "Go to church and say your prayers, or stay at home and take your dozen". Though these mongrel Russians have long since hoisted anchor and sailed, and sailed, farther up the coast, until they quitted the continent altogether a few years ago, and the Aleuts have gone in their *baidarkas*, and the neophytes alone remain, debauched and dwindled by this pseudo-civilization and this religion which was taught to them with the cat-tail and the knout, there still remain traces of the Russian occupation among them. After the rigorous rule of the Ivans, they are if possible a little more indolent and a little more worthless than those who were subject to the Spaniards. To this day they use the Russian word for "milk"—*malako*—which they have corrupted into *meluko;* and they sometimes use the Russian for "gun", which is *sooshyo*. But the grim Northmen have not left so many traces of their physiognomy as did the Spaniards.

They construct their conical wigwams principally with slabs of redwood bark. I saw in the possession of a Gualala squaw a fancy work-basket,

186

which evinced in its fabric and ornamentation quite an elegant taste and an incredible patience. It was of the shape common for this species of basket— that of a flat, round squash, to use a homely comparison—woven watertight of fine willow twigs. All over the outside of it the down of woodpeckers' scalps was woven in, forming a crimson nap which was variegated with a great number of hanging loops of strung beads and rude outlines of pine trees, webbed with black sprigs into the general texture. Around the edge of the rim was an upright row of little black quail's plumes gayly nodding. There were eighty of these plumes, which would have required 74 the capture of that number of quails, and it must have taken at least one hundred and fifty woodpeckers to furnish the nap on the outside. The squaw was engaged three years in making it, working at intervals, and valued it at $25. No American would collect the materials and make it for four times the money.

Charles Hopps, a veteran pioneer, told me that such richly-ornamented baskets were quite frequent among the California Indians, but the Americans were seldom permitted to see them.

These Indians make considerable account of the wild oats growing so abundantly in California, which they gather and prepare in the following manner: The harvester swings a large, deep, conical basket under his left arm, and holds in his right hand a smaller one furnished with a suitable handle. When the oats are dead ripe they shatter out easily, and he has only to sweep the small basket through the heads in a semicircle, bringing it around to the larger one, into which he discharges the contents at every stroke. When the hamper is full he empties it in a convenient place, and the squaws proceed to hull the grain. They place a quantity in a basket, moisten it slightly, then churn and stir the mass with sticks which causes the chaff to accumulate on the surface, when they burn it off by passing firebrands over it. This process is repeated until the grain is tolerably clean.

They then beat it into flour with stones, and roast it for pinole or manufacture it into bread; and the latter article is said by those who have eaten it to be quite palatable and nutritious.

Like all their brethren they are also very fond of acorns, and the old Indians still cling tenaciously to them in preference to the finest wheaten bread. To prepare them for consumption they first strip off the shells one by one, then place a large basket without a bottom on a broad, flat stone, pour into it the hulled acorns, and pound them up fine with long, slender, stone pestles. I had often noticed these bottomless baskets before, and wondered how the bottoms were worn out while the sides remained so good; but here I learned that they were so made for a good reason. The flour thus obtained is bitter, puckery, and unfit to be eaten, but they now take it to the creek for the purpose of sweetening it. In the clean, white sand they scoop out capacious hollows, and with the palms of their hands pat them down smooth and tight. The acorn flour is poured in and covered with water. In the course of two or three hours the water percolates through the sand, carrying with it a portion of the bitterness; and by repeating this process they render the flour perfectly sweet. The bread made from it is deliciously rich and oily, but they contrive somehow to make it as black as a pot, not only on the crust but throughout. Generally it is nothing but a kind of panada or mush, cooked with hot stones in baskets.

In a time of scarcity they cut down the smaller trees in which the woodpeckers have stored away acorns, or climb up and pluck them out of the holes.

And here I will make mention of a kind of sylvan barometer which Hopps told me he had learned from the Indians to observe. It is well known that a species of California woodpecker (*Melanerpes formicivorus*) drills holes in soft-wooded trees in autumn, into each of which the bird inserts an acorn, in order that when it gets full of worms in winter he may pull it out and devour the same. These acorns are stowed away before the rainy season sets in, sometimes to the amount of a half-bushel in a tree, and when they are wetted they presently swell and start out a little. So always when a rain-storm is brewing, the woodpeckers fall to work with great industry a day or two in advance, and hammer them all in tight. During the winter, therefore, whenever the woods are heard rattling with the pecking of these busy little commissary clerks heading up their barrels of worms, the Indian knows a rain-storm is certain to follow.

The Gualala also eat a considerable quantity of a wild potato, proba-bly cammas, which they call *hi-po*, and which is said to be quite good

eating when cooked and peeled.   There is a certain locality on Gualala
Creek, called by them Hí-po-wi, which signifies "potato place".   Unlike
the Atlantic tribes, those on this coast seldom consume anything raw,
except dried smelt and salmon.

Clams and mussels are great dainties in the season.   They also trap
ground-squirrels "and such small deer" by means of a noose attached to a
pole bent over, which springs up and hoists the animal into the air.

It will be observed by the traveler that the quality of aboriginal art,
as a general thing, is inferior in Southern and Central California to that in
the northern parts of the State.   The tobacco-pipe affords a convenient illustration.   Among the Hupâ it is made of beautiful manzanita or laurel wood,
and very elegantly, though plainly, carved into the form of a cigar-holder;
it is as round as if turned with a lathe, and is frequently encircled at the
outer end with a thin rim or band of stone.   But among these southern
tribes the rudest kind of a pipe answers all purposes.   The Indian takes
any straight stick he happens to find and whittles out of it a stem a foot
long and as large as one's little finger, with a rough lump of wood at the
end, which is burned or bored out a little to serve for a bowl, the whole
pipe being straight, so that the smoker must cant it up a good deal or lie on
his back.

While among the Gualala I had an excellent opportunity of witness-
ing the gambling game of *wi* and *tep*, and a description of the same, with
slight variations, will answer for nearly all the tribes in Central and Southern California.

After playing tennis all the afternoon they assembled in the evening
in a large frame-house of one room, made by themselves with tolerable
skill, and squatted on the ground around a fire, which it was the children's
task constantly to replenish with shavings.   There were about forty men,
women, and youngsters.   They first divided off in two equal parties, and
then proceeded to make up the grand sweepstake.   One Indian would lay
down a half dollar, and another of the opposite section would cover the
same.   Another would deposit a blanket or a pair of trousers, and one of
the other side would match it with an article agreed to be of equal value.
A squaw would contribute a dress, or a chemise, or a string of beads, which

would be covered as above, and so on until they deemed the stake large enough to be worth their while. It consisted of $8 in silver coin, a large hatfull of strings of shell-money, and an immense heap of clothing and blankets, some of them new and very good, and it was worth at least $150.

They gamble with four cylinders of bone about two inches long, two of which are plain and two marked with rings and strings tied around the middle. The game is conducted by four old and experienced men, frequently gray-heads, two for each party, squatting on their knees on opposite sides of the fire. They have before them a quantity of fine dry grass, and, with their hands in rapid and juggling motion before and behind them, they roll up each piece of bone in a little bale, and the opposite party presently guess in which hand is the marked bone. Generally only one guesses at a time, which he does with the word *"tep"* (marked one), *"wi"* (plain one). If he guesses right for both the players, they simply toss the bones over to him and his partner, and nothing is scored on either side. If he guesses right for one and wrong for the other, the one for whom he guessed right is "out", but his partner rolls up the bones for another trial, and the guesser forfeits to them one of the twelve counters. If he guesses wrong for both, they still keep on, and he forfeits two counters.

There are only twelve counters, and when they have been all won over to one side or the other the game is ended. Each Indian then takes out of the stake the article which he or she deposited, together with that placed on it, so that every one of the winning party comes out with double the amount he staked.

All this is extremely simple, but it took me a long time to penetrate into the whole mystery of it, such a wonderful amount of jugglery, mummery, and manipulation do the Indians encompass it with. As soon as they commence rolling up the bones in the hay they fall to whipping their arms to and fro, before and behind them, swaying their bodies backward and forward, and chanting *"Ha-man', ha-man', ha-man'!"* or *"Kai-yai', kai-yai', kai-yai'!"* or something similar, each chanting an independent refrain, but keeping perfect time the while with his companion. Then presently they bring up their hands to their breasts, with elbows akimbo, twist their bodies as if in mortal agony, and reduce the chant to a mere grunt " *Uh-uh'*, *uh-uh'*, *uh-uh'!*" though they still keep perfect time with the twisting motion. Then they interpolate divers and sundry highly superfluous shouts and roll their eyes, as if the very deuce were in them or a violent attack of colonitis.

Besides that, the old mustaches who are about to guess put on a wonderful amount of fancy flourishes. You shall see one with his eyes shining, almost glaring, as if he were possessed, slowly stretch out his hand, gradually extend his forefinger, lean far forward, and hiss out fiercely between his teeth, "*wi-i-i-i!*" or, more abruptly, "*tep!*" Sometimes he stretches one arm out, shakes it violently a while, hissing through his teeth or chanting in their strange, frenzied manner; then suddenly jerks it home as if pulling in a sturgeon, and shoots out the other, whereupon the open palms smite together in passing with a report almost like a pistol-shot, and out hisses "*wi-i-i-i!*" or "*tep!*"

All these things are conducted with that fanatic frenzy, that weird superfluity of unction, so characteristic of the California Indian. These multiplied manipulations and juggleries attract the stranger's attention so much that he forgets to notice the simple machinery of the matter for a long time. After contemplating it for a full half-hour my mind was still in about as lucid a condition as it is after reading the following quatrain:

> "The twain that, in twining, before in the twine,
> As twins were intwisted, he now doth untwine;
> 'Twixt the twain intertwisting a twine more between,
> He, twirling his twister, makes a twist of the twine."

But the Indians are so accustomed to all this blue fire that the circle of spectators look on with that stolid and imperturbable gravity peculiar to the race; and no matter how deeply any one may be involved in the issue, one can discern no indications of it in his countenance. This singular game was protracted until midnight, when we came away, and we learned next morning that it was not concluded till two o'clock. One thing is praiseworthy in the Indian gamblers, and that is the good nature with which they accept all their losses. They very seldom quarrel over a game, and never fight unless inflamed with the white man's *a'-ka bish-i-tu* (bad water).

But for all kinds of gambling both sexes and all ages have a positive passion. The Gualala wife of Hopps, although the mother of two little children, abandoned them utterly to her husband's care, watching the game until the "wee sma' hours", when it closed; and, in consequence, Hopps was obliged to get breakfast next morning, a task to which he seemed to be accustomed, and which he accepted with becoming resignation.

While sitting near these Gualala and looking at the circle of swarthy faces which the staggering blazes redly lighted up, I was not a little impressed with their resemblance to those calm, grand faces of old Egypt. Probably the reader will smile here, and I am well aware how greatly inferior these poor Diggers are to the mighty race who builded Cheops and Karnak, and whose wisdom was a beacon even to Athenian philosophy; but they are not much if any lower than the modern Fellahs who toiled in the sand of the Suez Canal, and who are said to retain the features of their great ancestors. I saw here the same scanty beard; the same full, voluptuous lips; the same straight, strong noses, with thick walls and dilated nostrils; the same broad cheek-bones; the same large and prominent eyes in most; the same expression of restful and placid strength that I have seen among the Egyptian sculptures of the Berlin Museums and the British Museum of London. The differences are that the Indians open their eyes more freely except in extreme old age, when they are shriveled and nearly burnt out by the smoke, and have lower foreheads and more shrunken cheeks.

It cannot be denied that there was a certain grave and savage strength of feature, perhaps due to a slight infusion of Russian blood, in that midnight circle of dark faces, such as one would little expect to find in men so entirely empty of mental force and originality, however imitative they may have been. Such faces joined to such intellects go hard to demolish all physiognomy theories. And yet these are elevated several degrees above the lowest savages. They reckon their beads "by the two hundred", as one explained to me, up to a thousand, the word for which is *tush-op'-te* (literally "five two-hundreds"). In marriage they observe strictly the Mosaic table of prohibited affinities, accounting it "poison", as they say, for a person to marry a cousin or an avuncular relative. True, they occasionally practiced infanticide formerly by their own confession, but they appear to have sacrificed generally only the weakest and deformed infants; and the amount of dancing which they can endure for ten or fifteen days together, day and night, is astonishing, when we remember that the manner of dance practiced by the men is terribly hard work; but like all savages they can stand the fatigue of amusements much better than they can the steady, hard grubbing which gets bread and meat.

It is a curious fact that there is no word for "lazy" in their language, and they have borrowed a word from the Spanish. Some qualities are known by themselves, and some only by their opposites; hence, as the Indian knew nothing of industry, he also knew nothing of laziness.

Besides their sweat-house heats and their regular cold-water baths in the morning, they have another habit which is on the side of cleanliness; they sleep stark naked, even when they have learned to wear civilized garments. I was first made aware of this fact by an amusing incident. Near the farmer's house there was a *campoody*, and in the night the swine became frightened and ran through the wigwams, and when we looked out we saw them come shooting out from the opposite door-hole, first an Indian on all-fours, then a pig, one as naked as the other. I afterward chanced to observe this fact several times in the central and southern parts of the State. What little aboriginal clothing they wore was of a material not comfortable to lie in; besides which, as they never washed it, it was a relief to lay it off at night, and doubtless conducive to health, as they themselves argue. Man and wife do not sleep apart, as in some Algonkin tribes, but lie down snugly together in a kind of nest, and draw a hare-skin rug over them.

The chieftainship is hereditary unless the heir is incompetent, though its functions are very nebulous, and their social system nowadays is patriarchal. But as on Russian River the remnant of them is so shrunken and narrowed down that it saddens their hearts, and they dwell all in one wigwam together for the comforting of their souls, though some who thus abide in common are nowise related.

Every year brings around the great autumnal games, which continue a matter of two weeks. Besides the spear dance, tennis, gambling, and the like, they amuse themselves with divers other entertainments. One of them is the devil dance, which is gotten up to terrify the women and children, like the *haberfeldtreiben* of the Bavarian peasants. In the midst of the ordinary dances there comes rushing upon the scene an ugly apparition in the shape of a man, wearing a feather mantle on his back reaching from the arm-pits down to the mid-thighs, zebra-painted on his breast and legs with black stripes, bear-skin shako on his head, and his arms stretched out at full length along a staff passing behind his neck. Accoutered in this harlequin rig he dashes at the squaws, capering, dancing, whooping; and they and the children flee for life, keeping several hundred yards between him and themselves. If they are so unfortunate as to touch even his stick all their children will perish out of hand.

The object of this piece of gratuitous foolery seems to be, as among most of the Pomo tribes, merely to exhibit to the squaws the power of their lords over the infernal regions and its denizens, and thereby remind them forcibly of the necessity of obedience.

Their fashion of the spear dance is different from the Gallinomero. The man who is to be slain stands behind a screen of hazel boughs with his face visible through an aperture; and the spearman, after the usual protracted dashing about and making of feints, strikes him in the face through the hole in the screen. He is then carried off, revives, etc.

The Gualala say the world was made by the Great Man above assisted by the Old Owl; here we doubtless have a Russian graft on their aboriginal belief. The lower animals were created first; man and woman after.

Around Fort Ross there is a fragment of the tribe called by the Gualala, E-rus'-si; which name is probably another relic of the Russian occupation.

THE E-RI'-O.

Such is the name given by the Spaniards to the tribe living at the mouth of Russian River. Both they and the Gualala have more affinity with the Pomo in language than with the Gallinomero, though a Potter Valley Pomo must associate with them a few weeks before he can understand them readily.

They practice cremation and give a reason for it which I had not heard before, that is, if the dead are not burned they will become grizzly bears. Probably some such reason prevails everywhere, though they are extremely loth to give any reason. Hence cremation is an act of religion, of redemption, of salvation, which it were a heinous impiety to the dead to pretermit.

In their autumnal games, which continue as long as the provisions they have brought hold out, they have the spear dance, the dance of seven devils, the black-bear dance, etc. The dance of seven devils is like the devil dance of the Gualala, only there are seven devils instead of one, and they are more devilish, having horns on their heads, forked tails, and the like. In the black-bear dance they dress a man in a black bearskin and dance around him with hideous noise, being naked, but zebra-painted with black, and wearing coronals of long feathers. Possibly this may be an act of fetichism, performed, as the Indians cautiously say of all such doings, "for luck"; because nearly all tribes regard the black bear in distinction from the grizzly as peculiarly of happy omen.

THE SAN RAFAEL INDIANS.

Under this name the Spaniards collected at the San Rafael Mission most of the Indians of the peninsula who spoke a different language from the Gallinomero. Among them were the Tá-mal from whom Mount Tamal- 75 pais is named, and the Li·kat'-u-it, whose last great chief was Ma-rin'. Having lost most of their aboriginal usages they are not of interest here.

THE CHO-KÚ-YEN.

The same is true of this tribe, who occupied Sonoma Valley, which was named from one of their celebrated chiefs.

CHAPTER XXI.

THE ASH-O-CHÍ-MI.

Probably this tribe would be more readily recognized under the Spanish name of Wappo. The Spaniards never forgot the keen and stinging defeat inflicted by old Colorado upon them under the lead of General M. G. Vallejo; and they embodied the qualities which worsted them in a name which the Ashochimi use yet in preference to their own—Wappo the Unconquerable. Although the battle-ground between them and the Spaniards was on the edge of Big Plains, northeast of Healdsburg, their ancient proper home was in the mountains. They ranged from the Geysers to the Calistoga Hot Springs, inclusive, and in Knight's Valley; and holding thus two of the great natural wonders of the State they disputed for their possession more heroically than did even the famous tribe of Yosemite.

The Geysers were discovered by means of one of their well-worn trails; and they were early aware of the healing virtues of the Calistoga waters. Their invalids were accustomed to wallow in the hot, steaming mud and pools, receiving benefit therefrom into their bodies.

There is an ancient tradition that the Wappos were once at war with their neighbors, and were by the latter hemmed in and straitly besieged in the head of Calistoga Valley. They were at last so sore pressed with hunger that they were fain to resort to cannibalism, and stripping off the flesh of their companions who died or were slain they boiled it in the springs. From this horrid use arose the name Carne Humana sometimes given to this celebrated spa by the early Spaniards. The Indians of to-day know nothing of this story.

After the Spanish conquest had decimated and enervated their lowland neighbors, the Gallinomero, the yet untainted Wappo descended from their mountain homes upon them, and worsted them in a pitched battle. The

196

two tribes then entered into a treaty by which the Gallinomero ceded to the Wappo a portion of Russian River Valley about ten miles long north and south, and reaching across from mountain-top to mountain-top. That portion of the Wappo who occupied this tract became known as the Rincons. In descending this valley, I was surprised to find a break in the Pomo dialects, beginning about Geyserville and reaching down to Healdsburg. It was accounted for by this recent Wappo conquest, by which a foreign language had been interjected into the Pomo. With this exception the Pomo dialects are continuous from the head to the mouth of Russian River; while along the mountain chain east of it runs a parallel body of language of nearly equal length, namely, the Yuki or Wappo.

That the Wappo and the Yuki are somewhat related is shown by the similarity of some words, thus:

	YUKI.	HŪCHNOM.	WAPPO.
One.	pong'-weh.	pú-weh.	pâ-wah.
Two.	ó-peh.		hó-peh.
Seven.		o-pi-dūn'.	o-pi-hūn'.
To go.	ko-āt'-tah.		chau-á-si.
Tree.	oal.		hoal.
Yesterday.	sūm.		su'-ma.

This resemblance and manifest relationship between the two languages is singular, when we consider that they are separated by an interval of at least sixty miles, with a branch of the Pomo (in the mountain gap leading over from Ukiah to Clear Lake) interpolated between them. This raises the question, Did the Yuki-Wappo once occupy the Russian River Valley and yield it to its present occupants"? What was the course of migration or conflict which some time or other in the past has disrupted and broken asunder these two languages so clearly of a common origin?

In regard of this treaty, Dr. E. Ely relates this: He was once out hunting in company with a Gallinomero, when he beat up a fine buck and shot it. He told the Indian to shoulder the carcass and carry it home, but to his great surprise the savage refused. It appeared that the buck had

76

dropped a few yards inside the Wappo territory, and though the Gallinomero had the powerful backing of a white man, and the lickerish sniff of
venison in his mind's nostril, he dreaded the possible divulgence of the
matter, and the Wappos' secret vengeance; so strictly are these Indian
treaties observed, through fear.

The Wappo presents a finer physique than the lowland Gallinomero.
He is shaded perceptibly lighter; has a more even and well-rounded head,
though it is large like the Yuki head; less angularity and coarseness of
feature; a much more prominent chin; a brighter eye; less protuberance
of belly.

The Wappo language, like its congener, the Yuki, is clear-cut, sharp,
and easy of expression to an American. The words are mostly short, and
seldom is there one that cannot be neatly and accurately spelled from the
Indian's lips. Thus *hell* is "fire"; *pi* is "white"; *poll* is "earth"; and
hell-pi-poll (literally, "fire-white-earth") is "ashes". The agglutinative
feature prevails, as usual. Thus *mi* is "you", *má-deh* is "father," and
mai'-ah is "your father". The verb takes a different form for the
past tense, but not for the future; thus *chau-á-sy, chau-á-ky, chau-á-sy*
are the three forms for the present, imperfect, and future of "go". The
Wappo display great readiness in learning their neighbors' tongues. Old
Colorado was said by the whites to have spoken in his prime fourteen languages and dialects. He is still alive, but blind, extremely shriveled and
helpless, probably a hundred years old—a pitiable shadow of a once great
warrior, who over and over again routed the brave Spaniards.

In the main the social customs of the Wappo are like those of the Gallinomero, but they do not commit parricide, and less frequently infanticide.
In regard to the latter, both whites and Indians have so often asserted its
existence that there is no room for incredulity; but I have seen only one
man who could affirm that he had actually witnessed the deed. A. S. Nelson
stated that he once saw a Wappo woman put her foot on the neck of her
healthy, new-born babe, and throttle it.

When a young man beholds a maiden who is beautiful in his eyes, he
goes to her father and lays down before him in the wigwam a quantity of
shell-money. Both of them maintain a profound silence, and the old man

feigns to take no notice whatever of the money, though he surreptitiously squints at it now and then. If he thinks there is not enough, or he does not like the youth, after a sufficient time has elapsed to suit the aboriginal ideas of dignity and red-tape, he reaches out his hands and returns it, and the suitor goes away without a word, or remains and adds another string. If accepted, the old Indian calls his daughter to him, joins her hand to her lover's, makes them sit down together on the ground before his knees, and addresses them a few words of advice. Thereupon they arise and go away husband and wife.

Their custom allows the wife unlimited rights in recovering a truant husband, if only she has the muscular force to exercise them. A Wappo once abandoned his wife at Cloverdale and journeyed down the river to the ranch of William Fitch where he abode for a season with a second love. But the lawful wife soon discovered his whereabouts, followed him up, confronted him before his paramour, upbraided him fiercely, and then seized him by the hair and led him away triumphantly to her bed and basket. Some author has said that love warmed up is not enduring. This love remained warm two years, when the Indian again met his enslaver and again eloped.

They worship the owl and the hawk; that is they regard them as potent and malignant spirits which they must conciliate by offerings and by wearing mantles of their feathers When a great white owl alights near a village in the evening and hoots loudly, the head-man at once assembles all his warriors in a council to determine whether Mr. Strix demands a life or only money (for they understand him to say, like the California foot-pad, "Your money or your life!"). If they incline to the belief that he demands a life, some one in the village is doomed and will speedily die. But they generally vote that he can be placated by an offering, and immediately a quantity of shell-money and pinole must be brought in by the squaws, whereupon the valorous trencher-men fall to and eat the pinole themselves, and in the morning the head-man decorates himself with owl feathers, carries out the shell-money with much solemn formality, and flings it into the air under the tree where the owl perched. The hawk is appeased in a different manner. A stuffed specimen of that bird is placed on top of a pole, and

long strings of shell-beads are stretched from the ground up to its feet.
Then, decorated with mantles and head-dresses of hawks' feathers, they
dance around the pole in a circle, with chanting and various gestures, and
afterward solemnly commit the money to the flames

In case of death the body is immediately incinerated, and the ashes
flung into the air. They believe that the spirit is thus borne aloft and flies
away to a grotto hard by the sea at Punta de los Reyes. In this grotto is
a fire which burns without ceasing, and which no living being may behold
without being instantly stricken blind The disembodied spirit enters,
hovers over and around this fire for a season, then flutters forth again and
wings its flight over the ocean to the Happy Western Land.

They have a legend of the Deluge which runs as follows: Long ago
there was a mighty flood which prevailed over all the land and drowned
all living creatures save the coyote alone. He set himself to restore the
population of the world in the following manner: He collected together a
great quantity of owls,' hawks', eagles', and buzzards' tail-feathers, and with
these in a bundle he journeyed over the face of the earth and carefully
sought out all the sites of the Indians' villages. Wherever a wigwam had
stood before the flood, there he planted a feather in the ground and scraped
up muck around the same. In due time the feathers sprouted, took root,
grew up, branched and flourished greatly, finally turning into men and
women; and thus was the world repeopled.

Like all mountaineers, they are much braver in pursuit of game than
the lowlanders. They snare even grizzly bears, and then boldly assault
and kill them with no weapons but sharp, fire-hardened sticks, with which
they pierce them. These snares are made of a species of wild flax (I saw
no samples of it), from which they twist out ropes, small, but very strong.

The following legend relating how the Geysers were discovered by
Indians pursuing a grizzly bear is taken from the San Francisco Bulletin:

A LEGEND OF THE GEYSERS.

In passing up the gorge in which are situated the Pluton Geysers you
will notice a human head carved in stone. It bears so striking a resemblance to a half-finished piece of statuary that the most casual observer

asks its history. This is the legend as told by the Indians who inhabit the Coast Range:

The discovery of the Geysers is a comparatively modern event. "From the time when the memory of man runneth not to the contrary" peaceful tribes of Indians inhabited the rich, luxuriant valley of Russian River and its tributaries. With hunting and fishing, with clover, wild oats, and acorns, with the various roots, berries, and fruits provided by Nature, they lived a happy, contented life. The dense chaparral which covers the mountains and lines the cañons of the region surrounding the Geysers effectually concealed these wonderful springs. It was since the Spaniards and Mexicans began to settle the country and fatten their immense herds upon the rank herbage that the Indians were compelled to put forth greater exertions for food. Two of their young men were hunting on the south side of the river, below where Cloverdale now stands, when they caught sight of an unusually large grizzly bear. Simultaneously they fired their sharp-barbed arrows into the monster's side. He dropped as if dead, but well knowing it to be a habit of the grizzly to fall to the ground upon receiving the slightest wound, they again let fly their flint-headed shafts, and again struck the bear. Sorely wounded, the animal instinctively staggered toward the thick underbrush, leaving a trail of blood behind. Sure of their game, the hunters followed the blood stains into the chaparral and up the cañon. Here and there the weary monster lay down to rest for a moment, and upon arising left a gory pool to attest the severity of his hurt. The thews and sinews of the California grizzly almost give him a charmed life. The eager hunters would several times have given up the chase, but fresh indications of the bear's weakness, the hope of so rich a prize, and the fear of the ridicule of their companions, spurred them forward. The wounded animal never once swerved from a direct course up the cañon. Mile after mile he tottered straight forward, although his fast-ebbing life frequently caused him to stumble and fall. Just as his merciless pursuers were ready to turn back, baffled and discouraged, they saw him writhing in agony on a little, open grassy plot half a mile distant. Most of their route, until now, had been through close-timbered forests, thick-set with chaparral and scrub-oak.

The sun had moved far down the heavens, and the lofty western mountain shut out his beams from the gorge. At sight of their dying game, the

Indians gave a loud, exultant shout. The grizzly startled by the sound rose from the ground, and with the last glimmering ray of life plunged into the ravine ahead. Running across the intervening space, the hunters saw his lifeless body in the bottom of the gorge. In their eager haste they had not noticed the thousand minute jets of steam issuing from the hillside, nor did they hear the hoarse, rushing sound that filled the cañon with a continuous roar, until just as they reached the body.

Halting, amazed, they found themselves standing on the brink of the Witches' Caldron, in the midst of the hissing, seething Geysers. One horrified, ghastly look at the smoky, steaming hillsides; one breath of the puffing, sulphurous vapor; one terrified glance at the trembling, springy earth, and the frightened hunters darted back down the cañon. With stoical skepticism the aged chief and council listened to the tale the hunters told as the tribe gathered around the camp-fire. Earth that smoked! Water that boiled and bubbled without fire! Steam that issued from holes in the ground with a noise like the rushing of the storm-wind! Impossible! But the two young braves were noted for courage and truthfulness, and at last they prevailed on a score of their fellows to return with them. It was all true. There lay the dead bear by the black, seething waters that were hotter than fire could make them. After a thorough examination, the medicine-men concluded that the strange mineral waters must have rare healing properties. Booths of willows were erected over the jets of steam, and the sick laid thereon. The cañon became a favorite resort of the red men, and all the Coast Range tribes came hither with their invalids Many wonderful cures were effected, and yet, occasionally, things happened that convinced the superstitious medicine-men that the place was under the control of an evil spirit.

Finally, one cloudy night, a strange, rumbling sound rose through the darkness, and the earth trembled violently. After that no one approached the spot for many days.

It is a common belief among the Coast Indians that evil spirits frequently dwell within the bodies of grizzlies. It was now universally believed that the spirit of the slaughtered bear had charge of the Geysers. There were many sick and dying with a strange plague, or pestilence that had suddenly appeared among the tribe. Something must be done. Many urged a return, at all hazards, to the medicinal springs; others held that the angry demon of the gorge had sent the pestilence upon them. At last a gray-haired seer whose hand was skilled in all cunning craft was persuaded to try to appease the spirit by making a graven image near the Witches' Caldron. Enough of the idolatrous traditions of their ancestors were remembered to enable them to have faith in this strange attempt at propitiation. Day after day the good old sculptor went all alone to the cañon, and chiseled away the rock until the semblance of a human face appeared. As the work neared completion, he often lingered later, in his anxiety to finish the statue. It was believed that when the task was entirely ended the demon would retire, and let the people be healed. A few more days and the finishing strokes would be made on the figure. Every one was full of hope The old man was working at the dawn, and when the evening came and the twilight shadows stole down the mountain and up the ravine he had not returned. Suddenly a weird, hollow moan seemed to tremble on the shuddering air, and at the next instant the earth shook so violently that the cliffs toppled from their base. The terrible shocks were felt several times during the night, and when the sun arose the old seer was gone from earth. The cold, stony face of the image alone remained. Not the slightest trace was ever discovered of the faithful sculptor, yet during the night new springs had burst forth three-quarters of a mile down the river. Here the sick were brought, and from that day to the present time the Indians used only the lower springs. Scaffolds are raised above the steam-jets three or four feet, and willows and brush are laid across. On these the sick are placed, and the mineral vapors encircle and heal them.

Years after, the white men came to the great valley of the Russian River, and in due time were guided to the springs. The Indian guides would not go farther than the lower springs, but the pale-faces found the image still guarding the ravine. Enterprise and love of gain have built a beautiful hotel across from the Geysers, and hundreds of tourists annually flock thither

The Indians, however, firmly believe that the wrathful demon still holds sway, and they can never be induced to approach the gorge of the main Geysers.

CHAPTER XXII.

THE KÁ-BI-NA-PEK.

In the Clear Lake Basin the Indians may be divided into two main bodies, those on the west side and those on the east. On the west they are related in language slightly to the Pomo; on the east, equally slightly, to the Patwin. In the northwest corner of the basin a constant communication was kept up with the Pomo; hence the villages about Lakeport speak a Pomo dialect, and are properly included with that large nation; but all the dwellers around the lake should be enumerated as distinct peoples, being divided into the two bodies above mentioned. Big Valley and Cobb Valley were the principal abode of the western lacustrine tribes; Höschla Island and the narrow shore adjacent that of the eastern.

The Ká-bi-na-pek living on lower Kelsey Creek may be taken as representative of the western division, though they formed only one village of the many in Big Valley. The myriads of fish in the lake and the abundance of acorns supported a dense population in this valley, estimated by the pioneers at many thousands. They were brave and independent mountaineers, even more infinitesimally subdivided and less coherent, if possible, than is the wont of the California Indians. They had no chiefs of general and large authority; nothing but head-men or captains of villages.

Coming up from Russian River to Clear Lake one receives at first the impression that the natives here are a sickly race on account of their lighter, brassy color and longer faces. Indeed some pioneers insist stoutly that they are altogether a different race from the "Diggers", perhaps a remnant of some ancient, indigenous people who were forced into these mountain valleys by an invasion of the lowlands. It will be shown further along that this theory is erroneous. Still they always were and yet are a much finer

204

race than the Russian River tribes, being tall and stalwart, often of a noble physical mould, weighing not unfrequently 180 to 200 pounds.   They have a quicker apprehension, readier imitation, and a brighter intelligence than their neighbors on the river, and they are as brave as the Wappo.   They are less dependent on the whites, more frequently cultivate their own patches of ground, or hire out for a wage.   Not long ago they held a barbecue whereat an ox and several sheep were roasted whole, and white spectators affirm that they ate there as fine pastry, puddings, and roast beef, all prepared by Indian women, as they ever saw at an American party; and that the tables were laid with the cleanest of linen and a full service of crockery.   Better than all, the leading Indians banished strong drinks from the place, and formed a police force from their own numbers to preserve order.   Whenever a drunken or disorderly fellow intruded on the premises, these officials arrested him at once, carried him out bound hand and foot, and laid him carefully away behind the bushes to cool off.

In the spring of 1872, on the occasion of a great festival to be described shortly, the Kabinapek dispatched a commission who traveled two or three months among the surrounding tribes examining different styles of assembly-house architecture.   On their return they reported voluminously in a council, and it was voted to build the new assembly-house on a model different from anything previously seen on Clear Lake.   Instead of con- 77 structing it in the shape of a blunt cone, only three or four feet excavated in the ground, they dug a circular cellar ten or twelve feet deep, timbered it up around the sides, and roofed it over nearly flat and level with the earth.   It is common to say that the California Indians never change any of their customs except at the instance of the Americans.   Whether this style of assembly-house was any improvement or not, I do not know; but it was wholly novel and of their own contriving.

They take three kinds of fish, mostly in the creeks in the spawning season, for they fish comparatively little in the lake.   The lake whitefish furnishes by far the greatest proportion of the catch.   In the spring they ascend the creeks in such vast numbers that the Indians, by simply throwing in a little brushwood to impede their motion, can literally scoop them out.   In 1872 there was a remarkable run.   I arrived in the valley too late to see it, but the sides and bottom of Kelsey Creek were yet strewn and malodorous with fish that had perished by reason of the crowding.

The Kabinapek language is extremely rugged, hirsute, and guttural, so that I was deterred from doing anything beyond getting a meager vocabulary; and even these few words were very difficult to spell. That it is an offshoot of the Pomo is clearly proven by the fact that it possesses in common with it a few such words of hourly occurrence as "water", "dog", "deer", etc. But the numerals are changed beyond all recognition. The personal pronouns are radically the same, but have been gutturalized by these mountaineer fish-eaters.

There is presented in this tribe an interesting but unanswerable inquiry. As the Kabinapek and the other villages are descended from the Pomos, their language must once have been identical with that spoken on Russian River. Let us suppose that the parent language had 3,000 words. At 78 this day, so widely have the two resultant languages departed from the original that, judging from the limited vocabularies I took, they have not above 100 in common. How long would it take each of them to change 1,500 words beyond the recognition of the other? It must have taken many hundreds, if not thousands, of years.

About the only act which can be considered religious is the *pu-i-si*, "raising the dead". It is the same as the custom which prevails on the east side, and will be described in speaking of that people.

Like all California Indians, these are extremely sensual. In the spring when the wild clover is lush and full of blossoms and they are eating it to satiety after the famine of winter, they become amorous. This season, therefore, is a literal Saint Valentine's Day with them, as with the natural beasts and birds of the forest.

A peculiarity of this tribe is the intense sorrow with which they mourn for their children when dead. Their grief is immeasurable. They not only burn up everything that the baby ever touched, but everything that they possess, so that they absolutely begin life over again—naked as they were born, without an article of property left. A young Indian was drowned at Lower Lake, and so great and bitter was the grief of his mother over his untimely death that she besought her friends to take away her life also. Moved by her passionate sorrow and her entreaties, they complied with her wishes; she was hanged, and then laid upon the funeral pyre beside her son, and together they were burned. Such is the tradition.

It is very generally asserted that unlike the river tribes they never committed infanticide before the advent of our countrymen. When whites took Indian women for wives, they were often mortified at the receipt of little pledges of love; and to their lasting shame and infamy be it written, (this fact is well authenticated,) they compelled them either to give them away or destroy them outright. But even if they were not originally addicted to infanticide, they were sometimes guilty of fœticide, which was accomplished, not by drugs, but by violent physical means. This fact was stated to me by an accomplished lady who had lived among them many years with her husband.

They are singular also in their devotion to the formality of incineration. Two Indians were once drowned in the lake near Kelsey, and their relations searched for them assiduously for weeks that they might reduce their bodies to ashes, without which they believed they would never behold the Happy Western Land. A lady described to me a scene of cremation which she once witnessed, and instead of the revolting exhibitions seen among some tribes it was conducted with seemly and mournful tenderness. The body was carefully wrapped in blankets, laid upon the pyre, and the torch applied, and as the flames advanced fresh blankets were continually thrown over the body to conceal its loathsomeness from sight until it was consumed. A woman, one of the chief mourners, sat at the head, with her eyes upturned to heaven, chanting, mourning, and weeping. The mother, bowed down and broken with grief, with close-cropped head, and face disfigured with the blackest pitch, as the emblem of mourning, sat at the foot, lamenting and lacerating her face until she was exhausted. She then rose, tottered away and fell at the feet of her husband who encircled her with his arm and tenderly stroked down her hair while he mingled his tears with hers. An Indian counts it no unmanliness to weep for his friends.

They believe, like all others, that the soul can be disembodied and set free by the agency of fire alone; hence the necessity of burning. Hence, also, when a person of a goodly fatness is burning, and his flesh sputters and pops in the flames, the spectators shout the loudest, believing that his spirit is enjoying a happy release.

The Kabinapek have a vague conception of a Supreme Being, whom they call Kin'-tash-i; but, as usual, he is a wholly negative person who takes no part or interest in mundane affairs—evidently a foreign graft upon their cosmogony.

AN INDIAN REVIVAL.

From time immemorial it has been the custom of the Clear Lake Indians to celebrate a large harvest of acorns, or a heavy run of fish in the spring, with a season of dancing, protracted for two or three weeks, an occasion in which the religious element manifestly mingled. For some years there had been neither one, hence no opportunity for the great dance; and the assembly chambers wherein they were held have partly been burned by accident, partly fallen into disuse at the instance of the Americans. In the autumn of 1871 the acorns were plenty, and the next spring the fish ascended the creeks in unprecedented numbers; and now there was double occasion for the long-neglected festival. The old Indians, who still clung tenaciously to the ancient traditions had often upbraided the younger generation for their impiety, and now they renewed with redoubled force their exhortations to them to rebuild the fallen assembly-houses, the *ædes labentes deorum*, and return to the pious and time-honored usages of their ancestors.

It was done. With all the ardor of the Israelites rebuilding the temple of Solomon the young men fell to cutting and peeling timbers, excavating pits, timbering them up, etc. As above recorded, a commission was sent out to study the best models. In a short time the new assembly-houses were completed and then they fell to dancing all around the lake with great enthusiasm. Night after night the assembly-houses sounded to the songs of the singers and the monotonous clacking of the sticks. Though the old Indians had persisted that their neglect of the dance was bringing on them the displeasure of the spirits, yet they had been healthy all these years; but now they began to cough and wheeze withal. When they went naked, these sweat-house heats were undoubtedly good, but after they had learned to wear clothes they were injurious. The Kabinapek danced so hard that two of them yielded up the ghost and went to the Happy Western Land.

By that subtle system of telegraphy which exists among them, all the surrounding tribes heard of the great revival of antique customs at Clear Lake; they heard of the singing and the dancing, of the fish and the eating thereof. About that time the Lone Pine earthquake occurred, and some of their prophets dreamed dreams and beheld visions of another which was to follow and destroy all the whites. By fleeing to Clear Lake the Indians would escape the *dies iræ*. More than that, in all waters except those of the lake there was a comparative scarcity. Hundreds of Indians round-about flocked to the lake to have a good time, a good mess of fish, and by the sight of a multitude of their race refresh the memory of better days. The coming earthquake was a vague matter, and disturbed them little; the fishing and the dancing were rare good things.

In all directions they came, but especially from Russian River. Half-way over the mountains from Cloverdale is a station called Ellis's Ranch, which they passed in almost continual procession. One stalwart Wappo slung a rawhide band across his forehead and down over his shoulders, like a swing, wherein his old and decrepit father sat and rode, clasping his son around the neck. Another bore two aged squaws this way, carrying first one to a resting-place, then returning for the other. In painful contrast to these instances of filial devotion, the Wappos of Knight's Valley abandoned a squaw thought to be 120 years old, in the valley, and she would have perished but for the compassion of Americans.

Toiling over the mountains on this pious pilgrimage they would arrive, faint and weary at this half-way house. Ragged and insolent young louts jingling their huge bell-spurs on their naked heels, two of them, perhaps, great, strapping fellows, bestriding the least mite of a mustang, and riding like Jehu up hill and down dale, would approach the gate and impudently demand food and tobacco. In beautiful contrast to this was the conduct of a squaw, who with her little one had no victual for the journey. Seeing the good matron of the station approach with a pan of milk, she ran and fell down on her knees before her, looked up into her face, and clasped her hands before her in silent thankfulness.

Thus they flocked to Clear Lake by hundreds. Some of them being "apprenticed" to white men, had written leaves of absence and passes, ranging from twelve to twenty days. Like children, they greatly over-stayed their time. With an Ethiopian passion for the dance, all these hundreds yielded themselves up to it with an absolute infatuation, and week after week slipped away unperceived. The time was going by for the planting of their own small crops and those of the whites who depended on their labor. Their best friends earnestly warned them to have done. Men and timid women were scared at the unwonted multitude of dusky faces in a feeble settlement. Citizens banded together in places and chased them away. The atmosphere began to be big with rumors of a removal to the dreaded reservation; but this cry of "wolf" had been so often sounded that the savages laughed it to scorn. The fascinations of the dance were irresistible, and Indians that had formerly been so industrious as to inspire their patrons with high hopes that they were reclaimed to civilization now danced all night for weeks together and slept all day. The halcyon days of savagery had returned, with all their pleasant and lazy witcheries.

But at last, after several months had elapsed, and some in a neighboring valley had actually been sent to a reservation, better counsel prevailed, the dancers gradually dispersed, and the whites around Clear Lake once more slept secure.

It only remains now to describe this dance, as I witnessed it one night among the Kabinapek. Some acquaintances and myself were on the ground at nightfall, but it was fully an hour before anything was done toward collecting the dancers, who after so many weeks' frenzied excite-ment were extremely sluggish until they got enlivened in the dance. A herald finally mounted half-way up the low dome of the assembly-hall, and with a hard and rattling loudness of voice made proclamation substantially as follows, uttering a sentence about once a minute:

"*He*, come to the sweat-house! *He*, make haste to the dance! *He*, make haste, everybody! *He*, be not angry with the strangers *He*, steal nothing from the strangers! *He*, give them plenty of food! *He*, make haste to the dance, men and women! *He*, do not steal the strangers' things while they dance!"

By "strangers" was meant any Indians who did not live in the Kabin-apek village. He proclaimed thus for about a half-hour, using a vast deal of repetition, and then he descended. It was about half an hour yet before anybody responded, when the dancers began to assemble, gliding with slow and noiseless tread through the darkness. It was fully an hour before a low humming inside announced that the performances were about to begin, whereupon we bowed our heads half-way to the ground, and advanced several feet along a narrow, sloping passage, and found ourselves in the circular arena of the assembly-hall. There were about sixty persons in it, squatting around in concentric circles, leaving a central space about 20 feet in diameter for the performers. There was a bright fire burning right at the entrance, and as there was only one other small air-hole at the opposite side the atmosphere was already horribly foul, and we had to stop in the passage and squat as low as possible to prevent ourselves from being stifled. The orchestra, eight in number, all young men, were squatted together opposite the entrance, four facing four. Between them was a hollow slab, serving as a kind of drum, to be beaten by a drummer with the naked foot, and each of them held in his right hand a little stick, split half-way down, to be used as a clapper in keeping time. The dancers were all young women, who stood in a curved row in front of the orchestra. All of them were decked out in their bravest apparel, and dancers and orchestra alike had a single ornament, which was the only thing aboriginal in their costume. The long feathers of the yellowhammer (the sacred ornamental bird of California) were evenly laid together, butt to tip alternately, and strung on strings, forming a bandeau about 4 inches wide and 15 long, which was passed across the forehead and tied behind the head with strings fastened to it half-way back, leaving the ends to flop backward and forward over the ears.

The orchestra hummed several little choruses, accompanied by the clacking of the sticks, before the dancers took their places. Then they sung a chorus, as follows:

Yo-hi-o-he-i, (four times,)
Le-lo-mu-he,
Hu-di-go.

In this the dancers joined, sometimes facing the orchestra, sometimes the audience, but each one always keeping in place. Like everything they sung, it has no meaning. They all sung in a high falsetto voice, the women especially, so that they were less agreeable to listen to than the men. The sharp, monotonous clacking of the sticks, and the dull tunk, tunk of the slab-drum were execrable. I am no judge of harmony, except to know that they kept perfect time, and am, as Wordsworth says of himself, "in music all unversed;" but I have listened to simple melodies that affected me even to tears; and I declare without hesitation that there was one short passage in this chorus which when chanted by the men alone was one of the most moving I ever heard. Those three rude, barbaric, and wholly unintelligible syllables, *hu-di-go*, were trilled and prolonged out with a sweet, soft, and wild melodiousness that I shall not forget to my dying hour. Never have I so regretted my inability to write down music by the ear, that I might make good this assertion by submitting the passage to musical critics.

About this time appeared on the scene the two performers, who were the principal characters of the evening. They wore richly ornamented and beaded buckskin tights, reaching from the hips half-way to the knees; mantles composed of long, black eagles' feathers netted together in successive courses, sweeping gracefully down from the shoulders to the knees, but leaving the arms free; and brilliantly bespangled head-dresses of feathers and beads. On the breast and face they were smeared with a number of black stripes, crossing in squares. But for this absurd use of the charcoal they would have presented really splendid figures, their smooth, round, finely molded limbs setting off the spangles handsomely. Their feet were bare.

They danced before the audience in lively fashion, sometimes stamping with one foot with great force, sometimes chasing one the other around the fire in a kind of hippity-hop, their magnificent mantles sailing and rustling, while their heads wagged from side to side, and their arms were brandished aloft in free and graceful gestures. The suppleness and agility of their softly-rounded, full, almost feminine forms were wonderful. Notwithstanding their violent motions, the eye perceives no hard, knotted contortions of the muscles as in an American athlete; all that rapid play of the tendons goes on beneath the skin with a snaky smoothness and strength.

They finally created quite a dust, and an aged "super" went around with a basket of water and sprinkled the course. At the termination of each chorus they would end off with a prodigious stamping, then suddenly wheel and bow to the women dancers with a profundity and elegance that would have done the highest honor to Chesterfield. But very unfortunately the women would wheel at the selfsame time toward the orchestra and slightly incline their heads, so that they would receive this magnificent compliment of the two performers, not facing toward them, but quite the reverse! The audience would then applaud with a loud "ho"! After each chorus, which would occupy about five minutes, there would be a pause of about a minute. Each chorus was chanted five or six times over, then some other was taken up. Another that I wrote down was as follows:

Hu-pé, hu-pé, hu-pé, la-ha.

The men would chant this once, then the women, then both together, then this together:

Hu-pe-lí, hu-pe-lá.

Once more I must assert, at whatever risk, that there were occasional passages in these barbaric chants which were very beautiful indeed.

We lingered till midnight, going out frequently to avoid being asphyxiated, and then took our departure. How these performers could endure to keep up such violent leaping and stamping for five hours longer, as they did, passes comprehension.

CHAPTER XXIII.

THE MAKH'-EL-CHEL.

This is the name by which they are known among the surrounding Indians and the Americans, but whether it originated with themselves I cannot state. Their principal, and formerly only, abode was an island on the east side of Clear Lake, a few miles above Lower Lake. In their language *hösch'-la* signifies "island", which has been corrupted and applied both to the island and the tribe; and our undiscriminating countrymen pronounce it with great impartiality Hessler, Kessler, Hesley, Kelsey, and several other ways.

The Makh'-el-chel are in some respects a remarkable race. So fine and almost Caucasian is their physiognomy, so light their color, so quick their intelligence, so exclusive and haughty are they (or once were), that many persons refuse to believe they are of the same blood with the degraded and miserable beings on the Lower Sacramento. Pioneers with a good eye for the fine points in a man, and knowing nothing of the subtle laws of philology, insist that they cannot be "Diggers", but must be a remnant of some previous, ancient race. But the indications of language cannot be disregarded. Words of such common occurrence as "water", "earth", "panther", and the personal pronouns, which they have in common with the Patwin or Wintūn, could not have been borrowed from the latter, but must have come to them by inheritance. They are undoubtedly descended from the Sacramento Valley tribes, and are a fine illustration of the ennobling effects of a mountain climate.

80

They are singular also for their exclusiveness. They are one of the very few tribes who would put a woman to death for committing adultery with or marrying an American. All blue-eyed and fair-haired children they destroyed without remorse, regarding the whites with the same disdain that

214

the Chinese do. In an early number of the *Overland Monthly*, under the title of "The King of Clear Lake", the reader will find an interesting story bearing on this feature. It relates how the chief, Salvador, hanged one of his subjects for adultery with a white man; and it has an additional interest as showing that in this tribe the chief exercised the power of life and death, which was unusual. But even among the Makhelchel the title "king" is hardly appropriate.

In their pride and haughtiness they insist on an indigenous origin for themselves, and refuse to believe that their mortal ancestors ever dwelt in any other country, though they admit that the Great Man, their divine creator, came from the west in a remote antiquity, and formed them from the soil of their beloved island. The primordial fire also came from the west, instead of the east, as in the traditions of other tribes. Further, they relate a curious legend about a glorious and resplendent beast which once existed in the west, and which no man, no living being, could destroy or injure. Its name was *pa'-teh*, from which it would seem to have been related to the panther, *pat'-ta*.

Their language is like the Kabinapek phonetically, even more harsh and difficult. It is full of hissing sounds, and at times there occurs a kind of click, apparently like that in certain African languages, produced by the tongue against the roof of the mouth. Sometimes a word is preceded both by a hissing and a click—a combination almost impossible for an American to imitate.

They construct cabins of slender willow poles set upright in the ground, with others crossing them horizontally, forming a square lattice-work. In the season of fish-drying each one of these apertures, hundreds in number, has a fish stuck in it—a singular spectacle. Wild fowl are slain by means of bullets of hard-baked clay projected from a sling, which they handle with great dexterity. They construct boats of tule, with indifferent skill. First, two or three long tule-stalks are sewed together for a keel, and hammered hard. Then others are laid alongside of them, each one overlapping the last a little in length, sewed on and beaten. When finished the bottom is twenty or thirty feet long, elliptical in shape, sharp at the ends, three or four layers of tule thick, and all hammered hard and water-tight. The sides are then built up perpendicular, but only one or two tules thick, and not ribbed. After being in the water awhile the thick bottom becomes water-logged, and if the boat is capsized it rights itself in an instant, like a loaded cork. One of these boats will last five years, and carry several men or a ton of merchandise in a heavy sea. The Makhelchel are bold watermen and skillful fishers. Yet they take most of their fish in the creeks in spring, which they frequently do by treading on them with their naked feet in the crevices of the rocks.

81   They burn the dead, and always if possible on their native island. W. C. Goldsmith described a funeral he once witnessed, where a squaw was conducted from the main-land where she had died, across the lake by night, followed by a long procession of boats in single file, carrying torchlights, and filled with mourning women, chanting and wailing as the cortege moved with noiseless paddles across the water—a mournful and impressive spectacle. The relations do no mourning, which is performed by hired mourners. But on the occasion of a funeral of some friend of Salvador, an irreverent American offered him a dollar if he would cry, whereupon the avaricious old chief moved by the seductive coin lifted up his voice and wept, though he may have done it from grief at the insult. As all good Indians are burned, so the wicked are "holed". Their neighbors on the east, the Patwin, whom they heartily despise, always bury; hence the greatest contumely these people can offer an Indian is to "hole" him.

     Once this tribe had occasion to make a treaty with the Cache Creek Indians for the privilege of fishing in a certain creek. Four captains, two for each tribe, squatted down together on some deer-skins, surrounded by a great circle of their followers. After an impressive silence of some minutes one of them lifted up his voice and chanted without ceasing for nearly three-quarters of an hour, gesturing the while toward the four quarters of heaven. Then one of the opposite party took up the refrain for an equal length of time. Altogether they were several hours crooning a wholly unmeaning farrago, simply as a solemnization of a matter already consummated. All such treaties as these they observe with religious scrupulosity—until they are strong enough to break them.

     One of their modes of medical practice deserves mention for its naive exhibition of human nature. The patient is wrapped tight in skins and blankets, deposited with his feet to the fire, a stake driven down near his head, and strings of shell-beads stretched from it to his ankles, knees, wrists, elbows, etc. These strings of money exercise the same magical effect on the valetudinary savage that a gold "twenty" does, placed in the palm of the doctor, upon the dyspeptic pale-face. The cunning Esculapian adjusts the distance of the stake, and the consequent length of the strings, according to the wealth of the invalid. If he is rich, then by the best divining and scrutation of his art the stake ought to be planted about five feet distant; if poor, only one or two. After he has powwowed sufficiently around the unfortunate person to make a sound man sick, or deaf at least, he appropriates the money.

One day in early spring seven Indians and a young squaw of this tribe set out in a small boat to cross the lake, near the upper end, and the boat was capsized three miles from land. They righted it, but as the lake was rough they could not bail it out, and while full of water it would not support more than one person. The men put the girl in and held on the edges of the boat, supporting themselves by swimming until exhausted and chilled through by the cold water, and then dropped off and sank one by one. They showed no thought of disputing the young woman's exclusive right to the boat, and she was saved by their heroic self-sacrifice.

CHAPTER XXIV.

THE PAT-WĬN'.

On the middle and lower Sacramento, west side, there is one of the largest nations of the State, yet they have no common government, and not even a name for themselves. They have a common language, with little divergence of dialects for so great an area as it embraces, and substantially common customs, but so little community of feeling that the petty sub-divisions have often been at the bitterest feud. For the sake of convenience, and as a nucleus of classification, I have taken a word which they all employ, *pat-wĭn'*, signifying "man", or sometimes "person".

Antonio, chief of the Chen'-po-sel, a very intelligent and traveled Indian, gave me the following geographical statement, which I found to be correct so far as I went. In Long, Indian, Bear, and Cortina Valleys, all along the Sacramento from Jacinto to Suisun, inclusive, on Cache and Puta Creeks, and in Napa Valley as far up as Calistoga, the same language is spoken, which any Indian of this nation can understand. Strangely, too, the Patwin language laps over the Sacramento, reaching in a very narrow belt along the east side from a point a few miles below the mouth of Stony Creek down nearly to the mouth of Feather River. In the head of Napa Valley were the Wappo, and in Pope and Coyote Valleys there was spoken a language now nearly, if not quite, extinct.

The various tribes were distributed as follows: In Napa Valley the Napa; on the bay named after them the Su-i-sun', whose celebrated chief was Solano. In Lagoon Valley were the Ma-lak'-ka; on Ulatus Creek and about Vacaville the Ol-u-lá-to; on Puta Creek at the foot-hills the Li-wai'-to. (These last three names were given to me by a Spaniard and I could find no Indians living by whom to verify them, except that the aboriginal name of Puta Creek was Li-wai'.) On Lower Puta Creek they were called by the Spaniards, on account of their gross licentiousness, Putos, and the stream Rio de los Putos. In Berryesa Valley were the To-pai'-di-sel; on upper, middle, and lower Cache Creek, respectively, the Ol'-po-sel, Chen'-po-sel, and Wí-lak-sel, which signify "upper tribe", "lower tribe", and "tribe on the plains". In Long Valley are the Lol'-sel or Lold'-la; *lol* denotes "Indian tobacco", and *sel* is a locative ending; hence the name means "Indian tobacco place", applied first to the valley, then to the people in it. 82 At Knight's Landing are the Yo-det'-a-bi; in Cortina Valley the Wai'-ko-sel (north tribe); at Colusa the Ko-rú-si (corrupted to the present form), whose most celebrated chiefs were Sai'-ok and Hu-kai'-leh. On Stony Creek the Patwin intermarried with the Wintūn and were called by the latter No-yú-ki (southern enemies).

If all the immense plains from Stony Creek to Suisun had been occupied the population would have been very great; but for several more or less obvious reasons they were not. In winter there was too much water on them, in summer none at all, and the aborigines had no means of procuring an artificial supply. Besides there was no wood on them, and the over-flowed portions in early summer breed millions of accursed gnats, which render human life a burden and a weariness. Hence they were compelled to live beside water-courses, except during certain limited periods in the winter, when they established hunting-camps out on the plains. Nor could they even dwell beside the Sacramento, save on those few low bluffs, as at Colusa, where the tule swamp does not approach the river. At a point about four miles south of Colusa there are indications in the shape of circular excavations that they once had somewhat substantial dwellings far from water; yet these may have been only permanent hunting-camps. They also had temporary camps in winter along the edge of the tule swamp for the purpose of snaring wild-fowl.

But along the streams the population was dense. General Bidwell states that, in 1849, the village of the Korusi contained at least one thousand inhabitants. In Spring Valley, on the Estes Ranch, a cellar was lately dug which revealed a layer of bones six or eight feet below the surface, lying so thick that they formed a white stratum all around the side of the cellar. At Vacaville great numbers of bones have been discovered in

various excavations.   Señor Piña, who was in the country ten years before
the gold discovery, states that on Puta Creek the Indians lived in multitudes.   They had an almost boundless extent of plains whereon to hunt
game and gather grass-seed; before the streams were muddied they swarmed
with untold myriads of salmon; and the broad tule swamps in winter were
noisy with the quacking and screaming flocks.

In addition to the modes of gathering and preparing food heretofore
described the Patwin had some different processes.   On the plains they
gathered the seed of a plant called yellow-blossom (*Ranunculus californicus*),
crushed it into flour with stones, then put it into baskets with coals of fire
and agitated it until it was cooked and burned pot-black, when they made
it into pinole.   The Korusi and probably others had an ingenious way of
capturing wild ducks.   They set decoy-ducks, carved and colored very life-
like, and when the living birds approached they rose from concealment and
scared them in such a manner that they flew into nets stretched above the
water.   The Suisun fashioned clumsy rafts of tule with which they cruised
about in pursuit of water-fowl.   When wild clover came into blossom they
frequently ate it so greedily as to become distressfully inflated with gas, (a
condition which when superinduced in his cattle by the same cause the
farmer calls "hooven").   A decoction of soaproot was administered for one
remedy, and careful squaw-mothers kept a quantity of it on hand against
any indiscretion on the part of their children.   But a more frequent treatment was to lay the sufferer on his back, grease his belly, and let a friend
tread it.   A gentler way was to knead it.   The Spaniards affirm that the
Solano plains were well covered with wild oats as early as 1838, but the
Patwin did not make very extensive use of it then.   Wild sunflower and
different kinds of grass were pulled or cut on the plains, thrashed out on
smooth ground, winnowed in the wind, the seed beaten up and made into
a kind of panada.   Along the Sacramento they gathered many blackberries
in the season.

On the plains all adult males, and children up to ten or twelve, went
perfectly naked, while the women wore only a narrow slip of deer-skin
around the waist.   In the mountains where it was somewhat cooler, the
women made for themselves short petticoats from the inner bark of the

cottonwood. In making a wigwam they excavated about two feet, banked up the earth enough to keep out the water, and threw the remainder on the roof dome-shaped. In a lodge thus covered a mere handful of sprigs would heat the air agreeably all day. In the mountains where wood was more *Fig. 21* abundant they frequently put on no roofing of earth. It has been thought by some that they used wood in the mountains in order to make a sharper roof as a precaution against the weight of snow, and in the Sierra this consideration had its weight also, but the real explanation is that they simply used the material which lay nearest to hand.

With the Lolsel a bride often remains in her father's house and her husband comes to live with her, whereupon half the purchase-money is returned to him. Thus there will be two or three families in one lodge. They are very clannish, especially the mountain tribes, and family influence is all-potent. That and wealth create the chief, with such limited power as he possesses. The chief of the Lolsel was and is Klai'-ty, but his brother at one time became more powerful than he through his family alliances, created an insurrection, involved the tribe in civil war, and expelled nearly half of it with Klaity to the head of Clear Lake. They remained there several years, but when the Americans arrived they intervened and secured a reconciliation. A man who is wealthy sometimes purchases "relatives" in order to augment his family influence; and one who has none at all does the same to secure himself protection.

This clannishness begets conspiracies, feuds, and secret assassinations. The members of a powerful Korusi family have been known to assemble in secret session, during which they appeared to determine on the death of some person who was considered dangerous, for immediately afterward that individual was shadowed and soon disappeared. The Lolsel and Chenposel are noted for the savage family vendettas which prevailed between them, some of which have been kept alive to this day.

In war the Patwin employed bows and arrows and flint-pointed spears, and often fought in open ground with much bravery. No scalps were taken from the slain, but the victors often decapitated the most beautiful maiden they had captured, and one held up the bloody head in his hand for his companions to shoot at to taunt and exasperate the vanquished. Men who had a quarrel about a woman or any other matter sometimes fought a duel with bows and arrows at long distances.

When a Korusi woman died, leaving an infant very young, the friends shook it to death in a skin or blanket. This was done even with a half-breed child. Occasionally a squaw destroyed her own babe when she was deserted by her husband and had no relations, for the sentiment that the men are bound to support the women—that is to furnish the supplies—is stronger even than among us, especially in these days of endless discussion of "woman's sphere". No American woman would be upheld in destroying her child because it had no supporter but herself, but the Indians uphold it always. In Long Valley a woman who was about to give birth to a child was so strongly threatened by its American father that she consented to make away with it; but the neighbors interfered, collected a sum of money and a quantity of supplies, and presented them to her on the condition that she should preserve its life—a condition to which she gladly assented. Afterward the child was bought of her for $10, and lived with one of its purchasers eighteen years.

Parents are very easy-going with their children, and never systematically punish them, though they sometimes strike them in momentary anger. On the Sacramento they teach them to swim when a few weeks old by holding them on their hands in the water. I have seen a father coddle and teeter his baby in an attack of crossness for an hour with the greatest patience, then carry him down to the river, laughing good-naturedly, gently dip the little brown smooth-skinned nugget in the waves clear under, and then lay him on the moist, warm sand. The treatment was no less effectual than harmless, for it stopped the perverse, persistent squalling at once.

The Patwin presents as good an illustration as any of the traditional Digger Indian physique, and it will be well to describe it somewhat minutely. There is a broadly ovoid face, in youth almost round, and in old age assuming nearly the outlines of a bow-kite. The forehead is low, but disproportionately wide, thickly covered with stiff, bristly hair on the corners, and often having a sharp point of hair growing down in the middle toward the nose; not retreating, but keeping well up toward a perpendicular with the chin, and frequently having the arch over the eye so strongly developed as to be a sharp ridge; the ciliary hairs sparse, never spanning across over the nose; beard and mustache very thin, almost totally lacking, and carefully plucked out; the head small and brachycephalic, often found to be startlingly small when the fingers are thrust into the coarse shock of hair enveloping it; but the skull phenomenally thick. So depressed is it that the diameter from temple to temple, judging by the eye, is equal to that from base to crown, if not greater. This gives the forehead its great width. Small as the cranium actually is, when a widow has worn tar in mourning, and then shaved her poll to remove it, the hair, growing out straight and stiff for two or three inches, gives her the appearance of having an enormous head. In youth the eyes are well-sized, often large and lustrous, but at a great age they became smoke-burnt and reduced to mere points, or else swollen, bleared, and disgusting. Probably there is no feature in this race so characteristic as the nose. So slightly is it developed at the root, and so broad at the nostrils that it outlines a nearly equilateral triangle upon the face. Perfectly straight like the Grecian, it is yet so depressed at the root that it seems to issue from the face on a level with the pupils of the eye. Owing to the great lateral development of the nares, their longer axes frequently incline so much as to form nearly one continuous line. In this case the outer axial line of the nose is foreshortened, so that the eye of the beholder is directed into the opening of the nostrils, a repulsive spectacle. The color varies from a brassy and a hazel almost to a jet black. In young women the breasts are full and round, but after they have borne children they hang far down, so far that a woman when traveling will suckle her babe over her shoulder. This may be partly due to the fact that they wear no dresses to assist in staying them up. Their frames are small, and the hands and feet might well be the envy of the Caucasian belle, being so delicate that in youth they seem out of all proportion to the body, and it is only when age has stripped off the gross mass of fat that they return to their normal relation of size. In walking the Indian throws more weight on the toes than an American, which is probably due in part to his stealthy, cat-like habits. There is a tendency to walk pigeon-toed, especially when barefoot, but it is by no means universal. As to the body, the most notable feature is the excessive obesity of youth, and the total, almost unaccountable collapse with advancing years. The watery and unsubstantial nature of their food doubtless has something to do with this; and it is this phenomenal shrinkage which causes them to become so hideously wrinkled and repulsive. I have seen nonagenarians who it seemed to me would scarcely weigh fifty pounds. An aged squaw of the Sacramento, with her hair close cropped, the wrinkles actually gathered in folds on the face, and smutched with blotches of tar, the face so little and weasened, and the blinking, pinched eyes, is probably the most odious-looking of human beings. On the other hand, take a Patwin girl of the mountains, at that climacteric when she is just gliding out of the uncomfortable obesity of youth, her complexion a soft, creamy hazel, her wide eyes dreamy and idle, and she presents a not unattractive type of vacuous, facile, and voluptuous beauty.

Klaity, the chief of the Lolsel, was turning white in spots. The process had been going forward slowly for several years—he was probably over eighty years old—not by any sloughing off, but by an imperceptible change from black to a soft, delicate white. The old captain appeared to be rather proud of the change than otherwise, hoping eventually to become a white man. When asked by the interpreter where he expected to go after death, he replied that he did not know, but he was going to follow the Americans wherever they went.

From the above descriptions, it will be guessed that the Patwin rank among the lowest of the race. Antonio told me that his people who could not speak English had no name or conception whatever of a Supreme Being, and never mentioned the subject, and that they never spoke of religion, a future state, or anything of the kind. But this must be taken *cum grano salis*. The Lolsel speak of a divinity whom they call Kem'-mi Sál-to (the white man of the clouds), but this is too manifestly a modern invention made to please their patron, Hanson.

Neither have they any ceremony that can be called worship. They have dances or merrymakings (*pó-noh*) in celebration of a good harvest of acorns or a plentiful catch of fish. The Patwin have a ceremony of raising the dead, and another of raising the devil, but both are employed for sordid purposes. The former was in early times used merely to keep the women in subjection, but now merely to extort from them the gains of the prostitution to which they are forced by their own husbands and brothers!

In the ceremony of raising the dead there is first a noisy powwow in the assembly-hall, and then a number of muffled forms appear, before whom the women pass in procession in the darkness, with fear and trembling and weeping, and deposit gifts in their hands. Thus their rascally and indolent masters get possession of their base earnings without using coercion.

In raising the devil there is a still greater ado. About the time of harvest it would appear that the Old Scratch had determined to get them all. They go out and kindle fires on all the hills about at night; they whoop, halloo, and circle around as if driving in game; finally they chase him in and tree him, then fling down shell-money underneath the tree to hire him to take himself off. Sometimes he makes for the assembly-house, fantastically dressed, and with harlequin nimbleness capers about it awhile, then bows his head low and shoots into the entrance backward. He is now intrenched in the stronghold of their power, and literally the devil is to pay. Presently they pluck up courage to follow him in, and for awhile there prevails the silence of the grave, when a pin could be heard to drop. Then they fling down money before him, and dart out with amazing agility After a proper length of time he steals out by some obscure trap-door, strips off his diabolical toggery, and reappears as a human being. The only object of this gratuitous and egregious foolery appears to be to assist them in maintaining their influence over the squaws.

A widow wears tar on her head and face as long as she is in mourning; sometimes two or three years, sometimes as many weeks. When she removes it, it is understood she wishes to remarry; but if an Indian makes advances to her before its removal, she considers herself insulted, and weeps.

The knowledge of medicine is a secret with the craft; to learn it a young man pays his teacher all that he possesses, and begins life without anything left. But he soon reimburses himself from his patients, charging them often from $10 to $20 shell-money for a single dose. For a felon, a Korusi shaman split a live frog and bound one portion on the affected part, which cured the same. When a person is manifestly sick unto death, the Korusi sometimes wind ropes tight around him to terminate his sufferings.

A mixed practice prevails in disposing of the dead, but most are buried. Those living near Clear Lake are somewhat influenced by the example of their neighbors in favor of cremation, but on the plains burial was and is almost universal. The Korusi thrust the head between the knees, wrap up the body with bark and skins, and bury it on the side in a round grave. Previous to interment, the body is laid outside of the assembly-hall, and each of the relatives passes around it, wailing and mourning, and calling upon the dead with many fond, endearing terms, then ascends the assembly-hall, smites his breast, faces toward the setting sun, and with streaming eyes waves the departed spirit a last, long farewell, for they believe it has gone to the Happy Western Land. But the souls of the wicked return into coyotes.

Of legends, there are not many to relate. It is a nation not very ingenious, though occasionally there is a shrewd head. An old chief in Napa Valley was once bored by a number of that description of men who appear to think the Indians know more of earthquakes and the like than our own scientists. Pointing to the mountains, he asked, "You see them mountains?" He was informed that they saw them. "Well, me not so old as them." Then pointing to the foot-hills, he asked again, "You see them little mountains?" Again they replied in the affirmative. "Well, me older than them."

The Liwaito relate that there was once a great sea all over the Sacramento Valley, and an earthquake rent open the Golden Gate and drained it off. This earthquake destroyed all men but one, who mated with a crow, and thus repeopled the world. The Korusi hold that in the beginning of all things there was nothing but the Old Turtle swimming about in a limitless ocean, but he dived down and brought up earth with which he created the world.

The Chenposel account as follows for the origin of Clear Lake: Before anything was created at all the Old Frog and the Old Badger lived alone together. The Badger wanted a drink and the Frog gnawed into a tree, sucked out and swallowed the sap and discharged it into a hollow place.

He created other little frogs to assist him and by their concentrated efforts they finally made the lake. Then he created the little flat whitefish, which voyaged down Cache Creck and turned into the great salmon, pike, sturgeon, and other fishes that swim in the Sacramento.

The Chenposel also tell this:

THE GREAT FIRE.

There was once a man who loved two women and wished to marry them. Now these two women were magpies (*atch'-atch*), but they loved him not and laughed his wooing to scorn. Then he fell into a rage and cursed these two women, and went far away to the north. There he set the world on fire, then made for himself a tule boat, wherein he escaped to the sea and was never heard of more. But the fire which he had kindled burned with a terrible burning. It ate its way south with frightful swiftness, licking up all things that are on earth—men, trees, rocks, animals, water, and even the ground itself. But the Old Coyote saw the burning and the smoke from his place far in the south, and he ran with all his might to put it out. He took two little boys in a sack and ran north like the wind. So fast did he run that he gave out just as he got to the fire and dropped the two little boys. But he took Indian sugar (honeydew) in his mouth, chewed it up, spat it on the fire, and so put it out. Now the fire was out, but the coyote was mighty thirsty, and there was no water. Then he took Indian sugar again, chewed it up, dug a hole in the bottom of the creek, covered up the sugar in it, and it turned to water, and the earth had water again. But the two little boys cried because they were lonesome, for there was nobody left on earth. Then the coyote made a sweat-house, and split out a great number of little sticks, which he laid in the sweat-house over night. In the morning they were all turned to men and women, so the two little boys had company, and the earth was re-peopled.

It seems probable that this story relates to some great volcanic eruption, perhaps to that of which an account was given by Professor Le Conte in a paper read before the California Academy of Sciences in the spring of 1874.

THE RE'-HO.

This was one name of the tribe in Pope Valley, derived from a chief. They were also called by the Patwin, Tu-lo-kai'-di-sel. They early became extinct. As far back as 1842 there were only three living. The Spaniards carried away a great portion of the tribe to the Sonoma Mission about the year 1838, and within a few weeks of their arrival hundreds perished of the small-pox. Nothing is preserved of their language, and almost nothing of their customs.

CHAPTER XXV.

THE WIN-TŪN'.

There is presented in this nation an illustration of the venerable saw, *flecti, non frangi.* Ranking among the lower types of the race; superstitious and grossly sensual, but industrious and well provisioned for savages; joyous, blithe-hearted, excessively fond of social dances and gayeties; averse to war and fighting; timid, peaceful, and gentle, they have nevertheless seen more heroic peoples melt away around them like the dew. With that toughness and tenacity of life characterizing some of the lower orders of beings, they have lived on and possess their homes while better and braver races have gone to oblivion. They early learned to let the Americans well alone, and they have dumbly and placidly beheld the latter sweep out of existence bold mountaineers who were wont of old to make their lives a terror. They have gone out widely from their ancient domain; I have seen them in Inyo County, in Yreka, and in various other parts of the State; and a small colony of them settled in Huerfano Park, Colorado. I saw a Wintūn who, as servant to a traveler, had visited New York, China, and other places; and another who had acquired a good education (for a born savage), including a remarkably correct and grammatical use of English.

Their name, Wintūn, denotes "Indians" or "people", and is one of which they are proud, and use constantly as if it were, The People, the Great People, whereas the Patwin never use theirs in a national sense. This interpretation seems to be sustained by the fact that *win-tú* means "chief".

Generally speaking, they occupy the whole of the Upper Sacramento and the Upper Trinity. In designating the various tribes, they always prefix the point of the compass *wai, nor, pu'-i, noam* (north, south, east, west), but they show much ingenuity in diversifying the terms, employing *bos, lak'-ki, su, mok, kekhl, yu'-ki* (house, tongue, nation, people, tribe, enemy), to avoid repetition. The nucleus or home of the nation is on Cottonwood Creek, and here they are Daú-pum Win-tūn (Valley Indians).   On Ruin River, a tributary of Cottonwood, are the Num'-mok (Western People). On Stony, Thomes, and Elder Creeks, in the mountains and on the edge of the plains, are the Noam'-lak-ki; on Lower Stony Creek, the Nu'-i-mok (Southern People).   The latter are intermarried with the No-yu'-ki (South-ern Enemies), living at Jacinto, who belong to the Patwin nation.   On Lower Elder and Thomes Creeks are the Pu'-i-mok (Eastern People), who also lap over on the east side of the Sacramento, and extend in a strip about a mile wide from Rock Creek up to the mouth of Pit River.   All these tribes above-mentioned were called, in general, by the Cottonwood Indians, Nor'-bos (Southern House or Branch); and the latter, in turn, called the Cottonwoods, and others above them, Wai'-lak-ki (North Tongue or Branch).   Both sections called the Indians over the Coast Range, Yu'-ki, a name which we have seen explained; and sometimes Noam'-kekhl (Western Tribe), corrupted by Americans into Noam'-kult.   The Noam'-lak-ki were forever at war with their lowland neighbors, the Pu'-i-mok, but were always obliged to confine themselves to the upper plains and mount-ains until after the whites arrived.   In 1855 they conquered at last, and followed down the streams which belonged to them, taking up their abode on their banks, as far down as the river.   The Wai'-lak-ki, who called themselves such (in distinction from the general appellation above-men-tioned), lived on both sides of the Sacramento, from the Cottonwood up to the Pit.   On McCloud's Fork are the Win'-ni-mim (from *wai, win'-ni,* "north", and *mem, mim,* "river"); and what few lived on Pit River were called the Pu'-i-mim.   On the extreme Upper Sacramento and in Squaw Valley there was originally a mixed race, the result of intermarriage between the Wintūn and the Pit River nations.   The latter are called by the Wintūn, Pu'-i-su, or Pu'-shūsh, who range down to the Big Bend of the Pit, called by the Indians Cher'-ri-paum (Sandy Place).

In the Trinity Valley is another large branch.   On the Upper Trinity, reaching up to Scott Mountain, are the Wai'-kēn-mok (People up North). From Douglas City, or thereabout, down to North Fork, lived a tribe called Ti-en'-Ti-en'.   This name is said to signify "Friends", and we can well believe it does since these peaceful Win-tūn living within reach of the incursions of the powerful and warlike Hupâ would be very likely to seek to avert peril by calling themselves friends. On Hay Fork, as far down as Hai'-en-pum (High Hill), are the Nor'-mok, or Nor'-rel-mok.

The Wintūn appear to have been originally a sort of metropolitan tribe for the whole of Northern California below Mount Shasta. An intelligent pioneer who had made himself well acquainted with their language told me he was inclined to believe, from its richness in forms and synonyms, that the Wintūn had attained a higher point of development than any of the surrounding tongues and might once have been, perhaps, a diplomatic or court language over a wide extent of territory, as the Hupâ is yet. The broad, rich and beautiful valley of the Cottonwood is a natural center for leagues upon leagues of the rolling, barren wastes that surround it, being to this day a chosen spot of reunion for the scattered and wasted tribes of the Wintūn—"a Mecca of the mind", the seat of power of The People; and we can easily believe that in the by-gone days of their glory and greatness it may have witnessed large assemblages of gay revelers, and the transaction of mighty affairs of state with savage pomp.

Physically considered the Wintūn are apt to be obese to a degree, though not more so than others living in Sacramento Valley. At an early day while the wild-clover pastures were yet good, when it was fresh and green in the spring, the nursing-women might be seen sitting on the ground covering nearly a yard square with their fat persons, "larding the lean earth", like Falstaff; gathering clover and putting it in baskets, while their little ones frolicked and tumbled on their heads in the soft sunshine, or cropped the clover on all-fours like a tender calf. They were very numerous, swarming on the face of the earth like the long-eared rabbits of the chaparral. They were a healthy race in this way; that is, a very large number of children were born, though many died young; but when a child once survived the hardships of savage rearing and arrived at years of discretion, the chances were good that it would live a tolerably long and healthy life. But there were few very old people.

It is the testimony of the pioneers that even before they were corrupted by the whites they were rather neglectful than otherwise of the sick and aged. About 1846 there was an epidemic among them which produced fever and raging thirst; and in a camp near Red Bluff several of the invalids crawled down to the river to drink and fell in, owing to their weakness, and were allowed to float away and drown.

A prominent disease among them, in aboriginal times, was various phases of lung complaint.

As a tribe they were indifferent hunters but good fishermen, and they kept their larders abundantly supplied with dried salmon. It is not too much to say that as fishermen they were industrious; they seem to take no small pleasure in waiting and watching for the approach of the fish; it is a lazy and a loafing occupation which is eminently congenial to the indolent nature of the California Indian. Their squaws were also industrious in collecting roots, nuts, berries, farinaceous seeds, etc.

Mrs. Wm. Shard, whose husband settled near Red Bluff in 1844, relates the following instance of infanticide witnessed by herself. In a camp near her husband's house a women died soon after confinement, and her young infant was buried alive in the grave with her, although Mrs. Shard begged them to give it to her and promised to rear it with the utmost care.

The Wintūn language has many words in common with the Patwïn, a third or more according to my brief vocabularies, though it would not so appear from the numerals:

	WINTŪN.	PATWĪN.
One.	ket'-tet.	e-té-ta.
Two.	pal'-lel.	pam'-pet.
Three.	pan-ó-khel.	po-nó-thle.
Four.	klâ'-wit.	i-mú-sta.
Five.	chan'-shi.	et-i-sem'-ta.
Six.	só-pan-oakh.	sēr-poat'-la.
Seven.	lo-lok'-it.	sēr-po-té-ta.
Eight.	só-klâ-wit.	pan-i-mos'-ta.
Nine.	chán-klâ-wit.	pan-i-me-té-ta.
Ten.	tí-kel-les.	pam-pa-sem'-ta.

In the Wintūn, five is literally "one-half hand" or "one side hand" (*shi*, from *sem*), that is, one hand, for by the simple word *sem* the Indian means both hands. In the Patwin, five is "one hand". The Wintūn, nine is "one side and four"; ten is "none lacking". In the Nummok dialect nine is "one lacking", that is one finger minus.

In the matter of dress a fashionable young woman sometimes makes for herself a very pretty habit, which consists simply of a broad girdle of deer-skin, the lower edge slit into long fringe with a polished pine-nut on the end of each strand, while the upper border and other portions are studded with brilliant bits of shell. An old Wintūn wife occasionally appears in the light and airy costume of a grass rope wound once or twice around. The squaws all tattoo three narrow lines, one falling from each corner of the mouth, and one between.

They are as remarkable as all Californians for their fondness for being in, and their daily lavatory use of, cold water. They are almost amphibious, or were before they were pestered with clothing. Merely to get a drink they would wade in and dip or toss the water up with their hands. They would dive many feet for clams, remain down twice as long as an American could, and rise to the surface with one or more in each hand and one in the mouth. Though I have never given special attention to the singular shell-mounds which occur in this State, I have often thought they might have been originated by an ancient race of divers like these Wintūn. I am not aware that the latter accumulate the shells in mounds, but they are seen scattered in small piles about their riparian camps. In ancient times, two rival rancherias might have striven to collect each the larger heap of shells, as to-day two hunting or fishing parties will carry their friendly contention to the verge of fool-hardiness to secure the greater amount of game or fish.

For a fishing-station the Wintūn ties together two stout poles in a cross, plants it in deep water, then lays a log out to it from the shore. Standing here, silent and motionless as a statue, with spear poised in the .ir, he sometimes looks down upon so great a multitude of black-backed salmon slowly warping to and fro in the gentle current, that he could scarcely thrust his spear down without transfixing one or more. At times,

he constructs a booth out over the water, but it is not nearly so ingenious
84 and pretty a structure as those on the Klamath. His spear is very long
and slender, often fifteen feet in length, with a joint of deer's bone at the
end about three inches long, fashioned with a socket to fit on to the main
spear-shaft, to which it is also fastened by a string tied around its middle.
The Indian aims to drive this movable joint quite through the fish, whereupon it comes loose, turns crossways, and thus holds the fish securely,
flouncing at the end of the string. The construction of this spear shows a
good knowledge of the gamy, resolute salmon; the string at the end allows
him to play and exhaust himself, while a stiff spear would be broken or
wrenched out of him. A party of six Indians on McCloud's Fork speared
over 500 in one night, which would at a moderate calculation give 500
pounds to each spearman. In view of this, although an exceptional case,
who can doubt that the ancient population of California may have been
very great?

When the fisherman is done in the morning he lays his fish head to
tail alternately, from the largest down to the smallest, runs two sharp twigs
through them, takes them on his back like a great mantle—the longest
overlapping his shoulders at both sides, the shortest dangling at his heels
perhaps—bows forward under his heavy burden, and goes off with the
point of his spear cutting strange hieroglyphics in the sand far behind him.
To his credit be it recorded he frequently also performs the work of disem-
boweling the salmon and hanging them on the bushes to dry instead of
compelling his squaw to do it. I have seen a bushel basketful of salmon
roe in a camp. This is the highest luxury the Indian mind can conceive of.

Manzanita berries are of two kinds. The kind they use are prepared
in three ways. They are gathered when very dry and floury, and then a
squaw puts a quantity into a basket, sits down on the ground before it and puts
her legs on top of the basket to steady it, then beats them with a stone
pestle. The beaten mass is put on a round mat in small quantities at a
time and the mat inclined in various directions to allow the seeds to roll off.
The flour thus obtained is cooked in a basket or a little sand-pool with hot
stones, and yields a panada which is sweet and nourishing, or a thinner porridge which is eaten with the shaggy knob of a deer's tail. In the hot

summer months they make a drink by soaking the mashed berries in cold water, and this is also imbibed with the deer's tail. It is the acme of hospitality in the host to swab this utensil in the liquid, put it into his mouth, and then hand it to his guest! An Indian would refuse to touch it unless the host did this, lest he should be poisoned.

Clover is eaten in great quantities in the season of blossoms. You will sometimes see a whole village squatted in the lush clover-meadow, snipping it off by hooking the forefinger around it and making it into little balls. After a long winter on short commons they are fain to allay the cravings of hunger by filling their stomachs with the sweet inner bark of the yellow pine. But the seasons formerly furnished them a very convenient and liberal rotation. Earliest and always was the bark of trees, then the eagerly awaited clover, then roots and wild potatoes lasting all summer, next salmon about June and July, now wild oats and grass seeds, then manzanita berries and piñon-nuts; last, acorns, finishing the harvest of the year, with game and vermin of many kinds at many seasons. Thus did the genial climate offer them an almost unbroken succession.

When the Wintūn were at peace with the mountaineers they carried on considerable traffic with them, exchanging dried salmon, clams, and shell-money for bows, arrow-heads, manzanita berries, and wild flesh or peltries. Nowadays they manufacture arrow-heads with incredible painstaking from thick, brown whisky-bottles, which are very deadly, but are principally used for fancy purposes, gambling, etc.

When a girl arrives at maturity, about the age of twelve or fourteen, her village friends celebrate the event with a dance in her honor, which may be called the puberty dance (*bath'-leschu'-na*), to which all the surrounding villages are invited. First, as a preparation for this festivity the maiden is compelled to abstain rigidly from animal food for the space of three days, and to allowance herself on acorn porridge. During this time she is banished from camp, living alone in a distant booth, and it is death to any person to touch or even to approach her. At the expiration of the three days she partakes of a sacred broth or porridge, called *khlup*, which is prepared from buckeyes in the manner following: The buckeyes are roasted underground a considerable time to extract the poison, then are boiled to a pulp in small sand-pools with hot stones. The eating of this prepares her for subsequent participation in the dance, and consecrates her to the duties of womanhood. The invited tribes now begin to arrive and the dance comes on. As each village or deputation from it arrive on the summit of a hill overlooking the scene, they form in line, two or three abreast or in single file, then dance down the hill and around the village, crooning strange, weird chants. When all the deputations are collected, which may not be for two or three days, they unite in a grand dance, passing around the village in solid marching order, chanting many choruses the while. One of these choruses used by the Nummok is as follows:

"Hen-no we-ai,
Hen-no we-ai,
Hen-no."

In conclusion of the ceremonies the chief takes the maiden by the hand and together they dance down the line, while the company sing songs improvised for the occasion. I tried to procure the Indian words of one of these songs, but could not because there is no fixed form. All the interpreter, David Baker, could do was to give me the substance of a refrain or sentiment very often heard, which I have cast into a form to indicate as nearly as possible the numerous repetitions and the rhythm or movement of these performances:

" Thou art a girl no more,
Thou art a girl no more;
The chief, the chief,
The chief, the chief,
Honors thee
In the dance, in the dance,
In the long and double line
Of the dance,
Dance, dance,
Dance, dance."

Sometimes the songs are not so chaste and innocuous as the above, but are grossly obscene. Every Indian utters such sentiments as he chooses in his song, though, strange to relate, they keep perfect time. But the women, it should be added, utter nothing impure on these occasions.

The Wintūn have a remarkable fondness for social dances and merry-makings. Whenever the harvest of field, forest, or waters is abundant, the heralds are kept running lively and the dance goes right merrily, first in one village, then in another. When a chief decides on holding one he dispatches the fleetest-footed man in his camp, who runs with all his might to the next, where a fresh man takes up the message and bears it forward. The news of a death is carried in the same manner and spreads with wonderful rapidity. When I was on the extreme upper Sacramento an Indian died on Cow Creek, fifty miles below, toward midnight, and the next morning at sunrise it was known to the Indians that I talked with. As soon as the appointed day for a dance arrives, every man, woman, and child sets out; even the decrepit are carried along; the squaws load their deep, conical baskets full of acorn panada; and they stay as long as it lasts at the usual rate of consumption, for feasting is nothing, but the dance is everything. And the number of choruses they have is wonderful—all stored away in the memory. I can give only two more, which sounded very pretty when sung in a low soft voice by an Indian girl and her sister. The first is a Nummok dance-song:

"Mi-i-hen-ne,
Mi-o-hen-ne,
Hu-ai-ker-hu-ne-he,
Hu-ai-ker-hu-ne-he,
Hu-ai-ker-hu-ne-he,
Mi-i-i."

The other is a Noam-lak-ki social song:

"Hil-li-shu-min-ah,
Hil-li-i-vi-wik-o-yeh,
Hai-ho-ho,
Hai-ho-ho,
Hai-ho-ho."

These songs are truly sweet and charming at first, but when they are repeated fifty or sixty times they become somewhat wearisome.

Among the numerous dances they observe is the pine-nut dance, celebrated when the pine-nuts (*Pinus edulis*) are fit to gather, and the clover dance in the spring, which is an occasion of much good feeling and rejoicing. Then there is the war dance, which is not much observed by this peaceful race. The Nuimok, however, have a magnificent costume for this dance, which consists of a long robe or mantle made of the feathers of different birds, arranged in rings or bands, and the head surmounted by a plume of the longest eagle feathers, the whole presenting a brilliant and gaudy appearance. In the scalp dance (*hupchu'-na*) a scalp was hoisted on top of a pole, on the head of an effigy made in the human figure. As each village deputation came to the top of the hill they formed in line, danced down hill, and around the pole, chanting and whooping, and after all the villages had assembled they danced around it together, yelling and discharging arrows at the effigy. That village was accounted victorious that lodged the most arrows in it.

Between the Nummok and the Norbos tribes there existed a traditional and immemorial friendship, and they occupied a kind of informal relation of cartel. This cartel found its chief expression in an occasional great gift dance (*dūr'-yu-pu-di*). There is a pole planted in the ground, near which stands a master of ceremonies dancing and chanting continuously while the exercises are in progress. The visitors come to the brow of the hill as usual, dance down and around the village, and then around the pole, and as the master of ceremonies announces each person's name he deposits his offering at the foot of the pole. Of course, a return dance is celebrated soon after at the other village, and always on these occasions there is displayed a great rivalry of generosity, each village striving to outdo the other, and each person his particular friend in the neighboring village. An Indian who refuses to join in the gift dance is despised as a base and contemptible niggard.

A Wintūn generally pays nothing for his wife, but simply "takes up with her", though the headman usually has a comely maiden selected for him and pays her parents money. This makes the marital relation extremely loose and easily sundered. The chief may have two or more wives, but when one of his subjects attempts to introduce into his lodge a second partner of his bosom there frequently results a tragic scene. The two women dispute for the supremacy, often in a desperate pitched battle with sharp stones, seconded by their respective friends. They maul each other's faces with savage violence, and if one is knocked down her friends assist her to regain her feet, and the brutal combat is renewed until one or the other is driven from the wigwam. The husband stands by and looks placidly on, and when all is over he accepts the situation, retaining in his lodge the woman who has conquered the territory. But if his heart follows the beaten one, he will presently abandon the victress and with the other seek a new and distant abode. It is very seldom that an Indian expels his wife. In a moment of passion he may strike her dead, or, as above, ignominiously slink away with another, but the idea of divorcing and sending away a wife does not occur to him.

A wife thus abandoned and having a young child is justified by her friends in destroying it on the ground that it has no supporter. A child orphaned by his father's desertion is called "the devil's own" (*lol'-chi-bus*, from *lol'-chet*, "the devil").

For most diseases the shaman sucks the affected part until it is black and blue. For a headache they bleed themselves with flints, or beat their noses until the blood flows profusely. Their practice in midwifery is sometimes terribly severe, though effectual. In a hard case the woman is caused to sit against the side of the wall or against a tree, and is kneaded with the hands, or laid on the floor and trodden upon! But severe as their treatment is, it is more sensible than civilized methods, so far as natural appliances are concerned. During *accouchement* the woman remains in a lodge remote from camp, and no man is allowed to see or even approach near her.

When death becomes inevitable they contemplate it without terror. There is a strange, morbid sentiment among them, which sometimes causes an aged woman to wear wound around her for months the rope wherewith she is to be wrapped when a corpse. There seems also to be in this act a piteous plea for a little span of toleration; or perhaps the poor old wretch, bitterly conscious that she has outlived her beauty and her usefulness as a slave, seeks thus to remind her relatives, impatient for release, that she will burden them now only a little longer. When dead, the body is doubled up and wrapped with grass ropes, skins, mats, and the like into a ball. A wealthy Indian will have enough strings of shell-money passed under one shoulder and over the other to make the corpse nearly round. All the possessions of the departed that can be conveniently got into the grave are cast in, nowadays including knives and forks, vinegar cruets, old whisky bottles, oyster cans, etc. In the case of an industrious squaw, several bushels of acorns will be poured over her in the grave. All is cast out of sight and out of mind, and whatever cannot be buried is burned. When an Indian of rank departs this life his wigwam is burned down. Squaws with tarry faces dance on the new rounded grave, with their arms now uplifted, now wildly wrung and waved toward the west, while their cries and ululations are mournful to hear. The name of the dead is never mentioned more, forever and ever. He has gone to the sky, he has ascended *ol'-lel hon ha'-ra*, and gone to the Happy Western Land. Standing beneath the blue, broad vault of heaven, little groups of mourners with bated breath and whispering voices will point out to one another imaginary "spirit-roads" (*klesh yem'-mel*) among the stars. With vague longings and futile questionings they seek to solve the time-old mystery of death and the grave. But the name is heard no more on earth. If some one in a group of merry talkers, assembled to while a weary hour and patter the gossip of the *campoody*, inadvertently mentions the name, another in a hoarse whisper cries out *"Ki-dach'-i-da!"* ("It is a dead person!") and straightway there falls upon all an awful silence. No words can describe the shuddering and heart-sickening terror which seizes upon them at the utterance of that fearful word.

Wicked Indians' ghosts (it would be difficult to determine exactly what is a wicked Indian) return into the grizzly bear, for that is the most evil and odious animal they can conceive of. Hence they will not partake of the flesh of a grizzly, lest they should absorb some wicked soul. The strongest cursing with which a Wintūn can curse another is, "May the grizzly bear eat you!" or, "May the grizzly bear bite your father's head off!" On the contrary, a black bear is lucky and a sacred beast. In former times the Yuki used to carry black-bear skins over the mountains and sell them to the Noamlakki at $20 or $30 apiece, to be buried in. Whenever a member of a village is so fortunate as to kill one, they celebrate the black-bear dance at which the lucky hunter is a hero. They suspend the hide and dance around it in a circle, beating it with their fists as if tanning it. Then they send it to a neighboring village that they may do likewise.

There is a word for the Almighty sometimes heard among them—*Noam-kles-to'-wa*—which, as nearly as it can be analyzed, signifies "Great

Spirit of the West". Among my vocabularies this is the only instance in California where the word for the Supreme Being denotes "spirit"; it is everywhere else "man". Thus the Trinity Wintūn say *Bo-hi'-mi Wi'-ta* (The Great Man). They have nothing that can be considered a religious ceremony, unless it is one of their fanatic dances in the assembly chamber, wherein they act in an extraordinary manner, running around naked, leaping and whooping like demons in the execrable smudge, and heat, and stench, until they are reeking with perspiration, when they clamber up the center-pole and run and plunge neck and heels into the river. Sometimes they fall in a swoon, like the plantation negroes in a revival when they are affected with "the power", and lie unconscious for two or three days. I cannot believe this is any religious frenzy, but simply the exhaustion resulting from their savage passion for the dance, combined perhaps with asphyxia brought on by the hellish stink of the sweat-house. Doubtless, also, they are subject to a contagious exaltation from the heat of the atmosphere, something like that described by Lady Montague as a sensation of the Turkish bath.

The Trinity Wintūn have a few customs different from those of the main body. For instance, the Tien-Tien take no scalps, wherein they resemble rather their neighbors, the Hupâ, with whom they intermarried. All of them, admonished by the same lesson that nature herself obeys in constructing her ancient Gothic, the yellow pine, to resist the weight of the snow, build lodges sharply conical, composed of bark and poles. They have therefore freer ventilation, and the features of their occupants are not so drawn and smoke-burnt in old age as those of the dwellers in the overgrown Dutch ovens of the lowlands. Being mountaineers, they are less sensual and adulterous than the Sacramento tribes, and are more faithful in marriage. A miner of '49 told me that the Normok of Hay Fork were anciently a splendid race, tall and well formed, and that they might almost be called a tribe of Anaks, not a few of them weighing 200 and 220 pounds.

It appears that these mountaineers added the sling to their weapons, and that their lusty arms could propel a pebble out of it further and with more deadly effect than they could project an arrow. There are miners living yet on the Fork who have had painful demonstration of this fact made on their own persons. To capture deer they construct long lines of brushwocd-fence converging to a point, or merely tie a slip of bark from tree to tree. When the deer approaches the bark and perceives thereon the smell of human touch it does not vault over, but flings back and passes along to go around it. Thus it is conducted along until it finally passes through the aperture prepared, and thrusts its head into the snare.

Among the Normok I saw a squaw who had had executed on her cheeks a couple of bird's wings, one on each cheek, done in blue, bottom-edge up, the butt of the wing at the corner of the mouth, and the tip near the ear. It was quite well wrought, both in correctness of form and in delicateness of execution; not only separate feathers, but even the filaments of the vane, being finely pricked in. Occasionally there will be seen among the Coast Range tribes a woman who has a figure of a tree tattooed on her abdomen and breast, sometimes eighteen inches or more in length, but very rudely done, the branches about as large as the trunk, and no attempt at representing twigs or leaves.

CHAPTER XXVI.

THE SHAS-TÍ-KA.

It is extremely difficult to learn from the Indians any comprehensive, national name; and in this case it was impossible. Only a mere handful of them are left, none of whom remembered their tribal designation, and *Fig. 22* only one white man had ever heard the above or any other, though this one is probably correct, being apparently the original of the name "Shasta", by which they are usually known. Sometimes they are called Sai'-wash, from their relationship to the Oregon Indians; sometimes also Wai-ri'-ka, from a corrupt pronunciation of *wai-i'-ka* (mountain), their name for Mount Shasta.

Their ancient dominion was as follows: On the Klamath from Bogus Creek down to Scott River; on the Shasta, Little Shasta, and Yreka Creek; and in Scott Valley. To this Mr. E. Steele adds the Upper Salmon and a   86 part of Rogue River in Oregon. He also states that before their organization was broken up by the whites, one chief exercised authority over all this territory, with his head-quarters in Scott Valley. As a nation they are different from the California Indians proper, being more related to the Oregon races, in that they had more solidarity, fewer infinitesimal subdivisions, (though there was always a fierce feud between the Scott and Shasta Valley sections); hence this statement as to the extended authority of the chief is probable, at least for war-times.

The Shastika are a small-boned race now, at least the men are, not averaging above five feet five inches in stature. Some of their names point to this, as Little John, Little Tom. The men are conspicuously smaller *Fig. 23* and weaker than the women, and not so numerous, which is unquestionably a result of the ferocious feuds formerly existing that destroyed the picked fighting men. Their features are not so coarse and cloddish as those of the

Modok; the faces are mostly small and compact; eyes keen and lively; noses a little better developed at the root than the Californian; color varying from a rich maple or hazel to a walnut, or still darker. As above remarked, the women are larger and stronger-featured and every way more respectable than the handful of dandies who lord it over them. In the physiognomy of the Shastika women there is a notable vigor comporting with their character; they bear age well; I have seen tough, old, weathered faces among them, long past the age of child-bearing, and yet with the cheeks etched only with fine spider-lines. With their willow skull-caps (used at pleasure as drinking-cups) fitting tight on their round heads, and walking with a brave, grenadier stride, they present quite an Amazonian appearance. They smear their faces all over daily with choke-cherry juice, which gives them a bloody, corsair aspect

But their foppish lords have dwelt so long amid the mining camps and about Yreka that they have become odiously "fast". They sport the daintiest calf-boots and have an Ethiopian passion for fancy shirt-fronts, breastpins, rings, and the like, which look strangely bizarre in a brushwood booth. Dapper little fellows, impertinent, dancing, card-playing, pony-racing, idle, thoroughly worthless—there is not another tribe in the State going out of existence so rapidly, in such good clothes, and with more elegance—the squaws excepted. Taken in all their qualities, apparent and traditional, they are the Athenians of Northern California, and the Modok the Bœotians (since the Modok war I will add, the Spartans).

They have no assembly chamber, as is the case with the California Indians; nothing but a kind of oven large enough that one person may stretch himself therein and enjoy a sweat-bath. Sometimes there is a family affair large enough for ten or twelve people, but it has not the other multiplied uses of the California sweat-house. Instead of it there is a kind of town-lodge, one for men, one for women.

Reference has already been made to the theory of Judge Rosborough, of Yreka, that there were three lines of migiation southward into California, one of which lodged and remained in Scott and Shasta Valleys. The Shastika have traditions that they came from the north and northwest, and found in these valleys a tribe (doubtless the Wintūn) who had the custom of making very large, circular sweat-houses or dance-houses, and also for general public purposes; whereas they, the Shastika, had no such custom. They say further, that these previous dwellers worshiped Mount Shasta, and always placed their villages where they could behold it. War ensued, of course, and these aborigines were expelled and driven south of Mount Shasta by the new-comers. In addition to the traditions mentioned above, there are evidences of the occurrence of this migration in the large, circular excavations found to this day in Scott and Shasta Valleys, showing the former existence of structures larger than any now constructed.

Salmon were once abundant and good in the streams owned by them, though nowadays the Scott Valley Shastika are compelled to go over the mountains to Salmon and Klamath Rivers in fishing-time. Acorns also are plenty in the western part of their domain, and roots along the streams. The great Shasta plains were anciently the most famous hunting-grounds in Northern California, abounding in elk, deer, antelope, and wild sheep, which grazed on the alfilerilla, and other grasses produced there. The possession of these made the Shastika the envy of surrounding tribes, and to retain them cost their owners many a bloody fight. They also produce great numbers of large and succulent crickets, which they consider toothsome when roasted. Choke-cherries furnish them juicy messes in autumn; cammas grows in abundance. For winter occupation they have conical bark lodges, but in summer, like most tribes in the State, they roam along the banks of the streams, and dwell in cool bush-arbors.

In the Introduction, the Shastika and the Modok were both excluded from the California Indians, and there are several reasons that may be given for this classification.

First. When the Wintūn come over on a visit, both tribes speak English together, just as is done when the Paiuti come over the Sierra. The Californians almost universally learn each other's languages or dialects, which is easy on account of their similarity in structure and their possession of words in common; but here the separating chasm is so wide that both prefer to use English.

Second. They have no assembly chamber, which is the one shibboleth of a Californian.

Third. All, or nearly all, of their shamins are women. Below Mount Shasta the women do whatever is required in midwifery, and make some little occasional use of roots and herbs, but they cannot be called the physicians of the tribe.

Fourth. The chief here exercises too great authority to suit the democratic clannish Californians. The latter sometimes rebel against their chief and chase him ignominiously out of camp, but nothing of the sort is attempted or thought of by the Shastika. An intelligent Indian told me that the chieftainship was hereditary, but E. W. Potter and J. A. Fairchild state that the position is acquired solely by prowess and common consent, in distinction from the rule of the gift-giver in California tribes. A Shastika chief has power to exact taxes of the village captains, to cede territory, to put a disobedient subject to death with his own hands if necessary, and to surrender criminals to the whites; none of which prerogatives, except the last, is exercised by a Californian chief unless he is a man of extraordinary force of character.

There is a war-chief and a peace-chief, the latter being simply the best orator in the tribe, without any very well-defined functions, and then a petty captain over every village. In a case of flagrant wrong-doing a general council is sometimes assembled by the chiefs, and the decision of the council is the law of the matter, which no individual may go behind. There is no appeal, no court of cassation, no bill of exceptions. When a married man commits adultery he is frequently condemned to be tied down naked to the ground for a certain number of nights near a stream of water, where it is always colder than it is on the plain. If his relations pity him sufficiently, public sentiment sometimes allows them to build a fire near him; otherwise he must lie and shiver through the frosty nights. The Indian theory seems to be that his blood and his passions require cooling. If a squaw is punished at all she is beaten by her husband.

For murder a tender of blood-money is made, from one up to five, or even ten horses, but almost always rejected. The Shastika are less easily placated with money than the Karok, and demand blood for blood.

A treaty is not accounted to be fully ratified and binding unless the high contracting powers exchange clothes (these Indians anciently wore warm clothing of skins). Sometimes they also swap names, which renders the treaty very sacred. The following amusing circumstance is related of the treaty made in 1852 by Col. Redick McKee with Tolo, for the possession of the upper part of Scott Valley. The colonel was vestured in a scarlet waistcoat and other raiment calculated to produce a profound impression on the aboriginal mind, while Tolo's skin shirts were frayed and otherwise very objectionable to a civilized man. The old savage considered it absolutely necessary to the solemnization of the treaty that he should get himself inside of that scarlet vest. But McKee's views did not coincide with his, and after much persuasion and the promise of a herd of beef-cattle as a 87 *douceur*, he secured Tolo's assent to the treaty merely on condition that they should exchange names. They *must* exchange something, else the treaty would be, and remain, null and void; so the old natural called himself McKee, and gave the American his name. He was quite proud of the change for a long time, and always strenuously insisted on being called McKee. But month after month passed away, and there came no beef-cattle. As he began to get hungry, and still no hoof ever arrived, the name did not seem to him so ornamental. At last the unwelcome conviction dawned upon him that he had been swindled. One morning he came into the American camp, and when addressed by his Christian appellation he repudiated it with indignation, and declared that he had no name, that it was "lost". Ever afterward, to the day of his death, he refused to be called anything, declaring that his name was "lost".

In 1874, Hon. J. K. Luttrell asserted in Congress that fifteen annual appropriations had been made for this tribe and that they never received a dollar of them all, the Indian agents having appropriated the money to themselves. Thus it was Tolo got nothing for his valley but a name.

A wife is purchased of her father for shell money or horses, ten or twelve cayuse ponies being paid for a maid of great attractions. The pioneers testify with much unanimity that the Shastika women were formerly more virtuous than those on the Sacramento; but now, like so many others living near mining camps, they are compelled by their indolent lords to go out on errands of prostitution, and then compelled again to give up the rewards of their infamy. They are to be pitied more than the California women, for they always had to slave for their masters more than these, and they are now driven correspondingly more into lives of prostitution.

One day a band of Indians were aimlessly strolling about Yreka, when some outrage was perpetrated upon them and they started to leave. They had hardly gained the suburbs, when a squaw came running after them furious with anger; caught up her calico dress and rent it from top to bottom, as if to show at once her impatience at being a woman, and her loathing of the hated race which it represented; seized a rifle off the shoulder of an Indian; leaped upon a little hillock by the roadside, and in words of the fiercest passion called upon them, if they were not recreants and dastards, to follow her and avenge the insult with blood. She started back, but the Indians had tasted rather oftener than she the quality of American cold lead, so they restrained her and took away the rifle and persuaded her to go home peaceably.

Often of old the women went out with their lords to the battle. Alvy Boles relates this story: In 1854, when Captain Judah was campaigning against the Shastika on the Klamath, north of Yreka, women were frequently seen among the Indians fighting, and sometimes found among the dead. One day the savages came suddenly upon him, advancing rapidly over the brow of a hill, and filling the air with a perfect shower of arrows. But not a male barbarian was in sight! Before them, in serried line of battle, their women were moving to the charge, while the warriors slunk along behind them, discharging their arrows between the women. For a moment the Americans were taken aback. Their traditional gallantry, not a whit diminished by residence on the frontier, forbade their firing on the tender sex. But what could be done? They could not shoot bullets around a corner, or over the women's heads at a right angle. Then the order rang out loud and clear, "Break down the breastworks!" It was done. In his report Captain Judah mentioned that "a few squaws were killed by accident."

I do not give entire credence to this story. It is the custom of the Modok, and perhaps also of this tribe, to go into battle in couples, one warrior crouching along behind another; and this circumstance may have originated the above anecdote.

Not only do the women go to war if they will, perform most of the labor, and practice medicine, but they own property in certain instances. A widow retains all the baskets and trinkets made by herself, and if she subsequently acquires a pony or two it is against the traditions of the tribe that they should be wrested from her. But money may be taken from her by any male relative, and if he has not the manliness to do it openly he may steal it, and it is accounted no crime to him.

One reason why the Shastika have hastened so rapidly toward extinction is the murderous ferocity with which feuds have always been prosecuted between the Scott and Shasta Valley sections. An assassination never rested long in either valley; it was bandied to and fro like a shuttlecock. As many as fifteen Indians have been known to be slaughtered in a year as the result of a single family vendetta.

Sweating and cold plunge-baths are less employed as remedial agencies than among the California tribes. This is a natural consequence of their colder climate and their more cumbrous dress. There is a class of priests or rain-makers, who have an occult language not understood by the common Indians.

One thing is especially noticeable of the Shastika, as it is more or less throughout California, and that is their strong yearning to live, die, and be buried in the home of their fathers. If an Indian is overtaken by sudden death away from his native valley, and must needs close his eyes far from home and kindred, the prayer which he breathes with his dying breath to his comrades is a passionate adjuration to them not to let his body molder and his spirit wander houseless, friendless, and alone in a strange country. He conjures them by all that is good and pleasant in this life, by all the mournful tenderness which is due to the awed and shuddering soul that is going down to the grave, by all the solemn obsequies that are owed to the unreturning dead, and as they themselves hope for like consolations when growing faint, and weak, and dim-eyed in the shadows of death, and for like common humanity at the hands of their tribe when all is ended, not to suffer alien hands to bring indignity upon his helpless corpse, and alien earth to press upon his stilled and silent lips. This request is religiously observed. As they anciently had no efficient means of transportation, so the scarred and arrow-pierced body of the warrior fallen on the battle-field within the enemy's country, as well as that of the captive maid who had yielded up her life beneath some white man's roof beyond the mountains, was first reduced to ashes, which were carefully gathered up and borne home to rest in the ancient patrimony of the Shastika. But when one dies at home he is buried, generally not in a grave, but upon a hill-top, or on some bold promontory overlooking the village, where the body is covered with a cairn of stones. This seems to be dictated by the idea so prevalent in California that if the body is buried in the earth the soul cannot escape from it.

This tribe have no clover, pine-nut, or acorn dances, and the like merry-makings. There is a "doctor dance" held nearly every night, but what it is I could not clearly discover; probably a combination of dancing, singing, and jugglery. The puberty dance is observed, and the maiden is compelled to fast quite rigorously, being obliged to abstain from animal food ten or twelve days.

Their language is a difficult one, many of the words being polysyllabic and harsh. A great many of the verbs assume a different radical in forming the oblique tenses, and in the imperative. The pronoun is agglutinated to the noun, and one substantive to another to form the genitive case. Agglutination prevails extensively, complicating the already forbidding language. The numerals in Scott Valley are as below:

One.	chá-mo.	Six.	cho-wé-ta.
Two.	hú-ka.	Seven.	ho-kó-da.
Three.	hats'-ki.	Eight.	hats-ki-wé-da.
Four.	id-i-hoi'-a.	Nine.	cham-i-dakh'-i-wa.
Five.	etch'-a.	Ten.	etch-é-weh.

They speak of a Great Man (*Yú-ma-chuh*), but his attributes are of a negative sort, as usual, for the world was created by the Old Mole (*id'-i-dok*), a huge animal that heaved creation into existence by burrowing underneath somewhere. A long time ago there was a fire-stone in the distant east, white and glistening like the purest crystal, and the coyote journeyed east, brought this stone, and gave it to the Indians; this was the origin of fire. Originally, the sun had nine brothers, all like to himself, flaming hot with fire, so that the world was like to perish; but the coyote slew nine of the brothers, and so saved mankind from burning up. The moon also had nine brothers, all like unto himself, made of ice, so that in the night people went near to freeze to death. But the coyote went away out on the eastern edge of the world with his knife of flint-stone, heated stones to keep his hands warm, then laid hold of the nine moons one after another and slew them likewise, and thus men were saved from death by freezing.

When it rains there is some Indian sick in heaven, weeping. Long, long ago there was a good young Indian on earth, and when he died all the Indians wept so much that a flood came on the earth, and rose up to heaven and drowned all people, except one couple.

Many hundreds of years ago, according to the old Indians, there existed on earth a horse and a mare which were extremely small. The Indians called them by a name (*sá-to-wats*), which they at once applied to the first horses brought by the Spaniards. They perished long before 90 white men ever saw California. It is possible that these liliputian ponies of the Indian fable refer to an extinct species of horse, of which the remains have been discovered by Mr. Condon, in Oregon.

CHAPTER XXVII.

THE MO'-DOK.

Some persons derive this name from Mo'-dok-us, the name o a former chief of the tribe, under whose leadership they seceded from the Klamath Lake Indians and became an independent tribe. Others assert that it was originated by the Shastika, being at first pronounced Mo'-a-dok, and that it denoted "aliens", applying in its earlier usage to all the enemies of the Shastika, and subsequently narrowed down to this one tribe. The first derivation is the more probable, for there are other instances in California where a seceding fragment of a tribe gradually came to be called by the name of the chief who led the movement.

Their proper habitat was on the southern shore of Lower Klamath Lake, Hot Creek, Clear Lake, and Lost River. They ranged as far west in summer as Butte Creek to dig cammas, and at long intervals made an incursion into the unoccupied and disputed territory around Goose Lake. The great plains south, east, and west of this lake were thickly inhabited of old, as is demonstrated by the number of stone mortars, fashioned with a sharp point, to be inserted into the ground, which have been found on Davis Creek and elsewhere; but within the historical period they have been deserted. The Indians relate that, long ago, the Modok, Pai-ú-ti, and Pit River tribes contended for their possession in many bloody battles, but none of them ever gained a permanent advantage, and at last they abandoned the ferocious and wasting struggle from sheer exhaustion. Always afterward, even when the all-equalizing Americans had arrived, none of them ever ventured into this Golgotha, except now and then a band of warriors on a brief hunting or fishing excursion, armed to the teeth, and slipping through with haste and with stealth.

They present a finer physique than the lowland tribes of the Sacra-

mento, taller and less pudgy, partly, no doubt, because they engaged in
the chase more than the latter.　There is more rugged and stolid strength
of feature than in the Shastika now living; cheek-bones prominent; lips
generally thick and sensual; noses straight as the Grecian, but depressed
at the root and thick-walled; a dullish, heavy cast of feature; eyes frequently yellow where they should be white.　They are true Indians in their
stern immobility of countenance.

What is singular, men as well as women paint their faces excessively
and every day with various pigments made of rotten wood, ocher, clay,　91
&c., so that they present a grotesque appearance.

On the whole, they are rather a cloddish, indolent, ordinarily good-
natured race, but treacherous at bottom, sullen when angered, notorious
for keeping Punic faith.　But their bravery nobody can impeach or deny;
their heroic and long defense of their stronghold against the appliances of
modern civilized warfare, including that arm so awful to savages—the
artillery—was almost the only feature that lent respectability to their
wretched tragedy of the Lava Beds.　As in the case of the Shastika, their
women often participate in the battle.　It is said that in one of the forlorn,
fool-hardy assaults on the Lava Beds in the spring of 1873, a soldier was
killed by a Modok woman.

Like several of their neighbor tribes, they generally fight in couples,
one going in advance to draw the enemy's fire, while his comrade creeps
along behind him.　When the one in front succeeds by stratagem and false
appearances in inducing the enemy to unload his bow or his gun, the latter
is apt to step out from concealment or from the smoke to reconnoiter for the
effect of his shot, and then it is that the seconder, having retained his fire,
has him at deadly disadvantage.

The story of the wars waged between the Oregonians and the Modok,
extending at intervals for a quarter of a century, is frightful to contemplate,
but it is not the province of this work to enter into its details.　There are
no more black and infamous massacres recorded in history than those of the
immigrants in 1852 and 1864, and that of General Canby and Commissioner Thomas in 1873.　But it is well not to forget that the butchery per-　92
petrated by Ben. Wright, even as related by a friendly countryman, was

committed under circumstances every whit as damning and treacherous as either of the above; and that the war of 1864, according to the old chief Skon'-chin, (an Indian universally believed and respected by the whites to this day), was begun by the whites simply in retaliation for the loss of some horses. The victims of Modok treachery lie in scores, ay, in hundreds, along the old emigrant-trail which leads up along the east side of Tule Lake, past Big Bloody Point and Little Bloody Point—terribly suggestive names! But, on the other hand, I have more than once when sitting at the fireside in winter evenings, listened to old Oregonians telling with laughter how when out hunting deer they had shot down a "buck" or a squaw at sight, and merely for amusement, although the tribe to which they belonged were profoundly at peace with the Americans! After that, let us say no more.

The Modok were always churlishly exclusive, having no cartel or reciprocity with other tribes like the joyous and blithe-hearted Wintūn, inviting none to their dances, and receiving no invitations in return. In fact they have hardly any merry-makings, chiefly the gloomy and truculent orgies of war, of the scalp, and of death. They were like Ishmael of old; their hand was against every man, and every man's hand was against them. They attained in early years to a great infamy as slave-dealers, their principal victims being the timid, simple, joyous races of California, especially the Pit River tribes. They and the Muk'-a-luk (Klamath Lake Indians) are said to have got their first stocks of cayuse ponies in exchange for slaves, which they sold to the Indians on the Columbia River, about The Dalles.

They have a toughness of vitality which corresponds to their character. About 1847 the small-pox destroyed 150 of their number; they were forever at war with the Shastika and other tribes until the whites intervened; and they fought two terribly decimating wars with the Americans; and yet in 1872 they were slowly increasing again. In 1851 they were less numerous than the Shastika; but just before the last great outbreak they numbered about 250 souls, while the Shastika had only 30 or 40. In 1864 brave old Skonchin said, when he signed the treaty, "Once my people were like the sand along yon shore. Now I call to them, and only the wind answers. Four hundred strong young men went out with me to war with the whites; only 80 are left. We will be good if the white man will let us, and be friends forever." And individually he kept his word.

For a foundation to his dwelling the Modok excavates a circular space from 2 to 4 feet deep, then erects over it a rounded structure of poles and puncheons, strongly braced up with timbers, sometimes hewn and squared. 94 The whole is warmly covered with earth, and an aperture left atop, reached by a center pole. Before the coming of the whites secured them against the constant assaults and incursions of their enemies, their dwellings were slighter, consisting generally of a frame of willow poles, with tule matting overspread. It was not worth their while to build very substantial structures, lest in the next marauding expedition they should lose all their labor.

On the great, arid, volcanic, and sage-bush plains which sweep over the northeast corner of California, and which make it geologically a part of Nevada, it was an object of prime importance to the aborigines to get a supply of water. Hence the lodges of the Modok always stand beside some lake or some sluggish desert stream, and they were notably fond of the pellucid, fresh, and wholesome waters of Lost River—that so singular phenomenon in this land of acrid sage-bush and lye-burnt soil.

Both sexes always dressed themselves warmly in skins and furs. For gala robes they took large skins and inlaid them with brilliant-colored duck-scalps, sewed on in various patterns, forming very beautiful if rather evil-smelling, raiment.

They formerly had "dug-outs", generally made from the fir, quite rude and unshapely affairs compared with those found on the Lower Klamath, but substantial, and sometimes capable of carrying a burden of 1,800 pounds. Across the bow of one of these canoes a fish-seine was stretched, bellying back as the craft was propelled through the water, until the catch was sufficiently large, when it was lifted up and emptied.

In these canoes they also gathered the *wo'-kus*. This is an aquatic plant with a floating leaf very much like that of the pond-lily, in the center of which is a pod resembling a poppy-head, full of rich farinaceous 95 seeds. These are pulled in great quantities, and the seed thrashed out on shore, forming an excellent material for bread or panada. Americans some-

times gather and parch them, then eat them in a bowl of milk with a spoon— a dish which is very relishable. It forms a large source of winter provisions for this tribe.

Another thing which is of much importance in their stores is the *kais*, or *kĕs*, a root about an inch long and as large as one's little finger, of a bitter-sweetish and agreeable taste, something like ginseng. I presume it is a variety of cammas. Early in June they quit their warm winter-lodges, and scatter about in small parties or families, camping in brush-wood booths, for the purpose of gathering this root. They find it in moist, rich places near the edge of swamps. With a small stick, fire-hardened at the end, a squaw will root out a half bushel or more in a day. It is eaten raw—the men and children are munching it all day—or dried and sacked up for winter.

They were formerly accustomed to cache large quantities of *wokus* and cammas in the hills for safe-keeping during the winter. Forty years ago or more, as they relate, there fell an unprecedented snow, 7 feet deep on the level plain, so that for many days and weeks together they were unable to reach the caches, and there came upon them a grievous famine. They ate up all their rawhides, thongs, and moccasins, and would all have perished if it had not happened that a herd of antelope, struggling through the snow down to Rhett Lake, got upon the ice and broke in, when they were captured, and their flesh saved one village alive to tell the tale.

In Lost River they find a remarkable supply and variety of fish. There are black, silver-sided, and speckled trout, of which first two species individuals are said to be caught weighing twenty-five pounds; buffalo-fish, from five to twelve pounds; and very large, fine suckers, such only in name and appearance, for they are no bonier than ordinary fishes. In spawning-time the fish run up from Clear Lake in extraordinary numbers, so that the Indians only have to place a slight obstruction in the stream to catch them by thousands. Herein lies one good reason for the passionate attachment which the Modok felt for Lost River. But the salmon, king of the finny tribes, they had not, for that royal fish ascends the Klamath only to the first rapids below Lower Klamath Lake. Above them there is no deposit of gravel suitable for it to spawn in. They do not smoke-dry for winter consumption any considerable amount of fish, the principal kind used for this purpose being the small white lake-fish.

The Modok women make a very pretty baby-basket of fine willow-work, cylinder-shaped, with one-half of it cut away, except a few inches at the ends. It is intended to be set up against the wall, or carried on the back; hence the infant is lashed perpendicular in it, with his feet standing *Fig. 24* in one end, and the other covering his head like a small parasol. In one I saw this canopy was supported by small standards, spirally wrapped with strips of gay-colored calico, with looped and scalloped hangings between. Let a mother black her whole face below the eyes, including the nose, shining black; thrust a goose-quill three inches long through the septum of the nose; don her close-fitting skull-cap, and start to town with her baby-basket lashed to her back, and she feels the pride of maternity strong within her. The little fellow is wrapped all around like a mummy, with nothing visible but his head, and sometimes even that is bandaged back tight, so that he may sleep standing.

From the manner in which the tender skull is thus bandaged back, it occasionally results that it grows backward and upward at an angle of about forty-five degrees. Among the Klamath Lake Indians I have seen a man,   96 fifty years old perhaps, whose forehead was all gone, the head sloping right back on a line with the nose, yet his faculties seemed nowise impaired.

The conspicuous painstaking which the Modok squaw expends on her baby-basket is an index of her maternal love. And, indeed, the Modok are strongly attached to their offspring—a fact abundantly attested by many sad and mournful spectacles witnessed in the closing scenes of the war of 1873. On the other hand, a California squaw often carelessly sets her baby in a deep, conical basket, the same in which she carries her household effects, leaving him loose and liable to fall out. If she makes a baby-basket, it is totally devoid of ornament; and one tribe, the Mí-wok, contemptuously call it "the dog's nest". It is among Indians like these that we hear of infanticide.

One ancient aboriginal custom observed by the Modok was rather pretty and poetical—that of intoning an orison in the morning before they rose. At early daylight, before any one had come out of his wickiup, they all sat up in their couches and chanted together, in the loud, harsh voice in which they are accustomed to sing, some unmeaning chorus. This was related to me by N. B. Ball, a soldier of Capt. Jesse Walker's company in 1854, who listened to it one morning with a thrill of strange and superstitious awe as he lay close on his face on the brow of an overlooking hill waiting for the daylight to reveal the nick in the sights of his rifle, preparatory to a charge on the village.

The Modok have a hereditary chieftainship, and are less democratic and independent than the California Indians, though there reveals itself occasionally a surly and intractable character. A casual observer cannot perceive any great difference between the nobility and the riffraff.

It is often asserted that the Indians improve in moral character after they become acquainted with the Americans. B. F. Dowell, for instance, states that twenty years ago the Modok were all roving, hostile, barbarous savages, while now more than half are loyal, very kind, and many of them speak good English. Their "loyalty", as with a great majority of Indians, is nothing else but fear; they are neither more nor less kind than they were as savages, if anything less generous to one another; and my observation, which is not limited, gives painful proof of the fact that the younger and English-speaking generation are less truthful, less honest, and less virtuous than the old simon-pure savages. And this is the testimony of everybody whose knowledge of the race has been gained by contact.

In a lecture delivered in San Francisco, Hon. A. B. Meacham made the following statement concerning Modok marriages:

"Within the confines of this State nearly all the young women are the wives of old men, because the old men have the money to pay for them. Remonstrance on the part of a young woman is out of the question, because she is threatened constantly with the spirit of her father. Young men all over the country have old wives. A poor young man has not fifty horses, and he must take an old woman. He accepts the situation and marries an old woman; but, becoming rich, he takes to himself a young woman. Polygamy is allowed, and the Indians give many reasons why it should be allowed. They say that in the spirit-land women are very small; that they are scarcely known at all; that one man is so much greater than a woman that he can take care of several female spirits; that in this life he requires one to keep house, another to do hunting, another to dig roots. Then the women themselves are opposed to any change, and are opposed to the idea of marrying unless they are bought."

Of the California tribes, this assertion that the old men all have young wives, and the young men old wives, is untrue. It may be true of the tribes in Oregon, but of the Modok I doubt if it is even partially true. Horses were not so numerous among the Modok that it required fifty to purchase a woman; farther up in Oregon they may have been.

Of their religion, he states that a new one had been introduced within a few years past.

The substance of the new religion is, that wherever a man is born there he ought to die. If he changes his habitation, his body will not go back to where it originated, and both body and soul will wander around.

The central idea of this "religion" is by no means new; it has always been one of the most passionate desires among the Modok, as well as their neighbors, the Shastika, to live, die, and be buried where they were born. Some of their usages in regard to the dead and their burial may be gathered from an incident that occurred while the captives of 1873 were on their way from the Lava Beds to Fort Klamath, as it was described by an eyewitness. Curly-headed Jack, a prominent warrior, committed suicide with a pistol. His mother and female friends gathered about him and set up a dismal wailing; they besmeared themselves with his blood, and endeavored by other Indian customs to restore his life. The mother took his head in her lap, and scooped the blood from his ear: another old woman placed her hand upon his heart, and a third blew in his face. The sight of the group, these poor old women whose grief was unfeigned, and the dying man, was terrible in its sadness. Outside the tent stood Bogus Charley, Huka Jim, Shacknasty Jim, Steamboat Frank, Curly-headed Doctor, and others who had been the dying man's companions from childhood, all affected to tears.

When he was lowered into the grave, before the soldiers began to cover the body, Huka Jim was seen running eagerly about the camp, trying to exchange a two-dollar bill of currency for silver. He owed the dead warrior that amount of money, and he had grave doubts whether the currency would be of any use to him in the other world—sad commentary on our national currency!—and desired to have the coin instead. Procuring it from one of the soldiers, he cast it in, and seemed greatly relieved. All the dead man's other effects, consisting of clothing, trinkets, and a half dollar, were interred with him, together with some root-flour as victual for the journey to the spirit-land.

It does not come within the purpose of this report to narrate the Indian wars of California; only those incidents are selected which throw some light on aboriginal customs, habits, and ideas. It was asserted by some writers, and by the Hon. A. B. Meacham in his lecture, that the Modok were led into their last terrible outbreak by a belief that their dead were about to be restored to life and come to their assistance, and at the same time the Americans would be swallowed up in the earth. This curious expectation prevailed not only among them, but among the Yurok, Karok, Shastika, and in fact all over Northern California, as far down as Lower Russian River and American River, and perhaps farther. The Shastika said a crow had imparted to them the information that all their dead were hovering about the top of Mount Shasta, waiting a favorable moment to descend. The Karok prophets announced that the re-embodied dead of their tribe were already on the march from the east, myriads of pigmies, coming to overthrow the Americans.

But I do not believe this prophecy had any active influence in driving the Modok into the rebellion. To their credit, a great majority of the Indians refused credence to their soothsayers in this thing. To be sure, there was infinite talk about it, as there always is among savages about any matter of superstition, but they took good care not to attempt any rash thing against the whites in the expectation that they would be sustained in it by the timely arrival of the revivified dead. The Modok simply drifted into the war through the force of circumstances—a war which had been prepared and made inevitable by events long antedating its outbreak.

There is no doubt, however, that their sorcerers exercised a baneful influence over them both before the war and after it was begun. For instance, when an attack was ordered to be made on the Lava Beds by 400

men, January 17, 1873, and a dense fog overhung the face of the earth
when the time arrived, the Modok believed firmly that their sorcerers had
brought it; that the spirits were favorable to them, and they were encour-
aged and kept hearty in the fight.

Of the consummate skill and daring with which they fought, when once
in the war, both soldiers and civilians bear abundant testimony. A careful
and conscientious correspondent, Mr. Bunker, who visited the famous Lava
Beds soon after they were captured, writes:

"The military engineers with whom I have talked upon the subject are
emphatic in their opinion that no man versed in military tactics could have
selected a fortress in the Lava Beds better adapted to the ends of defense   98
than this same stronghold. Where nature has not fulfilled the requirements
of the situation, the Indians have piled up the lava, and so remedied every
apparent defect. It is a fact that no soldier could have climbed within
fifty yards of the stronghold while the Indians were in possession without
looking into the muzzles of guns; and nothing but a gun would be seen.
The ingenuity of the Modok has surpassed all understanding. Their engi-
neering skill draws warm commendation from the best talent in the camps.
Every picket-post is thoroughly protected from assaults by riflemen, and
arranged to cover a retreat. The avenues are even more complicated than
the labyrinthian streets of Boston. Even the Modok could not trust to
memory in this fortification, and as a matter of precaution had localities
marked by bits of wood of different sizes. They could not familiarize themselves with a pile of rocks two hundred yards square!"

They merited a better leader than they had. Captain Jack was not a
hero, and does not deserve to be mentioned with Tecumseh and Pontiac
and Red Jacket. A full-blooded Modok (all idle tales to the contrary notwithstanding), born at the mouth of Lost River, he entered the last great
struggle of his tribe about thirty-five or forty years of age, in the full maturity of his powers.

A man about five feet eight inches high, compactly and strongly built;
a large, square head and massive cheek-bones; hair parted in the middle, and
reaching down to the shoulders, where it was cut off even all around; long
eyelashes, but no beard; dark, piercing, sinister eyes; the thin lips of an

insincere and cowardly man—such was his physique. He is described as having an undecided and irresolute air. At the last, when adversity began to overcloud his fortunes, he signally failed to command the obedience of his followers, and even in the height of his prosperity he rather followed than led the bolder spirits.

He had an evil record from the beginning, a record showing his native baseness. He ascended to the supremacy only by rebelling against his lawful chief, old Skonchin, and by pandering to the worst elements of his tribe on the reservation.

Soon after he left the reserve he gambled with Captain George, a Mukaluk chief, until he lost twenty-one ponies, then refused to give them up; and, finally, because his following was the larger of the two, and Captain George's was unarmed, he began to bluster, threatened George's life, and at last coolly drove the ponies away.

There is no doubt that he originally opposed the scheme of massacreing the commissioners, but he was overborne by the fiery young warriors of his band, and he weakly allowed himself to be led into the plot and become the chief actor in that perfidious butchery; and then, in his dying speech, he proposed that a relation should be executed in his stead; and when the proposition was rejected cravenly followed after General Wheaton to know if there was not yet a prospect that it would be accepted! Two passages in his speech reveal the man he was: "It is terrible to think I have to die. When I look at my heart I would like to live till I died a natural death." And this: "I always had a good heart toward the white people. Scarface Charley is a relative of mine; he is worse than I am, and I propose to make an exchange and turn him over to be executed in my place."

John Skonchin, brother to old Skonchin, desperado that he was, should go down to posterity as the real chieftain and moral hero of the Modok war. In his last speech he pleaded not for himself. He pleaded for his children, that they might be tenderly cared for and given into the charge of his brother. He expressed himself willing to die for the misdeeds of his young men. He was much moved by the words of the "Sunday Doctor", and said: "Perhaps the Great Spirit will say, 'Skonchin, my law, which was in force among the whites, has killed you.' * * * You have tried the law on me and know whether or not I am a good man. * * * I will try to believe that the President did according to the will of the Great Spirit in condemning me to die. * * * My heart tells me I should not die. You are doing a great wrong to take my life." Thus his natural love of life contended with his philosophic calm, sometimes getting the better of it; but he went to his death without any weakness.

Boston Charley displayed the nerve of a devil; he alone manifested that Indian stoicism of which poets and romancers tell us. And, fiend-incarnate though he was, let us do him the justice to say that he was the only Indian of the four who did not die with a falsehood in his mouth. A mere boy in years, but tall, athletic, and of a splendid physique; a face perfectly smooth ; a head small and round; little, fierce eyes, set deep in it and gleaming with a devilish expression—there never went to the scaffold a human being with a more cool and reckless unconcern, not feigned but real, than Boston Charley. In his speech he said: "Although I am a boy, I feel that I am a man. When I look at the others I feel that they are women. When I die and go to the other world I don't want them to go with me. I am not afraid to die. I am the only man in this room to-day."

Speculating on the purpose the Modok had in murdering the commissioners, an ingenious writer advanced the theory that, judging the Americans by themselves, they believed that the death of our leaders would strike terror into the hearts of their followers, and cause them to disperse in wild dismay. Probably the motive for this to us almost unaccountable act must be sought from two sources. First, they doubtless considered it, educated in savage ideas as they were, as only a righteous retaliation for the massacre perpetrated by Ben. Wright many years before, in which Captain Jack's father and the fathers or near relatives of many others perished. Second, there is a sentiment dwelling in the breast of every brave Indian that if he can only destroy the greatest, or at least a very great man out of the enemy's camp, he will die in battle content. In the case of Boston Charley, and perhaps of one or two others, it was undoubtedly pure, unreflecting, unreckoning malice and hatred. It is not at all probable that any of them expected by the deed to put all our hundreds of soldiers to incontinent flight. They had lived among the Americans too long and knew them too well for that. They knew us better than we knew them, so far as fighting qualities were concerned.

There was a burst of indignation on two continents when this bloody, treacherous thing was done; that the Modok had disregarded what all men, savage as well as civilized, have universally agreed to recognize as sacred, to wit, a flag of truce and the person of an ambassador. But when Ben. Wright did the same thing, the very same thing, in all essential particulars, where is the use of talking any more about the "code of warfare"? In fact, the plain and painful truth is that, since the day of Miles Standish, the "code of warfare" has been broken very many times on both sides, for the simple reason that when civilized men are arrayed against uncivilized men in a struggle for life, it ceases to be civilized warfare, or any other kind, except a war of extermination. Disguise it as we may, that is what the war has practically been on both sides from the settlement of the continent to this hour.

Notwithstanding their acts of barbarous ferocity there is something melancholy in the whole history of the Modok. Seceders in the first place from the Mukaluk, they drew down upon their heads the bitterest hatred of the parent stock, who became their irreconcilable enemies. Being an offshoot without hereditary prescriptive rights and a patrimony, they were regarded by all the surrounding nations as interlopers, and warred upon accordingly, as was the case with the Lassik in California. Thus they became outcasts and outlaws to the whole Indian world, and who shall doubt that in this fact lay the secret of much of the rancorous cruelty and implacable revenge with which they afterward always prosecuted their wars?

Finally they came upon the great enemy who leveled all tribes before him, and in two bitter, bloody wars, in which they saw their young men melt away before some strange and dreadful weapon, they were utterly broken down to the earth, and consented by treaty to go upon a reservation. But unhappily for them this reservation was situated on the ancestral soil of their old enemies, the Mukaluk, and their troubles began afresh. They had been able before to take care of themselves, and had established traditional rights on Lost River; but now a second time they were taunted as interlopers, and they were helpless to defend themselves. In every way that savages are so ingenious to invent their lives were made bitter to them. Their women were beaten and insulted whenever it could be done with impunity; their springs and streams were muddied or poisoned; their ponies were shot; their children were whipped; themselves were stoned and scoffed and flouted.

Their brave and honest old chief Skonchin had given his word to the Government, in 1864, that he would stay on the reservation, and he kept it to the letter. The cries and wails of his sorely-persecuted people came up to his ears as did the lamentations of the children of Israel in the desert to Moses. But he was helpless to save them. He could only appeal to the reservation authorities for relief, and when they did nothing he was forced therewith to be content.

Finally Captain Jack arose as a would-be deliverer. In fiery orations he pictured and magnified to the long-suffering Modok the griefs which they knew all too well. He gathered about him a band of reckless young men who chafed under the restraints of the reservation. He made common cause with them and united them to his fortunes. At length, in 1870, emboldened by the imbecility which reigned on the reserve, he struck camp and boldly marched away, taking with him one hundred and fifty followers, about three-fifths of the Modok tribe.

He went down to Lost River, the ancestral home of his race, and re-occupied the rich grazing lands which the Government had sought to secure to the settlers by the treaty of 1864. Troubles continually arose with the settlers. The air was burdened with their complaints. The Modok had become impudent and insolent; they had learned to despise the wretched farce of the reservation management.

Herein lay the great and fatal mistake of the American authorities, that they did not deal firmly with the savages. They sent agents to them to urge them to return; they threatened, they coaxed, they made promises, they wheedled, then they threatened again, and so on through all the inefficient and farcical round which has generally characterized the dealings of our reservations with the American Indians. They taught the Modok to contemn them. All their lives they have done nothing but read faces, and they are consummate judges of human nature. They know well when there is weakness in the enemy's camp. They judged the Great Father in Washington by the sons whom he sent.

In fact, Captain Jack went back to the reservation once on condition that the Mukaluk should not be allowed to insult him as a coward. But this guarantee was not kept, the old course of ignominious taunts and abuse began again. Jack withdrew a second time, declaring he would not remain in a home which was no home, and with an agent who had no heart.

There were changes of agents and changes of policies. The Indians knew not what to depend on. They were disgusted and defiant. Old Skonchin and his faithful hundred were removed to a new reservation at Yainax, where they were out of the reach of their hereditary tormentors, and were allowed to live in peace. But this change came too late.

In a sudden spasm of vigor a detachment of thirty-five soldiers was sent to Jack's camp, and on the fatal 29th of November, 1872, they took him by surprise. There was bloodshed. The torch of the Modok war was lighted, and it flamed up with a fearful burning. They fought with unparalleled heroism for their homes, but were crushed by superior power; and their fallen chiefs were held to a stern and awful accountability to laws which they had no hand or voice in making, and whose spirit and substance had been as wantonly violated by the conquering race as by themselves.

CHAPTER XXVIII.

THE A-CHO-MÂ'-WI.

The Pit River Indians are divided into a number of tribes, of which the principal are the following: In Fall River Basin, the A-cho-mâ'-wi; on the South Fork, the Hu-mâ'-whi; in Hot Spring Valley, the Es-ta-ke'-wach; in the same valley, below Hot Spring, the Han-te'-wa; in Round Valley, 99 the Chu-mâ'-wa; in Big Valley, the A-tu-a'-mih (also called sometimes the Ha-mef-kut'-tel-li). The first name is derived from *a-cho'-ma*, "the river"; and Estakewach is from *es-ta-ke'*, "hot spring".

Another tribe on the south side of the river, opposite Fort Crook, are called Il-mâ'-wi. Pit River is simply and pre-eminently "the river"; other streams have their special names. In accordance with that minuteness of geographical nomenclature so common in California, they are not content with designating the river as a whole, but every reach, every cataract, every bend, has a name to itself. Thus a little rapid above Burgettville is Cho-to'-keh, the next bend below Lo-ka'-lit.

There is a remarkable difference between the physique one sees in Hot Spring Valley and that in Big Valley, only twenty miles below. It is partly caused by the meager supply of aboriginal food in the former valley; partly the deplorable result of generations of slave-wars and slave-catching prosecuted against them by the Modok and the Mukaluk, and partly the result of the awful scourging given them by General Crook, and the deportation of the heart of the tribe to a distant reservation. The Hot Spring Valley Indians are the most miserable, squalid, peaked-faced, mendicant, and mendacious wretches I ever saw in California. Frequently their teeth project forward into a point, and when their lips are closed they are wrinkled tight over them like a drawn purse. When eating there is often the same rapid, mumbling motion one may observe in the lips of a squirrel. Squatted on their haunches in their odious tatters, they grin, and grin, and lie. Nibbling at a piece of bony fish with those puckered, prehensile lips, they look like nothing in the world so much as a number of apes. Their faces are skinny, foreheads very low and retreating, bodies lank, and abdomens protuberant. I dismounted and stood fifteen minutes watching a group of them eating one of those execrable Pit River suckers; and never in my life have I seen so saddening and so piteous a spectacle of the results which come from seizing out into bondage year after year all the comeliest maidens and bravest youths of a people. All the best young blood of the nation is filched out of it, and instead of physical advancement by the Darwinian principle of "selection", here is steady embrutement by the propagation of the worst.

But the tribe on the South Fork (whom I did not see) were perhaps made of better stuff, besides which they ate plenty of fat deer out of the mountains, and escaped the slave-raids of the Modok. It was these whose "nasty" fighting indirectly gave the name to Fort Damnation—a place well christened, where Crook jammed them at last against the wall. There is a deep, steep cañon into which they had escaped as a last resort, and barricading themselves with shards of rock and *débris* at the foot of the cañon walls, they made it death for any man to show his face at its mouth. A subaltern officer came back to report the situation to his superior, and demurred against further fighting. To him said the grim soldier: "We were sent here to fight Indians. When you are all killed I am going in there to fight them myself." Two detachments were sent out, and by making a long circuit they succeeded in reaching the brink of the cañon on opposite sides. Then their bullets shot slanting down, and came crashing upon the heads of the savages, while plenty of leaden leg-cutters were slung up the cañon with an infernal yelling, and the Indians found it getting hot. It was their last fight.

Let one remount at the Hot Spring and ride one easy day's journey down to Big Valley where the mountains helped to keep out the thieving 100 Modok slavers, and there is much improvement in the forms we meet. The faces are broad and black and calm, and shining with an Ethiopian unctuousness; the foreheads are like a wall; in those solid, round-capped cheek-bones, standing over against one another so far apart, and in those massive lower jaws, there is unmistakable strength, bred in the bone through tranquil generations. They laugh with a large and placid laugh which comes all the way up from their stomachs, soundless, but agitating their well-fed bodies with slow and gentle undulations. Here is a hearty and a lusty savagery which is pleasant to see.

There was one custom of the Pit River nation wherein they differed from all other California Indians, and that was their custom of digging pitfalls for the trapping of game. Selecting some trail where the deer passed frequently, they would, with no other implements but fire-hardened sticks, excavate pits ten or twelve feet deep, and carry all the earth away out of sight in baskets. Then they would cover the pits with thin layers of brushwood and grass, sprinkle earth over all, scatter dead leaves and twigs on the earth, restore the trail across it, and even print tracks in it with a deer's hoof; then back out and conceal their own tracks. Such an infinity of trouble would they give themselves to capture one deer—a fact which shows them to have been, as we otherwise know was the case, indifferent hunters. These pitfalls were very numerous along the river-banks where the deer came down to drink; and the early settlers lost so many cattle in them and fell in so often themselves that they compelled the Indians to abandon the practice. It is these pits which named the river.

Mention has been made of the meager diet of the Hot Spring tribes. They have no acorns, no salmon (acorns and salmon are the flour and pork of the California Indians). They have a fine range of game-birds—*Centrocercus urophasianus, Pediocœtes Columbianus, Bonasa Sabinii, Oreortyx pictus*—but they trap few of them and shoot fewer. Venison they are able to indulge in rarely. They have grasshoppers, very large and juicy crickets, the miserable suckers and a few trout from the river, cammas, clover in the spring, and the sickening, disgusting bear-berries (*Frangula Californica*). After the vast crystal volume of Fall River enters and overcomes the swampiness of the snaky Pit, then salmon are caught, the Indians say, though the whites assert that they do not ascend above a certain tremendous cataract which is said to exist on the lower river. When the salmon season arrives, a band of aged shamans abstain from fresh fish, flesh, or fowl for certain days, which they believe will induce a heavy run and a plentiful catch. Even the women and children at this time, if they wish to eat fresh salmon, must carry it back in the forest out of sight of the river. Like the Maidu of Sutter County, they call the salmon by sitting in a circle on some overlooking promontory, while a venerable shamin stands in the midst and earnestly addresses the finny multitudes for two or three hours, urging them to ascend the river.

Probably the squaws in this nation occupy as degraded and servile a position as in any other tribe in the State. A man's daughters are considered simply as his property, his chattels, to be sold at pleasure. He owns them not only when maidens, but when widows—either the father or the brothers. A widow does not pass into the possession of her husband's brother, as in some tribes, but of her own brother, who sells her and her children to her second husband. An intelligent squaw told me they were often cruelly beaten, and had no redress. If a wife deserts her husband's lodge and goes back to her father, the husband may strike her dead if she refuses to return. A squaw is seldom held responsible for adultery, even with white men. Polygamy prevails when the man is rich enough to buy wives. Tyee John, for instance, had three. When a man marries he gives presents to all the male members of his bride's family, but none to the female. Yet even here there were some mitigations to her position. A widow retains all the articles which she herself made; also sometimes a horse which she paid for out of her own earnings. A widower cannot keep his wife's personal property, such as baskets, &c.; but her relatives come and take them away. Though a slave herself, bought and sold, her right to these little personal articles is inviolable. There are many female shamins, and the rights and modesty of a woman in childbirth are sacredly respected, as they are not among civilized nations. Moreover, there is once in a while a good, healthy, natural instance of a thoroughly henpecked man. The Indians tell with great glee of a terrible termagant in the tribe, called "Old Squally". One day she quarreled with her husband when they were fishing, whereupon she faced him about toward the water, and kicked him into the same with violence, telling him to "go in swimming".

Notwithstanding their occasional ebullitions of brutality toward women and children, they are a race with strong affections. William Burgett relates that he has frequently seen them carry the aged long distances on their backs to bring them to a physician. An Indian employed by him once lost a cousin to whom he was much attached, and he wept and mourned for him daily for more than six months, refusing food to such a degree that he was reduced to a living skeleton. An aged Achomâwi lost his wife, to whom he had been married probably half a century, and he tarred his face in mourning for her as though he were a woman—an act totally unprecedented, and regarded by the Indians as evincing an extraordinary affection.

A woman speaking good English gave me some interesting glimpses of Indian social life on Pit River. An Achomâwi mother seldom teaches her daughters any of the arts of barbaric housekeeping before their marriage. They learn them by imitation and experiment after they grow old enough to perceive the necessity thereof. The parents are expected to establish a young couple in their lodge, provide them with the needful basketry, and furnish them with cooked food for some months, which indulgent parents sometimes continue for a year, or even longer, so that the young people have a more real honeymoon than is vouchsafed to most civilized people. As children are taught nothing, so they are never punished, but occasionally cuffed or banged. It is a wonder that they grow up with any virtue whatever, for the conversation of their elders in their presence is often of the filthiest description. But the children of savages far less often make wreck of body and soul than do those of the civilized, 101 because when the great mystery of maturity confronts them they know what it means and how to meet it.

In case of the birth of twins one is almost always destroyed, for the feeling is universal that two little mouths at once are too great a burden. Infanticide seems to prevail in no other instance but this. It is a singular fact that the Indians generally have no word for "milk". They never see it, for they never extract it from any animal, because that would seem to them a kind of sacrilege or robbery of the young. Hence, an Indian frequently sees this article for the first time among civilized people, and adopts the Spanish word for it.

The squaws spend a good deal of time in visiting each other, when the conversation runs on their youngest children, on how many strings of shells Hal-o'-mai-chi paid Sdem'-el-di for his daughter, on the last dance they, the squaws, had around the bloody head of a Modok, &c.

The language of Pit River is so hopelessly consonantal, harsh, and sesquipedalian, so utterly unlike the sweet and simple languages of the Sacramento, that to reduce it to writing one must linger for weeks, and cause the Indians to repeat the words many times. The reader may wonder at this, but I have only to say let him make the experiment. The personal pronouns show it to be a true Digger Indian tongue.

A mixed custom prevails as to the disposition of the dead. William Burgett affirms that they burn only those bodies which died of an unknown disease, as a sanitary measure, burying all others in a sitting posture; but this imputes to them more philosophy and more freedom from superstition than they are entitled to, I opine. One fact is peculiar: the Ilmâwi never have burned their dead at any time in their history, though belonging to a nation that did. It is probable that in the other tribes cremation prevailed almost exclusively before the Americans arrived. They believe that the spirits of the departed walk the earth and behold the conduct of the living; a belief common in Oregon, but not, as I am aware, in California. The good reach the Happy Western Land quickly; the wicked go out on the same road, but walk forever and never reach it. To walk forever—perpetual motion!—could anything be a fitter painting of hell to the indolent California Indian?

Some years ago an aged chief related to a settler on Fall River an ancient tradition respecting an extraordinary phenomenon which once occurred on Pit River. All the atmosphere was filled with ashes so that the heavens were darkened and the sun blotted out, and the Indians wept with fear and trembling, as they who stand before death. The birds of the air were stilled, and all the sweet voices of nature were hushed. This phenomenon continued for days, insomuch that some of the Indians attempted to find their way out to another country by creeping along the ground, in hope of beholding the sun once more. After they had crept on their knees for many miles the ashes began slowly to disappear, and the sun shone again, but at first it was like blood for color.

It is possible that this legend has reference to that tremendous out-pouring of lava (which must have been preceded by showers of ashes), which was recently described by Professor Le Conte in a paper read before the California Academy of Sciences.

LEGEND OF CREATION.

Our earth was created by the coyote and the eagle, or, rather, the coyote began and the eagle completed it.   First, the coyote scratched it up with his paws out of nothingness, but the eagle complained that there were no mountains for him to perch on.   The coyote made hills, but they were not high enough, so the eagle fell to work on it and scratched up great ridges.   When he flew over them his feathers dropped down, took root, and became trees, and his pin-feathers became bushes and plants.   But in the creation of animals and man the coyote and the fox participated, the first being an evil spirit, the other good.   They quarreled as to whether they should let men live always or not.   The coyote said, "If they want to die, let them die"; but the fox said, "If they want to come back, let them come back".   But nobody ever came back, for the coyote prevailed.   Last of all, the coyote brought fire into the world, for the Indians were freezing.   He journeyed far to the west, to a place where there was fire, stole some of it, and brought it home in his ears.   He kindled a fire in the mountains, and the Indians saw the smoke of it, and went up and got fire; so they were warmed and comforted, and have kept it ever since.

Following are the Pit River numerals, in Big Valley:

One.	ha-mis'.	Six.	má-shuts.
Two.	hak.	Seven.	há-kuts.
Three.	chast.	Eight.	ha-ta-mé-leh
Four.	ha-tam'.	Nine.	mo-losch'-i-jin.
Five.	lá-tu.	Ten.	mo-losch'-i.

The word for "nine" means "pretty near ten".

Such is the name applied to the tribe living on Hat Creek, the most warlike tribe in all the Pit River basin, and the one most dreaded by the timid aborigines of Sacramento Valley. The Achomâwi tell me their language is somewhat different from their own, though a good many words are identical, so that they easily learn each other's tongues; but that in Indian Valley, and as far east as Big Meadows, the Indians are substantially the same as the Maidu. Some years ago all the Pit River tribes and the Pakamalli hatched a conspiracy to go over in a body and remain with the Paiuti until the soldiers should be withdrawn from Pit River, when they would descend on it, massacre all the whites, and recover their ancient domain, together with many cattle and horses. From their geographical position these tribes are more friendly to the Paiuti than most California Indians are.

CHAPTER XXIX.

THE NO'-ZI, ETC.

One of the most dreaded enemies of the great Wintūn nation was the little tribe called Nó-zi or Nó-si—a whale pursued by a sword-fish. Though themselves inferior to the terrible Pakamalli of Hat Creek, they were a constant terror to the effeminate dwellers in the rich and sweltering valley of the Sacramento, and kept them hemmed in all along from Battle Creek nearly up to Pit River, on a margin only about a mile wide. Indeed, with this fierce and restless little tribe forever on their flank, always ready to pounce upon them, it is singular that the Wintūn maintained such a long and narrow ribbon of villages on the east bank, isolated from the main body of their nation on the west bank, especially when they had no means of communication but rafts. Every year during the salmon season, June and July, their days were spent in dread, and their nights in sleeplessness, on account of the tormenting Nozi, who were now making frequent dashes down on the river. Not content with the limited run of salmon up the creeks whose banks they occupied, they made forays under their celebrated chief, Polillis, on the Sacramento, and though coming for fish they never neglected an opportunity to carry away women and children into the foothills for slaves. For several years before 1849 Major Reading, living on the west bank, was largely engaged in trapping for furs, and the Nozi gave his trappers endless trouble.

Round Mountain and the valleys of Oak Run and Clover Creek were their principal habitat, though it is pretty certain that they formerly extended as far south as Battle Creek. The handful of them still living can give no information on the subject, but the above are their territorial limits as described by the pioneers.

Though living at a little higher altitude than the Wintūn they are not quite so tall as they, but are several shades lighter-colored. They are rather undersized, even for California Indians, and are quite a delicate, small limbed, handsome race. With their hazel complexions; smooth, polished skins; smallish, ovoid faces; and lithe, well-knit frames, they present a race-type different from any other to be seen in California. Pwi-es'-si, the present chief, a very polite, innocent little man, who had never been away from Oak Run in his life, as he stood in the hay-field at the head of his mowers, in his neat, well-fitting garments, leaning in a picturesque attitude on his scythe, presented a very pleasing view. His eye was soft and gentle, his voice was mild, his manners much more refined than is the wont of the hay-field, so that he seemed the farthest possible remove from his warlike progenitors whom the pioneers describe.

As the stature of the Nozi is short at best, so the children are slow in attaining it. They often remain mere dwarfs until they are ten or fifteen years old, when they start and shoot up suddenly eighteen inches or so.

They have a reputation for honesty above their neighbors. A ranchman states that he has frequently known them to bring in strayed cattle on their own motion. They adapted themselves early to the necessities of labor and the usages of civilization. Many years ago—so early in the history of the State that they were obliged to content themselves, master and man, with the primitive repast of boiled wheat and beef—John Love sometimes had a hundred Nozi in his employment at once; and they labored faithfully, as they do to-day.

As the Nozi were so early civilized, and are so nearly extinct, it is not easy to learn much concerning their aboriginal usages. The principal interest attaching to them is the question of their origin. There is an ancient tradition, related by themselves to Major Reading many years ago, that their ancestors came from a country very far toward the rising sun. They journeyed a great many moons, crossing forests, prairies, mountains, plains, deserts, and rivers so great, according to their description, that they could have been found nowhere except in the interior of the continent. At length they came to a delightful land and to a timid and feeble folk, where they conquered for themselves a dwelling-place, and rested therein. The narrator of this story states that Major Reading once showed him an old flint-lock musket which he had found in possession of the Nozi, and which had been so worn by being loaded with gravel that it was as thin as paper at the muzzle. It was not known how they could have obtained it, unless they had brought it with them from the Atlantic States; and it was Major Reading's conjecture that they were the descendants of the remnants of King Philip's tribe, of New England. I know not if this story is of   104 any importance. Pwiessi knew nothing whatever concerning it, but his information was very limited on all subjects. The one crucial test would be that of language. I have at hand nothing from which I can obtain a vocabulary of King Philip's nation. The Nozi numerals are very peculiar in their formation, unlike anything I have found in California. For the benefit of anybody who may have the means of making a comparision, I subjoin them:

One.	pai-kĭ-mo'-na.	Six.	pur-han-mo'-na.
Two.	o-mich-i-mo'-na.	Seven.	chu-mi-man-mo'-na.
Three.	pul-mich-i-mo'-na.	Eight.	taum-han-mo'-na.
Four.	tau-mi-mo'-na.	Nine.	paitsch-o-ma-ta'-na.
Five.	chi-man-mo'-na.	Ten.	hakh-hen-mo'-na.

THE KOM'-BO.

In writing of this tribe, I am compelled for once to forego the name employed by themselves. It is not known to any man living save them-   105 selves, and probably it will not be until the grave gives up its dead. The above is the name given to them by their neighbors of Indian Valley, a tribe of the Maidu Nation.

If the Nozi are a peculiar people, these are extraordinary; if the Nozi appear to be foreign to California, these are doubly foreign. They seem likely to present a spectacle which is without a parallel in human history— that of a barbaric race resisting civilization with arms in their hands, to the last man, and the last squaw, and the last pappoose. They were once a numerous and thrifty tribe. Now there are only five of them left—two men, two women, and a child. No human eye ever beholds them, except now and then some lonely hunter, perhaps, prowling and crouching for days over the volcanic wastes and scraggy forests which they inhabit. Just at nightfall he may catch a glimpse of a faint camp-fire, with figures flitting about it; but before he can creep within rifle-range of it the figures have disappeared, the flame wastes slowly out, and he arrives only to find that the objects of his search have indeed been there before him, but are gone. They cooked there their hasty evening repast, but they will sleep somewhere else, with no camp-fire to guide a lurking enemy within reach. For days and weeks together they never touch the earth, stepping always from one volcanic stone to another. They never leave a broken twig or a disturbed leaf behind them. Probably no day of the year ever passes over their heads but some one of this doomed nation of five sits crouching on a hillock or in a tree-top, within easy eye-shot of his fellows; and not a hare can move upon the earth beneath without its motions being heeded and recorded by the watcher's eye. There are men in and around Chico who have sworn a great oath of vengeance that these five Indians shall die a bloody death; but weeks, months, and years have passed away, and brought for their oaths no fulfillment. There is now wanting only a month of four years since they have ever been seen together so that their number could be certainly known. In February, 1870, some hunters had succeeded in capturing the two remaining squaws, whereupon they opened communication with the men, and promised them a safe-conduct and the release of their squaws if they would come in and promise to abandon hostilities. The two men came in, bringing the child. It was the intention of the hunters, as one of them candidly avowed to me, to have seized them and secretly put the whole five out of existence. While they were in camp, one of the hunters conceived an absurd whim to weigh himself, and threw a rope over a limb for that purpose, at which the wily savages took fright, and they all bounded away like frightened deer and escaped. But they had remained long enough for an American, as eagle-eyed as themselves, to observe that one of the two warriors had a gunshot wound in one hand, and many others on his arm, forming an almost unbroken cicatrix from hand to elbow. Probably no white man's eyes will ever again behold them all together alive.

When they were more numerous than now, they occupied both Mill Creek and Deer Creek; but nowadays they live wholly in the great volcanic terraces and low mountains west of Mill Creek Meadows. Down to 1858 they lived at peace with the whites, but since that time they have waged unrelenting and ceaseless war—ceaseless except for a casual truce like that above described. Their hostilities have been characterized by so many and such awful atrocities that there are men, as above-mentioned, who have sworn an oath that they shall die. All these seventeen years they have warred against the world and against fate. Expelled from the rich and teeming meadows which were their chosen home ; hemmed in on these great, hot, volcanic table-lands where nothing can live but a few stunted trees, and so destitute of water that this forms at once a security against civilized foes and their own constant menace of death—a region accursed of Heaven and spewed out even by the earth—they have seen one after another of the craven tribes bow the knee and make terms with the enemy; but still their voice has been stern and steady for war; still they have crouched and hovered in their almost disembodied life over these arid plains until all are gone but five. Despite all their bloody and hellish treacheries, there is something sublime in this.

So far as their customs have been observed, they have some which are Californian, but more which are decidedly foreign. They burn the dead, and are remarkably fond of bathing.

On the other hand, the customs which are foreign to California are numerous and significant. First, they have no assembly chamber and consequently no indoor dances, but only circular dances in the open air. The assembly chamber is the one capital shibboleth of the California Indian. Second, they did not erect the warm and heavily-earthed lodges which the Indians of this State are so fond of, but mere brush-wood shelters, and often they had no refuge but caves and dens. Third, they inflicted cruel and awful tortures on their captives, like the Algonkin races. Whatever abominations the indigenous races may have perpetrated on the dead, the torture of the living was essentially foreign to California. Fourth, they had a mode of capturing deer which no other California tribe employed, as far as known. Taking the antlers of a buck when they were green and velvety, they split them open on the under side and removed the pith, which rendered them so light that an Indian could carry them on his head. Then he would dress himself in the skin and go to meet the herd, or rather thrust

106 his head out from the bushes, taking care not to expose himself too much, and imitate the peculiar habit which a buck has of constantly groping about with his head, lifting it up and down, nibbling a little here and a little there. At a proper time he would shoot an arrow into one of them, and the stupid things would stare and step softly about, in their peering and inquisitive way, until a number of them were knocked over. Fifth, their unconquerable and undying determination to fight it out to the bitter end is not a California Indian trait. Sixth, their aboriginal habit of singeing or cropping off their hair within an inch of their heads contrasts strongly with the long locks of the Californians.

Several years ago this tribe committed a massacre near Chico, and Sandy Young, a renowned hunter of that country, with a companion, captured two squaws, a mother and a daughter, who promised to guide them to the camp of the murderers. They set out at nightfall in the dead of winter. It was sleeting, raining, and blowing that night as if " the de'il had business on his hands". But they passed rapidly on without halt or hesitation, for the squaws led the way boldly. From nightfall until long after midnight they held on their dreary trail, stumbling and floundering occasionally, but speaking scarcely a word; nor was there a moment's cessation in the execrable, bitter sleet and rain. At length they came to a creek which was swollen and booming. In the pitchy darkness it was manifestly impassable. They sounded it in various places, and could find no crossing. While the hunters were groping hither and thither, and shouting to each other above the raging of the torrent, the squaws disappeared. No hallooing could elicit a response from them. The two men considered themselves betrayed, and prepared for treachery. Suddenly there came floating out on the storm and the roaring a thin young squeal. The party had been re-enforced by one. The hunters then grasped the situation, and, laughing, set about collecting some dry stuff and making a fire. They were benumbed and half-frozen themselves, and supposed of course the women would come in as soon as they observed the fire. But no, they wanted no fire, or, if they did, their aboriginal modesty would not allow them to resort to it under these circumstances. The grandmother took the new-born babe, amid the almost palpable blackness of darkness, the sleeting, and the yelling winds, and dipped it in the ice-cold creek. Again and again she dipped it, while now and then the hunters could hear its stout-lunged protest above the roaring. Not only did the infant survive this unparalleled treatment, but it grew excellently well. In memory of the extraordinary circumstances under which it was ushered into this world, Young named it " Snow-flake," and it is living to this day, a wild-eyed lad in Tehama.

CHAPTER XXX.

THE MAI'-DU, OR MAI' DEH.

This is a large nation, extending from the Sacramento to Honey Lake, and from Big Chico Creek to Bear River. As usual in the case of an extensive nation in this State, they have no name of general application, except that they all call themselves *mai'-du, mai'-deh* (Indians). Of separate tribes or villages there are many. I give what I could collect, first premising that the same name is applied to the locality and to the inhabitants of it, though this is not always the case, for there is a village on Chico Creek whose inhabitants are called O-tá-ki, while the village itself is known as O-ta-kūm'-ni.

In Indian Valley, up in the mountains, are the To-sí-ko-yo; at Big Meadows, the Ná-kum; at Susanville, the Ku-ló-mum. On Feather River are the Ol'-la, opposite the mouth of Bear River; next above, on the same side, the Kūl'-meh, the Hoak (Hock), the Tí-shum, the Wí-ma, and the Yú-ba, the latter being opposite the mouth of Yuba River. Next, on the left bank, are the Toam'-cha and the Hoan'-kut, the latter being just below the mouth of the Honcut Creek. Then, on the right bank again are the Bó-ka, the Tai'-chi-da, the Bai'-yu, and the Hol-ó-lu-pai, the latter being opposite Oroville. The Taichida had a very large town, and their chief in early days was Ya-hai'-lum. On Honcut Creek, going up, are the Tó-to and the Hel'-to; on Butte Creek, the Es'-kin; on Chico Creek, the Mich-ōp'-do. In Concow Valley are the Kon'-kau, once a large and powerful tribe, and probably the best representatives of this nation. On the Yuba, at Nevada City, are the Us-tó-ma; lower down, the Pan'-pa-kan. All these tribes, in giving their full designation, add the word *maidu*, thus Ustoma Maidu. Bear River and all its tributaries were occupied by the Nishinam, so that

107

the real boundary between them and the Maidu was on the plains, midway between Bear River and the Yuba.

There is little to be said respecting the etymology of these geographical names. "Konkau" is from "Kó-yoang-kau", which is composed of *kó-yo*, "a plain", and *kau*, "the earth" or "a place". There are three creeks called by these Indians Chú-lam-shu (Chico Creek), Kim'-shu, and Nim'-shu; the second of these is from *ki-wĭm sé-u* (little water), and the last from *nem sé-u* (big water). The word *sé-u*, which appears in all these three names, is rendered by the Indians "river" ("water" being *mó-mih*); but I am inclined to believe it originally signified "water".

Although the California Indians perhaps lived as peacefully together as any tribes on the continent, they were careful so to place their camps or villages as to prevent surprise. Necessity compels them to live near a stream or a spring; so in the mountains they generally select a sheltered, open cove, where an enemy could not easily approach within bow-shot without being discovered, and where there is a knoll in the cove to afford good drainage. But there are frequently what might be called hill-stations, or out-posts, commanding a still wider prospect, though often some distance from water, in which either the warriors alone or the whole village took up their residence when war was raging. These are generally on bold promontories overlooking the stream, but there are indications that they contained substantial lodges, and even the dance-house, or council-house, wherein the warriors would assemble for deliberation, and perhaps for safety.

The Paiuti always made their camps on hill-tops, compelling the squaws to bring up water in willow jugs; and Kit Carson used to say that the reason so many emigrants were killed in early days was because they would camp by the stream, where the Indians were able to pounce down upon them. Some account for these hill-stations in California on the ground that when the miners made their irruption into the country and followed up all the streams, the Indians who were timid or hostile moved back into the hills, where they sometimes lived several years before they finally became reconciled; but the true explanation is that above given.

The old camping-grounds are always marked by a layer of rich, black mold, accumulated from the leavings of years. They seem sometimes to live on these spots, off and on, so long that they become foul and unwholesome from the exhalations (for they are not nice, and use no disinfectants); then they abandon them, and years elapse before they camp on them again. Sometimes, and perhaps more frequently, they abandon them on account of deaths, though these deaths may have been caused by noxious effluvia.

108

A few words will suffice to describe a hamlet. It stands on a gentle knoll beside a small, living stream, the bed of which is a dense jungle of willows and aquatic weeds. Back of the village the low, rounded hills spread away in the arid, sweltering air, tawny-colored, and crisped in the pitiless drought, with here and there a wisp of faded poison-oak, or a clump of evergreen chaparral, or a low, leaden-green, thin-haired silver-pine, scarcely able to cast a shadow in the fierce, blinding glare of a California summer. Crowning the knoll, the dome-shaped assembly or dance house swells broadly up—a barbaric temple—in the middle of the hamlet, and an Indian is occasionally seen passing on all-fours in or out the low arched entrance; hard by which stands a solitary white-oak, that swings its circling shadow over the village. Half a dozen conical, smoke-blackened lodges are scattered over the knoll, each with its open side on the north to protect the inmates from the sunshine, and rude wickiups or brush-awnings stretch raggedly from one to another, or are thrown out as wings on either side. One or more acorn-granaries of wicker-work stand around each lodge, much like hogsheads in shape and size, either on the ground or mounted on posts as high as one's head, full of acorns, and capped with thatch.

Fig. 25

Drowse, drowse, mope, is the order of the hour. All through the long sweltering days there is not a sound in the hamlet unless it is the eternal thump, thump of some squaw pounding up acorns. Within the heavily-earthed assembly-house it is cool and dark, and here the men lie on the earth-floor with their heads pillowed on the low bank around the side; but the women do not enter, for it is forbidden to them except on festival days. They and the children find the coolest places they can outside. The younger Indians are mostly dressed in clothing in which it is possible to recognize the civilized cut and fit; the old men, if the weather is not immoderately hot, wear mostly assemblages of picked-up raiment; but the old women have a single garment much the shape of a wool-sack, sleeveless, and gathered at the neck with a string, more or less white once, but now, after the lapse of unnumbered washing-days when they did no washing, taking on the rich color known as isabel. When they are sitting on top of some great rock, pounding acorns between their legs in their clumsy way, they lay aside even this garment. There is nothing so intensely stupid and vacuous 109 as the Indian's daily life—the man's part of it.

The Maidu have two contrivances for snaring wild-fowl that I have not seen elsewhere. One of them is a loose-woven net which is stretched perpendicularly on two rods running parallel with the surface of the water. The lower rod is lifted up a few inches so that the net is not taut, but hangs down in a fold or trough. When the ducks are flying low, almost skimming the water, they thrust their heads through the meshes of the net, while 110 their bodies drop down into the fold, which prevents them from fluttering loose. The other contrivance is also a net, stretched on a frame projecting up out of the water in a shallow place. The Indian fastens decoy-ducks close by the net, or sprinkles berries on the bottom to attract the fowl. He has a string attached to the frame and leading to the shore, where he sits holding the end of it behind the bushes. When the ducks are swimming about close to the net, he twitches it over them, and they thrust their heads up through it, which prevents them from diving or flying away. The Indian runs down quickly, treading at every step on the string, to hold the fowl securely until he can reach them. With either of these contrivances they would sometimes snare a whole flock at once.

Of dances the Hololupai Maidu have a large number, each being celebrated in its yearly season. One of the most important of these is the acorn dance (*ka-mi'-ni kon-pe'-wa la-loam'*, literally "the all-eating dance"), 111 which is observed in autumn, soon after the winter rains set in, to insure a bountiful crop of acorns the following year. Assembled together throughout their villages, from fifty to a hundred or more in a council-house, men, women, and children, they dance standing in two circles, the men in one the women in the other. The former are decorated with all their wealth of feathers, the women with beads, etc. After a certain length of time the dance ceases, and two venerable, silver-haired priests come forward with gorgeous head-dresses and long mantles of black eagle's feathers, and take their stations on opposite sides of one of the posts supporting the roof. Resting their chins on this, with their faces turned up toward heaven, each, in turn, makes a solemn and earnest supplication to the spirits, chanting short sentences in their occult priestly language, to which the other occasionally makes response. At longer intervals the whole congregation respond "*Ho!*" equivalent to "amen", and there is a momentary pause of profound silence, during which a pin could be heard to drop. Then the dance is resumed, and the whole multitude join in it, while one keeps time by stamping with his foot on a large hollow slab. These exercises continue for many hours, and at intervals acorn-porridge is handed about, of which all partake liberally without leaving the dance-house. Of the religious character of these exercises there can be no doubt.

Then there is the clover dance (*he'-lin ka-mi'-ni*, "the great dance"), which is celebrated in the blossom-time of clover, in concentric circles like the above, but outdoors, and not attended with anything that could be called religious ceremonies. The men often dance with a fanatic violence and persistence until they are reeking with perspiration, and then plunge into cold water or stretch themselves at full length on the ground in a manner that would insure a white man the rheumatism.

Upon the ripening of manzanita berries comes the manzanita dance, (*wi'-du-kan ka-mi'-ni*, "the little dance"), which is about like that last described.

Then there is the great spirit dance (*he'-lin ka-ki'-ni ka-mi'-ni*), which is held in propitiation of the demons. The reader must not for a moment confound this great spirit with the being so called by the Algonkin races, for he has nothing whatever to do with their cosmogony; he created nothing, is powerful only for evil, and is nothing more nor less than the chief of the imps or goblins supposed to haunt certain hills or other localities.

The dance for the dead (*tsi'-pi ka-mi'-ni*, "the weeping dance") will be found described in the last chapter.

Lastly there is a dance called *walin-hu'-pi ka-mi'-ni*, (this will not bear translation), which is held in the open air at pleasure, chiefly in the clover season. The maidens dance this alone in the evening. They join hands in a circle and swing merrily around an old man seated upon the grass, chanting to a lively step; then presently they break the circle with screams and laughter, and flee in every direction. The young men waiting near pursue and capture each his mistress, and kindly, liberal night draws her sable curtain over the scene that ensues.

Many of them believe in the annihilation of the soul, or as Blind Charlie expressed it to me, "that they will never live any more". It is not annihilation, pure and simple, of which the Indians are probably incapable of conceiving; but they think that many departed spirits enter into inanimate forms, as the mountains, rocks, trees, or into animals, especially the grizzly bear and the rattlesnake. In this latter case it is simply transmigration.

They have a conception of a Great Man (*he'-lin mai'-du*), who created the world and all its inhabitants. The earth was primarily a globe of molten matter, and from that the principle of fire ascended through the roots into the trunk and branches of trees, whence the Indians can extract it by means of their drill. The Great Man created woman first, and then cohabited with her, and from their issue the world was peopled. Lightning is the Great Man himself descending swiftly out of heaven, and rending the trees with his flaming arm. According to another and prettier fancy, thunder and lightning are two malignant spirits, struggling with all their fearful and incendiary power to destroy mankind. The rainbow is a good spirit, mild and peaceful, which overcomes them with its gentle sway, mollifies their rage, and permits the human race to occupy the earth a little longer.

Besides the wholly unmeaning choruses which they have in common with all, they possess also some songs which are really entitled to the name, having a body of intelligible words and expressing sentiments. I heard an Indian at Oroville sing one, called "a song of rejoicing" (*so'-lim wuk'-tem tu'-lim-shim*), which was a schottish, and very pretty. But it was still prettier when played on the flute by an American, and I deeply regretted my inability to write down music from the ear. It was a most gay and tripping little sprite, sweet, and wild, and wayward, with bold dashes across an octave, and seeming to be wholly out of joint, because of having hardly any two consecutive notes on the same line. It was quite lengthy, requir-

ing about two minutes in the playing. What would I not have given to
be able to preserve for better musicians this sweet, weird piece of savage
melody!

WO'-LOK-KI AND YO'-TO-WI.

Wo'-lok-ki and Yo'-to-wi were Konkau Indians, brother and sister, and
112 young children when their tribe first became acquainted with the whites.
One morning at daylight a foray was made on their native village, their
parents put to flight, many were killed, and these children with others were
carried away into captivity. The boy had, in ten minutes' time, torn away
a hole in the chaparral, and hidden himself and his little sister therein so
completely that they would not have been discovered if their dog had not
followed and revealed their hiding-place. By some good fortune they were
not separated, but were carried, first, in a pair of huge saddle-bags, made
for the purpose, one suspended on each side of the horse, with their heads
just peeping out; and afterward in a wagon, with a number of others, all
snugly packed on the floor, and covered with deer-skins, bear-skins, and
other peltries. In passing through a town the wagon attracted suspicion,
and was halted and slightly searched by the officers of the law, but nothing
was discovered contraband. With the strange instinct of their race, the
young captives did not cry out, or whimper, or move a muscle, but lay as
still as young quails lie in the chaparral when the hawk is hovering overhead. The wagon was suffered to proceed, but in another town it was
halted and searched again, more thoroughly, and the young Indians brought
to light. For the vindication of the excellent majesty of American law, it
was necessary that there should be a prosecution of the kidnapper, and he
was gently mulcted in the sum of $100, and the good citizens of the place
took away his captives from him, and they became "apprenticed" unto
them! It chanced that our little hero and heroine thus passed into the possession of a great philanthropist of those regions, whose voice had often
been mightily lifted up in denunciation of the infamies of this "Indian slave-
trade". He kept them some time, and finally transferred them to a negro
barber in exchange for a stove, did this philanthropist! The barber did not
keep them long, but sold them for $25 apiece, the usual price of an Indian

boy in those times. Thus they passed from one to another until seven or eight years had elapsed, and they were grown nearly to maturity; but they still remained unseparated.

At the end of this period they regained their liberty, and at once they set out together to return to their native valley. It was many days' journey for them, for they traveled afoot, but at last they arrived in sight of the village wherein they were born. By some means the news of their escape and return had preceded them, and the parents now learned for the first time that their long-lost children were still alive.

The wanderers now approach the village. They enter, and are guided by friends to the paternal wigwam, for there are many changes since they saw the village last. Ascending the earthen dome, they go down the well-worn ladder in the center, and seat themselves without a word. The father and mother give one hasty glance at them, but no more, and not a word is uttered. What the exceeding great joy of their hearts is, heaven and themselves alone know; but from all the spectator can read in their still, passionless faces, he would not know that they had ever borne any children, or mourned them for years with that great and unforgetting sorrow that savages sometimes know. An hour passes away, and still not a word is spoken, not even a single glance of recognition exchanged. The returned captives sit in motionless silence, while the father and mother move about the lodge on their various duties. An hour and a half is gone. The parents turn now and then a sudden and stolen look upon their waiting children. Two hours or more elapse. The glances become more frequent and bolder. It is now perhaps three hours since the captives entered, and yet not a whisper. But at last all the fullness of time of savage custom and savage etiquette is rounded and complete. The waiting hearts of the aged father and mother are full to bursting. Their eyes are filled with tears. They turn and speak to their children by name. They rush to them, they fall upon their necks, and together they mingle their tears, their strange outcries of joy, and their sobs.

To the reader this may seem extravagant and impossible, but, with the exception of a few minor particulars, it is a true story, illustrating a social custom of this singular race. In receiving a guest, the Konkau frequently

wait two or three hours before they address him. The substance of the
above story was related to me by an American, who was an eye-witness of
the captives' return.

LEGEND OF THE FLOOD.

Of old the Indians abode tranquilly in the Sacramento Valley, and
were happy. All on a sudden there was a mighty and swift rushing of
waters, so that the whole valley became like the Big Water, which no man
can measure. The Indians fled for their lives, but a great many were overtaken by the waters, and they slept beneath the waves. Also, the frogs
and the salmon pursued swiftly after them, and they ate many Indians.
Thus all the Indians were drowned but two, who escaped into the foot-hills.
But the Great Man gave these two fertility and blessed them, so that the
world was soon repeopled. From these two there sprung many tribes, even
a mighty nation, and one man was chief over all this nation—a chief greatly
known in the world, of large renown. Then he went out on a knoll overlooking the wide waters, and he knew that they covered fertile plains once
inhabited by his ancestors. Nine sleeps he lay on the knoll, turning over
and over in his mind the thoughts of these great waters, and he strove to
think how they came upon the land. Nine sleeps he lay without food, for
he lived on his thoughts alone, and his mind was always thinking of this
only: "How did this deep water cover the face of the world"? And at
the end of nine sleeps he was changed. He was no more like himself before,
for now no arrow could wound him. Though a thousand Indians should shoot
at him, not one flint-pointed arrow would pierce his skin. He was like the
Great Man in heaven, for no man could slay him forevermore. Then he
spoke to the Great Man, and commanded him to let the water flow off from
the plains which his ancestors had inhabited. The Great Man did this; he
rent open the side of the mountain, and the water flowed away into the Big
Water.

The following legend is taken from Bean's "History and Directory of
Nevada County":

THE LION AND THE CAT.

It was a long time ago. A California lion and his younger brother, the wild-cat, lived in a big wigwam together. The lion was strong and fleet of foot. He was more than a match for most of the animals he wanted to eat. But he could not cope with the grizzly, or the serpent that crawled on the earth. His young brother was wise. He had a wonderful power. From a magical ball of great beauty he derived an influence potent to destroy all the animals his older brother was afraid of. They hunted together, the cat going before. One day—it was a long time ago—the two went out to hunt. "There is a bear", said the lion. The cat, pointing to the bear, said, "Die", and the bear fell dead. They next met a serpent, and he was killed in like manner. They skinned the snake and took along his skin for its magical power. A little farther on two large and very beautiful deer were found feeding together. "Kill one of these for yourself", said the boy brother to his man brother, "but catch me the other alive." The lion gave chase, and at night he returned to his wigwam. "Did you bring me back one of the beautiful deer"? said the cat. "No", said the lion, "it was too much work; I killed them both." Then the cat was sorry, and did not love his brother. They were estranged. The cat would not go out to slay the bear and the snake any more, and the lion would not go out for fear of the bear and the snake. He thought he would use the magical ball of his brother, the cat, and learn to kill the bear and the snake himself. One day—it was a long time ago—the lion was playing with the ball, and, tossing it up, he saw it go up and up, and out of sight. It never came down. Then the deer scattered all over the earth and the hunting has been poor ever since. The cat was disconsolate for the loss of the magical ball. He left the wigwam to wander alone. He sorrowed for his loss and looked to find the ball again. It was a long time ago. Big water run all around from "Lankee" Jim to Humbug, and away up to the high mountains. The wild-cat went north. He climbed a tree by the water. He wished for the lost ball. By and by he saw a beautiful ball hanging, like a buckeye, on a limb. He picked it off. It was very pretty. He put it in the snake-skin to keep it so it would not get away. He went along the shore of the big water till he could see across it. Two girls were on the other side cooking. The ball jumped out of the snake-skin and rolled over in the water. It went across the river. One of the girls came down to the stream to get some water in her basket, and saw the beautiful ball rolling and shining in the water. She tried to dip it up in her basket. But it would roll away. She said, " Sister, come and help me catch this beautiful ball." The sister came. They tried a long time, but finally caught it in the basket. It was bright and very pretty. They were afraid it would get away. One held it for a time, and then the other. They were very glad. At night they put it between them in the bed. They kept awake a long time and talked about their prize. But at last they fell asleep. They woke in the morning—the ball was gone—there was lying between them a full-grown young man. And that was the first man that ever came on the earth. This was a long time ago.

CREATION AND FALL OF MAN.

Kó-do-yam-peh, the world-maker, and Hel'-lo-kai-eh, the devil, came from the east to We-lé-u-deh. Kodoyampeh said he would make a man, but Hellokaieh told him he could not do it, and dared him to attempt it. But Kodoyampeh repeated that he could do it. So he went out and got two smooth, yellow sticks (*yo-kó-lon-cha*), and laid them on the bed beside him at evening, and said they would turn into a man and woman during the night, but they would not by day.

So the world-maker and the devil went to bed. Through the night the devil often waked up his companion and asked him if the two sticks had turned to a man and a woman yet. He made fun of him, and asked him if he felt them move about in the bed. But Kodoyampeh replied that he must not trouble him, or it would not happen.

Thus the night passed away, and early in the morning Kodoyampeh felt two touches on his body. Looking up quick, he saw a man and a woman. He rose from his bed, and made them get up and go bathe themselves and then come and eat. When Hellokaieh came in he claimed the woman as his sister and the man as his brother-in-law. Kodoyampeh suffered this for the time.

Then the devil said to Kodoyampeh that if he would give him two sticks he would do the same thing, and create a man and a woman. Kodoyampeh did so, and the devil took the two sticks and laid them beside

him on his bed. Many times during the night he looked to see if a man
had appeared yet, but saw nobody. At last, about daybreak, he fell asleep.
Presently he was awakened by two lusty thumps in the ribs, when he
jumped up quickly, laughing, and saw two women, one with two eyes
and the other with only one. He asked each one in turn, "Are you a
man"? But each replied, "No, I am a woman ; we are two sisters."

Then the devil was sorely perplexed, because he could do nothing
without a man. He asked Kodoyampeh why he had not succeeded, and
Kodoyampeh said it was because he had laughed, whereas he had expressly
charged him not to laugh. The devil answered that he could not help it
when he got two such sharp digs in the ribs. He asked Kodoyampeh if he
would not make a man for him, but he refused. Then he asked him at
least to make him a two-eyed woman ; but Kodoyampeh said he could not
do it until they were dead. This, then, is the reason why one-eyed men
and women are seen in the world to-day.

After this Kodoyampeh sent on the earth the man whom he had
created to gather food from the face of it. Now, before this all the game
and all the fish, the grasshoppers, the birds of the air, and the insects of
the earth had been tame, so that a man had only to reach forth his hand
among them and take whatever he wished for his food. Also the soil had
been prolific up to this time, yielding all products, acorns, manzanita berries, pine-nuts, and many kinds of rich grass-seed for the sustenance of
man. So when Kodoyampeh sent forth the man whom he had made he
told him to take freely of all that he saw and desired—of the game and the
fish and the birds and the nuts, seeds, and berries—for all these things he
had created for him. One injunction only he laid upon him, and that was
that he should bring home to his house whatever he wished to cook, and
not kindle a fire in the woods.

So the man went out to catch game, but the devil saw him and told
him to cook in the woods whatever he wished. And he did so. Therefore
all the game and the fish, all the grasshoppers, the birds, and the insects,
when they saw the smoke in the woods, became wild, as they are to-day.
More than that, the ground was changed, so that the oaks yielded no more
acorns, and the manzanita bushes no more berries, nor was there anything

left for the food of man on the face of the earth, save only roots, clover, and earth-worms. These three things were all that men had to eat.

Also Kodoyampeh changed the air so that it was no longer always the same the year round, but now there was frost, and rain, and fog, and wind, and heat, and drought, together with the pleasant days. As a recompense he gave them fire to warm themselves, whereas before they had had only stones to press against their bodies. He established the seasons—Kum'-men-ni (the rain season); Yo'-ho-men-ni (the leaf season); I'-hi-lak-ki (the dry season); Mat'-men-ni (the falling-leaf season). He also instituted the sacred *ku'-meh*, the assembly-hall, and gave the Konkau songs to sing, but he did not yet give them any dances. Before this time they had had no diseases and no deaths, but after they cooked and ate in the woods they became subject to fever and pestilences, and many died. But Kodoyampeh told them that if they were good, at death they would go away to the spirit-land by the right-hand path (*yim'-dūm-bo*), which is light; but if they were bad they would go away by the left-hand path (*dak'-kūm-bo*), which leads away into darkness.

LEGEND OF OAN-KOI'-TU-PEH.

An old man named Pi-u'-chun-nuh, long ago, lived at We-le'-u-deh (above Oroville near Cherokee Flat). In those days the Indians lived wholly on clover, roots, and earth-worms; there was no game, no fish, no acorns, no nuts, no grasshoppers. Piuchunnuh went about everywhere, praying to hear a voice; he prayed to the woods, and to the rocks, and to the river. He prayed in the assembly-house, and listened if perchance he might hear a voice answering his prayer. But he heard nothing. He went to the oak and looked to see if it bore acorns, but it had only leaves; he went to the manzanita bush and looked for berries, but it had only leaves. He brought the leaves in the house and he prayed three days and nights; but still no answer, no voice.

Far away to the north, in the ice-land, there lived two old men, Hai'-kut-wo-to-peh (the great one), and Woan'-no-mih (the death-giver). Piuchunnuh resolved to send for them. He sent a boy to see them, and the boy went like a humming-bird, and reached the ice-land in one day. These two old men lived in a house and they were asleep inside (it was in the daytime), each in his own bed, placed on poles which reached across overhead—the attic of the wigwam. Their hair was so long that as they lay it reached down to the floor. The boy went in. The old men awakened and asked him what he had come for. He told them he was sent by Piu-chunnuh to ask them to come to him. They asked him if he had no other errand. He said he had not. They knew all this before, but they asked the boy to see what he would answer. The boy offered to wait and show them the way, but they told him to go on back for they knew the way and would come alone. They told him they would be there that night; that they must wait until evening before starting, because they never traveled in the daytime and did not wish to be seen by anybody.

So the boy started home, and as soon as he went out of the house the two old men got down out of their beds, and the noise of their alighting was like thunder. They shook out their long hair which reached to the earth, and put on their mystic garments, and prepared for their flight to the south.

But the boy sped on his homeward way like a humming-bird all day long, and at night he reached home. They asked him, "Did they let you in"? "Yes", he said. "They were asleep in high beds placed on poles overhead, each in his own bed; and their hair reached to the ground. Their house was full of all kinds of food—acorns, pine-nuts, manzanita berries, grasshoppers, dried flesh and fish; but there were no women and no cooking." And he said further, "They will come to-night at midnight. When they come the assembly-house must be ready for them; the old men must be in it, and all must be silent and dark. There must be no light and no voice. If any light is made and any one beholds those two old men he shall die."

That night all the old Indians came together into the assembly-hall; but some were on top of it looking and waiting for the two old men. A fire was made at one side of it, but when it burned low it was covered over with ashes lest it should give a light.

That night the two old men left their home in the far north, in the ice-land. Their house was not like a house at all, but it was like a little low mountain. They came out of it and set their faces to the south, and they sped on their way like a humming-bird; and at midnight they reached the home of Piuchunnuh. They alighted on the assembly-house wherein the Indians were assembled; and, as they touched the top of it, it opened and parted asunder in every direction, so that those who were within beheld the blue heavens and the stars. They cried out, "Make room for us", and they came down and stood in an open space before the fire. And when they lifted up their voices to speak the house was full of sweet sounds, like a tree full of singing blackbirds. The heart of Piuchunnuh was filled with joy.

One of the old men had in his hand the sacred rattle (*sho'-lo-yoh*), from which all others since have been modeled—a stick whereon were tied a hundred cocoons, dry, and full of acorns and grass-seed. He said to them, "Always when you sing have this rattle with you, and let it be made after the pattern which I now show you. The spirit of sweet music is in this rattle, and when it is shaken your songs will sound better." Always before this, when Piuchunnuh had prayed, he had held leaves in his hand and waved them. But the old men said, "The leaves are not good. Have this rattle with you when you pray for acorns, and you will get them; or when you pray for grasshoppers, and you will get them. The leaves will bring no fruit when you pray with them."

Now, it was Woannomih who uttered all these words; the other old man was not so eloquent, but he stood behind Woannomih and sometimes put a word in his mouth. Woannomih further said to Piuchunnuh, "Heretofore you have let all your boys grow up like a wild tree in the mountains; you have taught them nothing; they have gone their own way. Henceforth you must bring every youth, at a proper age, into your sacred assembly-house, and cause him to be initiated into the ways and knowledge of manhood. You shall teach him to worship me, and to observe the sacred dances which I shall ordain in my honor." (Before this there had never been any dances among the Konkau, nothing but songs.) He further said, "Three nights we shall teach and instruct you. There must be no light and no voice in this house or you will die. Three nights you must be silent and listen. We need no light; we have light in us. You shall know us in your hearts; you need neither to see nor to touch us."

Thus for two nights they taught the Konkau, and the heart of Piu-chunnuh was full of joy continually so that he could not utter it. But on the third night, before the old Indians had come together, there crept into the assembly-house two wicked boys, whose hearts were black and full of mischief. Standing outside of the house they had overheard some of Woannomih's words, and they said one to another, "Let us get in and take some pitch-pine and make a light in the night; then we can see these old men and see what they look like." Thus they wickedly devised in their hearts and so did they. Secretly they crept into the house and carried with them some pitch-pine.

In the night when Woannomih was talking these boys raked open the fire and threw on the pitch-pine, when suddenly the house was filled with a strong light, and the old men stood out plain in the sight of all. They had on their heads woven nets (*bo-noang'-wi-la)* covered all over with bits of abalone-shell shining like the sun; they wore long mantles (*wu'-shim-chi*) of black eagle's feathers reaching below the knees, with acorns around the edges; shell-spangled breech-cloths; tight leggings of buckskin; and low moccasins (*sho'-loh*) covered with red woodpecker's scalps and pieces of abalone-shell. Their flesh was salmon in one place; in another, grasshopper; in another, deer; in another, antelope, etc. They stood revealed in clear, bright colors, and they shone like fine obsidian.

Near Piuchunnuh there was standing a harlequin or herald (*pe'-i-peh*); it was his office to stand on top of the assembly-house in the evening and proclaim the approaching dance to the villagers. Also, when his chief made a speech, he stood behind him and repeated all his words to the people. When he saw the two boys making the light, he grasped them in his hands and flung them to the ground; but it was too late, the light flamed up in the house. Piuchunnuh covered his face with his hands, so as not to behold Woannomih, and he groaned aloud a groan of bitter despair. But Woannomih spoke quietly on a moment more: "Keep the sacred dance-house, as I have told you, while the world endures. Never neglect my rites and my honors. Keep the sacred rattle and the dances. Worship me in the night, and not in the daylight. In the daytime I will none of it. Then shall your hills be full of acorns and nuts; your valleys shall yield plenty of grass-seed and herbs; your rivers shall be full of salmon, and your hearts shall be rejoiced. Farewell."

Then he ceased speaking, and the two old men rose through the roof, and went up to the valley of heaven (*hi-pi-ning' koy-o-di'*). Very soon the two boys who had kindled the fire were stricken with death; they lay still on the floor, and breathed no more. There was also a woman who had not restrained her curiosity, but had groped about the house, feeling with her hands, if perchance she might touch the two old men   She also fell on the floor quickly and died.

The people went out in the morning, and washed their bodies, and rejoiced. When the sun was up they took food and were glad. But at noon there fell fire out of the sun upon the village, and burned it up to the uttermost house, and all the villages of that land round about, and all the men, women, and children, save Piuchunnuh alone. He escaped because he covered his face with his hands when the fire was kindled by the two boys, but he was dreadfully burned, almost unto death.

Now, long before all these things happened, there lived at Ush'-tu-ped-di (near Chico) a tribe of Indians whose chief was Ki-u-nad'-dis-si. But Hai'-kut-wo-to-peh, one of the two old men of the north, came down and gambled with him. They had four short pieces of bone, two plain and two marked. They rolled them up in little balls of dry grass; then one of the players held up one of them in each hand, and the other held up his. If he matched them, he counted two; if he failed to match them, the other counted one. There were sixteen bits of wood as counters, and when one got the sixteen he was winner. Haikutwotopeh used a trick; his arms were hollow, and there was a hole through his body, so that he could slip his pieces across from one hand to the other and win every time. Kiunaddissi wished to bet bows, arrows, shell-money, etc., as usual; but Haikutwoto-peh would not bet anything but men and women. So he won Kiunaddissi's whole tribe from him, and carried them away to the north, to the ice-land. There remained only Kiunaddissi, his daughter, and an old woman.

So Piuchunnuh went down to Ushtupeddi, and abode there, because they spoke the same language as himself. He taught them all the things which Woannomih had told him, and they observed them, and had plenty of acorns and fish to eat, and were happy.

One day, as the sun was setting, Kiunaddissi's daughter went out and saw a beautiful red cloud, the most lovely cloud ever seen, resting like a bar along the horizon, stretching southward. She cried out to her father, "O, father, come and see this beautiful cloud!" He did so. When they went back into the house they heard, right in their ears, it seemed to them, the sweetest music man ever heard. It continued all the time without stopping, and none of them could tell what caused it.

Next day the daughter took a basket and went out into the plain to gather clover to eat. While picking the clover she found a very pretty arrow, trimmed with yellow-hammer's feathers. After gazing at it awhile in wonder, she turned to look at her basket, and there beside it stood a man who was called Yang-wi'-a-kan-ūh (the Red Cloud), who was none other than the cloud she had seen the day before. He was so bright and resplendent to look upon that she was abashed; she modestly hung down her head and uttered not a word. But he said to her, " I am not a stranger. You saw me last night; you see me every night when the sun is setting. I love you; you love me; look at me; be not afraid." Then she said, "If you love me, take and eat this basket of grass-seed pinole" He touched the basket, and in an instant all the pinole vanished in the air, going no man knows whither. Thereupon the girl fell away in a swoon, and lay a considerable time there upon the ground. But when the man returned to her, behold she had given birth to a son And the girl was abashed, and would not look in his face, but she was full of great joy because of her new-born son. And Yangwiakanuh was glad when he looked at the babe, and he said to her: " You love me now; that is my boy, but he is not of this world. You were born in Ushtupeddi; your father was born in Ushtupeddi. I know all that, but this, my son, is not of this world." Then he placed the babe in her basket, and with him he put in also all weapons which are used by Indians—bows, arrows, spears, slings—but no man saw it. And he said to the mother again: " In less than five days he shall come forth from the basket. He shall be greater than all men; he shall have power over all, and not fear any that lives. Therefore shall his name be Oan-koi′-tu-peh (the Invincible). Whenever you see him, think of me. This boy has no life apart from me; he is myself."

Then his mother took this basket, in which the babe lay, and started to go to her father's house, but when she had gone a little way she turned to look back, and behold Yangwiakanuh was gone out of sight, and no man ever saw him more.

She took her babe home, and secretly went into the assembly-house, and hid him in the basket behind the great basket of acorns. But the child's heart was quick with life, and the beating of it was like the ticking of a bug on the wall. When Kiunaddissi, the child's grandfather, heard the noise, he said to his daughter, "What noise is that? I never heard such a noise as that before." At that the girl was greatly ashamed, but she held her peace.

On the fourth night Kiunaddissi made a sacred dance in the assembly-house, and there was a hot fire of willow-wood. A coal snapped out from it, and fell upon the basket in which was hidden the young child. It burned through the basket, and the child came forth a man full grown, and came down and stood upon the floor. He knew his grandfather, and called him by name. But the old man was overcome with astonishment. He ran and called to his daughter, saying, "Come to me quick; there is a stranger here; he calls me grandfather, but I know nothing of him." His mother came in all haste, weeping, moaning, and wringing her hands, because she knew the five days were not expired, and she feared evil would befall her child. When the lad spoke to the old man again, he replied, "You are not my grandson. My daughter has no husband."

But when the mother entered, she cried out, "My son! my son!" She led him and seated him on a clean board, washed his face and hands, and her heart was full of joy. He sat there; he looked all around; he knew all things beforehand. He took note of all the deadly snakes, the deadly beasts, the diseases, the fatal quagmires wherein men sank and perished, and he said to them that all the men who had perished by these means in other times had gone to the land of good spirits. He asked his grandfather what meant all the round pits about them. He told him that once a great people had lived there, but their chief had gambled them all away in captivity, and these pits were the places where their houses had stood. He told him also the story of Piuchunnuh and his people. Oankoitupeh knew all this before, but he asked, to hear what they would reply. He wanted to know the way in which this gambling was done, and his grandfather showed him. He wished to try his luck with Haikutwotopeh, but they earnestly warned him against it, and begged him with tears not to do it. But he said, "I fear no man. I am greater than all." He wanted to show them the trick by which Haikutwotopeh had won all the tribe, but they besought him not to attempt it. But his mother did not, for she knew in her heart that he could not die, because his father had said it.

There was an old she-devil, as tall as a great pine in the mountains, who could at pleasure assume the form of man or woman. She wanted to kill Oankoitupeh. She could, when she pleased, look young and beautiful as a speckled fawn. She called to him, "Oankoitupeh! Oankoitupeh!" and lured him to the forest, though his grandfather earnestly begged him not to follow her. But he went with all his war-weapons (which have been models to the Konkau ever since), and met the old she-devil. He touched her, and she fell to the earth before him. She said to him, "Poor child! you were born with a crooked back. I saw you; nobody helped you; you were born without a father. But I can straighten your back if you will let me."

There was, in the foothills near Chico, a straight, smooth rock, just the length of a man, which had a hole in the middle of it, made by pounding acorns in it, This rock can be seen here to this day. She led him to it, and told him to lay off his bow and arrows, his sling, spear, belt, and feathers. He did so. Then he went a little aside, knelt down by a rock, and prayed; and he listened for the great voice of Nature to tell him what to do. The voice told him that she meant to kill him, but that he must do as she bade him, and have an eye in his back to put him on his guard. He came back, and lay down on the rock face upward; but the old hag told him he must lie down back upward. This he did, and then she came and stood over him, and lifted a stone far up almost to the sky, and brought it down as if to crush him with one tremendous blow. He did not wince. A second time she lifted the great stone into the sky, but again he did not wince when she brought it down. A third time she brought it down in earnest, but just before it reached him he turned quickly on his side, and the mighty stone, descending, smote on the rock close beside him with the noise of thunder, and splintered it into a thousand pieces. The hag was stricken with amazement and fear; she fell prone upon the earth. Oankoitupeh, drawing his knife of flint, with one plunge cut out her heart and lungs, and taking them on his spear carried them home and gave them to his grandfather; but the old hag he burned.

There was a large and fierce black eagle in that country which had killed many Indians in former times. Oankoitupeh wished to go and kill it, but his grandfather begged him with tears not to attempt it. But again he prayed and listened for the great voice of Nature to tell him what to do. Before that they had sought to snare the eagle with a net, but he always broke it and destroyed many Indians. Now Oankoitupeh prepared a trap, with which he caught him as he issued from the hole in the tree where he lived, and so he killed him. Then he ripped out his heart and lungs and carried them to his grandfather; but the body he burned, and out of the ashes there arose the woodpecker as we see it to-day.

These two exploits of Oankoitupeh were received by his friends with unbounded joy; each time, as he returned home after it, he was welcomed with a dance and with songs of triumph.

He was now ready to go on his great mission to the north, to expose the trick of Haikutwotopeh, and recover his grandfather's lost tribe from bondage. All four of his friends wished to go with him, but he said they could not go with him unless they first died. So they died, three of them, and they set out together with him, leaving the old woman behind. They traveled far over the earth, then waded on the bottom underneath the great and deep sea, then across the ice to the home of Haikutwotopeh. Haikutwotopeh knew that he was come, and felt in his heart that he was greater than himself. He said to Oankoitupeh, "I felt in my heart that you had come. Perhaps you are greater than I." But Oankoitupeh said, "No; I have done nothing great." Kiunaddissi said, "You won all my tribe by gambling, and all your land is full of people." Haikutwotopeh answered,

"You may gamble and win them back if you can. You are free to do that, but you cannot carry them away by force or fraud."

So they sat down together in the assembly-house, Oankoitupeh and Haikutwotopeh, to gamble for the lost tribe. First, Oankoitupeh staked his grandfather and Piuchunnuh against the tribe. They played a quick game, and Oankoitupeh lost. Then he had only his mother left, and he staked her. Oankoitupeh lost one counter after another, until all the sixteen were gone but one. The fate of his mother and of her tribe hung on that one counter. Haikutwotopeh became bold; he played recklessly. At this moment Oankoitupeh asserted his secret power. He stopped the hole through his opponent's arm and body, and opened one in his own. He now won back piece after piece; he gained the whole sixteen. The game was won; his mother was saved, and the whole tribe redeemed. They came over to their rescuer with shouts of great joy; they were as numerous as the trees of the thick forest.

So they came out of the icy assembly-house, and the friends of Oankoitupeh rejoiced over his splendid victory. Then Oankoitupeh proposed a second game, and offered to bet his tribe against Haikutwotopeh's own tribe. He said to him, "You gambled with my grandfather in other days, and won his whole tribe. You ought to have been satisfied to bet bows, arrows, money, etc., but you would bet only men and women. You might as well have bet the earth itself, the rivers, the mountains, the rocks; only you could not have carried these away if you had won them. I will not gamble with you for your lands and your rivers, but only for your people."

They sat down in the assembly-house again and played, and Oankoitupeh won. Even before the game was ended, the tribe of Haikutwotopeh were eager to go over to Oankoitupeh, but he said to them, "No; you must wait; my people did not wish to come over before they were won".

Then they all set out together for the far distant Ushtupeddi. But long before they arrived, the old woman who was left behind knew that Oankoitupeh was alive and had gained the victory. There was a quail's-head plume in her house, and she saw it waver and flutter; also, when she went out-doors, she saw the grass and flowers in a gentle tremor. If he had been dead or beaten in the game, all these things would have been lifeless.

When they arrived at Ushtupeddi there was great rejoicing among the long-lost tribe over their restoration. Oankoitupeh was then surely known as the son of the Red Cloud, and he was held in great honor. Every tribe was restored to its old original place, and every village to its own place on the face of the earth, and there was no confusion. Every valley received back its own proper inhabitants, as was ordained at the first by Ko'-do-yam-peh (the World-Maker), who was also called Woan'-no-mih.

Oankoitupeh now assembled all the people together in a great convocation, and pointed out to them Piuchunnuh and Kiunaddissi as examples for their perpetual imitation or avoidance. He related to them the sad history of both these two men's tribes, and showed them how disobedience to the commands of Woannomih had brought ruin and death upon them. He rehearsed to them their history in the dreary ice-land, and pointed out the beautiful contrasts of their own land, to which they were now happily restored. He adjured them to remember the precepts of the religion which they were now to receive from Woannomih through the lips of these two old chiefs and himself. Let them never return to the brutish worship of their ancestors, who prayed to the rocks, the rivers, and the hills; but let them rather pray to Woannomih. He told them never to forget or neglect the assembly-hall, the house of religion and of the sacred song and dance; they should never suffer any village to be without one while the world endures. If they continued faithful in the worship of Woannomih, and at any time their oak trees did not yield acorns, or their rivers did not afford them salmon, and their prophets prayed to him, they should receive abundance.

He said it would be allowed to them to have their pleasures as before; to have all kinds of songs and dances—dances of war and of friendship, scalp dances and acorn dances; to indulge in foot races and in trials of skill with the bow and arrow and the sling, and all kinds of plays with the ball and racket, with gambling and betting, etc. But in betting they must bet only such articles as were counted property, and must never more wager men and women, as their foolish ancestors did, thereby losing their tribe.

Let the man be accursed who should ever bet his father or mother or any of his tribe in a game of chance.

He told them also that they must no longer burn their dead, but bury them in the earth. Last of all, he appointed unto them four great dances or festivals, to be held once a year as long as the world endures, namely these: Hōk'-tŏm-we-dah (the open-air festival), in the spring; I'-lak-kum-we-dah (the dry-season festival), about the first of July; Ush'-ti-moh (the burning to the dead), about the first of September; and Yak'-kai-we-dah (the winter festival), about the last of December.

When Oankoitupeh had made an end of speaking to his people, he disappeared from before their eyes, rose upward toward the valley of heaven, and was seen no more on earth in human form. But when his people cried out and wailed in bitterness of heart, and ran after him, wringing their hands, to comfort them he appeared once more in the form of a great and splendid rainbow, spanning the earth from side to side. He lingered before them a moment in this form, then faded away in the skies.

In accordance with the injunctions in the above legend, the Konkau established and have maintained to this day a secret society which is called Ku'-meh (literally the "assembly-house" or "dance-house", though it may be rendered the "Order of Manhood"). Boys are initiated into it at the age of about twelve, or, in case of sober, thoughtful boys, a year or two younger. Not all youths are taken into membership, although the older members are good propagandists, and use strenuous exertions to bring in the youngsters of their acquaintance. They tell them that if they do not join they will be devoured by wild beasts, or fall over precipices, or be drowned, and their spirits will go the left-hand path into darkness. Nothing is revealed to them beforehand, and boys are often reluctant to join, having heard from outsiders fearful stories of the doings inside.

There is no grip or password for admission into the sacred house. When a member approaches he simply says to the doorkeeper, "Ni'-hai ye'-pom-mi ku'-meh" (I belong to the order). The services are called wa-tai'-i-teh. When a neophyte is initiated, after the services are over the old members in turn place their right hands on his left shoulder. A new name, his virile name, which is generally that of his father or some other near relative, is then added to his baby-name. For ten days following the initiation he must refrain from all flesh meat, and eat nothing but acorn-porridge.

113 As a special favor the Konkau on Round Valley Reservation permitted a few of us to witness (or rather hear) one of their secret meetings, for everything is shrouded in profound darkness. When we entered the lodge of Tūm′-yan-neh (Captain George)—they had no assembly-house—they requested us to extinguish our lanterns. There was a feeble fire in the middle of the house, but before anything was done one of the sextons covered it all up, and several times during the exercises, when the smallest possible spark of fire became visible through the ashes, we would see something creep stealthily over it and it would wink out.

There was a silence of some minutes in the impenetrable darkness, then the sacred rattle (described in the above legend) began a low, ominous quivering close to the ground, in which there was sufficient suggestion of a rattlesnake to make one feel chilly about the scalp. Presently one of the four performers, apparently lying on his belly and holding his mouth close to the ground, began to give forth a series of blubbering, gurgling sounds and nasal whining, with frequent intermissions, growing shorter all the while as the tone of his voice rose. At the same time the rattle rose up slowly, gaining a little in force, until finally it shot up all at once, and seemed to dart about the top of the room with amazing rapidity, giving forth terrific rattles and low, buzzing quavers, now and then bringing up against the post with a thud of the holder's fist.

One of the performers now begins to utter petitions with a rapid mumbling, to which another responds simply *heh!* (yes), or with a few words, or by repeating the petition. This strange fanfaronade goes on for several minutes, then all of the four performers strike up a verse of the sacred songs (given below), which they repeat six or eight times, accompanied by all in the house, in a low voice ; then there is a sharp *sh!* quickly followed by a "tiger". This is done four or five times ; then another verse of the song is taken up. When they have sung for about half or three-quarters of an hour without cessation the rattle grows fast and furious, the performer's fist goes tunk, tunk, tunk on the post with great violence, the singers' voices sink into a long-drawn, dying wail; then all at once comes a sharp *sh!* and a tremendous "tiger". The rattle drops to the ground and seems to hover close over it, darting in every direction, and only two of the performers are heard, groveling on the ground and muttering petitions and responses, until finally the rattle dies slowly out, the voices hush, and all is over. The fire is quickly raked open, straw and splinters are thrown on it, a blaze springs up, laughing and talking begin again, and cigarettes are lighted.

The Indians seize this breathing time to interpret to us the songs, and to explain that the petitions were for the blessings of Woannomih on their tribe, and the petitions last heard were for blessings on the fire about to be uncovered. After smoking and chatting a few minutes they cover up the fire again, and the programme above given is repeated; but the second time we find it monotonous and wearisome. The reader will understand, if he knows anything about Indian habits, that there was a great deal introduced into this performance which no man can describe or imitate—unutterable groans, hissings, mutterings, and repetitions, with which the savage so delights to envelop his sacred exercises.

SACRED SONGS OF THE KONKAU.

RED CLOUD'S SONG.

[Heard by the mother of Oan-koi'-tu-peh]

Yang-wi'-a-kan-u mai'-dum-ni.
I am the Red Cloud.
Hi-pi-ning' koi-o-di' nik bai'-shum yan'-u-nom mai'-dum-ni.
My father formed me out of the sky.
Lu'-lūl yan'-dih oi'-yih nai.
I sing [among] the mountain flowers.
Yi'-wi yan'-dih oi'-yih nai.
I sing [among] the flowering chamize of the mountains.
Wēk'-wēk yan'-dih ci'-yih nai.
I sing in the mountains [like] the *wēk'-wēk*.
Wēk'-wēk o'-di so'-liu nai.
I sing [among] the rocks [like] the *wēk'-wēk*.
Lai'-dam yan'-dih we'-we nai.
In the morning I cry in the mountains.
Lai'-dam bo u'-ye nai.
In the morning I walk the path.
Lai'-dam lūl'-luh we'-we nai.
I cry [to] the morning stars.

OAN-KOI'-TU-PEH'S SONG.

Yu-dik-no' hel-ai-no', na'-kum yo'-wo, ha'-le ni.
I go to the north. I will win all, I begin [to gamble].

Yo'-wo, yo'-wun nim, yun' ni-ni.
I will win, I will win, I will win.
Dūm'-lan-no di kŭl'-leng wo'-man-di.
The women weep in the shadows [of the assembly-hall].
Lai'-dam lĭl'-lim win nai'-nai ku'-lem ni.
I twinkle [like] the morning star, my father (i. e., I am vanishing in the sky).
Hi-pi-ning' koi-o-di', ko-wi'-cho-nung koi-o-di'.
The valley of heaven, I approach the valley [of heaven].
Hi-pi-ning' koi-o-di' ye'-wo nai.
[Now] I run up the valley of heaven.
Hi-pi-ning' koi-o-di', nĭk'-ki koi-o-di'.
The valley of heaven, mine [is] the valley [of heaven].
Hi-pi-ning' koi-o-di' lel'-ūng-ku-ku wuh'-wuh toan nai.
I strike the heaven-reaching, sounding string, (literal, *wuh-wuh*-string).

THE ACORN SONG.

Hu'-tim yo'-kĭm koi-o-di'.
The acorns come down from heaven.
Wi'-hi yan'-ning koi-o-di'.
I plant the short acorns in the valley.
Lo'-whi yan'-ning koi-o-di'.
I plant the long acorns in the valley.
Yo-ho' nai-ni', hal-u'-dom yo nai, yo-ho' nai-nim'.
I sprout, I, the black-oak acorn, sprout, I sprout.

PI-U'-CHUN-NUH'S SONG.

We-le'-u-deh Pi-u'-chun-nuh nai'-i-ni.
I, Pi-u'-chun-nuh, am in We-le'-u-deh.
Wi'-no mai'-keh we'-we nai.
I cry everywhere, like the boys (i. e., the young choristers).
We-le-leh' tūm-bo'.
Foggy is the path to We-le'-u-deh.
Win'-na, win'-na koi-o-di'.
Bright, bright is the valley.
Lu'-yeh, lu'-yem yan'-dih.
All, all [are in] the assembly-hall.
Pal'-a-kum bo u'-ye nai.
I walk the red-feather path.
Pok'-al-mam bo u'-ye nai.
I walk the white-feather path.
Ko'-i me'-lu me'-lu nai.
[Like] the white goose I sing, I sing.
Yu'-yem yan'-dih yu'-yem nai.
I put out all from the assembly-hall.
Tai-u-man -ing ya-ma-na' loi'-e-mo to nai'-i-nih.
I throw together the mountains and the west mountains (i. e., the Sierra Nevada and the Coast Range).

KI-U-NAD'-DIS-SI'S SONG.

Yo-iu' nin-nin' yo-iu' nin-nim'.
I am the only one, the only one [left].
Wa'-pum dat'-pan ka'-no-mai, si'-wing ku'-no ka'-no-mai, en'-ak wi'-wung ka'-no-mai.
An old man, I carry the gambling-board; an old man, I sing the gambling song.
Wai'-i pen'-noam so-loap'-kum.

The roots I eat of the valley.
Su'-i-bang kut-dul-lul'.
The pepper-ball is round.
Mo'-mih til-lak' til-lak'-keh.
The water trickles, trickles.
Ta-a'-ti-ti yin-no-di' ti'-is bum'-bum.
The water-leaves grow along the river bank.
Wi-li-pesh-o-yeh' nau'-nih, būk-wi-lai'-lai.
I rub the hands, I wiggle the tail (*i. e.*, I am gambling, from the motions made).
Yo'-mih mai'-i-ni, yo'-mih mi'-mi-teh.
I am a doctor, I am a doctor.

HAI'-KUT-WO-TO-PEH'S SONG.

[Sung when Oan-kol'-tu-peh approached.]

Yu-dik-noam' bo u'-ye ni ?
Do you come from the north ? (lit., the path to the north).
Ko-mo-wim' bo u'-ye ni ?
Do you come from the east ?
Tai bo u'-ye ni ?
Do you come from the west ?
Ka'-nai bo u'-ye ni ?
Do you come from the south ?
Hi-pi-ning' bo-o-di' u'-ye-ni ?
Do you come from above ?
Ko'-do ka'-na-neh u'-ye ni ?
Do you come from below ?

In the acorn song, as above given, it will be observed that it appears to be spoken by two different persons. The first three verses are attributed by some Indians to Oankoitupeh, and by others to the Red Cloud. The latter would seem to be more poetically correct. Then the last line is evidently spoken by the acorn personified. I have grouped both these together, and called it all the acorn song, but the Indians sing them somewhat confusedly, as indeed they do the other songs more or less. It required a great deal of patient labor to construct order out of their chaos; and even now I am not always positive, for some Indians will attribute a given verse to one of the personages and others to another. Besides that, the interpretation is sometimes a little uncertain, principally, I think, for the reason that a number of the words either belong to an occult, priestly language, or are so antiquated that the modern Indians, in the absence of most of their old men and prophets, are unable to agree absolutely upon their meaning. I have tabulated below all the archaic forms occurring in these songs, the meaning of which the Indians were agreed upon.

	MODERN.	ARCHAIC.
Sing.	so′-lin.	oi′-yih, me′-lu.
Flowering chamize.	hi′-bi.	yi′-wi.
Everywhere.	i′-bi-deh.	wi′-no.
Bright.	yo′-nak-muk-ka.	win′-na.
Level.	muh′-pi-teh.	yo′-nah.
North.	no′-to	yu-dik-no′.
East.	ko′-mo.	ko-mo-wim′.
Path.	bo.	bo-o-di′.
Throw.	hoal′-yeh.	loi′-e.
Together.	wik′-koh.	mo′-to.
All.	lak′-o.	lu′-yeh.
Grow.	hü′-no.	bum′-bum.
I.	ni′-hai.	nai.

The reader has doubtless observed the great number of forms for the pronoun of the first person—*nai, mai′-dum-ni, nim, ni′-ni, nai-nim′, nai-ni′, nan′-nih, mai′-i-ni, mi′-mi-teh.*

The white goose is sacred among the Konkau; they call it "God's bird". Its name *ko′-i* is formed from its cry *kauh!* They and other tribes of the Maidu (especially about Yuba City) make beautiful robes of its down.

The Indians use the same word, *yandih,* in the song, to denote "assembly-house" and "mountain"; it is abbreviated from *ya′-man-deh.*

In the same assembly-hall where these sacred rites are observed they sometimes have comic entertainments which correspond to the acrobatic part of our circuses. It is necessary to state, however, that they are inferior even as purely muscular performances to the corresponding displays of civilization. Among other things the Indians themselves admit that they never witnessed or conceived of either a handspring or a somersault before they became acquainted with the Americans; and that the gymnastic feats which they see in our circuses surpass anything ever compassed by their own athletes.

The performer in those shows is called *pé-i-peh,* which is also the title

of the prompter or repeater to the chief. He is more properly a clown than 114
a tumbler or an athlete. One of his most "taking" performances is to pretend that a bear has crawled under the hollow slab which is used for a drum,
whereupon he fastens him in, and seizing something which is supposed to
represent his tail he twists it until Bruin roars lustily. Then he binds
up straws and splinters into a bundle about as large as one's little finger,
and with prodigious effort, grunting and staggering, he lifts it on his back,
and tries to carry it, but falls sprawling all along on his belly, crushed to
the earth by his enormous burden. Next, he offers somebody an (empty)
basket of soup, pretending that it is very, very heavy. He smells it and
smacks his mouth over it, and makes motions as if taking swallows of it
and licking his lips. Then when the receiver takes it and places it to his
lips he raises it up so far in the effort to get some soup out of it that he falls
over backward. Now, perhaps, he mounts the roof of the house with a
fish-gig in his hand, and after many false starts and absurd flourishes he
thrusts his spear into a fish prepared for the purpose, driving it in with a
comically surperfluous force all the way through from its snout to the uttermost tip of its tail, and perhaps a yard beyond. The fish flounces about to
such a degree that he requires the assistance of eight or ten men to land
him, and these all tug frantically at the spear, and finally they get their
legs tangled up and fall in a heap together. Another performance they have
which is more properly acrobatic than those previously described. The
clown (sometimes two), showily and fantastically arrayed in feathers and
paint, climbs a pole and hangs head downward from a cross-bar and sings,
while a company dance underneath. Four men stand close together and
join hands; then four others climb up on their shoulders, standing up, and
four more on top of these; then those underneath walk about, and the
twelve join in singing.

All this tumbling and tomfoolery goes under the general name of
kuk'-kun, and "brings down the house" with irrepressible laughter, for the
simple savages are very easily amused.

Another feat, called *yan'-i-nih*, is executed in the following manner:
Three or more men stand in a ring, and by bending their legs they hook
them together in such a manner that each of them stands on one foot. In

this attitude they hop around the house, singing and making grimaces, and generally end by falling down in a heap. There is still another resource which these aboriginal merry-andrews draw upon, and that is to call nick-names. Thus Captain George was called by the name O-kú-dik-noam (he who prays to the rocks). They generally bring into these nicknames some humorous allusion to an idiosyncrasy, which produces much merriment.

These performers are not professionals, and no stated admission-fee is charged, but the audience are expected to give them presents—shell-money, painted arrows, ear-ornaments, etc.

CHAPTER XXXI.

THE NI-SHI-NAM.

Several pioneers, including General Bidwell, classify as one nation all the Indians from Big Chico Creek to American River or the Cosumnes. They were chiefly acquainted with the tribes on the plains, and so far as these are concerned I do not object to the classification; but I prefer to group together all the mountain Indians from Bear River to the Cosumnes as a separate nation for several reasons:

1. Difference in the names used by the Indians. North of Bear River, it is *mai'-du, mai'-deh;* south, it is *ni-shi-nam, má-na, mai'-dek.* All these words denote simply "men" or "Indians", though *nishinam* seems to mean "our people", from *ni-sham,* a dialectic form for "we".

2. The criterion of the numerals is not infallible, though it is a tolerably correct guide in determining linguistic affinities. In a language abounding in dialects the numerals sometimes are more subject to change than any other words in equally common use; sometimes less. I give below a table of numerals, both Maidu and Nishinam, taken in the following places respectively: the first column in Concow Valley, the second at Chico, the third at Auburn, the fourth at Latrobe.

	KONKAU.	YUBA.	NISHINAM.	WAPUMNI.
One.	wuk'-teh.	wuk'-teh.	wut'-teh.	wit'-ti.
Two.	pe'-nim.	pa'-nem.	pen'.	pen'.
Three.	sha'-pwi.	sha'-pwi.	sa'-pwi.	sa'-pwi.
Four.	ch'u'-yeh.	chu'-yeh.	chu'-i.	chu'-i.
Five.	ma-cha'neh.	ma-cha'-nem.	mauk.	mâ'-wek.
Six.	sai'-so-ko.	shai'-cho-ko.	tim'-bo.	tum'-bo.
Seven.	pen-nem'-bo.	pa'-nem-boh.	top'-wi.	pe'-nem-boh.
Eight.	s'u'-ye-so-ko.	ma'-hi-cho-ko.	pent'-swi.	pen'-chu-i.
Nine.	ch'e'-nem-a-cho-ko.	he'-wal-li.	pel'-loh.	chu'-im-boh.
Ten.	ma'-cho-ko.	ma'-cho-ko.	ma'-chum.	ma'-chum.

115

3. South of Bear River, the tribes are designated almost entirely by the points of the compass, while north of it they have fixed names.

4. The customs of the Nishinam are different from those of the Maidu in important respects, and especially in that very few of the former observe the great annual dance for the dead.

As to language, the Maidu shades away so gradually into the Nishinam that it is extremely difficult to draw the line anywhere. But it must be drawn somewhere, because a vocabulary taken down on Feather River will lose three-fourths of its words before it reaches the Cosumnes. Even a vocabulary taken on Bear River will lose half or more of its words in going to the Cosumnes, which denotes, as is the case, that the Nishinam language varies greatly within itself. It is probably less homogeneous and more thronged with dialects than any other tongue in California. Let an Indian go even from Georgetown to American Flat, or from Bear River to Auburn, and, with the exception of the numerals, he may not at first understand above one word in four or five or six. But with this small stock in common, a great many others nearly the same and recognizable after being spoken a few times, and the same laws of grammar to guide them, they pick up each others' dialects with amazing rapidity. It is these wide variations which have caused some pioneers to believe that there is one tongue spoken on the plains around Sacramento and another in the mountains; whereas they are as nearly identical as the mountain dialects are.

So long as the numerals remain the same, or nearly the same, I count it one language, and so long as this is the case the Indians generally learn each others' languages; but when the numerals change utterly they often find it easier to speak English together than to acquire another tongue.

As to the southern boundary of the Nishinam there is no doubt, for at the Cosumnes the language changes abruptly and totally. As to the northern, the Yuba River villages could be classed indifferently with the Nishinam or the Maidu.

Like all others, the Nishinam name every camp, spring, flat, prominent hill, river, etc, but they very seldom use the name of a camp or village, as others do, to denote the inhabitants of it. Whatever Indians live east of them they call easterners, and if there is a rancheria a little farther east, they vary the form. Thus they use No'-to, No-to-nan', and No-toang'-kau which may be rendered "easters", "easterns", and "easterners". So contracted are their journeyings and their knowledge that they do not need a complicated system of names. If there are any people living twenty miles away they are not aware of their existence. In consequence of this it was almost impossible for me to learn any fixed names of tribes. There are the Pu-su'-na, at the mouth of American River, north side; the Kwoto'-a, at Placerville; the Ko-lo'-ma, at Coloma; and the Wa-pum'-ni, near Latrobe. Indeed, I doubt if there is any considerable number of tribal names, for they are such a nomadic nation (within small limits) that they exist in a continual chaos. They move their camps so often that they have not even names for them, properly speaking; that is, no name separate and apart from that of the spring, bowlder, tree, creek, or what not, where they happen at any particular time to be camping. Hence, in designating one another, they always use the points of the compass—*to'-shim, ko'-mo, no'-to, tai* (north, south, east, west)—in various forms; and those living near Bear River always add *kau* (place), as Tâ'-sing-kau, Ko-moang'-kau, No-toang'-kau, Taing'-kau.

There are also some curious peculiarities in regard to personal names. One can very seldom learn an Indian's and never a squaw's Indian name, though they will tell their American titles readily enough. It is a greater breach of decorum to ask a squaw her name than it is among us to ask a lady her age. I have often made the attempt and never yet have learned a squaw's Indian name from her own lips. A husband never calls his wife by name on any account, and it is said that divorces have been produced *Fig. 27* by no other provocation than that. It is amusing to note the resemblances between feminine human nature in the aboriginal and the civilized state. No squaw will reveal her own name, but she will tell all her neighbors' that she can think of. For the reason above given many people believe that half the squaws have no names at all. So far is this from the truth that every one possesses at least one and sometimes two or three. Hel'-la Ni-o'-chi-chit was mentioned as an instance of two; and He'-wal-la Kle'-gli Num'-num of three. As usual in California a great majority of the names have no significance, being merely such collections of sounds as are euphonious to their ears.   If one has any meaning it is generally the name of some animal.

Following is a formidable list of villages which once lined the banks of Bear River from Sacramento up to the foot-hills, a list which shows that the population must have been dense: Ha'-mi-ting-Wo'-li-yuh, Le'-li-ki-an, Ta'-lak, In'-tan-to, Mu-lam'-cha-pa (long pond by the trees), Lid'-li-pa, So'-lak-i-yu, Ka'-lu-plo, Pa'-kan-chi, Sho-kum-im'-lep-pi (wild potato place), Bu'-sha-mül (this was near the California and Oregon railroad crossing), Shu'-ta-mūl, Chu'-em-duh, O'pel-to (the forks), Pu'-lak-a-tu, Ka'-pa-ka, Yo-ko'-lim-duh and Toan'-im-but-tuk (little pine).

These are, in fact, only the names of localities where camps once stood; and the list may not include a half or a third of all the camp-sites which an old Indian of good memory could recall.   On Bear River, and in fact along all the low bottom-lands in the Sacramento Valley, there are frequently to be seen flat, wide mounds which were raised by the Indians for house-sites to keep them above the reach of floods in the rainy season.

116   It is often asserted by Californians that the malarial diseases now prevalent along Bear River and other streams in the great interior basin date only back to the beginning of the mining operations, which caused great masses of *débris* to accumulate in the river-beds, thereby throwing the water out over the lowlands.   On the contrary, it is asserted by the earliest pioneers, among others Claude Cheney, who settled on Bear River about 1846, that the Indians even at that day were much subject to fever and ague and other diseases resulting from malarial influences.   To avoid these they not only built the low mounds for their houses above mentioned, but the lowland tribes, by permission of those living in the foot-hills and mountains, went up into the latter regions to spend a portion of the hotter months of the summer.   But, of course, it was only a part of any tribe that could make this annual migration, and that principally the hunters, for the women had to remain behind in sufficient force to gather the wild grain and seeds which were their principal food-supply, and which they required for exchange with the mountaineers in return for acorns and mazanita berries.

And yet, notwithstanding the rather unhealthy condition of the lowlands, large families of children were common in early days.

Bear River they call Nem Se'-u (great river); the Sacramento, Nep'-em Se'u (greater river); the plains, Tu'-kü-di; the timber-land, Cha'-pa, Cha'-pa-di; the foot-hills, Ya'-mun, Ya'-mun-di; the Sierra Nevada, Nep'-em Ya'-mun (greater hills); the Coast Range, Tai'-a-mun (western hills).

Both in their social customs and in their political organization the Nishinam must be ranked on a low grade, probably the lowest in the State. They had the misfortune to occupy the heart of the Sierra mining region, in consequence of which they have been miserably corrupted and destroyed. Indians in the mining districts, for reasons not necessary to specify, are always worse debauched than those in the agricultural regions. And the fact that most observers and writers have seen the Indians of the diggings more than any others has contributed to bring the whole California race into unmerited opprobrium.

Let the following facts bear witness to their low aboriginal estate: Robert Gordon, a responsible citizen of Auburn, states that in 1849 he was surface-mining from Auburn as far up as the North Fork of Feather River, and that a great proportion of the men and women who entered his camp were costumed strictly after the fashion-plates of Eden. This was in a region pretty well up in the mountains, where the aborigines had not yet come in contact with Europeans. Both sexes and all ages moved about his camp, absolutely *in puris naturalibus*, with that perfect freedom and innocence which betoken unconsciousness of any impropriety. But these simple, unswathed mountaineers, according to the same good authority, were often of a magnificent physique, tall, sinewy fellows, who would have made the scale-beam kick at 180.

Most tribes in the State lay considerable emphasis on the formal establishment of marital relations in their way, that is by purchase, whether those relations are faithfully observed afterward or not. But the Nishinam may be said to set up and dissolve the conjugal estate almost as easily as do the brute beasts. No stipulated payment is made for the wife. A man seeking to become a son-in-law is bound to cater (*ye'-lin*) or make presents to the family, which is to say, he will come along some day with a deer on his shoulder, perhaps fling it off on the ground before the wigwam, and go his way without a single word being spoken. Some days later he may

bring along a brace of hare or a ham of grizzly-bear meat, or some fish, or
a string of hâ'-wok. He continues to make these presents for awhile, and
if he is not acceptable to the girl and her parents they return him an
equivalent for each present (to return his gifts would be grossly insulting;)
but if he finds favor in their eyes they are quietly appropriated; and in
due course of time he comes and leads her away, or comes to live at her
house, for both practices prevail.

When a Nishinam wife is childless her sympathizing female friends
sometimes make out of grass a rude image of a baby, and tie it in a minia-
ture baby-basket, according to the Indian custom. Some day, when the
woman and her husband are not at home, they carry this grass baby and
lay it in their wigwam. When she returns and finds it, she takes it up,
holds it to her breast, pretends to nurse it, and sings it lullaby-songs.
All this is done as a kind of conjuration, which they hope will have the
effect of causing the barren woman to become fertile.

I will relate an incident which shows the despotic and arbitrary power
that a husband, even before marriage, exercises. A man living on Wolf
Creek, a tributary of Bear River, had performed the simple acts which
entitled him to his wife, and the day had arrived when he determined to
bring her home. But she loathed him, and when she saw him coming she
fled from her father's wigwam and sought refuge, trembling and weeping,
with a motherly old widow who sympathized with her. The widow concealed her as well as she could, then hastened out to confront her pursuers.
When they came up she told them the girl had passed that way and escaped
from the village. They hurried on in pursuit, but returned after a long
search, baffled and angry, and asked the widow's little girl if she knew
where the fugitive was. The child innocently told them she was hidden in
her mother's wigwam. As soon as they had dragged her forth, they drew
their bows and arrows and shot the widow to death in the middle of the
village. They were not molested, for the general feeling was that the
bridegroom owned the girl, and that the widow in concealing her was guilty
of kidnapping, for which the penalty is death.

The Nishinam are the most nomadic of all the California tribes within
narrow bounds. They shift their lodges perpetually, if only a rod, prob-

ably to give the vermin the slip ; and always after a death has occurred in one they abandon it.   Nomadic habits among savages of a low grade are little better than death to the aged and infirm, for they cannot readily follow, and the few poor conveniences and comforts which they collect around themselves when stationary have often to be abandoned.   In fact, it would be hard for a tribe to devise a better way of ridding themselves of those whom they accounted burdensome.   The spectacle which is sometimes presented among the mining towns of poor, old, purblind, tattered wretches, perhaps laden with all they can carry, feebly tottering after the stronger ones, is a melancholy and pitiable one indeed.   They wander about much more now than they did before the Americans came among them, because they have been jostled out of their ancient narrow limits, are fewer in number, and can roam widely without trespassing on the soil of some neighboring little village.   Then, too, let it be remembered that these removes really amount to nothing, for they go to and fro, and it is very seldom that a Nishinam, after all his infinite little migrations, dies a mile from the place 117 of his birth.   They are thoroughly home-loving and home-keeping (counting a certain valley or flat a home), like all California Indians.

As for their political organization, like the snakes of Ireland, it can be described in three words : there is none.   True, they have their hereditary captains, or headmen, in the villages, but their authority is the most shadowy thing in the world.

The origin of government is something like this : We will suppose there is a secession, and a village establishes an independent existence.   A large, round dance-house is built, and the prominent men entertain their friends in it in a succession of feasts, which are very bald affairs indeed, so far as the viands are concerned.   They make presents to their followers according to their wealth—shell-money, bows and arrows, etc.   Always at these gatherings there is a great deal of petty bickering and quarreling.   The more earnest and grave old men of the tribe notice these matters ; they observe the aspirant whose personal influence is most successful in keeping order among the young fellows.   He is finally pitched on as the leader, and on a certain day he is informally proclaimed in the dance-house and makes a talk to them, wearing or displaying all his beadery.   If he has not enough to enable him to make a suitable appearance, his friends lend him a few strings, and they are returned to them after the proclamation.

For murder there is no punishment but individual revenge. That must be had within twelve moons after the murder, for there is a kind of statute of limitations which steps in then and forbids any further seeking of blood. They consider that the keenest and most bitter revenge which a man can take is not to slay the murderer himself, but his dearest friend. This, however, is probably only the sentiment of casual Indians, though it would comport well with the subtle Asiatic character of the race.

For kidnaping, as above mentioned, the punishment was death. It is related that a chief, named Ba-kal'-lim-pun, living near Bear River, in 1851, kidnaped a number of women from his own tribe, and sold them to the Spaniards for infamous uses. On detecting him in his villainies the Indians put him to death, and then hacked him into a thousand little pieces. They would throw an eye to one of his fellow-villagers, a finger-joint to another, a toe-joint to another, etc. It should, however, be borne in mind that the California Indians did not torture persons while alive.

For adultery with a foreigner the penalty was also death; and there are few other tribes in the State of whom this can be affirmed. In 1850, a squaw was sacrificed by her people on Dry Creek, near Georgetown, for this offense, committed with an American, though there was really no criminality on her part. The profanation of the loathed foreigner was upon her, and all her tears and cries were of no avail.

They did not mark their boundaries by artificial signs, though they had them defined with the greatest strictness by springs (*pokkan*), hills (*yamun*), valleys (*húnumchuka*), etc. They did not ordinarily destroy a member of another tribe for trespassing on their territory, but if he caught fish or game, or gathered acorns on it, they demanded reparation in kind They were frequently at war with the Pai-u'-ti, whom they called Moan'-au-zi, and whom they greatly dreaded. The Paiuti were always the aggressors, and came over armed with savage wooden knives, with which they slaughtered the feeble Californians (they seldom cared to take prisoners), and scalped the dead by cutting off a small round patch of hair on top of the head.

In war, upon coming into close quarters, the Nishinam sought to stab the enemy under the arm, aiming at the heart. They took no scalps. When going into battle they frequently waxed and twisted out the fore-hair of their heads into two devilish-looking horns, topped their heads with feathers, and painted their breasts black. I once heard an aged Indian describe with wonderful vividness a fight which his nation had by appointment with the Maidu, many a long year ago, when they were yet so numerous that their hosts darkened all the plains beside the beautiful Yuba. They fought a great part of a summer-day, and, according to his account, there was a mighty deal of thwacking, prodding, and hustling, though it was not a very bloody affair at all. He killed a Maidu; then presently he turned his back and ran away himself, and got a spear jabbed into his heel. He described both circumstances with the same simple honesty and remarkable vivacity, which showed he was telling the truth, and which contrasted so strongly with the boastful arrogance of the Algonkin, that never acknowledges defeat. Their male captives they tied to trees and shot to death without lingering tortures, and the women they sometimes whipped and then married, and sometimes put to death. A chief named Sis'-ko told me that when California tribes had a battle they occasionally exchanged prisoners afterward, but did not do so with the Paiuti. This may have been done since the whites have had an influence among them, but I doubt if it was before.

Their war-spear was quite a rude affair, consisting simply of a rough shaft of wood, eight or ten feet long, a little split at the end to receive a flint-head similar to the arrow-head, which was fastened to the shaft with sinew wrapped around it in a crease cut for the purpose.

They have a curious way of collecting debts When an Indian owes another, it is held to be in bad taste, if not positively insulting, for the creditor to dun the debtor, as the brutal Saxon does; so he devises a more subtle method. He prepares a certain number of little sticks, according to the amount of the debt, and paints a ring around the end of each. These he carries and tosses into the delinquent's wigwam without a word and goes his way; whereupon the other generally takes the hint, pays the debt, and destroys the sticks. It is a reproach to any Indian to have these dunning

sticks thrown into his wigwam, and the creditor does not resort to the measure except in case of a hard customer.

That their treatment of superannuated parents is not remarkable for
tenderness may be gathered from the following fact: In 1858 there was an
immense concourse of them at a place called Spenceville, some coming even
from the Coast Range, the purpose of all being, as was then supposed, a
concerted attack on the whites. Preparatory to this gathering and what
should follow it, numbers of them put to death the aged and decrepit
of their camps who would have been an incumbrance, though it was said
this was done at the instance of many of the victims themselves.

Being so nomadic in their habits, they have brought the savage field-
commissary to perfection. They discovered the substantial principle of the
famous Prussian pea-sausage long before the Pickelhauben did. When
about to go on a journey the squaws pack in their deep, conical baskets a
quantity of acorn-mush, made by processes heretofore described, which is
food in as condensed a form as they could make it without scientific appliances. They generally start from camp late in the morning, an hour or
two by sun (the Californians are poor travelers), and rest once or twice
during the forenoon, always by a spring. Taking out some of this panada
they dilute it with large additions of water, making a cool, thick, rich
porridge, which they drink from small baskets. In this manner a squaw
will carry enough to last two persons nearly or quite a fortnight, and that
while they are dancing—the hardest work an Indian does—nor will her
burden exceed thirty pounds. About 11 o'clock they call a halt for the
heat of the day, then they do not break camp again until 2, 3, or even 4
o'clock, but when started march until night-fall or long after.

As it was from the Nishinam that Captain John A. Sutter procured
most of his laborers, I wish here to make mention of a matter which falls
properly within the scope of this narrative. It is related by several men
who came here in 1849 and subsequently (there is to this day frequently a
slight pique between the ante forty-niners and the forty-niners, the land
pioneers and the gold pioneers) that the captain was accustomed in clover-
time to compel his " slaves", as they call them, to go out into the clover-
field for their rations. In view of the amount of labor they performed for

him, this charge, if true, would be a grave one. But it is a fact abundantly substantiated that Indians who have been reared all their lives in American families will, if permitted, in the season when the savor of the blossoms is wafted sweet as honey on the breeze, go afield for dinner in preference to the most lickerish viands ever cooked. I have been told by Americans that they themselves had often eaten California clover boiled and salted, and accounted it altogether a desirable mess of the season. Without doubt, then, this story is a true one; that is, Captain Sutter's Indians 119 preferred to eat clover for a change and a relish, and he simply—let them do it. That he was a kind master to them let the following document attest. It was shown to me by the owner of it, who had it wrapped in many folds of paper and inserted inside the lining of his hat, where he had carried it nearly ten years as a sacred treasure. He was said to have been one of the captain's major-domos, and to have had charge at one time of nearly two hundred Indians:

" The bearer of this, Tucollie, chief of the Wapumney tribe, has presented himself before me with the request to give him a certificate of his good behavior, and it is with pleasure that 1 comply with his wishes, as I know him over (22' twenty-two years as a good and honest Indian ; therefore I can recommend him to the benevolence and kindness of my fellow-citizens, and particularly to those residing in his native country.

"Very respectfully,

"J. A. SUTTER,
" *Special Indian Agent.*

" HOCK FARM, *August* 11*th*, 1862."

Unlike several tribes in the northwest part of the State, these are not misers, but quite the contrary, as are all the Southern California Indians. They never hoard up shell-money, beads, trinkets, or anything of a merely factitious value, unless it is for the purpose of burning them in honor of some great chieftain on his funeral pyre. In a bountiful acorn harvest they gather and store up in wicker granaries (*sukin*) sufficient to last them two or three years; but they frequently use the surplus above the winter's supply to gamble on, and often gamble away even the provisions which are immediately necessary. No Indian is despised so much as one who is close-fisted;

nothing is more certain than that, if an Indian comes along hungry, they will divide with him to the uttermost crumb.

The Indians immediately south of Bear River observe the following fixed dances: The most important is the first-grass dance (*kam'-min*, the generic word for "dance", hence *the* dance of the year), which is held in autumn or winter, after the rains have fully set in and started the grass. None but a resident of California can appreciate the joyfulness of the feeling which gives rise to this festival, when, after the long, weary summer of drought, the first cool rain commences trickling down on the parched plains and the naked foot-hills, and they clothe themselves again with a soft, pale green. Assembled in the dance-house together, both men and women, the men dance with such extraordinary enthusiasm and persistence that they sometimes fall exhausted and lie in a trance for hours.

The next is the second-grass dance (*yo'-mus-si*), which is celebrated in the spring, when the grass takes its second growth, after the dry season is well established, but before the clover has faded from its blossoming glory. Hence this is held in the open air—a *fête champetre*. Otherwise it is like the first, the dancers being in two concentric circles, the men in one inside, the women in the other—the former decorated with feather mantles, the latter more modestly with beads, etc. It continues three or four days, accompanied with plenty of good eating. The musicians at this dance play on whistles of reeds, and the more of them an Indian can get in his mouth the more sweet and ravishing his strains are held to be. If he has his mouth full from corner to corner, all pitched on the same key, and giving forth blasts from alternate sucking and blowing of the breath, then he has attained the perfection of art.

Pretty early in the spring there comes a gala-day, which is the occasion of a great deal of enjoyment. It is called *we'-da*, though that is only one and the most important of the exercises of the day. Its purpose is to prevent the snakes from biting them during the summer, and though held for so momentous a purpose it is a very gay and sportive affair. First, the sports are initiated in the morning by the *han'-pa-wa-ho*, a grand spectacular ballet-dance, performed by the women and girls in the open air (as all the sports are). There is extremely little art in it, and nothing is represented except the wild, extravagant joy of this genial season. Collected in some sequestered mountain glade, where the grass is green and the trees throw a grateful shade around, with flowers in fillets encircling their heads and woven in their hair, and habited (aboriginally) only with narrow cinctures of woven bulrushes about the waists, a great company of girls join hands in a circle and begin a voluptuous, dithyrambic dance. Faster and faster, wilder and wilder grows the motion, keeping time with the accelerating chant, until finally they run riot over the whole place. They break asunder with screams and laughter, and every one of the spectators finds himself pelted with girls and flowers.

The second act in the spectacle is the *kau'-da*, a dance performed by men alone. After it is over, a number of women go around with baskets to solicit presents of acorn-bread, fish, shell-money, and other articles, wherewith to pay the singers, and on the liberality with which the spectators contribute depends their immunity from snake-bites during the coming summer. The third act, toward the close of the day, is the *weda*. A bevy of young maidens dance around two young men in succession, singing a very gay and lively chorus, and ever and anon they make a dash at him, catching him by the shoulders, laughing, stretching out their arms toward him, tantalizing him, etc. After this dance is ended, some old fellows go around among the women, soliciting presents for the singers, as above, and when the women are about to contribute, they are frequently seized themselves by the old fellows and dragged along sportively, to the vast amusement of the bystanders.

But, with all this fun and horse-play, they entertain a very genuine terror of rattlesnakes. When an Indian is bitten by one, or lacerated by a bear, they exclude him rigorously from camp for certain days, believing that the bear or the snake, having tasted his blood, will follow him to camp and play havoc.

On the American River and below there is an indoor dance called *lo'-leh*, held in the winter, simply for amusement. Then there is an acorn-dance (*pai'-o*) held in autumn, which is like the grass-dances above described, only there are different steps and choruses for each. It is made the occasion of a " big eat ".

120

There is no regular secret organization like that described among the Konkau, but there are wandering prestidigitators who, for a gift, initiate young men into the mysteries of juggling described further along. There are also Indians who are versed in spiritualism, and who are scarcely inferior to the wonderful Fox sisters in their influence over the spirits of the vasty deep. More than that, they make practical use of the spirits to excellent purpose. When an Indian gets troublesome to manage, the headmen invite him to the assembly-house some evening, a dance is held, then all the fires are extinguished, and the congregation sit profoundly still in the darkness. Presently the gates of hell yawn open, and there issues forth a specter, who rustles his pinions and feathers, raps and ramps over the floor, and then addresses the company in the best English, "Good evening, gentlemen". He speaks as many words in that language as he can command well, adds a little Spanish perhaps, then makes a long discourse in Indian, which always happens to fit excellently well upon the back of the offender. Most Indians are thoroughly convinced of the genuineness of these apparitions, and that these grim familiars have the gift of tongues, also power to hang them by the neck in the apex of the lodge, or disembowel them instantly if they do not make presents to the chief and look well to their p's and q's. Americans are rigorously excluded from these proceedings, but a man named William Griffin, understanding the language, overheard from the outside what was said and done.

There is a kind of assembly-house called the *toad'-lam kŭm* which is devoted exclusively to female occupation. Deputations of women from different sections meet together in it occasionally and engage in contests of vocal music. It is held that that band of women who are victorious will thereby secure to their neighborhood the most abundant harvest of acorns. Of course, it is not to be supposed that these musical rivalries are decided in accordance with those principles of high art which would regulate the award in a German Liederkranz, but they are accounted triumphant whose song is loudest and longest.

There is a social gathering which may be called the soup-party, answering to our dinner-party or tea-party. The inhabitants of two or more villages meet at a designated place in the open air, bringing acorn-flour (nowadays frequently wheat-flour), a little salt, and baskets to cook and eat the soup in—nothing else. Nothing is *en regle* except the soup, an article somewhat thicker than gruel, and thinner than mush. After they have eaten a great quantity of this, the young people amuse themselves in dancing, while their elders indulge in the gossip and scandal of which the Indians are so inordinately fond.

Among many California Indians it is usual for a man requiring the services of a shaman to pay him in advance, but these hold to the principle " No cure, no fee ". The benefit which the man of drugs renders his patient generally consists in sucking from him certain sticks and stones, which he alleges were lodged just under the skin, to his great detriment. When it is manifest to all beholders that the sufferer has been marked by Death for his own, and that he cannot long survive, his friends and relatives collect around him in a circle, and stand awaiting the final event in awe-stricken silence. As his breath grows stertorous, showing that he is passing through the last grim struggle, one of them approaches reverently and kneels by his side. Holding his hand over the region of the heart, he counts its feeble pulsations as they grow slower and weaker. When it ceases to beat and all is ended, he turns to the waiting relatives and silently nods. Whereupon they commence the death-dance, with frightful wails and ululations. Every family have their own burning-ground, and as soon as the corpse is cold it is conveyed thither for incremation. Around Auburn, a devoted widow never speaks, on any occasion or upon any pretext, for several months, sometimes a year or more, after the death of her husband. Of this singular fact I had ocular demonstration. Elsewhere, as on the American River, she speaks only in a whisper for several months. As you go down toward the Cosumnes this custom disappears, and only the tarred head is observed. It is only fair to remark that the widow is generally more faithful to the memory of her husband than the widower to his wife's, and seldom disgraces human nature by remarrying in a week or two, as he not infrequently does.

Apropos, the following story : An Indian woman, living on Wolf Creek, lost her husband, and went to live with her mother, who was also a widow. One day before the customary period of mourning had expired, during which a widow is forbidden to do any work or attend a dance, her mother requested her to go down into the ravine and gather some clover. She went, accompanied by a young girl, one of her unmarried companions. Going afield with her basket, she was observed by an Indian named Pwi'-no, her husband's brother, who watched where she went and for what purpose. He reported to his father, and by him was charged to follow and strike her dead. He did so, following her for several hours, but he had no heart for the butcherly business, and he finally returned home without accomplishing his errand His father upbraided him bitterly as a coward and an ingrate for not avenging the insult to his brother's memory. Stung to madness by the paternal reproaches, in a moment of furious passion he rushed away, fell upon the offending widow, and smote her unto death.

When a mother dies, leaving a very young infant, custom allows the relatives to destroy it. This is generally done by the grandmother, aunt, or other near relative, who holds the poor innocent in her arms, and while it is seeking the maternal fountain, presses it to her breast until it is smothered. We must not judge them too harshly for this. They knew nothing of bottle-nurture, patent nipples, or any kind of milk whatever other than the human.

Some Nishinam hold that the dead linger on earth a while; hence it is that they have such a mortal terror of ghosts. If they are good spirits, after they have traveled toward the Happy Western Land until they are weary, other good spirits who have preceded them thither come to meet them, and bear them away from earth in a whirlwind. When an Indian sees one of those little dust-columns which are frequent in this windy climate, he thinks some beatific soul is ascending in it to the Happy Western Land.

As above recorded, the dance for the dead is observed as far south as American River (not below), through the influence and example of the Maidu, who observe it annually. As soon as life is extinct the body is burned, with all the person's possessions. Then the ashes are conveyed to some tribal burying-ground, and slightly covered up in the earth. When the dance for the dead is held by appointment at each place, generally in the spring, the ashes are uncovered and a fire is made directly over them. The first evening and morning the mourning-women dance in a circle around the fire, holding in their hands their votive offerings; the second evening and morning they burn the offerings during the dance.

But the southern Nishinam custom is to hold a "cry" at various villages and various times throughout the year, according to appointment, at which they sit in a circle on the ground, weeping and wailing. An effigy or effigies of the dead are rudely made of skins and cloths, and carried about over the hills and through the valleys, wherever the departed were most accustomed to resort during life, to recall the memory of the absent ones, and fill the breasts of the mourners with a more piercing sorrow. After this is done the effigies are burned, as the real bodies would have been.

I witnessed a scene of cremation on Bear River that was one of the most hideous and awful spectacles of which the human mind can conceive. The mourners leaped and howled around the burning pyre like demons, holding long poles in their hands, which ever and anon they thrust into the seething, blistering corpse, with dismal cries of "*Wu-wu-wu!*" On American River, after the body is reduced to a little smouldering lump, the women draw it out of the fire, then each one in succession takes it in her hands, holds it high above her head, and walks around the pyre, uttering doleful wails and ululations.

A touching story is related of old Captain Tom, of Auburn. His son Dick was an incorrigible rascal, and it finally fell out that he was arrested for something or other, tried, proved guilty, and sentenced to San Quentin for ten years. This was a terrible blow to Captain Tom, for he loved his boy, with all his wickedness. When Dick was manacled and taken away out of his sight, the old man turned away his head and wept. Dick became to him as one who is dead. Nevermore (for ten years to an Indian seems like eternity), nevermore should his old eyes behold him. The white man had bound his wrists and ankles with iron, hobbled him like a horse, carried him away to the uttermost ends of the earth, and buried him alive. He turned sadly away, and went back to his wigwam. Mingling their tears together, he and his family mourned for Dick as for one dead. Then they arose, gathered together all the things that had ever belonged to him, carried them out to the family burning-ground, erected a pyre, and placed them on it. Years ago, a brother to Dick had died while they were living in another place, and his ashes rested where they were burned. They were now brought and sprinkled over the pyre (for such a grievous calamity had never befallen the Indians before, that they should be compelled to burn one's possessions without his own body to accompany it). They were sadly troubled to think how they could send Dick's clothing to him in the Happy Western Land, or wherever else he was gone, and they thought, they hoped, if his brother's ashes were sprinkled on the pyre, perhaps his spirit might convey them. With these feelings in their breasts, but with many tears and sad misgivings, they applied the torch, and prayed their son whose ashes they had sprinkled on them to waft the clothes and money quickly to poor Dick in that undiscovered country to which the white man had conveyed him.

CHAPTER XXXII.

THE NISHINAM—CONTINUED.

There are numerous games with which old and young, men and women, amuse themselves. All of them, except one perhaps, are very simple, and several are quite puerile; but they all comport well with the blithe-hearted, simple-minded, joyous temper of the people—so fond of gayeties, so fond of gambling—who originated them.

Shooting at a target with bow and arrow, a game called *he'-u-to*, is a favorite diversion of men and boys. A triangular wicket about two feet high is set up, and under it is placed a wooden ball which constitutes the target. The contestants stand about fifty yards distant. In the *ha'-dang-kau ol-om-wi'-oh* (shooting at long range) there is no ball, and the wicket is higher. The men stand several hundred yards off, sometimes a quarter of a mile, so that the wicket is not visible. He is victor who lodges most arrows within the wicket. Frequently an arrow flies high and wide of the mark, so that it is lost. This long-range shooting is to give them skill against the day of battle.

The *pos'-kà huk'-um-toh kom-peh'* (tossing the ball) is a boys' game. They employ a round wooden ball, a buckeye, or something, standing at three bases or corners, and toss it around from one to the other. If two of them start to exchange corners, and the third "crosses out" or hits either of them, he scores one, and they count up to a certain number, which completes the game. Little boys and girls play *chi'-wi oi'-doi to'-ko-peh* (catching clover in the mouth). A large number of them stand in a circle, a few paces apart, and toss from one to the other a pellet of green clover, which must be caught in the mouth. This game produces a vast deal of merriment among the little shavers, and he who laughs loudest, and consequently

331

has his mouth open widest, is most likely to catch the clover, which he is then entitled to eat. As a variation, one will stand with his eyes shut and mouth open, while another fires wads at the port-hole, or occasionally harder substances, and he is not particular whether he hits the mouth, the nose, or some other portion of his physiognomy.

The most common mode of gambling (*hi'-lai*), used by both men and women, is conducted by means of four longish cylinders of bone or wood, which are wrapped in pellets of grass and held in the hand, while the opposite party guesses which hand contains them. These cylinders are carved from several materials, but the Indians call them all bones. Thus they have the phrases *pol'-loam hi'-lai hĭn, toan'-cm hi'-lai hĭn, du'-pem hi'-lai hĭn, gai'-a hi'-lai hĭn,* which mean respectively to gamble with buckeye bones, pine bones, deer bones, and cougar bones. There is a subtile difference in their minds in the quality of the game, according to the kind of bones employed, but what it is I cannot discern. This game, with slight variations, prevails pretty much all over California; and as I had opportunity of seeing it on a much larger scale on Gualala Creek, the reader is referred to the chapter on the Gualala. The *su'-toh* is the same game substantially, only the pieces are shaken in the hand without being wrapped in the grass.

The *ha* is a game of dice, played by men or women, two, three, or four together. The dice, four in number, consist of two acorns split lengthwise into halves, with the outsides scraped and painted red or black. They are shaken in the hands and thrown into a wide, flat basket, woven in ornamental patterns, sometimes worth $25. One paint and three whites, or *vice versa*, score nothing; two of each, score one; four alike, score four. The thrower keeps on throwing until he makes a blank throw, when another takes the dice. When all the players have stood their turn, the one who has scored most takes the stakes, which in this game are generally small, say a "bit". As the Indians say, "This is a quick game, and with good luck one can very soon break another."

The *ti'-kel ti'-kel* is also a gambling game, for two men, played with a bit of wood or a pebble, which is shaken in the hand, and then the hand closed upon it. The opponent guesses which finger (a thumb is a finger with them) it is under, and scores one if he hits, or the other scores if he misses. They keep tally with eight counters.

The *ti'-kel* is almost the only really robust and athletic game they use, and is played by a large company of men and boys The piece is made of rawhide, or nowadays of strong cloth, and is shaped like a small dumb-bell. It is laid in the center of a wide, level space of ground, in a furrow hollowed out a few inches in depth. Two parallel lines are drawn equidistant from it, a few paces apart, and along these lines the opposing parties, equal in strength, range themselves. Each player is equipped with a slight, strong staff, from four to six feet long. The two champions of the parties take their stations on opposite sides of the piece, which is then thrown into the air, caught on the staff of one or the other, and hurled by him in the direction of his antagonist's goal. With this send-off there ensues a wild chase and a hustle, pell-mell, higgledy-piggledy, each party striving to bowl the piece over the other's goal. These goals are several hundred 122 yards apart, affording room for a good deal of lively work; and the players often race up and down the champaign, with varying fortunes, until they are dead blown and perspiring like top-sawyers.

There is a performance which may appropriately be described here, though it is not a game, but a sort of public entertainment. The Indians call it "learning the rules", but that gives only a partial and indefinite idea of the whole. It occurs every spring, just before the trees put forth their leaves, sometimes in one village, sometimes in another. It combines jugglery, spiritual manifestations, ventriloquy, concerts, and perhaps other features. White men are excluded, but I was smuggled in after night-fall by the friendly Paung'-lo. An Indian who is celebrated as a magician makes his appointment for the year some time in advance, and there are generally deputations present from the vicinal villages. The performances continue uninterrupted for eight days, or rather nights, and that, too, all night, for they are as interminable as a Chinese drama. This magician is called *ka'-kin-nos'-kit* (Spirit-dweller), or *ka'-kin-mai'-dek* (Spirit-man). There is generally a novitiate present, who has been practicing the black-art for years, and has now arrived at sufficient skill to be initiated. The magician, as stated, carries forward the performances all night, but during the daytime he sleeps, rousing near meridian to take the only repast he allows himself in twenty-four hours. There is also a repeater, frequently a boy of good voice, whose function is to repeat after him all his utterances. The repeater and the novitiate are allowed to eat twice a day. In this case the repeater, being a boy, got sore hungered and fagged out by the long-drawn exercises, and he ran away. A dose of raw acorn-flour and water was administered to him, which was considered a specific against any desire to run away.

The great round dance-house is gorgeously decorated for this occasion; with black bear-skins hanging from the roof; with streamers and festoons of different lengths, some of them twelve feet long, all made of yellow-hammers' feathers, and with a pair of garlands (*yok'-kol*) encircling the whole house. The upper garland, passing around about at the height of one's head, consists of many kinds of acorns, alternating at short intervals on a string with brilliant wild-duck feathers. The lower one, at the floor, is composed of various plants, savory herbs, mints, leaves, etc. It is death to any person, in passing underneath the garland, to touch it; he must bow his head, and walk circumspectly.

When evening comes on, men, women, and children assemble in the dance-house, the fire is put out, all lights are extinguished, and darkness reigns profound. Exactly what the magician does nobody knows; of course I could not see him, and the interpreter dared not interrupt him by explaining to me. He sits cross-legged like a tailor, one Indian holds his knees down, another embraces him tight in his arms, yet he melts out of their gripe like an insubstantial vision. He goes through the roof where there is no orifice. His voice, or somebody's voice, floats about the rafters, or wells up from the ground. There are mysterious rappings in the air.

123

The Indians regard all these things with that impenetrable and impervious solemnity with which they accept everything especially intended for their amusement. They doze awhile, then they sit up awhile and listen to the interminable goings-on. Now and then a bright point of fire in the pitchy darkness reveals a cigarette burning. The Indian is absolutely the most *nil admirari* being in the world. He believes everything, and—gambles, or would if it were not dark. " It is the wind ", he says. "Of course, nobody can't go through the roof where there is no hole; but the spirit-man did."

Occasionally there is a break, and then the women contribute their quota to the entertainment by "singing the garland". First, there is a jingling overture, repeated many times:

Then follows:

Then this:

"U-we-we-toan-hai."

"Ta'-lim yok'-kol woi'-a-toh" *(quoties vis).*

Hol'-li-woh yok'-kol woi'-a-toh" *(quoties vis).*

The first means "The feather garland waves"; the second, "The leafy garland waves". Thus they sing the various ornaments of the house in succession, giving a verse to each, and when they have exhausted the list of all the streamers, garlands, bear-skins, etc., the magician resumes.

The credulous Paunglo paid the magician $3 American money, and twenty painted arrows trimmed with yellowhammer's feathers, worth $15, making $18 for his eight nights' entertainment. John, the novitiate, paid him $10 gold; others, various amounts.

But now he is gone from our gaze. The dance-house is deserted and silent. The *yokkol* are hid on the hill. If any rash American should look upon them, they would blast his eyes. If he should touch one his bowels would turn to acorns within him.

The subject of shell-money has hitherto received little more than casual mention. Immense quantities of it were formerly in circulation among the California Indians, and the manufacture of it was large and constant, to replace the continual wastage which was caused by the sacrifice of so much upon the death of wealthy men, and by the propitiatory sacrifices performed by many tribes, especially those of the Coast Range. From my own observations, which have not been limited, and from the statements of pioneers and the Indians themselves, I hesitate little to express the belief that every Indian in the State, in early days, possessed an average of at least $100 worth of shell-money. This would represent the value of about two women (though the Nishinam never actually bought their wives), or two grizzly-bear skins, or twenty-five cinnamon-bear skins, or about three average ponies. This may be considered a fair statement of the diffusion of wealth among them in their primitive condition.

The manufacture of large quantities of it nowadays by Americans with machinery has diminished its purchasing power by increasing its amount. The younger, English-speaking Indians scarcely use it at all, except in a few dealings with their elders, or for gambling. One sometimes lays away a few strings of it, for he knows he cannot squander it at the stores, and is thus removed from temptation and possible bankruptcy; and when he wishes for a few dollars American money he can raise it by exchanging with some old Indian who happens to have gold. Americans also sometimes keep it for this purpose. For instance, I have known an American, who associated a good deal with the Indians, buy a pony for $15 gold, and sell it to an old Indian for $40 shell-money. By converting this amount into gold in small sums at a time he cleared $25 in the course of a few months. It is singular how the old Indians cling to this currency when they know that it will purchase nothing from the stores; but then their wants are few and mostly supplied from the sources of nature; and, besides that, this money has a certain religious value in their minds, as being alone worthy to be offered up on the funeral pyre of departed friends or famous chiefs of their tribe.

125   It is my opinion, from its appearance, that the staple currency of all the tribes in Central and Southern California is made of the same material, but I am not positive of that material except among the Nishinam. Here it is a thick, white shell (*Pachydesma crassatelloides*), found on the coast of Southern California, and the money they make from it is called *hä'-wok*. It consists of circular disks or buttons, ranging from a quarter inch to an inch in diameter, and varying in thickness with the shell. These are pierced in the center, and strung on strings made of the inner bark of the wild cotton or milkweed (*Asclepias*); and either all the pieces on a string, or all in one section of it, are of the same size. The strings are not of an invariable length. The larger pieces rate at about twenty-five cents (though when an Indian saw I was anxious to secure a specimen he charged me fifty cents); the half inch pieces at 12½ cents; and the smaller ones generally go by the string. A string of 177 of the smallest pieces was valued by its owner at $7, and sold for that. The women often select the prettiest pieces,

about one-third of an inch in diameter, and string them on a string for a necklace.

This may be called their silver, and is the great medium of all transactions; while the money answering to gold is made from varieties of the ear-shell (*Haliotis*), and is called *ül-lo*. (Dr. R. E. C. Stearns, to whose kindness 126 I am indebted for the identification of the shells, suggests that this may be a corruption of the Spanish *aulon*. This is possible, although the Indians accent the first syllable and give it a sound somewhere between the German *ö* and *uh*). They cut these shells with flints into oblong strips from an inch to two inches in length, according to the curvature of the shell, and about a third as broad as they are long. Two holes are drilled near the narrow end of each piece, and they are thereby fastened to a string of the material above named, hanging edge to edge. Ten pieces generally constitute a string, and the larger pieces rate at $1 apiece, $10 a string; the smaller in proportion, or less, if they are not pretty. Being susceptible of a high polish this money forms a beautiful ornament, and is worn for necklaces on gala-days. But as money it is rather too large and cumbersome, and the Indians generally seek to exchange it for the less brilliant but more useful *hâwok*. The *üllo* may be considered rather as jewelry.

In preferring the former to the latter the California squaws are consistent with the character they maintain throughout of setting utility before beauty. In this regard they manifest more good sense than is usual for savages.

A third kind of money, very rarely seen, is made of the *Olivella biplicata*, and is called by them *kol'-kol*.

When I was in Auburn, Captain Tom showed me nearly half a bushel of shell-money and trinkets belonging to himself and family, and I had the *Fig. 29* curiosity to take an exact inventory of the same, with the values attached to the articles by the Indians.

CAPTAIN TOM'S TAX-LIST.

Hâwok, 10 yards	$230
Üllo, 10 pieces	10
Üllo, 10 pieces	10

Üllo, 12 pieces	$24
Üllo, 12 pieces	18
Üllo, 10 pieces	20
Üllo, 15 pieces	30
Üllo, 10 pieces	5
Üllo, 10 pieces	10
Üllo, 14 pieces	14
Chi'-lak	24
Shek'-ki	20
Pa'-cha	14
Pa'-cha	8
Pa'-cha	6
Pa'-cha	5
Two abalone gorgets	10
Alabaster	5
Kolkol, 14 yards	14
One grizzly-bear skin	50
One cinnamon-bear skin	4
One bear-skin robe	75
Total	$606

The *háwok* was all in one string, and contained 1,160 pieces. Tom
Fig. 28 was very proud of this, and would suffer no one but his wife to be photo-
graphed wearing it. The *kolkol* was strung in a double string, the shells
lying face to face; it is slightly esteemed. The "red alabaster", brought
from Sonoma, was in the form of a cylinder, about as large as one's little
— 127 finger, an inch long, drilled lengthwise, and forming the front piece in a
string of shell-beads worn by Captain Tom's baby. One of the girdles,
pacha, was decorated with 214 small pieces of abalone; the hair-net contained about 100.

Following is a list of articles of dress and ornament worn by the
Nishinam, which with a change of names would answer for nearly all the
tribes in Central California: (1) The hare-skin robe, often trimmed with
Fig. 26 ground-squirrel tails, generally used as bedding, but sometimes worn in the
rainy season. (2) The breech-cloth of hetcheled and braided tule-grass,

worn by women. (3) *Shek'-ki*, a hair-net, made of the inner bark of the milkweed, woven with large meshes, fitting the head like a skull-cap, drawn tight by a string running around the edge The hair was twisted into a hard knot behind the head, and into this was stuck a plume. (4) *Mok'-kus*, about a foot long, consisting of a stick wreathed with red woodpecker scalps and having at the end a cluster of pieces of abalone-shell or a little flag of yellowhammer's feathers. Worn only by the men when going to *Figs.* a dance. (5) *To'-lai*, the mantle of black, long feathers, eagle's or hawk's, *30, 31* often mentioned in these pages, worn on the back, from the armpits down to the knees, only by men and those generally shamans. (6) *Pa'-cha*, the wide deer-skin girdle, studded with bits of abalone, worn by women around the waist; nowadays generally made of scarlet cloth and covered thick with bead-work. (7) *Chi'-lak*, the bandeau of yellowhammer's feathers, laid butt to tip alternately, and strung on two strings; worn by both sexes in the dance (8) *Kak'-ki*, the narrow bandeau of fur, worn tight around the head by both sexes in the dance. Seen all over California, nowadays generally supplanted by a handkerchief. (9) *Bon'-noh*, ornaments, generally made of a large bird's wing-bones, with red woodpecker's down and pieces of abalone at one end ; worn thrust through the lobe of the ear or the septum of the nose by both sexes. (10) *Wuk'-tem-hin* ("one-hanger" or "single-hanger"), the large abalone gorget worn by men in a dance. The shell-money, often worn by women, has been already described. In the *yomussi* dance the women carry bows and arrows for ornaments.

First of all things existed the moon. Next came the coyote, but whether as a kind of protoplasm for other beings or as a creator of them, the Indians are not clear. But it is certain that the California Indians anticipated Darwin by some centuries in the development theory, only substituting the coyote for the monkey. The moon and the coyote created all things, including man, who, some say, was in the form of a stone; others in the form of a simple, straight, hairless, limbless mass of flesh, like an enormous earth-worm.

AÍ-KUT AND YO-TÓ-TO-WI.

The first man thus created was called Aikut. His wife was Yototowi. In process of time the woman fell sick, and though Aikut nursed her tenderly, she gradually faded away before his eyes and died. He had loved her with a love passing the love of brothers, and now his heart was broken with grief. He dug a grave for her close beside his camp-fire (for the Nishinam did not burn their dead then), that he might daily and hourly weep above her silent dust. His grief knew no bounds. His life became a burden to him; all the light was gone out of his eyes. He wished to die, that he might follow his beloved Yototowi. In the greatness of his grief he fell into a trance. There was a rumbling, and the spirit of the dead woman arose out of the earth and came and stood beside him. When he awoke out of his trance and beheld his wife he would have spoken to her, but she forbade him, for in what moment an Indian speaks to a ghost he dies. She turned away and set out to seek the spirit-land (*ūsh'-wūsh-i kŭm*, literally "the dance-house of ghosts"). He followed her, and together they journeyed through a great country and a darksome—a land that no man has seen and returned to report—until they came to a river that separated them from the spirit-land. Over this river there was a bridge of but one small rope, so very small that a spider could hardly crawl across it. Here the spirit of the woman must bid farewell to her husband, and go over alone to the spirit-land. When he saw her leaving him, in an agony of grief he stretched out his arms toward her, beckoning her to return. She came back with him to this world, then started a second time to return to the invisible land. But he could not be separated from her, so she permitted him and he spoke to the spirit. In that self-same instant he died, and together they took their last departure for the land of spirits.

Thus Aikut passed away from the realm of earth, and in the invisible world became a good and great spirit, who constantly watches over and befriends his posterity still living on earth. He and his wife left behind them two children, a brother and a sister; and to prevent incest the moon created another pair, and from these two pairs sprang all the Nishinam.

Their land of spirits is the Happy Western Land of all the California Indians, and thither go the souls of all good Indians, to live forever in indolent enjoyment. (As the Nishinam reckon the points of the compass rather by the trend of the Sierra Nevada than by the sun or the stars, their west is nearly southwest. Most other Sierra tribes seem to do the same.)

ORIGIN OF INCREMATION.

The moon and the coyote wrought together in creating all things that exist. The moon was good, but the coyote was bad. In making men and women, the moon wished to so fashion their souls that when they died they should return to the earth after two or three days, as he himself does when he dies. But the coyote was evil disposed, and he said that this should not be, but that when men died their friends should burn their bodies, and once a year make a great mourning for them. And the coyote prevailed. So, presently when a deer died, they burned his body, as the coyote had decreed, and after a year they made a great mourning for him. But the moon created the rattlesnake, and caused it to bite the coyote's son, so that he died. Now, though the coyote had been willing to burn the deer's relations, he refused to burn his own son. Then the moon said unto him: "This is your own rule. You would have it so, and now your son shall be 128 burned like the others." So he was burned, and after a year the coyote mourned for him. Thus the law was established over the coyote also, and, as he had dominion over men, it prevailed over men likewise.

This story is utterly worthless for itself, but it has its value, in that it shows there was a time when the California Indians did not practice cremation, which is also established by other traditions. It hints at the additional fact that the Nishinam to this day set great store by the moon, consider it their benefactor in a hundred ways, and observe its changes for a hundred purposes.

THE BEAR AND THE DEER.

At first all the animals ate only earth, but afterward the clover grew, and then they ate that also. There were no men yet, or rather all men were yet in the forms of animals. One day the bear and the deer went out together to pick clover. The bear pretended to see a louse on the deer's neck, and the deer bent down her head to let the bear catch it, but the bear cut her head off, scratched out her eyes, and threw them into her basket among the clover. When she went home and emptied her basket, the deer's children saw the eyes, and knew they were their mother's. So they studied revenge.

On another day, when the bear was pounding earth in a mortar for food, as acorns are now pounded, the deer's two children enticed the bear's children away to play, and persuaded them to enter a cave beneath the great rock Oamlam (high rock) on Wolf Creek, near Bear River. Then they fastened them in with a stone, and made a fire which roasted them to death. When the bear came and found them, she thought they were asleep and sweating, but it was the oil on their hair, and when she pawed them the hair came off. Thereupon she flew into a great passion, tore them to pieces, and devoured them.

Then she pursued the deer's two children to destroy them. She called out to them that she was their aunt and would do them good, but they fled and escaped up the great rock Oamlam, and it grew upward with them until the top of it was very high. The bear went round behind the rock and found a narrow rift where she could crawl up, but the deer's children saw her coming, and they had a stone red-hot, which they cast down her throat and slew her. Then they took this same stone and threw it to the north, and manzanita-berries fell down; to the east, and pine-nuts fell down; to the south, and one kind of acorns fell down; to the west, and another kind of acorns fell down. Thus they had now plenty of food of different kinds, and they ate earth no more.

After this, while they were yet on the rock, the deer's children thought to climb into heaven, it had grown so high. The big one made a ladder that reached the sky, and, with bow and arrow, he shot a hole up through, so that the little one could climb up into heaven. But the little one was afraid, and cried. So the big one made tobacco and a pipe, and gave them to the little one to smoke as he went up the ladder, whereby the smoke concealed the world from him, and his heart was no longer afraid. And this is how smoking originated. So the little one climbed up through the hole into heaven, and went out of sight; but presently he returned down the ladder, and told his brother that it was a good country above the sky, with plenty of sweet browse, and grass, and buds of trees, and pools of water, and flowers for them to sleep on. Upon that they both climbed the ladder and went above the sky.

Presently they saw their mother by a pool of water cooking, and they knew it was she, because she had no eyes. Now, the big brother was a deer, but the little one was a sap-sucker.   So these two made a wheel to ride on, that they might pursue their mother, for they were not well pleased to see her without eyes.   But they were punished for this act of wickedness, for the wheel went contrary with them, turned aside, and plunged into a pool of water, so that they were drowned.

This story contains a considerable part of the Nishinam cosmogony. In common with most California tribes, these Indians regard all animals, including men, as having a common original, and being intimately related. Thus the bear calls herself aunt to the deer's children, and one of the latter is a bird.

There is another tradition to the same effect substantially, that men were once on the same level with the beasts of the forest, and habitually devoured their own dead, as the coyote is said to do.

ORIGIN OF FIRE.

After the coyote had created the world and its inhabitants, there was still one thing lacking—fire.   In the western country there was plenty of it, but nobody could get it; it was so far off and so closely hidden.   So the bat proposed to the lizard that he should go and steal some.   This the lizard did, and he got a good coal of it, but found it very hard to bring home because everybody wanted to steal it from him.   At length he reached the western edge of the Sacramento Valley, and he had to be extremely careful in crossing with it, lest he should set the country on fire.   He was obliged to travel by night to prevent the thieves from stealing the fire, and to keep the dry grass from catching fire.   One night when he had nearly reached the foot-hills on the east side of the valley, he was so unfortunate as to come upon a company of sand-hill cranes (*ko'-dok*), who were sitting up all night gambling.   He crept slyly along on the side of a log, holding the fire in his hand, but they discovered him and gave chase.   Their legs were so long he had no hope of escape, so he was obliged to set fire to the grass, and let it burn into the mountains.   Thus he soon had a roaring fire, and he had to run like a good one to keep ahead of it.   When the bat saw the fire coming, being unused to it, he was half-blinded and had sharp pain in his eyes.   He cried out to the lizard that his eyes would be put out, and

129

asked him to cover them up with pitch. The lizard took pitch and rubbed it on so thick he could see nothing, which got the bat into a bad scrape. He hopped, jumped, and fluttered; he flew this way, he flew that way; he burnt his head, he burnt his tail. Then he flew toward the west and cried out loud, "*Mo-nu', shu-le'-u-lu!*" ("Blow, O wind!") The wind heard him and blew in his eyes, but he could not blow off all the pitch, and that is the reason the bat sees so ill to this day. And because he was in the fire, that is the reason he is so black and singed-looking.

THE OLD MAN-EATER.

Long, long ago there lived an old man and his wife who made it their especial business to kill and eat Indians. They had their wigwam thirty or forty miles down on the Sacramento Plains, and the ground all around it was covered a foot deep with blood. They made stone mortars, carved and polished inside and out, much better than the mortars the women use nowadays to pound acorns in; and in these mortars they pounded up their victims, and made them into hash (as the Indians express it), so that they might be tender to eat. The Indians warred for their lives against this terrible old man and his wife, but they could do nothing against them, and were disappearing from the earth. Then at last the Old Coyote took pity on his offspring, the people whom he had made, and he determined to kill this old man. It was his habit to go into the dance-house when it was full of Indians, the chiefs and the great men of the tribe, and of these he would catch and kill the fattest and the juiciest for himself. So the coyote dug a great hole outside of the dance-house, close beside the door, and hid himself in it with a mighty big knife, and covered himself up so that the old man could see nothing but the point of the knife. As he passed into the dance-house he saw the point of the knife and kicked at it, but went on in. Then the coyote leaped out of the hole, rushed in after him, caught the old man, and slew him.

This legend is very interesting, on account of the probable reference to a supposed pre-aboriginal race, who were the makers of the superio stone mortars occasionally found in many places in California, and of whic the Indians universally acknowledge that they were not the author

Other Indians say that these mortars were given to them by the same one who gave them the acorns, and that they subsequently learned to fashion for themselves the rude mortar-holes on the top of great bowlders, the same that they use to-day.

THE ROAD-WOMAN (BO'-HEM–KÜL'-LEH).

There dwells in the forests and upon the hills a ghost which is both man and woman. It is called by the Indians bo'-hem kül'-leh (from boh, bohem, "road", and külleh, "woman"). It is a bad spirit, and only bad men and women resort to it. Sometimes in the night its strange, wild, shrill cry is heard in the forest, and then some one in the camp will answer it and go out to meet it. When a woman is about to be overtaken in dishonest childbirth and her pangs are upon her, she goes to and fro in the forest crying that this bad spirit overcame her and that she conceived by it; also, a man who has wrought an evil thing and been detected in it accuses this double-sexed spirit of having tempted him.

This is one of those strange, subtle Indian superstitions which are scarcely intelligible to us. I suspect this spirit must be connected with the phenomenon of insanity. It has often been said that there never were any cases of insanity among the Indians before they became acquainted with the Americans and learned to love strong drink. This statement is doubtful. Like all people of a low grade of culture, they attribute insanity to demoniacal possession. They have a word, hon'-tai, which they apply to people who have become infatuated with this ghost, and which undoubtedly can only be translated "insane".

I have never discovered among the Indians any trace of beings like the swan-maidens or were-wolves of medieval legends. They have the words "quail-women", "deer-women", and the like, but that is their only way of expressing the feminine gender. There is a story of a famous shaman who, when about to exercise his art in a very difficult case, would turn into a bear. They also believe in hermaphrodites, and declare they have seen them.

Some Nishinam have heard of a Great Being, the white man's God, whom, on the American River, they call Sha; at Placerville, Lūsh. They have the name only, nothing more.

CHAPTER XXXIII.

THE MI'-WOK.

By much the largest nation in California, both in population and in extent of territory, is the Miwok, whose ancient dominion extended from the snow-line of the Sierra Nevada to the San Joaquin River, and from the Cosumnes to the Fresno. When we reflect that the mountain valleys were thickly peopled as far east as Yosemite (in summer, still further up), and consider the great extent and fertility of the San Joaquin plains, which to-day produce a thousand bushels of wheat for every white inhabitant, old and young, in certain districts; then add to this the long and fish-full streams, the Mokelumne, the Stanislaus, the Tuolumne, the Merced, the Chowchilla, and the San Joaquin encircling all, along whose banks the Indians anciently dwelt in multitudes, we shall see what a capacity there was to support a dense population. Even the islands of the San Joaquin were made to sustain their quota, for on Feather Island there are said to be the remains of a populous village. The rich alluvial lands along the lower Stanislaus, Tuolumne, and Merced contained the heart of the nation, and were probably the seat of the densest population of ancient California.

And yet, broadly extended as it was, and feeble or wholly lacking as was the feeling of national unity, this people possess a language more homogeneous than many others not half so widely ramified. An Indian may start from the upper end of Yosemite and travel with the sun 150 miles, a great distance to go in California without encountering a new tongue, and on the San Joaquin make himself understood with little difficulty. Another may journey from the Cosumnes southward to the Fresno, crossing three rivers which the timid race had no means of ferrying over but casual logs, and still hear the familiar numerals with scarcely the change of a syllable, and he can sit down with a new-found acquaintance

346

and impart to him hour-long communications with only about the usual supplement and bridging of gesture (which is great at best). To one who has been traveling months in regions where a new language has to be looked to every ten miles sometimes, this state of affairs is a great relief.

There are, as always, many and abrupt dialectic departures, but the root remains, and is quickly caught up by the Indian of a different dialect. There are not so often whole cohorts of words swinging loose from the language. A ride through the Nishinam land is like the march of a regiment through a hostile country; every half-day's journey there is a clean breach of a whole company of words, which is replaced by another.

For instance, north of the Stanislaus they call themselves *mi'-wok* ("men" or "people"); south of it to the Merced, *mi'-wa;* south of that to the Fresno, *mi'-wi.* On the Upper Merced the word "river" is *wa-kal'-la;* on the Upper Tuolumne, *wa-kal'-u-mi;* on the Stanislaus and Mokelumne, *wa-kal'-u-mi-toh.* This is undoubtedly the origin of the word "Mokelumne", which is locally pronounced mo-kal'-u-my. So also *kos'-sūm, kos'-sūm-mi* (salmon) is probably the origin of the word "Cosumnes", which is pronounced koz'-u-my. For the word "grizzly bear" there exist in different dialects the following different forms: *u-zu'-mai-ti, os-o'-mai-ti, uh-zu'-mai-ti, uh-zu'-mai-tuh.*

Their language is not lacking in words and phrases of greeting, which are full of character. When one meets a stranger he generally salutes him, *wu'-meh?* "[Whence] do you come"? After which follows, *whi-i'-neh?* "What are you at"? Sometimes it is *wi'-oh u-kūh'?* about equivalent to "How do you do?" How like the savage! Instead of inquiring kindly as to the new comer's health and welfare, with the inquisitiveness and suspicion of his race he desires to know from what quarter he hails, whither he is going, what for, etc. After the third or fourth question has been asked him, the stranger frequently remarks *he'-kang-ma,* "I am hungry", which never fails to procure a substantial response, or as substantial as the larder will permit. Perhaps he will acknowledge it by *ku'-ni,* "Thank you"; more probably not. When the guest is ready to take his departure, he never fails to say *wūk'-si-mus-si,* "I am going". To which the host replies *ko-to-el-le',* "You go ahead", an expression which arises from their custom of walking single file. These rudely-inquisitive greetings are heard only when two Indians meet abroad. At home the stranger is received in silence.

Some of the idioms are curiously characteristic of that point-no-point way of talking which savages have in common with children. Thus, *hai'-em* is "near", and *hai'-et-kem* is also "near", but not quite so near; and *kotun* is a "long way off", though that may be only on the opposite bank of the river. *Chu'-to* is "good"; *chu-to-si-ke'* is "very good", the only comparative expression there is.

While this is undoubtedly the largest, it is also probably the lowest nation in California, and it presents one of the most hopeless and saddening spectacles of heathen races. According to their own confession, in primitive times both sexes and all ages went absolutely naked. All of them north of the Stanilaus, and probably many south also, not only married cousins, but herded together so promiscuously in their wigwams that not a few white men believe and assert to this day the monstrous proposition that sisters were often taken for wives. But this is unqualifiedly false. The Indians all deny it emphatically, and not one of their accusers could produce an instance, having been deceived into the belief by the general circumstance above mentioned.

They eat all creatures that swim in the waters, all that fly through the air, and all that creep, crawl, or walk upon the earth, with a dozen or so exceptions. They have the most degraded and superstitious beliefs in wood-spirits, who produce those disastrous conflagrations to which California is subject; in water-spirits, who inhabit the rivers, consume the fish; and in fetichistic spirits, who assume the forms of owls and other birds, to render their lives a terror by night and by day.

In occasional specimens of noble physical stature they were not lacking, especially in Yosemite and the other mountain valleys; but the utter weakness, puerility, and imbecility of their conceptions, and the unspeakable obscenity of some of their legends, almost surpass belief.

But the saddest and gloomiest thing connected with the Miwok is the fact that many of them, probably a majority of all who have any well-defined ideas whatever on the subject, believe in the annihilation of the soul after death. When an Indian's friend departs the earth, he mourns him with that great and poignant sorrow of one who is without hope. He will live no more forever. All that he possessed is burned with him upon the funeral pyre, in order that nothing may remain to remind them afterward of one who is gone to black oblivion. So awful to them is the thought of one who is gone down to eternal nothingness that his name is never afterward even whispered. If one of his friends is so unfortunate as to possess the same name, he changes it for another, and if at any time they are compelled to mention the departed, with bated breath they murmur simply *it'-teh*, "him". Himself, his identity, is gone; his name is lost; he is blotted out; *itteh* represents merely the memory of a being that once was. Like all other tribes in California, they are gay and jovial in their lives; but while most of the others have a mitigation of the final terrors in the assured belief of an immortality in the Happy Western Land, the Miwok go down with a grim and stolid sullenness to the death of a dog that will live no more. It is necessary to say, however, that not all entertain this belief. It seems to prevail more especially south of the Merced, and among the most grave and thoughtful of these. Throughout the Sacramento and San Joaquin Valleys one will occasionally meet an Indian who holds to annihilation; but the creed is no where so prevalent as here.

The Miwok north of the Stanilaus designate tribes principally by the points of the compass. These are *tu'-mun, chu'-much, he'-zu-it, ol'-o-wit* (north, south, east, west), from which are formed tribal names as follows: Tu'-mun, Tu'-mi-dok, Ta-mo-le'-ka; Chu'-much, Chūm'-wit, Chu'-mi-dok or Chim'-i-dok, Chūm-te'-ya; Ol'-o-wit, Ol-o'-wi-dok, Ol-o-wi'-ya, etc. Ol-o'-wi-dok is the general name applied by the mountaineers to all the tribes on the plains as far west as Stockton and the San Joaquin.

But there are several names employed absolutely. On the south bank of the Middle Cosumnes are the Kâ'-ni; on Sutter Creek, the Yu-lo'-ni; in Yosemite, the A-wa'-ni; on the South Fork of the Merced, the Nūt'-chu; on the Stanislaus and Tuolumne, the extensive tribe of the Wal'-li; on the Middle Merced, the Chūm-te'-ya; on the Upper Chowchilla River, the Heth-to'-ya; on the Middle Chowchilla, the Chau-chil'-la; on the north bank of the Fresno, the Po'-ho-ni-chi.   There were probably others besides on the plains, but they have been so long extinct that their names are forgotten.   Dr. Bunnell mentions the "Potoencies", but no Indian had ever heard of such a tribe; also, the "Honachees", which is probably a mistake for the Mo-na'-chi, a name applied by some Indians to the Paiuti.

How extremely limited were their journeyings of old may be judged by the fact that all of them, no matter what two rivers they live between, always employ the same phrases: *wa-kal'-u-mi tu'-mun* (north river), and *wa-kal'-u-mi chu'-much* (south river).   The only fixed name I was ever able to learn was O-tūl'-wi-uh, which is the Tuolumne.

The name "Walli" has been the subject of a great deal of discussion among white men, as to its meaning and derivation.   Some assert that it is a word applied by the pioneers to the Indians, without any signification; others, that it is an aboriginal word, denoting "friends".   Probably the latter theory is due to the fact that the Indians, in meeting, frequently cry out "Walli! Walli!"   As a matter of fact, it is derived from the word *wal'-lim*, which means simply " down below "; and it appears to have been originated by the Yosemite Indians and others living high up in the mountains, and applied to the lower tribes with a slight feeling of contempt.   The Indians on the Stanislaus and Tuolumne use the term freely in conversing among themselves, but on the Merced it is never heard except when spoken by the whites.

For houses, the Miwok construct very rude affairs of poles and brushwood, which they cover with earth in the winter; in summer, as the general custom is, they move into mere brushwood shelters.   Higher up in the mountains they make a summer lodge of puncheons, in the shape of a sharp cone, with one side open, and a bivouac-fire in front of it.

Perhaps the only special points to be noted in their physiognomy are the smallness of many heads, and the flatness on the sinciput, caused by their lying on the hard baby-basket when infants.   I felt the heads of a rancheria near Chinese Camp, and was surprised at the diminutive balls which lurked within the masses of hair.   The chief, Captain John, was at least seventy years old, yet his head was still perceptibly flattened on the back, and I could almost encircle it with my hands.

For food they depend principally on acorns. They had, in common with many tribes both in the Sierra and in the Coast Range, a kind of granary to store them in for winter. When the crop was good and they harvested more than they wished to carry to camp just then, with a forethought not common among barbarians they laid by the remainder on the *Fig. 32* spot. Selecting a tree which presented a couple of forks a few feet from the ground, but above the reach of wild animals, they laid a pole across, and on that as a foundation, wove a cylinder-shaped granary of willow wickerwork, three or four feet in diameter and twice as high, which they filled with acorns and covered with thatch. There they remained safe. As these were often miles from a village, the circumstance denotes that they reposed no small confidence in each other's honesty. It goes near to refute altogether the frequent allegations that they are a nation of thieves. Nowadays, they make most of their granaries close to camp, either right on the ground or elevated on top of some posts.

It is generally asserted of these Indians that they will eat anything. But there is one exception, and that is the clean, sweet flesh of the skunk. Old hunters assert that it is such, but the aborigines detest it beyond measure. So uncompromising is their horror of this animal that they have never examined one; consequently they have an erroneous impression of its anatomy. They believe that the effluvium is produced, not by any peculiar secretion, but by the emission of wind! An old hunter related an amusing method of capturing this animal which he had seen among the Nishinam. One man attracted its attention in front while another ran up quickly behind, seized it by the tail, and by a blow with his hand on the back of the neck broke that organ before the beast could become offensive. The Miwok utilize it in one way at least; they sometimes hang the carcasses on trees along a trail difficult to follow, so that they can be guided by one sense if not by another. I have seen this myself.

They are very fond of hare, and make comfortable robes of their skins. They cut them into narrow slits, dry them in the sun, then lay them close together, and make a rude warp of them by tying or sewing strings across at intervals of a few inches.

Soap-root is used in the manufacture of a kind of glue, and the squaws make brushes of the fibrous matter encasing the bulb, wherewith they occasionally sweep out their wigwams and the earth for a small space around. Although there were millions of tall, straight pines in the mountains, the Miwok had no means of crossing rivers, except logs or clumsy rafts. All the dwellers on the plains, and as far up as the cedar-line, bought all their bows and many of their arrows from the upper mountaineers. An Indian is ten days in making a bow, and it is valued at $3, $4, and $5, according to the workmanship; an arrow at 12½ cents. Three kinds of money were employed in this traffic. White shell-buttons, pierced in the center and strung together, rate at $5 a yard (this money was less valuable than among the Nishinam, probably because these lived nearer the source of supply); "periwinkles" (olivella?) at $1 a yard; fancy marine shells at various prices, from $3 to $10 or $15 a yard, according to their beauty.

Their chieftainship, such as it is, is hereditary when there is a son or brother of commanding influence, which is very seldom; otherwise he is thrust aside for another. He is simply a master of ceremonies, except when a man of great ability appears, in which case he sometimes succeeds in uniting two or three of the little, discordant tribelets around him, and spends his life in a vain effort to harmonize others, and so goes down to his grave at the last broken-hearted. It is of no use; the greatest savage 131 intellect that ever existed could not have banded permanently together fifty villages of the California Indians.

When he decides to hold a dance in his village, he dispatches messengers to the neighboring rancherias, each bearing a string wherein is tied a number of knots. Every morning thereafter the invited chief unties one of the knots, and when the last one is reached they joyfully set forth for the dance—men, women, and children.

Occasionally there arises a great orator or prophet, who wields a wide influence, and exerts it to introduce reforms which seem to him desirable. Old Sam, of Jackson, Calaveras County, was such a one. Sometimes he would set out on a speaking tour, traveling many miles in all directions, and discoursing with much fervor and eloquence nearly all night, according to accounts. Shortly before I passed he had introduced two reforms, at which the reader will probably smile, but which were certainly salutary so far as they went. One was that the widows no longer tarred their heads in mourning, but painted their faces, which would be less lasting in its loathsome effects. The other was that instead of holding an annual "cry" in memory of the dead, they should dance and chant dirges.

In one of his speeches to his people he is reported to have counseled them to live at peace with the whites, to treat them kindly, and avoid quarrels whenever possible, as it was worse than useless to contend against their conquerors. He then diverged into remarks on economy in the household: "Do not waste cooked victuals. You never have too much, anyhow. The Americans do not waste their food. They work hard for it, and take care of it. They keep it in their houses out of the rain. You let the squirrels get into your acorns. When you eat a piece of pie, you eat it up as far as the apple goes, then throw the crust into the fire. When you have a pancake left you throw it to the dogs. Every family should keep only one dog. It is wasteful."

Tai-pok'-si, chief of the Chimteya, was a notable Indian in his generation, holding undisputed sovereignty in the valley of the Merced, from the South Fork to the plains. Early every morning, as soon as the families had had time decently to prepare breakfast, he would step out before his wigwam and lift up his sonorous voice like a Stentor, summoning the whole village to work in the gold-diggings, and himself went forth to share the labor of the humblest. Men, women, and children went out together, taking their dinners along, and the village was totally deserted until about three o'clock Every one worked hard, inspired by the example of their great chieftain, the men making dives in the Merced of a minute or more, and bringing up the rich gravel, while the women and children washed it on shore. They got plenty of gold and lived in civilized luxury so long as Taipoksi was alive. He was described by one who knew him well as a magnificent specimen of a savage, standing fully six feet high, straight and sinewy, shiny-black as an Ethiopian, with eyes like an eagle's, a lofty forehead, nostrils high and strongly chiseled, each of them showing a clean, bold ellipse. He died in 1857, and was buried in Rum Hollow with unparalleled pomp and splendor. Over 1,200 Indians were present at his funeral. After this grand old barbarian was gone his tribe speedily went to the bad; their industry lagged; their gold was gambled away; their fine clothing followed hard after it; dissension, disease, and death scattered them to the four winds.

Among the Miwok a bride is sometimes carried to the lodge of her husband on the back of a stalwart Indian, amid a joyous throng, singing songs, dancing, leaping, and whooping. In return for the presents given by the groom, his father-in-law gives the young couple various substantial articles, such as are needful in the scullery, to set them up in housekeeping. In fact, here, as generally throughout the State, it is a pretty well established usage that the parents are to do everything for their children, and the latter nothing until they marry. The father often continues these presents of meat and acorns for several years after the marriage. And what is his reward? Making himself a slave, he is treated substantially as such, and when he has become old, and ought to be tenderly nurtured, he frequently has to shift for himself.

Mention is made of a woman named Ha-u-chi-ah', living near Murphy's, who, in 1858, gave birth to twins and destroyed one of them, in accordance with the universal custom.

Some of their shamans are men and some women. Scarification and prolonged suction with the mouth are their staple methods. In case of colds and rheumatism they apply California balm of Gilead (*Picea grandis*) externally and internally. Stomachic affections and severe travail are treated with a plaster of hot ashes and moist earth. They think that their male shamans or sorcerers can sit on a mountain top, fifty miles distant from a man whom they wish to destroy, and accomplish that result by filliping poison toward him from their finger-ends. The shaman's prerogative is that he must be paid in advance; hence a man seeking his services brings his offering with him, a fresh-slain deer, or so many yards of shell-money, or something, and flings it down on the ground before him without a word, thereby intimating that he desires the equivalent of that in medicine and treatment. The patient's prerogative is that if he dies his friends may kill the physician.

In the acorn dance the whole company join hands and dance in a circle, men and women together—a position of equality not often accorded to the weaker sex. They generally have to dance by themselves in an outside *Fig. 33* circle, each woman behind her lord. Besides this fixed anniversary there are many occasional fandangoes, for feasting and amusement. They resemble a civilized ball somewhat, inasmuch as the young men of the village giving the entertainment contribute a sum of money wherewith to procure a great quantity of hare, wild-fowl, acorns, sweet roots, and other delicacies (nowadays generally a bullock, sheep, flour, fruit, etc.). Then they select a sunny glade, far within some sequestered forest where they will not 134 be disturbed by intruders, and plant green branches in the ground, forming a large circle. Grass and pine-straw are scattered within to form at once a divan and a dancing-floor. Here the invited villagers collect and spend frequently a week; gambling, feasting, and sleeping in the breezy shade by day, and by night dancing to lively tunes, with execrable and most industrious music, and wild, dithyrambic crooning of chants, and indescribable dances, now sweeping around in a ring beneath the overhanging pine-boughs, and now stationary, with plumes nodding and beadery jingling. It is wonderful what a world of riotous enjoyment the California Indians will compress into the space of a week.

They observe no puberty dance, neither does any other tribe south of 135 Chico.

There is no observance of the dance for the dead, but an annual mourning (*nŭt'-yu*) instead; and occasionally, in the case of a high personage, a special mourning, set by appointment a few months after his death. One or more villages assemble together in the evening, seat themselves on the ground in a circle, and engage in loud and demonstrative wailing, beating themselves and tearing their hair. The squaws wander off into the forest wringing their arms piteously, beating the air, with eyes upturned, and adjuring the departed one, whom they tenderly call "dear child", or "dear cousin" (whether a relative or not), to return. Sometimes, during a kind of trance or frenzy of sorrow, a squaw will dance three or four hours in the same place without cessation, crooning all the while, until she falls in a dead faint. Others, with arms interlocked, pace to and fro in a beaten path for hours, chanting weird death-songs with eldritch and inarticulate wailings—sad voicings of savage, hopeless sorrow.

On the Merced the widow does not apply pitch over the whole face, but only in a small blotch under the ears, while the younger squaws singe off their hair short. When some relative chances to be absent at the time of the funeral some article belonging to the deceased (frequently a hat nowadays) is preserved from the general sacrifice of his effects and retained until the absent member returns, that the sight of it may kindle his sorrow and awaken in his bosom fresh and piercing recollections of that being whom he will never more behold.

On the Lower Tuolumne, after dancing the frightful death-dance around the fresh-made grave into which the body has just been lowered, they go out of mourning by removing the pitch until the annual mourning comes round, when they renew it. On the latter occasion they make out of clothing and blankets manikins to represent the deceased, which they carry around the graves with shrieks of sorrow.

As soon as the annual mourning is over in autumn all the relatives of the departed are at full liberty to engage in their ordinary pursuits, to attend dances, etc., which before that were interdicted. That solemn occasion itself too frequently winds up with a gross debauch of sensuality. The oldest brother is entitled to his brother's widow, and he may even convey her home to his lodge on the return from the funeral, if he is so disposed, though that would be accounted a very scandalous proceeding.

Although cremation very generally prevailed among the Miwok there never was a time when it was universal. Captain John states that long before they had ever seen any Europeans, the Indians high up in the mountains buried their dead, though his people about Chinese Camp always burned. As low down on the Stanislaus as Robinson's Ferry long ranks of skeletons have been revealed by the action of the river, three or four feet beneath the surface, doubled up and covered with stones, of which none of the bones showed any charring.

In respect to legends, they relate one which is somewhat remarkable. First it is necessary to state that there is a lake-like expansion of the Upper Tuolumne some four miles long and from a half mile to a mile wide, directly north of Hatchatchie Valley (erroneously spelled Hetch Hetchy). It appears to have no name among Americans, but the Indians call it O-wai'-a-nuh, which is manifestly a dialectic variation of a-wai'-a, the generic word for "lake". Nat. Screech, a veteran mountaineer and hunter, states that he visited this region in 1850, and at that time there was a valley along the river having the same dimensions that this lake now has. Again, in 1855, he happened to pass that way and discovered that the lake had been formed as it now exists. He was at a loss to account for its origin; but subsequently he acquired the Miwok language as spoken at Little Gap, and while listening to the Indians one day he overheard them casually refer to the formation of this lake in an extraordinary manner. On being questioned they stated that there had been a tremendous cataclysm in that valley, the bottom of it having fallen out apparently, whereby the entire valley was submerged in the waters of the river. As nearly as he could ascertain from their imperfect methods of reckoning time this occurred in 1851; and in that year, while in the town of Sonora, Screech and many others remembered to have heard a huge explosion in that direction which they then supposed was caused by a local earthquake.

136

On Drew's Ranch, Middle Fork of the Tuolumne, lives an aged squaw called Dish-i, who was in the valley when this remarkable event occurred. According to her account the earth dropped in beneath their feet and the waters of the river leaped up and came rushing upon them in a vast, roaring flood, almost perpendicular like a wall of rock. At first the Indians were stricken dumb and motionless with terror, but when they saw the waters coming they escaped for life, though thirty or forty were overtaken and drowned. Another squaw named Isabel says that the stubs of trees, which are still plainly visible deep down in the pellucid waters, are considered by the old superstitious Indians to be evil spirits, the demons of the place, reaching up their arms, and that they fear them greatly. This account, if authentic, is valuable as throwing some light on the origin of Yosemite and other great cañons of the high Sierra.

An Indian of Garrote narrated to me a myth of the creation of man and woman by the coyote, which contained a very large amount of aboriginal dirt. When the legends of the California Indians are pure, which they generally are, they are often quite pretty; but when they diverge into impurity they contain the most gratuitous and abominable obscenity ever conceived by the mind of man.

The following is a fable told at Little Gap:

CREATION OF MAN.

After the coyote had finished all the work of the world and the inferior creatures he called a council of them to deliberate on the creation of man. They sat down in an open space in the forest, all in a circle, with the lion at the head. On his right sat the grizzly bear, next the cinnamon bear, and so on around according to the rank, ending with the little mouse, which sat at the lion's left.

The lion was the first to speak, and he declared he should like to see man created with a mighty voice like himself, wherewith he could frighten all animals. For the rest he would have him well covered with hair, terrible fangs in his claws, strong talons, etc.

The grizzly bear said it was ridiculous to have such a voice as his neighbor, for he was always roaring with it and scared away the very prey he wished to capture. He said the man ought to have prodigious strength, and move about silently but very swiftly if necessary, and be able to grip his prey without making a noise.

The buck said the man would look very foolish, in his way of thinking, unless he had a magnificent pair of antlers on his head to fight with. He also thought it was very absurd to roar so loudly, and he would pay less attention to the man's throat than he would to his ears and his eyes, for he would have the first like a spider's web and the second like fire.

The mountain sheep protested he never could see what sense there was in such antlers, branching every way, only to get caught in the thickets. If the man had horns mostly rolled up, they would be like a stone on each side of his head, giving it weight, and enabling him to butt a great deal harder.

When it came the coyote's turn to speak, he declared all these were the stupidest speeches he ever heard, and that he could hardly keep awake while listening to such a pack of noodles and nincompoops. Every one of them wanted to make the man like himself. They might just as well take one of their own cubs and call it a man. As for himself he knew he was not the best animal that could be made, and he could make one better than himself or any other. Of course, the man would have to be like himself in having four legs, five fingers, etc. It was well enough to have a voice like the lion, only the man need not roar all the while with it. The grizzly bear also had some good points, one of which was the shape of his feet, which enabled him easily to stand erect; and he was in favor, therefore, of making the man's feet nearly like the grizzly's. The grizzly was also happy in having no tail, for he had learned from his own experience that that organ was only a harbor for fleas. The buck's eyes and ears were pretty good, perhaps better than his own. Then there was the fish, which was naked, and which he envied, because hair was a burden most of the year; and he, therefore, favored a man without hair. His claws ought to be as long as the eagle's, so that he could hold things in them. But after all, with all their separate gifts, they must acknowledge that there was no animal besides himself that had wit enough to supply the man; and he should be obliged, therefore, to make him like himself in that respect also—cunning and crafty.

After the coyote had made an end, the beaver said he never heard such twaddle and nonsense in his life. No tail, indeed! He would make a man with a broad, flat tail, so he could haul mud and sand on it.

The owl said all the animals seemed to have lost their senses; none of them wanted to give the man wings. For himself, he could not see of what use anything on earth could be to himself without wings.

The mole said it was perfect folly to talk about wings, for with them the man would be certain to bump his head against the sky. Besides that, if he had eyes and wings both, he would get his eyes burnt out by flying too near the sun; but without eyes he could burrow in the cool, soft earth, and be happy.

Last of all, the little mouse squeaked out that he would make a man with eyes, of course, so he could see what he was eating; and as for burrowing in the ground, that was absurd.

So the animals disagreed among themselves, and the council broke up in a row. The coyote flew at the beaver, and nipped a piece out of his cheek; the owl jumped on top of the coyote's head, and commenced lifting his scalp, and there was a high time. Every animal set to work to make a man according to his own ideas; and, taking a lump of earth, each one commenced molding it like himself; but the coyote began to make one like that he had described in the council. It was so late before they fell to work that nightfall came on before any one had finished his model, and they all lay down and fell asleep. But the cunning coyote staid awake and worked hard on his model all night. When all the other animals were sound asleep, he went around and discharged water on their models, and so spoiled them. In the morning early he finished his model and gave it life long before the others could make new models; and thus it was that man was made by the coyote.

Many authors, in writing of the California Indians, use the term "sweat-house" loosely and inaccurately, applying it not only to the sudatory proper, but also to the public structure which I have variously designated "assembly-house", "assembly-hall", "dance-house", etc. Among the tribes of *Fig. 34* Southern California, south of Sacramento City, for instance, the sweat-house is made in the same way as the assembly-house, that is, a dome-shaped structure of poles and wicker-work, thatched and then heavily covered with earth; but it is much smaller. It is seldom used for any but purely sudatory purposes. In Northern California (except on the Klamath) the sweat-house is sometimes nearly as large as the assembly-house; and as it is made in the same way, and is sometimes used for certain religious or ecstatic dances, it has come to be a wide-spread popular error to confound it with the assembly-house.

Following are the Miwok numerals, as spoken in Yosemite. There are slight variations everywhere, but the only one of importance is found on Calaveras River, where *lu'-teh* is substituted for *keng'-a.*

One.	keng'-a.	Six.	ti-mok'-a.
Two.	o-ti'-ko.	Seven.	tit-oi'-a.
Three.	to-lok'-o.	Eight.	kâ-win'-ta.
Four.	o-i'-sa.	Nine.	el-le'-wa.
Five.	ma-cho'-ka.	Ten.	na-a'-cha.

CHAPTER XXXIV.

YOSEMITE.

There is no doubt the Indians would be much amused if they could know what a piece of work we have made of some of their names. As stated in the Introduction, all California Indian names that have any significance at all must be interpreted on the plainest and most prosaic principles; whereas the great, grim walls of Yosemite have been made by the white man to blossom with aboriginal poetry like a page of "Lalla Rookh". From the "Great Chief of the Valley" and the "Goddess of the Valley" down to the "Virgin Tears" and the "Cataract of Diamonds", the sumptuous imaginations of various discoverers have trailed through that wonderful gorge blazons of mythological and barbarian heraldry of an Oriental gorgeousness. It would be a pity, truly, if the Indians had not succeeded in interpreting more poetically the meanings of the place than our countrymen have done in such bald appellations as "Vernal Fall", "Pigeon Creek", and the like; but whether they did or not, they did not perpetrate the melodramatic and dime-novel shams that have been fathered upon them.

In the first place the aborigines never knew of any such locality as Yosemite Valley. Second, there is not now and there has not been anything in the valley which they call Yosemite. Third, they never called "Old Ephraim" himself Yosemite, nor is there any such a word in the Miwok language.

The valley has always been known to them, and is to this day, when speaking among themselves, as A-wá-ni. This, it is true, is only the name of one of the ancient villages which it contained; but by prominence it 138 gave its name to the valley, and, in accordance with Indian usage almost everywhere, to the inhabitants of the same. The word "Yosemite" is simply a very beautiful and sonorous corruption of the word for "grizzly bear".

On the Stanislaus and north of it the word is *u-zú-mai-ti;* at Little Gap, *o-só-mai-ti;* in Yosemite itself, *u-zú-mai-ti;* on the South Fork of the Merced, *uh-zú-mai-tuh.*

Mr. J. M. Hutchings, in his "Scenes of Wonder and Curiosity in California", states that the pronunciation on the South Fork is "Yohamite". Now, there is occasionally a kind of cockney in the tribe, who cannot get the letter "h" right. Different Indians will pronounce the word for "wood" *su-sú-eh, sú-suh, hu-hú-eh;* also, the word for "eye", *hun'-ta, hun'-tum, shun'-ta.* It may have been an Indian of this sort who pronounced the word that way; I never heard it so spoken.

In other portions of California the Indian names have effected such slight lodgment in our atlases that it is seldom worth while to go much out of the way to set them right; but there are so many of them preserved in Yosemite that it is different. Professor Whitney and Mr. Hutchings, in their respective guide-books, state that they derived their catalogues of Indian names from white men. The Indians certainly have a right to be heard in this department at least; and when they differ from the interpreters every right-thinking man will accept the statement of an intelligent aborigine as against a score of Americans. The Indian can very seldom give a connected, philosophical account of his customs and ideas, for which one must depend on men who have observed them; but if he does not know the simple words of his own language, pray who does?

Acting on this belief, I employed Choko (a dog), generally known as Old Jim, and accounted the wisest aboriginal head in Yosemite, to go with me around the valley and point out in detail all the places. He is one of the very few original Awani now living; for a California Indian, he is exceptionally frank and communicative, and he is generally considered by Americans as truthful as he is shiftless, a kind of aboriginal Sam Lawson. His statements and pronunciations I compared with those of other Indians, that the chances of error might be as much reduced as possible. In the following list the signification of the name is given whenever there is any known to the Indians.

Wa-kal'-la (the river). Merced River.

Kai-al'-a-wa, Kai-al-au'-wa, the mountains just west of El Capitan.

Pūt′-pūt-on, the little stream first crossed on entering the valley on the north side.

Lung-u-tu-ku′-ya, Ribbon Fall.

Po′-ho-no, Po-ho′-no, (though the first is probably the more correct), Bridal-Veil Fall. In Hutchings's Guide-Book, it is stated that the Indians believe this stream and the lake from which it flows to be bewitched, and that they never pass it without a feeling of distress and terror. Probably the Americans have laughed them out of this superstition, as it certainly is not now perceptible. This word is said to signify "evil wind". The only "evil wind" that an Indian knows of is a whirlwind, which is *poi-i′-cha* or *kan′-u-ma*.

Tu-tok-a-nu′-la, El Capitan. This name is a permutative substantive formed from the verb *tūl-tak′-a-na*, to creep or advance by degrees, like a measuring-worm. This may, therefore, be called the "Measuring-worm Stone", of which the origin will be explained in the legend given below.

Ko-su′-ko, Cathedral Rock.

Pu-si′-na, Chuk′-ka (the squirrel and the acorn-cache), a tall, sharp needle, with a smaller one at its base, just east of Cathedral Rock. *Pu-si′-na* is "squirrel", and *chuk′-ka* is "acorn-cache". A single glance at it will show how easily the simple savages, as they were pointing out to one another the various objects, imagined here a squirrel nibbling at the base of an acorn granary.

Fig. 35

Kom-pom-pe′-sa, a low rock next west of Three Brothers. This is erroneously spelled "Pompompasus", applied to Three Brothers, and interpreted "mountains playing leap-frog". The Indians know neither the word nor the game.

Loi′-a, Sentinel Rock.

Sak′-ka-du-eh, Sentinel Dome.

Cho′-lok (the fall), Yosemite Fall. This is the generic word for "fall".

Ūm′-mo-so (generally contracted by the Indians to Ūm′-moas or Ūm′-mo), the bold, towering cliff east of Yosemite Fall. According to Choko, there was formerly a hunting-station near this point, back in the mountains, where the Indians secreted themselves to kill deer when driven past by others. If we may credit him, they missed more than they hit. In his jargon of English, Spanish, and Indian, supplemented with copious and expressive pantomime, he described how they hid themselves in the booth, and how the deer came scurrying past; then he quickly caught up his bow and shot, shot, shot; then peered out of the bushes, looked blank, laughed, and cried out, "All run away; no shoot um deer!"

Ma'-ta (the cañon), Indian Cañon. A generic word, in explaining which the Indians hold up both hands to denote perpendicular walls.

Ham'-mo-ko (usually contracted to Ham'-moak), a generic word, used several times in the valley to denote the broken *débris* lying at the foot of the walls.

U-zu'-mai-ti Lâ'-wa-tuh (grizzly-bear skin), Glacier Rock. The Indians give it this name from the grayish, grizzled appearance of the wall and a fancied resemblance to a bear-skin stretched out on one of its faces.

Tu-tu'-lu-wi-sak, Tu-tūl'-wi-ak, the southern wall of South Cañon.

Fig. 36   Cho-ko-nip'-o-deh (baby-basket), Royal Arches. This curved and overhanging canopy-rock bears no little resemblance to an Indian baby-basket. Another form is *cho-ko'-ni;* and either one means literally "dog-place" or "dog-house".

Tol'-leh, the soil or surface of the valley wherever not occupied by a village; the commons. It also denotes the bank of a river.

Pai-wai'-ak (white water?), Vernal Fall. The common word for "water" is *kik'-kuk,* but *a-wai'-a* means "a lake" or body of water. I have detected a conjectural root, *pai, pi,* denoting "white", in two languages.

Yo-wai'-yi, Nevada Fall. In this word also we detect the root of *awaia.*

Tis-se'-yak, South Dome. This is the name of a woman who figures in a legend related below. The Indian woman cuts her hair straight across the forehead, and allows the sides to drop along her cheeks, presenting a square face, which the Indians account the acme of female beauty; and they think they discover this square face in the vast front of South Dome.

To-ko'-ye, North Dome. This rock represents Tisseyak's husband. On one side of him is a huge, conical rock, which the Indians call the acorn-basket that his wife threw at him in anger.

Shun'-ta, Hun'-ta (the eye), the Watching Eye.

A-wai'-a (a lake), Mirror Lake.

Sa-wah' (a gap), a name occurring frequently.

Wa-ha'-ka, a village which stood at the base of Three Brothers; also, that rock itself. This was the westernmost village in the valley, and the next one above was

Sak'-ka-ya, on the south bank of the river, a little west of Sentinel Rock. The only other village on the south bank was

Hok-ok'-wi-dok, which stood very nearly where Hutchings's Hotel now stands, opposite Yosemite Fall.

Ku-mai'-ni, a village which was situated at the lower end of the great meadow, about a quarter of a mile from Yosemite Fall.

A-wa'-ni, a large village standing directly at the foot of Yosemite Fall. This was the ruling town, the metropolis of this little mountain democracy, and the giver of its name, and it is said to have been the residence of the celebrated chief Ten-ai'-ya.

Ma-che'-to, the next village east, at the foot of Indian Cañon.

No-to-mid'-u-la, a village about four hundred yards east of Macheto.

Le-sam'-ai-ti, a village standing about a fifth of a mile above the last-mentioned.

Wis-kul'-la, the village which stood at the foot of the Royal Arches, and the uppermost one in the valley.

Thus it will be seen that there were nine villages in Yosemite Valley, and, according to Choko, there were formerly others extending as far down 140 as Bridal-Veil Fall, which were destroyed in wars that occurred before the whites came. At a low estimate these nine villages must have contained four hundred and fifty inhabitants. Dr. L. H. Bunnell indirectly states that the valley was not occupied during the winter, and was used only as a summer resort and as a stronghold of refuge in case of defeat Fig. 37 elsewhere; but the Indians now living say it was occupied every winter. This is quite possible, for Mr. Hutchings and others tarry there throughout the year without inconvenience. Moreover, the assertion of the Indians is borne out by the locations of the villages themselves, which Choko pointed out with great minuteness. With the exception of the two on the south bank they were all built as close to the north wall as the avalanches of snow and ice would permit, in order to get the benefit of the sunshine, just as Mr. Hutchings's winter cottage is to-day. If they had been intended only for summer occupation they would have been placed, according to Indian custom, close to the river. And the fact that the Indians all leave the valley in the winter nowadays makes nothing against this theory, for they have become so dependent on the whites for the means of making a livelihood that they would go near to perish if they remained.

LEGEND OF TU-TOK-A-NU'-LA.

There were once two little boys living in the valley who went down to the river to swim. After paddling and splashing about to their hearts' content they went on shore and crept up on a huge bowlder that stood beside the water, on which they lay down in the warm sunshine to dry themselves. Very soon they fell asleep, and slept so soundly that they never wakened more. Through sleeps, moons, and snows, winter and summer, they slumbered on. Meantime the great rock whereon they slept was treacherously rising day and night, little by little, until it soon lifted them up beyond the sight of their friends, who sought them everywhere weeping. Thus they were borne up at last beyond all human help or reach of human voice, lifted up into the blue heavens, far up, far up, until they scraped their faces against the moon; and still they slumbered and slept year after year safe amid the clouds. Then upon a time all the animals assembled together to bring down the little boys from the top of the great rock. Every animal made a spring up the face of the wall as far as he could leap. The little mouse could only jump up a handbreadth; the rat, two handbreadths; the raccoon, little further, and so on, the grizzly bear making a mighty leap far up the wall, but falling back in vain, like all the others. Last of all the lion tried, and he jumped up further than any other animal had, but he too fell down flat on his back. Then came along an insignificant measuring-worm, which even the mouse could have crushed by treading on it, and began to creep up the rock. Step by step, a little at a time, he measured his way up until he presently was above the lion's jump, then pretty soon out of sight. So he crawled up and up through many sleeps for about one whole snow, and at last he reached the top. Then he took the little boys and came down the same way he went up and brought them safely down to the ground. And so the rock was called after the measuring-worm (*tultakana*) Tutokanula.

This is not only a true Indian story, but it has a pretty meaning, being a kind of parallel to the fable of the hare and the tortoise that ran a race. What all the great animals of the forest could not do the despised measuring-worm accomplished simply by patience and perseverance. It also has its value as showing the Indian idea of the formation of Yosemite, and that they must have arrived in the valley after it had assumed its present form. It should be remarked that the word *tultakana* means both the measuring-worm and its way of creeping.

We turn now to the legend of Tis-se'-yak. As it stands in Hutchings's Guide-Book it was written by S. M. Cunningham, one of the earliest settlers in the valley, who first printed it in an eastern newspaper. It is a thousand pities to hack and slash in such a miserable way this somewhat tropical legend, but fidelity to aboriginal truth compels me to do it. In its present shape it is a production quite too embellished to have originated in a California Indian's imagination, hence it is not representative, not illustrative. Tisseyak, instead of being a "goddess of the valley", was a very prosaic and commonplace woman, who was beaten by her husband because she drank the water before him; and the picture of Indian life revealed in that action, however rude and brutal it may be, is wholly concealed in the story as Mr. Cunningham wrote it.

LEGEND OF TIS-SE'-YAK.

Tisseyak and her husband journeyed from a country very far off, and entered this valley foot-sore and weary. She came in advance, bowing far *Fig. 38* forward under the heavy burden of her great conical basket, which was strapped across her forehead, while he followed easily after, with a rude staff in his hand and a roll of skin-blankets flung over his back. After their long journey across the mountains they were exceedingly thirsty, and they now hastened forward to drink of the cool waters. But the woman was still in front, and thus it fell out that she reached the lake Awaia first. Then she dipped up the water of the lake in her basket and quaffed long and deep. She even drank up all the water and drained the lake dry before her husband arrived. And thus, because the woman had drunk all the water, there came a grievous drought in that land, and the earth was dried up so that it yielded neither herb nor grass. But the thing which the woman had done displeased her husband, and his wrath was greatly moved because he had no water, so that he beat the woman with his staff full sore. She fled from before him, but he pursued after her and beat her yet the more. And the woman wept, and in her anger she turned about and reviled the man and flung her basket at him. So it befell that, even while they were in this attitude, one standing over against the other, facing, they were turned into stone for their wickedness, and there they have remained to this day. The basket lies upturned beside the husband, while the woman's face is tear-stained with long dark lines trailing down.

South Dome is the woman and North Dome is her husband, while beside the latter is a lower dome which represents the basket. The acme of female beauty is reached in the fashion of cutting off the hair straight across the top of the forehead, and allowing the side-locks to droop beside the ears; and the Indians fancy they discover this square-cut appearance on the face of the South Dome. Probably the only significance of this little story is a reference to some severe drought that once prevailed in the valley.

There are other legends in Yosemite, including one of a Mono maiden who loved an Awani brave and was imprisoned by her cruel father in a cave until she perished; also one of the inevitable lover's leap. But neither Choko nor any other Indian could give me any information touching them, and Choko dismissed them all with the contemptuous remark, "White man too much lie."

CHAPTER XXXV.

THE YO'-KUTS.

In the language of this nation *yo'-kuts* denotes " Indian" or "Indians", and *no'-no*, "man". (It is a singular fact that nearly every language has different words for " man " and " Indian".) As often before, so here again it is necessary to adopt a word in common use as a basis of classification, since they have no national name.

We have seen how the California Indians in the extreme northern part of their domain were, at the time of the American advent, being driven back and crushed out by the stronger and fiercer Athabascan races. Likewise in the southern part of their habitat this peaceful race was slowly giving way before the incursions of the more powerful and warlike Paiuti of Nevada. All along the eastern side of the great interior basin the Sierra Nevada interposes an effectual barrier against the latter, protecting the Californians on that side; but the passes which occur at the northern and southern points of junction between the Sierra and the Coast Range allowed the Athabascan tribes and the Paiuti, respectively, to swarm in toward the rich and tempting plains of California, dispossessing the feebler peoples who were there before them.

Living as they do at the lower end of the great basin, the Yokuts received the brunt of the Paiuti attacks. So severe were the latter that the Yokuts, as a geographically solid body of allied tribes, were cut in two in one place and nearly in another. Their habitat stretched originally from the Fresno River to Fort Tejon; but the Paiuti tribes, swarming through Ta-hi'-cha-pa, Tejon, and Walker's Passes, seized and occupied Kern River, White River, Posa Creek, and Kern Lake, thus completely severing the Yokuts nation, and leaving an isolated fragment of it at Fort Tejon, in

369

142 a nook of the mountains. Doubtless they would eventually have seized
all the streams emptying into Tulare Lake, but they seem to have become
enervated by the malaria, and reduced to the same condition of sluggishness as the people whom they displaced.

At the time of the American advent, therefore, the Yokuts occupied
the south bank of the Fresno; the San Joaquin, from Whisky Creek down
to the mouth of the Fresno; King's River, from Mill Creek down to the
mouth; the Kaweah, Tule River, and Deer Creek; the west shore of
Tulare Lake, and the isolated mountain-nook at Fort Tejon.

Their tribal distribution was as follows: On the San Joaquin, from
Whisky Creek down to Millerton, are the Chŭk'-chan-si; farther down, the
Pit'-ka-chi, now extinct. On King's River, going down stream, are the fol-
lowing bands, in their order: Tis-e'-chu, Chai-nim'-ai-ni, It-i'-cha, Wi'-chi-
kik, Ta'-chi, No-toan'-ai-ti, the latter on the lake, the Tachi at Kingston.
143 On Dry Creek are the Kas-so'-vo; in Squaw Valley the Chu-kai'-mi-na.
On the Kaweah River, beginning in the mountains, are the Wik'-sach-i,
Wik-chum'-ni (in the foot-hills), Kan-i'-a (on the edge of the plains),
Yu'-kol (on the plains), Te'-lum-ni (two miles below Visalia), Chu'-nut (at
the lake). On Tule River are the O-ching'-i-ta (at Painted Rock), Ai'-a-pai
(at Soda Spring), Mai-ai'-u (on South Fork), Sa-wakh'-tu (on the main
river), Ki-a-wet'-ni (at Porterville). At Fort Tejon are the Tin'-lin-neh
(from tin'-nilh, "a hole"), so called on account of some singular depressions
in the earth in that vicinity. A little further north, near Kern Lake, are
the Po-hal'-lin-Tin'leh (squirrel-holes), so named on account of the great
number of ground-squirrels living in that place.

In the Yokuts nation there appears to be more political solidarity, more
capacity in the petty tribes of being grouped into large and coherent
masses, than is common in the State. This is particularly true of those
living on the plains, who display in their encampments a military precision
Fig. 39 and regularity which are remarkable. Every village consists of a single
row of wigwams, conical or wedge-shaped, generally made of tule, and
just enough hollowed out within so that the inmates may sleep with the
head higher than the feet, all in perfect alignment, and with a continuous
awning of brushwood stretching along in front. In one end-wigwam lives

the village captain; in the other, the shaman or *si-se'-ro* (Spanish, *hechizero*). In the mountains there is some approach to this martial array, but it is universal on the plains.

But it is more especially in their actual organization, and in the instances of great leaders who have arisen, that this quality is manifested. Every large natural division of territory possessing a certain homogeneity constitutes the domain of one tribe and one chief—for instance, a river-valley, from the snow-line down to the plains, or from the foot-hills to the lake—though nowadays this system has been disturbed by the whites. In this domain every village has a captain, who stands to the central chief in the relation of a governor to the President, and is generally distinguished from his subjects by his long hair. At certain annual meetings and other occasions each captain reports to his chief the general condition of his village as to morals, as to quarrels, as to the acorn-crop, etc. In return, the chief delivers a long oration of advice and counsel; warns, instructs, and admonishes his subalterns; and, if necessary, berates soundly any delinquent. Both the chiefship and the captaincy are hereditary, that is, if the son does not prove to be a fool. But either can appoint his successor as he likes. For instance, Santiago, captain of the Tachi, had two sons, Ka'-teh and Ku'-to-mats, of whom Kateh was the first-born, but he designated the other to succeed him, because, as Kateh ingenuously acknowledged, "he was the smartest".

Instances of this harmonious hierarchy of ranks exist yet in Chi-wi'-ni, who is chief over all the villages in Squaw Valley; in Wa-tu'-ga, who is chief of the three upper villages on King's River; and in Slōk'-nich, chief of the Chukchansi.

The captain has no substantial authority, even to appoint the time for a special mourning or a fandango; he must request the chief to do so in his behalf. But nowadays there are many villages which have broken away and become independent, and their captains exercise all the power the tribe will bear, which is small. In early days the chief sometimes wielded considerable authority, as the following instances will evince:

Ten or fifteen years ago Pascual consolidated all the villages on King's River, except the one at the mouth, into a robust little kingdom;

and he made his name feared and dreaded for many a score of miles around. He "bound out" his subjects at will, adults and children alike, to the ranchmen, on life-long indentures.

Nai-ak'-a-we was a famous prophet of the Chukchansi, who died in 1854. It is said that his name was known and his power was acknowledged from King's River as far north as Columbia; but this seems hardly probable. Naiakawe had a lofty ambition, and he meditated great and benevolent designs for his people, but he was doomed to disappointment. He sought to mollify those miserable janglings and that clannishness which have been so fatal to the California Indians from time immemorial; to reconcile the warring captains of villages and chiefs of tribes, and thereby harmonize them into one powerful nation, peaceful at home and respected and feared abroad. But the question of a food-supply was one which this savage statesman, however able and far-sighted, could not master. In ancient times they had immense herds of elk and deer, and, sweeping over the plains on their swift mustangs, they could shoot down at any time a fat bronco bogged by the lake (for the Indians of this State used to eat horse-flesh, until the influence of the Americans gradually induced them to abandon it); but now all these were gone, they had to scatter into families to collect food, the wretched feuds of the petty captains were eternally breaking out afresh, and Naiakawe beheld one hope after another and one noble design after another pass away; so he died at last broken-hearted. He said he did not wish to survive the ruin of his people.

Another notable characteristic of the Yokuts is the great influence and extensive journeyings of their wizards or rain-makers (*tēss*). Ke'-ya, who lives at Woodville, is one instance; but the most remarkable is Hop-ōd'-no. Though living at Fort Tejon, he has by his personal presence, his elo-quence, and his cunning jugglery, made his fame and authority recognized for two hundred miles northward, to the banks of the San Joaquin. In 1870, the first of two successive years of drought, he made a pilgrimage from the fort up as far as King's River, and at every centrally-located vil-lage he made a pause and sent out runners to collect all the Indians of the vicinal villages to listen to him. In long and elaborate harangues he would promise them to bring rain on the dried-up earth, if they would contribute

liberally of their substance.   But he was yet an unknown prophet.   They
were incredulous, and mostly laughed him to scorn, whereupon he would
leave the village in high dudgeon, denouncing war upon their heads, and
threatening them with a continuance of the drought another year far worse
than before.   Sure enough, the enraged Hopodno brought drought a second year, and the Indians were smitten with remorse and terror, believing
him endowed with superhuman power; and when next year he made a second pilgrimage, offerings were showered upon him in abundance, and men   144
heard him with trembling.   He compelled them to pay him fifty cents
apiece, American money, and many gladly gave much more.   And he
made rain.

As to their implements and weapons, there are some interesting particulars to be noted.   Here, as everywhere on the Sacramento and Joaquin
plains, the Indians make no bows, but purchase them all from the mountaineers.   This is because they have no cedar.   This wood is extremely
brittle when dry, and is then the poorest possible material for bows; but   *Fig. 40*
by anointing it every day with deer's marrow while it is drying the Indian
overcomes this quality and renders it the best.   The bow is taken from the
white or sap wood, the outside of the tree being also the outside of the bow.
It is scraped and polished down with wonderful painstaking, so that it may
bend evenly, and the ends are generally carved so as to point back slightly.
Then the Indian takes a quantity of deer's sinew, splits it up with flint into
small fibers, and glues them on the outside or flat back of the weapon until
it becomes semi-cylindrical in shape.   These strings of sinew, being lapped
around the end of the bow and doubled back a little way, impart to it its
wonderful strength and elasticity.   The glue is made by boiling the joints
of various animals and combining the product with pitch.

I saw a bow thus carefully made in the hands of an aged chief, and it
was truly a magnificent weapon.   It was about five feet long, smooth and
shining—for when it becomes a little soiled the fastidious savage scrapes
it slightly with flint, then anoints it afresh with marrow—and of such great
strength that it would require a giant to bend it in battle.   For lack of
skins the owner carried it in a calico case.   The string, composed of twisted
sinew, was probably equal in strength to a sea-grass rope of three times its

diameter. When not used the bow was unstrung, and the string tied around the left limb of the bow, and to prevent the slightest lesion of either the bow or the string the former had a section of fur from some animal's tail, about four inches long, slipped on to it.

Of arrows, the Indians living on the plains made some for themselves out of button-willow, straight twigs of the buckeye, and canes, but the most durable came from the mountains. There are two kinds, war-arrows and game-arrows; the former furnished with flint-heads, the latter not. The shaft of the war-arrow consists of a single piece, but that of the game-arrow is frequently composed of three pieces, furnished with sockets so adjusted as to fit into each other snugly. When the hunter, lurking behind the covert, sees the quarry approaching, he measures quickly with his eye the probable length of the shot he will have to make, and if it is a long one he couches his arrow with three pieces; but if a short one, with extraordinary quickness he twitches it apart, takes out the middle section, claps the two end sections together again, and fires. An arrow made of what we should pronounce the frailest of all woods, the tender shoot of a buckeye, and pointed with flint, has carried death to many a savage in battle. I have seen an Indian couch a game-arrow, which was pointed only with a section of arrow-wood, and drive it a full half-inch into the hardest oak! An old hunter says he has seen an Indian stand a hundred paces distant from a hare, slowly raise his long, polished bow, shoot a quick glance along the arrow, then send it whizzing through both his enormous ears, pinning him fast to a tree behind him.

Some mention was made in Chapter XI of the manner in which flint arrow-heads are made. Mr. E. G. Waite, in a communication to the *Overland Monthly*, gives the following description of the method employed both in Central California and among the Klamaths, as he witnessed it in an early day:

"The rock of flint or obsidian, esteemed by the natives for arrow-pointing, is broken into flat pieces, after the manner usually described. When the pieces have reached a proper size for arrow-heads the mode of finishing it is in this wise: The palm of the left hand is covered with buckskin held in its place by the thumb being thrust through a hole in it. The inchoate arrow-head is laid on this pad along the thick of the thumb, the points of the fingers pressing it firmly down. The instrument used to shape the stone is the end of a deer's antler, from four to six inches in length, held in the right hand. The small round point of this is judiciously pressed upon the edge of the stone, cleaving it away underward in small scales. The buckskin, of course, is to prevent the flesh from being wounded by the sharp scales. The arrow-head is frequently turned around and over to cleave away as much from one side as the other, and to give it the desired size and shape. It is a work of no little care and skill to make 145 even so rude an instrument as an arrow-head seems to be, only the most expert being very successful at the business. Old men are usually seen at this employment."

Mr. B. P. Avery, in an article entitled "Chips from an Indian Workshop", published in the same magazine, gives a very pleasant account of a visit made by him, near the summit of the Sierra, to what had evidently been the spots selected by the aborigines for the manufacture of these arrow-heads. They were generally so chosen as to show that the Indians had an eye for the picturesque and the romantic, on bold, overlooking promontories, commanding prospects far and wide down the mountain slope and over the plains; and the brilliant-colored chips of obsidian, jasper, chert, cornelian, and other flints, lying in piles, completed a very pleasing picture.

Most California Indians go now, and always have gone, barefoot; but some few were industrious enough to make for themselves moccasins of a very rude sort, more properly sandals. Their method of tanning was by means of brain-water. They dried the brains of deer and other animals, reduced it to powder, put the powder into water, and soaked the skins therein—a process which answered tolerably well. The graining was done with flints. Elk-hide, being very thick, make the best sandals.

The usual shell-money is used among them, and a string of it reaching from the point of the middle finger to the elbow is valued at 25 cents. A section of bone, very white and polished, about two and a half inches long, is sometimes strung on the string, and rates at 12½ cents. They uniformly undervalue articles bought from the Americans; for instance, goods which cost them at the store $5 they sell among themselves for $3, or thereabout. This is done by the old Indians, who consider an Indian dollar better than an American.

They say that, in remote times, they were accustomed to rub their acorns to flour on a stone slightly hollowed, like the Mexican *metate*, which was a suggestion of the mouse; but nowadays they pound them in holes on top of huge bowlders, which was a suggestion of the wiser coyote. On a bowlder in Coarse Gold Gulch, I counted eighty-six of these acorn-holes, which shows that they must have been used many centuries.

For snaring quail, rabbits, and other small game, they employ cords made of a kind of "wild flax" found in the Sierra. I presume this "wild flax" is milkweed (*Asclepias*).

Manzanita cider is made of a much better quality than the wretched stuff seen among the Wintūn. After reducing the berries to flour by pounding, they carefully remove all the seeds and skins, then soak the flour in water for a considerable length of time. A squaw then heaps it up in a little mound, with a crater in the center, into which she pours a minute stream of water, allowing it to percolate through. In this way she gets about a gallon an hour of a really delicious beverage, clear, cool, clean, and richer than most California apple cider. The Indians consume it all before it has time to ferment, so that they do not get intoxicated on it.

In the mountain streams which empty into Tulare Lake they catch lake trout, chubs, and suckers. Sometimes they construct a weir across the river with a narrow chute and a trap set in it; then go above and stretch a line of brushwood from one bank to the other, which they drag down stream, driving the fish into the trap. Another way is to erect a brushwood booth over the water, so thickly covered as to be perfectly dark inside; then an Indian lies flat on his belly, peering down though a hole, and when a fish passes under him he spears it. The spear is pointed with bone, and is two-pronged. Still another method is employed on Tule River and King's River. An Indian takes a funnel-shaped trap in his teeth and hands, buoys himself on a little log, and then floats silently down the rapids, holding the net open to receive the fish that may be shooting up. On Tulare Lake they construct very rude, frail punts or mere troughs of tule, about ten feet long, in which they cruise timidly about near the shore.   There is a margin where the bottom is almost level and the waves run light; but the middle of the lake is of immense depth, and the billows sometimes lash themselves into oceanic proportions.

Around the lake and on King's River one will often find a family using a tolerably well-made stone mortar. They always admit that they did not manufacture these implements, but happened on them in digging or found them on the surface, and that they belonged to a race other than their own. They sometimes have the ingenuity to improve on them by fastening a basket-hopper around the top to prevent the acorns from flying out. On the west side of Tulare Lake these mortars are very numerous, and of course they must have been carried thither from the mountains.

On Tule River I saw the process of basket-weaving. Instead of willow twigs for the framework or warp, the squaw takes long stalks of grass, *Fig. 41* (*Sporobolus*); and for the threads or the woof various barks or roots split fine—pine root for a white color, willow bark for a brown, and some unknown bark for a black. The process of weaving is like that heretofore described; the awl or needle was the sharpened thigh-bone of a hawk.

The Gualala style of gambling prevails all over the State, but the Yokuts have another sort, which pertains exclusively to the women. It is a kind of dice-throwing, and is called *u-chu'-us*. For a dice they take half of a large acorn or walnut shell, fill it level with pitch and pounded charcoal, and inlay it with bits of bright-colored abalone shells. For a dice-table they weave a very large, fine basket-tray, almost flat, and ornamented with devices woven in black or brown, mostly rude imitations of trees and geometrical figures. Four squaws sit around it to play, and a fifth keeps tally with fifteen sticks. There are eight dice, and they scoop them up in their hands and dash them into the basket, counting one when two or five flat surfaces turn up.

The rapidity with which the game goes forward is wonderful, and the players seem totally oblivious to all things in the world beside. After each throw that a player makes she exclaims *yet'-ni* (equivalent to "one-y"), or *wi-a-tak*, or *ko-mai-éh*, which are simply a kind of sing-song or chanting One old squaw, with scarcely a tooth in her head, one eye gone, her face all withered, but with a lower jaw as of iron, and features denoting extraoi dinary strength of will—a reckless old gambler, and evidently a teacher of the others—after each throw would grab into the basket, and jerk her hand across it, as if by the motion of the air to turn the dice over before they settled, and ejaculate *wiatak!* It was amusing to see the savage energy with which this fierce old hag carried on the game. The others were modest and spoke in low tones, but she seemed to be unaware of the existence of anybody around her.

Following are the Yokuts numerals, taken at three places:

	KINGSTON.	KAWEAH RIVER.	FORT TEJON.
One.	yet.	yet.	yet.
Two.	po-no'-eh.	pūng'-o-eh.	poan'-oikh.
Three.	so'-pin.	so-o'-pin.	so-o'-pin.
Four.	ha'-to-po-noh.	ha-to-pang-ih'.	ha-to-poan'-oikh.
Five.	yit'-sen-it.	yi-tsing'-ut.	yi-tsin'-et.
Six.	cha'-lip-eh.	chu'-di-peh.	tso'-li-pih.
Seven.	nōm'-chil.	noam'-chin.	noam'-chikhl.
Eight.	mo-noas'.	mu'-nūsh.	mu'-nus.
Nine.	se'-po-noat.	no'-nip.	so'-pon-hut.
Ten.	tsi'-oh.	ti'-i-hoh.	ti'-i-hoh.

On the Tule River Reservation they have coined names for the days of the week. They are these: Wu-lo'-a, Po'-ni-o, So'-pi-o, Hots'-po, Ya'-ti-so, Chol'-po, Hu-lo'-sa.

Their theory of disease is, that it all resides in the blood. To prove this, they cite the fact that the blood always collects underneath a bruise and makes it dark; and also the fact that drawn blood coagulates. Hence their favorite remedy was scarification with small flints. And when they became acquainted with the process of cupping, they wearied the reservation surgeon with applications to have it performed on them for every little ailment. For diseases of the bowels they boil up a mess of a large and very stinking ant, and give it internally.

Their range of food is extensive. Around the lake they cut and dry the seed-stalks of a kind of flag (*Typha*) which has a head something like a teasel, thresh out the seed and make flour of it; also wild rye and wild sunflower seed. They eat grass-nuts (*Cyperus*) and the seeds of the same, a plant with a triangular stalk. In the mountains they used to fire the forests, and thereby catch great quantities of grasshoppers and caterpillars already roasted, which they devoured with relish, and this practice kept the underbrush burned out, and the woods much more open and park-like than at present. This was the case all along the Sierra. But since about 1862, for some reason or other, the yield of grasshoppers has been limited. They are fond of a huge, succulent worm, resembling the tobacco-worm, which is roasted; also the larvæ of yellow-jackets, which they pick out and eat raw. Dogs are reared (or were) largely for the flesh which they supply, which 146 is accounted by them a special dainty, and which comes well in play, like the farmer's yellow-legged chicken, when other meat is scarce. Unlike the Miwok, they eat skunks.

Among the animals which are, in some sort, sacred to them, is the rattlesnake (*te'-el*), which they never destroy. A story is related of an Indian who captured one on the plains and carefully conveyed it into the mountains, where he released it, that it might be less liable to the attacks of white men; and of another, who, seeing an American about to destroy one, scared it into the rocks that it might escape. The coyote also moved among them with perfect impunity, for he is revered as the creator of the universe. Before the impious American came, these animals swarmed thick about every mountain rancheria, and they often chased the dogs into the village itself. An old hunter says he has seen Indian dogs more than once turn on a coyote and drive it off a few rods, when it would fall on its side, turn up its legs, and commence playing with them. It is a singular fact that, in the Gallinoméro language, *hai'-yu* denotes "dog", while in the Yokuts *kai'-yu* means "coyote". Indeed, to judge from his appearance to this day, the Indian dog is an animal in whose genealogy the coyote largely 147 assisted. In the Wintūn language the word for "coyote" is literally "hill-dog".

Some of the medical practice, and all of the midwifery, are performed by the women. In cases of severe travail they frequently employ a decoction of scraped bear's claws. Again, the nurse will smear her palms with

pine sugar, hold them before the fire until it is melted, then lay them gently
on the abdomen of the parturient. The sweat-house everywhere prevails,
of course, but it is smaller among these southern out-door people than it is
farther north, being never used for a council-house or a dance-house.

The rain-maker, or wizard, though very potent, can be put to death
by vote of a council, in case a patient dies under his treatment. Occasionally the manner of his taking-off is still more tragic. The Mono, being
unsophisticated mountaineers, originally had no professional wizards, and
in 1864 a Yokuts, named Sacate, went up from the plains to them, and
for a time prosecuted an extremely lucrative practice. But he finally lost
a case, and thereupon the simple and sincere Mono, being unable to comprehend how a man whose function was to save life could lose it and be
guiltless, crushed in his skull with a stone.

These wizards sometimes chew the seeds of the jimson-weed (*Datura
meteloides*) to induce delirium, which their dupes regard as the touch of an
unseen power, and their crazy ravings as divinely-inspired oracles. It is
related that an ambitious wizard once chewed too much seed and yielded
up the ghost.

An old Indian, named Chu-chu'-ka, relates that many years ago there
was a terrible plague which raged on both sides of the Fresno, destroying
thousands of lives. According to his account it was a black-tongue disease.
Abundant evidences of his truthfulness have been discovered in the shape
of bones. A man named Holt was digging a ditch on Ray's ranch, near
Sand Creek, and found such an immense number of bones about eighteen
inches under the surface that, after digging three hundred yards, he was
forced to abandon the undertaking. On Hildreth's ranch, near Pool-of-
Water, a large box of human bones was collected in making a garden.

It is the custom of the wizards to hold every spring the rattlesnake
dance (*ta-tu'-lo-wis*), which is a source of great profit to the cunning rogues.
They plant green boughs in a circle, inclosing a space fifty or sixty yards
in diameter, wherein the performances are held, as are most of the Yokuts'
dances. The great audience is congregated in the middle, while the wizards dance around the circle, next to the arboreal wall. Besmeared with
numerous and fantastic streaks of paint, and gorgeously topped with feath-

ers, four of them caper around like clowns in a circus, chasing each other, chanting, brandishing rattlesnakes in their hands, twining them about their arms, and suffering them to bite their hands. It is supposed that they have either plucked their fangs, or have not allowed them to drink any water for a number of days beforehand, which is said to render them harmless. But the credulous savages believe them invulnerable, and they eagerly press forward with their offerings, in return for which the wizards give them complete immunity from snake-bites for the space of a year. The younger Indians, somewhat indoctrinated in American ideas, have become sadly skeptical and heretical in regard of these dances, which they contemptuously term "skunk meetings", to the great scandal of their pious elders.

Formerly the step danced by the men on most occasions might not inappropriately be called the piston-rod dance, as they seemed intent on driving their legs alternately into the earth. Of late they have adopted from the Mono the grand walk-round, in a single circle, men and women together, and with an entirely different and less violent step.

Although they have a form of war-dance, and the Chukchansi warred a great deal with the Pohonichi of old, as a race they are peaceful, and they take no scalps. But of late years, under the aggravation of aggressions by white men, they have adopted from the warlike Mono the red paint (instead of black), which has so terrible a significance in a savage dance, and the appearance of which always makes the frontiersmen uneasy. From them, also, they have learned to talk of war, to bluster, to threaten darkly, to hold secret conclaves far within the depths of the mountains, from which the whites were rigidly excluded. But nothing has come of them. These things are foreign to the peaceful Yokuts, and the Monos, though they are supposed to have attempted it many times, have never succeeded in screwing their neighbors' courage up to the sticking-point of joining them in a war on the whites.

Nowadays $20 or $30 in gold is paid for a wife, but this only for a virgin. For a widow or a maid suspected of unchastity no man will pay anything or make any presents; and it is due to the Yokuts to state that a pioneer who has lived among them twenty-one years affirms that before the arrival of the Americans they were comparatively virtuous. Dr. E. B. Bateman, physician to the Tule River Reservation, gives me the information that both males and females, though bathing quite apart, never enter the water without wearing breech-cloths at least; and this is corroborated by an old resident on King's River, who observed it of them in their native condition. Mr. Charles Maltby, agent of the above reservation, and at one time Indian agent for the whole State, and well acquainted with aboriginal habits, also affirms that the Yokuts are purer than the northern tribes, and that the Indians throughout Southern California are less given to the infamous practice of selling the virtue of their women to white men than those of Northern California. They may not have been any better originally, but they have not been so shamefully debauched by miners. That is probably the explanation.

Their language has what is generally considered a good indication, separate words for "woman" (*mo-kel'-la*), and wife (*mo-ki'*); also, for "man" (*no'-no*) and "husband" (*lo'-wit*).

We find also the singular custom noticed in some other tribes, that a man marrying goes to live at his wife's or father-in-law's house, though he still has power of life or death over her person.

Infanticide is practiced in case of deformity.

Many years ago the Indians dwelling on the lake at the mouth of King's River were carried away captives by the Spaniards, and taken to San Luis Obispo. After a long residence there, upon the breaking up of the missions, they returned to their native land; but meantime a new generation had grown up, to whom the old mission was their home. They yearned to return, and to this day they make an annual pilgrimage to San Luis, where they remain a month; and they would by preference live there all their remaining days, only their children, born on the shores of Tulare Lake, will not consent. By some this may be considered a convincing proof of their attachment to the old Jesuit padres, who used to lasso them in the name of the church; but it is not necessary to resort to this explanation at all. It is easily enough accounted for by the California Indian's proverbial love of his birthplace, just as the slave-born children of Israel lusted for the flesh-pots of that Egypt which had scourged them.

If an Indian dies on a trail far from home he is buried beside it. Every

one who passes the mound casts upon it a stone, or a string of shell-money, 151
or some other offering, which pious service will secure him from the dire
calamity of dying away from home and friends.

Incremation is pretty general, though the Chukchansi are said to burn
only those who die a violent death or are snake-bitten, and bury all others.
A widow or widower is expected to mourn one year, and if they remarry
within that time they are discountenanced.   This is not saying that they do
not sometimes nowadays, since they have become debauched by "civilization", remarry in a week, even, occasionally; but there is good reason to
believe that in their better days of savagery they observed this period with
much scrupulosity.   But as soon as the first dance for the dead occurs it
releases all the mourners in the tribe from further seclusion, even if it should
happen only a few days after some death, and then they are free to enjoy
all the gayeties as before.

As there has been some sharp discussion of the existence of an aboriginal belief in annihilation of the soul after death, it is worth while to adduce
the testimony of one who should know.   J. H. Bethel, who lived among
the Chukchansi twenty-one years, and spoke their language fluently, affirms
that this belief is very generally diffused, both among the Yokuts and the
Mono.

ORIGIN OF THE MOUNTAINS.

Once there was a time when there was nothing in the world but water.
About the place where Tulare Lake is now, there was a pole standing far
up out of the water, and on this pole perched a hawk and a crow.   First
one of them would sit on the pole awhile, then the other would knock him
off and sit on it himself.   Thus they sat on top of the pole above the
waters for many ages.   At length they wearied of the lonesomeness, and
they created the birds which prey on fish such as the kingfisher, eagle,
pelican, and others.   Among them was a very small duck, which dived
down to the bottom of the water, picked its beak full of mud, came up,
died, and lay floating on the water.   The hawk and the crow then fell
to work and gathered from the duck's beak the earth which it had brought
up, and commenced making the mountains.   They began at the place
now known as Ta-hi'-cha-pa Pass, and the hawk made the east range,

while the crow made the west one. Little by little, as they dropped in the earth, these great mountains grew athwart the face of the waters, pushing north. It was a work of many years, but finally they met together at Mount Shasta, and their labors were ended. But, behold, when they compared their mountains, it was found that the crow's was a great deal the larger. Then the hawk said to the crow, "How did this happen, you rascal? I warrant you have been stealing some of the earth from my bill, and that is why your mountains are the biggest." It was a fact, and the crow laughed in his claws. Then the hawk went and got some Indian tobacco and chewed it, and it made him exceedingly wise. So he took hold of the mountains and turned them round in a circle, putting his range in place of the crow's; and that is why the Sierra Nevada is larger than the Coast Range.

152   This legend is of value as showing the aboriginal notions of geography. In explaining the story, the Indian drew in the sand a long ellipse, representing quite accurately the shape of the two ranges; and he had never traveled away from King's River.

153   While in Coarse Gold Gulch, it was my good fortune to witness the great dance for the dead (*ko-ti'-wa-chil*), which was one of the most extraordinary human spectacles I ever beheld. It was not the regular annual dance, but a special one, held by request of Ko-lo'-mus-nim, a subchief of the Chukchansi; but it was in all respects as strange, as awful, as imposing an exhibition of barbaric superstition and barbaric affection as is afforded by the formal anniversary. Not to my dying hour will the recollection of that frightful midnight pageant be effaced.

First, it will be well to explain that among the Yokuts the dance for the dead is protracted nearly a week. The first two or three nights, while they are waiting for the assembling of the tardy delegations, are occupied only in speech-making, story-telling, etc., until a late hour; but during the last three nights they dance throughout the night until morning, and on the third night, about daybreak, they burn the offerings consecrated to the dead. This happened to be the first of the last three nights, hence no burning occurred, but in every other respect it was complete, and all the exercises were conducted with more energy and with fuller choruses than they would have been after the Indians had become exhausted.

When Tueh, the Indian interpreter, and myself entered the camp it was already an hour after nightfall, but there were yet no indications of a beginning of the dark orgies that were to be enacted. We found about three hundred Indians assembled, in a place remote from any American habitations, and encamped in light, open booths of brushwood, running around three sides of a spacious quadrangle. This quadrangle had been swept and beaten smooth for a dancing-floor, and near one of the inside corners there was a small, circular embankment, like a circus-ring, with the sacred fire brightly burning in the center. Kolomusnim and his relatives, the chief mourners, occupied the corner-booths near this ring, and near by was Sloknich, the head-chief of the Chukchansi, by whose authority this assembly had been convened. Here and there a fire burned with a staggering, sleepy blaze just outside the quadrangle, faintly glimmering through the booths; at intervals an Indian moved stealthily across the half-illuminated space within; while every few minutes the atmosphere was rendered discordant and hideous, as indeed the whole night was, during the most solemn passages, by the yelping, snarling, and fighting of the hordes of dogs.

For fully half an hour we slowly sauntered and loitered about the quadrangle, conversing in undertones, but still nothing occurred to break the somber silence, save the ever-recurring scurries of yelps from the accursed dogs. Now and then an Indian slowly passed across and sat down on the circular embankment, while others in silence occasionally fed the sacred fire. But at last, from Kolomusnim's quarter, there came up a long, wild, haunting wail, in a woman's voice. After a few minutes it was repeated. Soon another joined in, then another, and another, slowly, very slowly, until the whole quarter was united in an eldritch, dirge-like, dismal chorus. After about half an hour it ceased, as slowly as it began; and again there was profound, death-like silence; and again it was broken by the ever-renewed janglings of the dogs.

Some time again elapsed before any further movement was made, and then Sloknich, a little, old man, but straight as an arrow, with a sharp face and keen, little, basilisk eyes, stepped forth into the quadrangle and began to walk slowly to and fro around its three sides, making the opening proclamation. He spoke in extremely short, jerky sentences, with much repetition, substantially as follows:

"Make ready for the mourning. Let all make ready. Everybody make ready. Prepare your offerings. Your offerings to the dead. Have them all ready. Show them to the mourners. Let them see your sympathy. The mourning comes on. It hastens. Everybody make ready."

He continued in this manner for about twenty minutes, then ceased and entered his booth; after which silence, funereal and profound, again brooded over the encampment. By this proclamation he had formally opened the proceedings, and he took no further part in them, except in a short speech of condolence. By this time the Indians had collected in considerable numbers on the embankment, and they kept slowly coming forward until the circle was nearly completed, and the fire was only visible shooting up above their heads. A low hum of conversation began to buzz around it, as of slowly awakening activity. The slow piston-rod of aboriginal dignity was beginning to ply; the clatter and whizzing of the machinery were swelling gradually up. No women had yet come out, for they took no part in the earlier proceedings. It was now quite ten o'clock, and we were getting impatient.

Presently the herald, a short, stout Indian, with a most voluble tongue, came out into the quadrangle with a very long staff in his hand, and paced slowly up and down the lines of booths, proclaiming:

"Prepare for the dance. Let all make ready. We are all friends. We are all one people. We were a great tribe once. We are little now. All our hearts are as one. We have one heart. Make ready your offerings. The women have the most money. The women have the most offerings. They give the most. Get ready the tobacco. Let us chew the tobacco."

This man spoke with an extraordinary amount of repetition. For instance, he would say: "The women—the women—the women—have the most—have the most—the most money—have the most money—the women—the women—have the most offerings—the most offerings—give the most—give the most—the women—the women—give the most."

He spoke fully as long as Sloknich had done, and while he was speaking they were preparing a decoction of Indian tobacco by the fire. When he ceased he took his place in the circle, and all of them now began to sip 154 and taste the tobacco, which seemed to be intended as a kind of mortification of the flesh. Sitting along on the embankment, while the nauseous mess was passing around in a basket, and others were tasting the boiled leaves, they sought to mitigate the bitter dose with jokes and laughter. One said, "Did you ever see the women gather tobacco for themselves ?" This was intended as a jest, for no woman ever touches the weed, but nobody laughed at it. As the powerful emetic began to work out its inevitable effect, one Indian after another arose from the circle and passed slowly and silently out into the outer darkness, whence there presently came up to our ears certain doleful and portentous sounds, painfully familiar to people who have been at sea. After all the Indians in the circle, except a few tough stomachs, had issued forth into the darkness and returned to their places, about eleven o'clock, the herald went around as before, making a third proclamation :

"Let all mourn and weep. O, weep for the dead. Think of the dead body lying in the grave. We shall all die soon. We were a great people once. We are weak and little now. Be sorrowful in your hearts. O, let sorrow melt your hearts. Let your tears flow fast. We are all one people. We are all friends. All our hearts are one heart."

For the last hour or so the mourners and their more intimate friends and sympathizers, mostly women, had been collecting in Kolomusnim's quarter, close behind the circle, and preparing their offerings. Occasionally a long, solitary wail came up, trembling on the cold night-wind. At the close of the third proclamation they began a death-dance, and the mourners crowded promiscuously in a great, open booth, and held aloft in their hands or on their heads, as they danced, the articles they intended to offer to the memory of the departed. It was a splendid exhibition of barbaric gew-gaws. Glittering necklaces of *Haliotis* and other rare marine shells ; bits of American tapestry ; baskets of the finest workmanship, on which they had toiled for months, perhaps for years, circled and furred with hundreds of little quail-plumes, bespangled, scalloped, festooned, and embroidered with beadery until there was scarcely place for the handling; plumes, shawls, etc. Kolomusnim had a pretty plume of metallic-glistening ravens' feathers in his hand. But the most remarkable article was a great plume, nearly six feet long, shaped like a parasol slightly opened, mostly of ravens' feathers, but containing rare and brilliant plumage from many birds of the forest, topped with a smaller plume or kind of coronet, and lavishly bedecked through all its length with bulbs, shell-clusters, circlets of feathers, dangling festoons—a magnificent bauble, towering far above all, with its glittering spangles and nodding plume on plume contrasting so strangely with the tattered and howling savages over whom it gorgeously swayed and flaunted. Another woman had an image, rudely constructed of shawls and clothing, to represent the dead woman, sister to Kolomusnim.

The beholding of all these things, some of which had belonged to the departed, and the strong contagion of human sorrow, wrought the Indians into a frenzy. Wildly they leaped and wailed; some flung themselves upon the earth and beat their breasts. There were constant exhortations to grief. Sloknich, sitting on the ground, poured forth burning and piercing words: "We have all one heart. All our hearts bleed with yours. Our eyes weep tears like a living spring. O, think of the poor, dead woman in the grave." Kolomusnim, a savage of a majestic presence, bating his garb, though a hesitating orator, was so broken with grief that his few sobbing words moved the listeners like a funeral knell. Beholding now and then a special friend in the circle, he would run and fall upon his knees before him, bow down his head to the earth, and give way to uncontrollable sorrow. Others of the mourners would do the same, presenting to the friend's gaze some object which had belonged to the lamented woman. The friend, if a man, would pour forth long condolences; if a woman, she would receive the mourner's head in her hands, tenderly stroke down her hair, and unite her tears and lamentations with her's. Many an eye, both of men and women, both of mourners and strangers, glistened in the flickering fire-light with copious and genuine tears.

But amid all this heart-felt mourning there were occasional manifestations of purely mechanical grief that were amusing. The venerable
Sloknich, though he was a gifted and thrilling orator, a savage Nestor, preserved a dry eye; but once in a while he would arise in his place and lift
up his voice in mourning like a sandhill-crane, then presently sit down and
calmly light a cigarette. After smoking two or three, he would stand up
and fire away again. Cigarettes were burning everywhere. An Indian
would take one out of his mouth and give a prolonged and dolorous bellow,
then take a few whiffs again.

Yet even these comical manifestations were so entirely in earnest that
nobody thought of laughing at the time; and though one's sense of humor
could not but make silent note of them the while, they were greatly overborne by the outpouring of genuine, unmistakable grief. So far even from
smiling, one might, without being accused of sentimental weakness, have
dropped a tear at the spectacle of these poor wretches, weeping not more
perhaps for the loved and lost than over their own miserable and hapless
destiny of extermination.

These demonstrations continued a long time, a very long time, and I
began to be impatient again, believing that the principal occasion had
passed. It appeared afterward that they are compelled by their creed and
custom to prolong the proceedings until daylight; hence this extreme deliberation.

But now, at last, about one o'clock in the morning, upon some pre-
concerted signal, there was a sudden and tumultuous rushing from all
quarters of the quadrangle, amid which the interpreter and myself were
almost borne down. For the first time during the night the women
appeared conspicuously on the scene, thronged into the sacred circle, and
quickly formed a ring close around the fire—a single circle of maidens,
facing inward. The whole multitude of the populous camp crowded about
them in confusion, jostling and struggling. A choir of male singers took
their position hard by and commenced the death-song, though they were
not audible except to the nearest listeners.

At the same instant the young women began their frightful dance, which consisted of two leaps on each foot alternately, causing the body to rock to and fro; and either hand was thrust out with the swaying, as if the offering it held were about to be consigned to the flames, while the breath was forced out with violence between the teeth, in regular cadence, with a harsh and grinding sound of *heh!* The blaze of the sacred fire flamed redly out between the bodies of the dancers, swaying in accord, while the disheveled locks of the leaping hags wildly snapping in the night wind, the blood-curdling rasp of their breath in concert, and the frightful ululations and writhings of the mourners, conspired to produce a terrible effect. At the sight of this weird, awful, and lurid spectacle, which was swung into motion so suddenly, I felt all the blood creep and tingle in my veins, and my eyes moisten with the tears of a nameless awe and terror. We were beholding now, at last, the great dance for the dead.

All the long remainder of that frenzied night, from one o'clock to two, to three, to four, to five, those women leaped in the maddening dance, through smoke, and choking dust, and darkness, and glaring light, and cold, and heat, amid the unceasing wail of the multitude, not knowing or heeding aught else on earth. Once in five or ten minutes, when the choir completed a chorus, there was a pause of a few seconds; but no one moved from her place for a moment. What wonder that only the strongest young maidens were chosen for the duty! What wonder that the men avoided this terrible ordeal!

About four o'clock, wearied, dinned, and benumbed with the cold of the mountains, I crept away to a friendly blanket and sought to sleep But it was in vain, for still through the night-air were borne up to my ears the far-off crooning, the ululations, and that slow-pulsing, horrid *heh!* of the leaping witches, with all the distant voices, each more distinct than when heard nearer, of the mourning camp. The morning star drew itself far up into the blue reaches of heaven, blinking in the cold, dry California air, and still all the mournful riot of that Walpurgis-night went on.

Then slowly there was drawn over everything a soft curtain of oblivion; the distant voices blended into one undistinguishable murmur, then died away and were still; the mourning was ended; the dancers ceased because they were weary.

For half an hour, perhaps, I slept. Then awaking suddenly I stood up in my blankets and looked down upon the camp, now broadly flooded by the level sun. It was silent as the grave. Even the unresting dogs slept at last, and the Indian ponies ceased from browsing, and stood still between the manzanita bushes to let the first sunshine warm and mellow up their hides, on which the hair stood out straight. All that wonderful night seemed like the phantasmagoria of a fevered dream. But before the sun was three-quarters of an hour high that tireless herald was out again, and going the rounds with a loud voice,.to waken the heavy sleepers. In a few minutes the whole camp was in motion; not one remained, though many an eyelid moved like lead. The choir of singers took their places promptly, squatting on the ground; and a great company of men and women, bearing their offerings aloft, as before, joined in the same dance as described, with the same hissing *heh!* only it was performed in a disorderly rush-round, raising a great cloud of dust. Every five minutes, upon the ceasing of the singers, all faced suddenly to the west, ran forward a few paces, with a great clamor of mourning, and those in the front prostrated themselves, and bowed down their faces to the earth, while others stretched out their arms to the west, and piteously wrung them, with imploring cries, as if beckoning the departed spirits to return, or waving them a last farewell. This is in accordance with their belief in a Happy Western Land. Soon, upon the singers resuming, they all rose and joined again in the tumultuous rush-round. This lasted about an hour; then all was ended for that day, and the weary mourners betook themselves to their booths and to sleep.

Perhaps the only feature that mars this wonderful exhibition, in a moral point of view, is the fact that any mourner, when about to consign a funeral plume or other ornament to the flames in honor of the dead, will accept money for it from a by-stander (provided he is an Indian), if only enough is offered. But they have scruples against selling objects on these occasions to a white man.

At Kern Lake, there was a small tribe which I am at a loss where to place in my classification. There are only a very few of them left, having been removed to Tule River Reservation; and at this latter place I saw only one old man who was able to give me, through a Spanish interpreter, his numerals, but nothing more. Following are the ten numerals:

One.	kil'-leh.	Six.	tukh'-tu.
Two.	cho-yo'-chi.	Seven.	po-ko'-i-chin-tin'-li.
Three.	u-yat'-si.	Eight.	pus'-in-tin'-li.
Four.	chu'-i-chau.	Nine.	hōs'-che.
Five.	loap'-chin-tin'-li.	Ten.	chi'-wa.

CHAPTER XXXVI.

TRIBES RELATED TO THE PAI·U'·TI.

I have above intimated that there is a large infusion of Paiuti elements in the lower end of the great California basin, arising from early invasions. Among these tribes are the Pal-li-ga-wo-nap' (from *pal-up'*, "stream", and *e-ke'-wan*, "large") on Kern River; the Ti-pa-to-la'-pa on the South Fork of the Kern; and the Wi-nan-gik' on the North Fork. Another name for the Tipatolapa was the Ku-chi-bich-i-wa-nap' Pal-up' (little stream). At Bakersfield was a tribe called by the Yokuts, Pal-e'-um-mi. In the famous 156 Tahichapah Pass was a tribe called by themselves Ta-hi-cha-pa-han'-na; by the Kern River Indians, Ta-hichp'; and by the Yokuts, Kâ-wi'-a-suh. They are now extinct. The Kern River Indians were called by the Yokuts of Fort Tejon, Pi-tan'-ni-suh; and the Indians at Kern Lake, Pal-wu'-nuh (which denotes "down below"). On Kern River Slough are the Po-e'-lo; at Kern River Falls, the To-mo'-la; on Posa Creek, the Be'-ku. On White River there are no Indians, neither have there been any for many years, owing to the prevalence of malaria; but there are indications that the lands along this stream were once inhabited.

THE PAL-LI-GA-WO-NAP'.

As above stated, these Indians lived on Kern River; this one tribe may stand for all on the branches of this stream, and also for those formerly occupying Posa Creek and White River. All the lower waters of the Kern and of these other streams flow through a low malarious region which is very unhealthy. It is related by the Indians that all the aborigines living about Kern Lake perished in one year with the scourge of chills and fever. 157 The dwellers on Posa Creek and White River often suffered terribly from the same disease, and finally, within the American period, or very soon before it, they all removed to a place called Whisky Flat, in the more salubrious region of the foot-hills, from which they went down to their old home only once a year, in the spring, to gather food-seeds.

158   The Palligawonap have the Paiuti custom of burying the dead. They have no sweat-houses, but there are ruins of old ones in various places in their domain, which were doubtless made there by the California Indians proper, whom they expelled.

They live in wigwams made of tule, woven and matted into various fashions. Tule is also the material from which they construct a rude water-craft. This is only about six feet in length, with the bow very long and sharp-rounded, and the stern cut nearly square across; sides perpendicular;
159 a small tule keel running along the middle, dividing the bottom into two sides. It will carry only one man, and he has to be very careful when standing up to keep his feet one on each side of the keel, or the bobbing thing will capsize. It is used principally in fishing, for which purpose they employ a three-pronged gig pointed with bone. They show much more skill in balancing themselves in the boat than they do in making it.

I saw only one of the tribe, named Chico, on the Tule River Reservation, and he presented the traditional physique of the Californian—very dark-skinned, pudgy in stature, large cheek-bones, nose depressed at the root, brachycephalic head, etc. He was a singular Indian, a real philosopher; had traveled much over Southern California, Nevada, Utah, and Arizona, broadening the range of his intellectual vision; spoke English and Spanish fluently, besides several Indian tongues; and was as full of curious, quaint, barbaric superstitions, poetical conceits, common sense, and inflated egotism as an egg is of meat, though these various knowledges and fancies were wofully mingled in his brain. I will attempt to give only a few of his ideas.

Po-koh', the Old Man, created the world. He was a being of a capacious head, full of many and great thoughts, and in his voluminous blankets he found room to carry about enough gifts for all men. He created every separate tribe out of soil taken from the place where they now live; hence it is that the Indian's desire is so strong to live and die in his native place. Pokoh intended that men should not wander and travel, but should be con-

tent in their birthplace. In the folds of his great blankets he carried around
an immense number of gifts, with which he endowed every man according 160
to his will, and every tribe according to his pleasure, with which gifts every
one ought to be content.

Long ago the sun was a man, and was bad, but the moon was good.
The sun's rays are arrows, and he has a quiver full of them. These arrows
are deadly, for the sun wishes to kill all things. He gave an arrow to
every animal according to his power; to the lion the greatest; to the
grizzly bear the next, and so on, though no animal received an arrow that
would kill a man. The man is lord of all.

The sun has two daughters (Venus and Mercury), and twenty men 161
kill them; but after fifty days they return to life again.

The rainbow is the sister of Pokoh, and her breast is covered with
flowers. Other Indians say, whenever they see a rainbow, that at that very
hour some maiden has reached that first mysterious and momentous event
which marks her transition from girlhood to womanhood.

Lightning strikes the ground and fills the flints with fire, which is the
source of fire. A "California diamond" will be found wherever it strikes
the ground. Some say the beaver brought fire from the east, hauling it on
his broad, flat tail, and that is the reason why it has no hair on it to this day.

The carved stone mortars found in many parts of California were made
by a race of men that lived long ago. There is one book for the father,
and another for the son. Men pass away, and others come in their places.

There are many worlds, some that have passed, and some that are to
come. In one world the Indians all creep, in another they all walk, in
another they all fly, etc. They may even begin by swimming in the water
like fish; in the next, they may walk on four legs; in the next, on two,
etc. Other men may walk in this world, and in another crawl like a snake
or swim like a fish. These are bad men.

THE SUN AND THE COYOTE.

A long time ago the coyote wanted to go to the sun. He asked Pokoh
the road, and he showed him. He went straight out on this road, and 162
traveled in it all day, but the sun went round, so that the coyote came back

at night to the place where he started in the morning. The next morning he asked Pokoh the road, and he showed him, but he traveled all day, and came back at night to the same place again. But the third day he started early, and went right out to the edge of the world and sat down on the hole where the sun came up. While waiting for the sun he pointed with his bow and arrow toward various places, as if he were about to shoot, and pretended not to see the sun. When the sun came up he told the coyote to get out of his way. But the coyote told him to go round, that it was his road, and he would not get out of the way. But the sun came up under him, and he had to hitch forward a little. After the sun came up a little way it began to get hot on the coyote's shoulder, and he spit on his paw and rubbed his shoulder. Then he wanted to ride up with the sun. The sun tried to persuade him not to do it, but he would go. So he got on, and the sun started up a path in the sky which was marked off into steps like a ladder, and as he went up he counted "one, two, three", etc. Presently the coyote got very thirsty, and he asked the sun for a drink of water. He gave him an acorn-cup full, and the coyote asked him why he had no more. Toward noon he got impatient. It was very hot, and the sun told him to close his eyes. He did so, but opened them again, and so kept opening and shutting them all the afternoon. At night, when the sun came down, the coyote took hold of a tree, clambered off, and got down to the ground.

In this pathway of the sun, with steps like a ladder, there is undoubt-edly a trace of an ancient zodiac myth. Some persons insist that the In-dians must have learned this from the Mexicans or the early Jesuits. The story is sufficiently poor, certainly, but such as it is it must be the inven-tion of the Indians in everything except the one little particular of the graded pathway, at any rate, for no civilized person would have conceived such a fable. These critics, then, would leave the Indians everything but this item; but this they would take away from them because it has a faint suspicion of civilization about it ! Such reasoning is contemptible.

THE MONO.

In their own language these Indians call themselves Nūt′-ha. Why the Spaniards named them Mono (monkeys) is not very clear. Although rather an undersized race, they by no means justify the appellation, either in appearance or in character, for they are a manly, warlike people, and were anciently a great terror to the Yokuts. They are several shades lighter than the latter; and with their raven-black hair worn quite down to the shoulders, their smallish features, and their quick, suspicious eyes glancing out from under their great Spanish *sombreros*, they present a rather singular appearance. They still retain many of the simple virtues of a race of hardy, honest mountaineers, and are mostly free from those brutish practices which disgrace the lowlanders. For years they resisted the inroads of whisky, the great leveler which laid low their valley neighbors. They are a healthy people, and are said to be increasing even now. They do not bathe the entire person daily, like the lowland tribes, but they sometimes take sweat-baths, then run and plunge into cold water. Probably owing largely to their isolated position they are exclusive, and refuse to intermarry with other tribes.

The Mono are an offshoot of the Nevada Indians, and should be properly classified with them, but they have been so long on the western slope of the Sierra, and acquired so many California habits and usages, that they may be included here. Many years ago—it is impossible to ascertain how long ago—they came over from Owen's River Valley, and conquered for themselves a territory on the upper reaches of the San Joaquin and King's River, the lower boundaries of which were indicated in the previous chapter.

They are not such a joyous race as the Californians, and have no annual merry-makings, though they sometimes celebrate a good harvest of acorns; and they think that a certain great being in the east, who is nameless to them, must be propitiated at times with a grand hunt and a feast following it, else there will be disease and bad luck in their camps. Their business is with war, and fighting, and hunting; hence they have more taciturnity, more stern immobility of feature, than the Californians. It was they who introduced among the Yokuts, in recent years, the red paint, the terrible emblem of war and bloodshed, which appears to have been unused by the latter before that. They pursue and slay the grizzly bear in single-handed combat, or in companies, with bows and arrows, but

163

the Yokuts hold that animal in mortal terror, and refuse even to partake of its flesh when slain.

164 The black eagle is sacred to them, and they never kill one, but they pluck out the feathers of those that die, and wear them on their heads as one of their most valuable ornaments. When they succeed in capturing a young one, after two weeks they have a great dance and jubilation around it, then sell it to another village, that they may do likewise.

165 The California big tree is also in a manner sacred to them, and they call it *woh-woh'-nau*, a word formed in imitation of the hoot of the owl, which is the guardian spirit and deity of this great monarch of the forest. It is productive of bad luck to fell this tree, or to mock or shoot the owl, or even to shoot in his presence. Bethel states that they have often, in earlier years, tried to persuade him not to cut them down—pity they could not have succeeded!—and that when they see a teamster going along the road with a wagon-load of lumber made from these trees, they will cry out after him, and tell him the owl will visit him with evil luck.

The hunter who penetrates into the great forests of the high Sierra sometimes notices a tree which looks scratched about the base. The Mono account for this appearance in the following manner: Once in awhile the grizzly bears assemble in a council, great and small together, and sit down in a circle in the forest with some huge Old Ephraim occupying the post of honor as chairman. There they sit a long time, bolt upright on their tails, in a silence as profound as that of a Quaker meeting. After awhile the old chairman drops down on all-fours and goes to the tree, rears up and hugs it with his fore-paws, and dances around it. After him the next largest one takes his turn, then the next, and so on, down to the cubs. When a Mono hunter sees them in a council thus, or perceives by the indications that they have recently held one, he hastens home and notifies his companions of the circumstance. They consider that the bears hold these councils for the purpose of making war on them, and for a certain number of days after the discovery is made they carefully refrain from hunting the animals, or even from firing off a gun where they would be likely to hear it, lest they should enrage them. The younger Indians laugh at this story.

Subjoined are the numerals of some of those tribes, taken at the locali-

ties indicated. As the Tahichapahannah are extinct, I was obliged to pro- 166
cure their numerals from the Kern River Indians.

	KERN RIVER.	MILLERTON.	TEJON PASS.
One.	chich.	si'-muh.	pau'-kŭp.
Two.	wâh.	wo'-hat-tuh.	wah.
Three.	pai.	pait.	pa'-hai.
Four.	na-nau'.	wa'-tsu-kit.	wa'-tsa.
Five.	ma-hai-ching'-a.	ma'-lo-kit.	ma-hats'.
Six.	nap'-pai.	na'-vait.	pâ'-wa-hi.
Seven.	noam'-chih.	ta'-tsu-it.	wats-ka-pi'-ga.
Eight.	na-pūn-ching'-a.	wa'-su-it.	wa-wat'-sa.
Nine.	la'-kih.	kwa'-nu-kit.	ma-ka-bi'-ka.
Ten.	um-hai-ching'-a.	se'-wa-nu.	we'-ma-hat.

CHAPTER XXXVII.

GENERAL FACTS.

It has been the melancholy fate of the California Indians to be more vilified and less understood than any other of the American aborigines. They were once probably the most contented and happy race on the continent, in proportion to their capacities for enjoyment, and they have been more miserably corrupted and destroyed than any other tribes within the Union. They were certainly the most populous, and dwelt beneath the most genial heavens, and amidst the most abundant natural productions, and they were swept away with the most swift and cruel extermination.

Pity for the California Indian that he was not a Christian born, instead of a "Gentile", as the good God made him, for therefore he was written down by the Jesuit padres near to the lowest levels of humanity, that the more conspicuous might appear that self-sacrificing beneficence which reached down to pluck him up to salvation. Pity for him that his purple-tinted and snowy mountains were ribbed with silver and fat with gold-dust, for thereby he became to the American a vagabond thief and a liar, "uncanny and repulsive". Pity for him that his shining valleys, lying warm and genial in the sun, were capable of making the greedy wheat-grower rich in seven good harvests, for thereby he became to him "a mean, thieving, revengeful scoundrel, far below the grade of the most indifferent white".

It is small concern to pioneer miners to know aught of the life-story, customs, and ideas of a poor beggar who is so fatuously unwise as to complain that they darken the water so he can no longer see to pierce the red-fleshed salmon, and his women and children are crying for meat. And when, persisting, he is shot down and lies stark and stiff in the arid gulch, where the pitiless sun of California shakes above him the only winding-sheet that covers his bloody corpse, he is not prolific in narration of his people's legends and traditions.   Dead men tell no tales.

Besides that, the California Indians, above all others, are a shy, foxy, secretive race, who will not impart whatever information they possess until confidence has been grounded on long acquaintance, and even then not completely unless one shows sufficient regard for them to learn their language.   This singular secretiveness has kept the great body of the whites in profound ignorance of their ideas, whatever they may have observed of their customs.

The multitude of tongues is another serious obstacle.   One may spend years in acquiring an Indian tongue, then ride a half-day's journey and find himself adrift again.

It is frequently difficult also to clear away the *débris* created by the white man during twenty years and get down to the bed-rock of the old tribal organization.   So morally feeble and self-abnegative were they that their tribes crumbled under the touch of the pale-face, and their members were proud to group themselves about some prominent pioneer and call 169 themselves by his name.   They frequently accounted it greater honor to be called Bidwell's Indians or Reading's Indians, or so, than Wintūn or whatever the vernacular title might happen to be.   Then, again, it is seldom that a tribe call their neighbors by the name the latter themselves use; and 170 there are some tribes that have no name taken from their own language, as they have adopted the one bestowed by their neighbors.

Physically considered the California Indians are superior to the Chinese, at least to those brought over to America.   There is no better proof of this than the wages they receive for labor, for in a free and open market like ours a thing will always eventually fetch what it is worth.   Chinamen on the railroad receive $1 a day and board themselves; Indians working in gangs on public roads receive seventy-five cents a day, sometimes $1, and their board, the whole equal to $1.25 or $1.50.   But on the northern ranches the Indian has $1.50 to $2 a day and his board, or $1 a day when employed by the year.   Farmers trust Indians with valuable teams and complicated agricultural machinery far more than they do the Chinese. And the Indian endures the hot and heavy work of the ranch better than even the Canton Chinaman, who comes from a hot climate but wants an umbrella over his head. The valley Indians are more willing to labor and more moral now than the mountain Indians, because the latter have better opportunities to hunt game and can pick up small change and old clothes about the mining towns.

There is a common belief among the prejudiced and ignorant that the Indian is such an enormous eater as to overbalance his superior value as a laborer over the Chinaman. This is untrue. It is the almost universal testimony of men who have employed them and observed their habits to any purpose, that when they first come in from the rancheria with their stomachs distended from eating the innutritious aboriginal diet, for a day or two they eat voraciously until they become sated on our richer food; and after that they consume no more than an American performing the same labor.

I am inclined to attribute something of the mental weakness of the California aborigines to the excessive amount of fish which they consumed 171 in their native state; also, perhaps, to the quantity of bitter acorns they ate. It is generally accounted that fish is rich in brain-food, but it is an indisputable fact that the grossest superstitions and lowest intellects in the 172 race are found along the sea-coast.

Another erroneous impression generally prevails among Americans as to their physique, because they have seen only the wretched remnants of the race, the inferior lowlanders, whereas the nobler and more valorous mountaineers were early cut off. On the Round Valley Reservation the Pit River men wear shoes averaging five and six in size, the women two and three. The Potter Valley men are, however, a little larger in the feet; their shoes run from seven to ten, averaging eight and nine; the women of the same tribe range from four to seven, averaging five and six. The men's hands are as small and handsome as their feet, and so are the women's when young, but the hard and unremitting toil of after-life makes their hands grow large, coarse, and ugly.

Old pioneers, especially on the upper waters of the Trinity and the higher foot-hills of the Sierra, have frequently spoken with enthusiasm of giants they had seen in early days weighing one hundred and eighty, two hundred, even two hundred and fifty pounds; tall, fine fellows, not gross, but sinewy, magnificent specimens of free and fighting savagery. On the other hand the desiccation of body in old age, especially in the women, is something phenomenal. In a wigwam near Temecula I have seen an aged man who certainly would not have weighed over fifty pounds, so extraordinarily was he wasted and shrunken. Many others have nearly equaled him. This fact accounts for the repulsively wrinkled appearance of the aged, that which has made them so odious in the eyes of superficial writers and the fastidious tourists. There is probably no other race so excessively fat in youth and so wasted in old age.

All of them emit an odor peculiar to themselves as that of the Chinese is to them. Although they are filthy in their wigwams and in their apparel, yet of the many hundreds I have seen there was not one who still observed the aboriginal mode of life that had not white teeth and a sweet breath. This is doubtless due to the fact that before they became civilized they ate their food cold; when they drink hot coffee and eat hot bread they are liable to toothache and offensive breath like ourselves.

There is another singular and apparently paradoxical fact connected with their habits of body. Though they are so generally uncleanly about their lodges and clothing, there is no nation, unless it was the ancient Romans, who bathed oftener than they. They were almost amphibious, and rival the Kanakas yet in their capacity to endure prolonged submergence. They had no clothing to put off and on, and they were always splashing in the water. They never neglected the morning bath, and many of them do not to this day, though pestered with clothing.

And never since the fatal hour when Adam and Eve tied about them the fig-leaves in Eden has clothing been a symbol so freighted with evil portent as to these people. On excessively hot days they would lay off the miserable rags of civilization which hampered and galled their free-born limbs; and then would come colds, coughs, croups, quick consumption, which swept them off by thousands.

It is a curious fact which has frequently come under my observation, and has been abundantly confirmed by the pioneers, that among half-breed children a decided majority are girls. There is a reason for this which would be a proper subject of explication in a medical work but not in these pages. Suffice it to say that the Indian women thus chosen for wives were generally the finest and most ambitious of their race, while their white husbands were the lowest of theirs. The above-named fact certainly seems to indicate that the California Indian is not without a certain aggressiveness of vitality.

It has been said that the two cardinal tests of national greatness are war and women—prowess in one and progress in the other. Tested by this ordeal, the California Indians seem to fall short. They certainly were
173 not a martial race, as is shown by the almost total absence of the shield, and the extreme paucity of their warlike weapons, which consisted only of bows and arrows, very rude spears, slings, and stones and clubs picked up on the battle-field. It is unjust to them to compare their war record with that of the Algonkins. Let it not be forgotten that these latter tribes gained their reputation for valor, such as it is, through two long and bloody centuries, wherein they contended, almost always in superior force, with weak border settlements, hampered with families, and enfeebled by the malarial fevers which always beset new openings in the forest. Let it be remembered, on the other hand, that after the Republic had matured its vast strength and developed its magnificent resources, it poured out hither a hundred thousand of the picked young men of the nation, unincumbered with women and children, armed with the deadliest steel weapons of modern invention, and animated with that fierce energy which the boundless lust for gold inspired in the Americans, and pitted them against a race reared in an indolent climate, and in a land where there was scarcely even wood for weapons. They were, one might also say, burst into the air by the suddenness and the fierceness of the onslaught. Never before in history has a people been swept away with such terrible swiftness, or appalled into
174 utter and unwhispering silence forever and forever, as were the California Indians by those hundred thousand of the best blood of the nation. They were struck dumb; they crouched in terror close around the few garrisoned forts; if they remained in their villages, and a party of miners came up, they prostrated themselves and allowed them to trample on their bodies to show how complete was their submission. Let a tribe complain that the

miners muddied their salmon-streams, or steal a few pack-mules, and in twenty days there might not be a soul of them living.

It is not to this record that we should go to form any fair opinion of the California Indians' prowess, but rather back to those manuscript histories of the old Spaniards, every whit as brave and as adventurous as ourselves, who for two generations battled so often and so gallantly, and were so often disastrously beaten by "*los bravos Indios*," as the devout chroniclers of the missions were forced against their wills to call them. The pioneer Spaniards relate that at the first sight of horsemen they would flee and conceal themselves in great terror; but this was an unaccustomed spectacle, which might have appalled stouter hearts than theirs; and this fact is not to be taken as a criterion of their courage. It is true also that their battles among themselves, more especially among the lowlanders of the interior—battles generally fought by appointment on the open plain—were characterized by a great deal of shooting at long range, accompanied with much voluble, Homeric cursing; but the brave mountaineers of the Coast Range inflicted on the Spaniards many a sound beating. It is only necessary to mention the names of Marin, Sonoma, Solano, Colorado, Quintin, 175 Calpello, and the stubborn fights of the Big Plains, around Blue Rock, at Bloody Rock, on Eel River, and on the Middle Trinity, to recall to memory some heroic episodes

And it is much to the credit of the California Indians, and not at all to be set down to the account of cowardice, that they did not indulge in that fiendish cruelty of torture which the Algonkin races practiced on prisoners of war. They did not generally make slaves of female prisoners, but destroyed them at once.

But if on the first count they must be allowed to rank rather inferior, in the second, I think, they were superior to the Algonkin races, as also to the Oregon Indians. For the very reason that they were not a martial race, but rather peaceable, domestic, fond of social dances, and well provisioned (for savages), they did not make such abject slaves of their women, were far less addicted to polygamy (the Klamaths are monogamists), and 176 consequently shared the work of the squaws more than did the Atlantic Indians. The husband always builds the lodge, catches all the fish and game and brings most of it home, and brings in a considerable portion of the fuel. In a company of fifty-seven who passed through Healdsburgh, there were twenty-four squaws riding on horseback and only three walking, while there were thirteen braves riding and seventeen walking. The young boy is never taught to pierce his mother's flesh with an arrow to show him his superiority over her, as among the Apaches and Iroquois; though he afterward slays his wife or mother-in-law, if angry, with very little compunction. But there is one fact more significant than any other, and that is the almost universal prevalence, under various forms, of a kind of secret league among the men, and the practice of diabolical orgies, for the purpose of terrorizing the women into obedience. It shows how they were continually struggling up toward equality, and what desperate expedients their lords were compelled to resort to to keep them in due subjection.

The total absence of barbarous and bloody initiations of young men into secret societies was a good feature of their life. They show sufficient capacity to endure prolonged and terrible self-imposed penances or ordeals, but these seldom take any other form than fasting, and that principally among the northern tribes. In their liability to intense religious frenzy, or rather, perhaps, a mere nervous exaltation and exhaustion, resulting from their passionate devotion to the dance, they equal the African races. The same religious bent of mind reveals itself in the strange, crooning chants which they intone while gambling.

As they were not a race of warriors, so they were not a race of hunters. They have extremely few weapons of the chase, but develop extraordinary ingenuity in making a multitude of snares, traps, etc. At least four-fifths of their diet was derived from the vegetable kingdom.

If there is one great and fatal weakness in the California Indians, it is their lack of breadth and strength of character; hence their incapacity to 177 organize wide-reaching, powerful federative governments. They are infinitely cunning, shrewd, selfish, intriguing; but they are quite lacking in grasp, in vigor, and boldness. Since they have mingled with Americans they have developed a Chinese imitativeness, and they take rapidly to the small uses of civilization; but they have no large force, no inventiveness. Their history is painfully deficient in mighty captains and great orators.

But I venture the assertion that no Indians on the continent have learned to copy after civilization in so short a time. I will give a few instances. Shasta Frank, a Wintūn, born and bred to savagery, was a perfect gentleman in the neatness and elegance of his dress, in his manners, and in his speech. For instance, having inadvertently said "setting", he instantly corrected himself with "sitting". He gave me a brief account of his language, which delighted me by its accuracy, clearness, and philosophic insight. I was told of another Wintūn who had become a book-keeper and was drawing a good salary as such. Matilda, a Modok woman, living in the wildest regions of the frontier, showed me a portfolio of sketches, made by herself with a common pencil upon letter-envelopes and such casual scraps of paper, which were really remarkable for their correctness. She would strike off, at first sight, an American, an Englishman, a German, a Chinaman, or any odd and eccentric face she happened to see, with a fidelity and expressiveness that were quite amusing. If she had ever had any advantages, she would have been heard of in the art-world. The pioneers acknowledge that they speedily acquire a subtileness of cheating in card-playing which outwits even themselves, and would have done honor to the "heathen Chinee". Again, it is the testimony of the reservation agents that the Indian children pick up simple Sunday-school melodies and the like with the facility of the plantation pickaninny down South.

There is a curious feature of aboriginal character, which is manifested more particularly in their games. An Indian seems to be very little chagrined by defeat. I have often watched young men and boys, both in native and American games, and have never failed to remark that singularly lymphatic good-nature with which everything is carried forward. American boys will contend strenuously, and even fight, for nice points in the game, down to a finger's breadth in the position of a marble; but Indian youths are gayly indifferent, jolly, easy, and never quarrel. They appear to be just as well pleased and they laugh just as heartily when beaten as when victorious. Everything goes on with a limp and jelly-like hilarity, which makes it extremely stupid to an American to watch their contests very long. When engaged in an athletic game, it is true, they exert themselves to their utmost, and accomplish truly wonderful feats of agility and bottom;

but they do all this purely for the physical enjoyment and the satisfaction of the animal spirits, not for the joy of conquest at all, so far as anybody can perceive. They never brag, never exult.

An Indian will gamble twenty hours at a sitting, losing piece after piece of his property, to his last shirt, which he takes off, hands to the winner, and emerges naked as he was born; yet he exhibits no concern; he passes through it all, and comes out with the same gay and reckless stoicism. There is not a tremor in his voice, not a muscle quivers, his face never blanches; when he takes off the shirt, his laugh is just as vacuously cheerful and untainted with bitterness as it was when he commenced. He borrows another, throws himself on his face, and in five minutes he sleeps the untroubled, dreamless sleep of an infant. It is difficult for a white man to comprehend how one can be so absorbed in the process and so indifferent to the result.

There is another notable defect in their character, that is their lack of poetry, of romance. Though a very joyous and blithe-hearted race, they 178 are patient, plodding, and prosaic to a degree. This is shown in their names, personal and geographical, the great majority of which mean nothing at all, and when they do have a signification it is of the plainest kind. The burden of their whole traditional literature consists of petty fables about animals, though some of these display a quaint humor and an aptness that would not do discredit to Æsop. And it must always be borne in mind that they are forbidden by their religious ideas to speak of the dead, which fact may account for the almost total lack of human legends.

There is not even enough poetry in them to make them tawdry in dress. There is hope of gaudy savages who are thoroughly wasteful and thoroughly devoted to beauty, as they understand it. But these are not wasteful enough even to have feasts, that is, downright, gluttonous "feeds". Their feasts, such as they are, are not held for the purpose of eating, pure and simple; they merely carry to a common rendezvous a store of provisions a little better than the every-day allowance, which they endeavor to make hold out as long as possible, in order that they may enjoy the dance for many days, which is the one great object of desire, while the feast is secondary. Food is gambled away recklessly, but not thrown away, though civilized men and women are apt to consider their prodigal hospitality as little better than sheer wastefulness. All Indians are "cousins" when they come to a camp hungry.

I have said that they are not tawdry in their dress. Young Indians who have mingled with the whites a few years show uniform good taste in their dress, especially in the northern counties; and even old Indians are never seen with those grotesque medleys of all conceivable objects, pepper-casters, patent-medicine labels, oyster-cans, and the like, heaped about their necks, such as may be seen in the interior of the continent.

Mention was made above of their ready adaptation of themselves to the uses of civilization. Who would ever have seen an Algonkin brave offer to go to work for his conquerors? In 1850–'51, before the Indians of the Sacramento Valley had any knowledge whatever of civilization, an adventurous pioneer went to the Upper Sacramento and commenced chopping wood on the banks, for which he received $16 a cord. Sometimes it was necessary to carry the wood a few rods to cord it up close to the water, and he had no trouble in getting Indians to do this work for him for a pittance of flour and bacon. The headman of the village, distinguished only by a feather or a green sprig in his hair, would lay three or four sticks on the back of each squaw or brave, to the number of thirty or forty, then take a stick himself, and with great importance and gravity march with the procession to the river.

There are not lacking instances which show that the California Indians have a sense of humor that the grave, taciturn Iroquois did not possess. The Nishinam of Bear River have several cant or slang names for the Americans, which they use among themselves with great glee. One is the word *boh*, "road", hence, perhaps, derivatively, "road-maker" or "roadster", which they apply to us in a humorous sense, because we make so many roads, which to the light-footed Indians seem very absurd, indeed. Another is *ka'-kin*, "spirit", which is given in compliment to the subtle and mysterious power the American possesses of doing many things beyond their comprehension. Perhaps as common an appellation as any is *chu'-pup*, "red" or "red-faced". Here we have a reversal of the traditional "Paleface" of the eastern dime-novel. But the most humorous name they give us, and the one which amuses them most, is *wóhah*, which is formed from the "whoa-haw" that they heard the early immigrants use so much in driving their oxen. Let an Indian see an American coming up the road, and cry out to his fellows, "There comes a *wóhah!*" at the same time swinging his arm as if driving oxen, and it will produce convulsive laughter. At Healdsburgh they call a locomotive *toot-toot-toot*. A Chinaman is called by the Nishinam, *chó-li-i*, which means "shaved head". There are other names which they apply to us, which are very amusing, but they will not bear translation.

Felicitously characteristic of one feature of Indian life, as well as humorous within itself, was the remark of an observing old man, "Injun make a little fire and set close to him; white man make a big fire and set 'way off."

Frequently their humor is of the kind that may be called unconscious, and is none the less pleasing on that account. One day I applied to an Indian for certain information, and he began to give me the desired names in "American". I interrupted him, and told him I wanted him to talk Indian talk. At that he pulled a black, scowling face, and said, "Guess mebbe bimeby all white man want to learn to talk Injin talk." To any one knowing the peculiar relations which exist between many whites and the aborigines, the satire of this remark is delightful.

They are great thieves, whenever it is safe to be so. Like ill-mannered white people, to use the mildest phrasing, they are fond of borrowing small articles, knives, pipes, pencils, and the like, which they will presently insert into their pockets, hoping the owner may forget to ask for them. One means of protection which old pioneers advised me to take, was, in journeying anywhither, always to keep at my tongue's end the names of several prominent citizens of the vicinity, to impress the savages with the belief that I was well acquainted there, had plenty of friends, and ample means of redress if they did me any wrong. They are strongly attached to their homes, and they have learned by tough experience that if they commit any thievery it will be the worse for them, and that it will go hard but the whites will burn their rancherias and requite the stealing double. Hence they are proverbially honest in their own neighborhood; but a stranger in the gates who seems to be friendless may lose the very blankets off him in the night. They resemble the fox, which never steals near its nest.

The northern tribes are much the most miserly and given to hoarding treasure, and none of them do a white man the smallest service without expecting payment. For instance, Ta'-kho Kol'-li, chief of the Ta-ta-ten', refused to count ten in his language unless I paid him for the service in advance. Once I was sitting with three stalwart and sinister-looking Yurok on a rugged promontory, waiting for the tide to ebb; and when lunch-time arrived we fell to—they on their dried smelt, I on some sandwiches. They had no claim on me, and therefore asked for nothing; but presently I commenced talking with one about Indian matters, and in an instant the crafty savage perceived the drift, saw he had established a claim, and said, "Me talk you Injun talk, you give me piece of bread and meat." No Indian in Southern California ever thought of driving such petty bargains as this.

White men who have had dealings with Indians, in conversation with me have often bitterly accused them of ingratitude. "Do everything in your power for an Indian," they say, "and he will accept it all as a matter of course; but for the slightest service you require of him he will demand pay." These men do not enter into the Indian's ideas. This "ingratitude" is really an unconscious compliment to our power. The savage feels, vaguely, the unapproachable elevation on which the American stands above him. He feels that we had much and he had little, and we took away from him even his little. In his view giving does not impoverish us, nor withholding enrich us. Gratitude is a sentiment not in place between master and slave; it is a sentiment for equals. The Indians are grateful to one another. Sambo did not feel that he was stealing when he took his owner's chickens; it is very much so with the Indian.

Though not by any means a warlike people, and therefore generally laying very little stress on the taking of scalps, they have the usual treachery, revengefulness, and capacity for rancorous hate of all savages. I have before me as I write a terrible memento, and one that opens up a dark and bloody picture of savage life. It is only a stone, a longish stone, rudely blocked out to be made into a pestle, with which a Nishinam woman beat out her sister's brains, while the husband of the murderess looked on. But, worse still, a niece of the murdered woman, in addition to this aunt, lost at various times her mother, a cousin, and a brother, all cut off in cold-blooded murder by her own tribe, and that before they became acquainted with the Americans, and while they were living in "primitive innocence". It is not pleasant to think of these things, and they dispel whole volumes of the romantic nonsense written about aboriginal Arcadias. Still, we must not judge savages by our standard, but bear always in mind that revenge is taught to them as a virtue from the baby-basket to the grave, and that anything which will secure the getting of that revenge is justifiable.

Notwithstanding all that has been said to the contrary by false friends and weak, maundering philanthropists, the California Indians are a grossly licentious race. None more so, perhaps. There is no word in all their languages that I have examined which has the meaning of "mercenary prostitute", because such a creature is unknown to them; but among the unmarried of both sexes there is very little or no restraint; and this freedom is so much a matter of course that there is no reproach attaching to it, so that their young women are notable for their modest and innocent demeanor. This very modesty of outward deportment has deceived the hasty glance of many travelers. But what their conduct really is, is shown by the Argus-eyed surveillance to which women are subjected. If a married woman is seen even walking in the forest with another man than her husband she is chastised by him. A repetition of the offense is generally punished with speedy death. Brothers and sisters scrupulously avoid living alone together. A mother-in-law is never allowed to live with her son-in-law. To the Indian's mind the opportunity of evil implies the commission of evil. He cannot comprehend the case of Joseph and Potiphar's wife, or else he is totally incredulous. If a brother and a sister should chance to dwell together a short time after their parents' death, and are reproached for it, the ready answer is, "Well, what of it? You Americans do it", mentioning some citizen whose bachelor household is presided over by his sister, and against whose fair reputation not the faintest breath of suspicion was ever blown. They cannot understand such a case, and refuse to believe in the blamelessness of the parties.

But while they thus carefully avoid the appearance of evil, the daily conversation of most of them, even in the presence of their wives and children, is as foul as the lowest white men indulge in when alone together. It is a marvel that their children grow up with any virtue whatever. Yet they far less often make shipwreck of body and soul than do the offspring of the civilized, because when the great mystery of maturity confronts them they know what it means and how to meet it.

Marriage frequently takes place at the age of twelve or fourteen. Parents desire to marry their children young, to remove them from temptation, and they willingly provide them with food for a year or two, so as to lighten the matrimonial yoke. Since the advent of the Americans the husband often traffics in his wife's honor for gain, and even forces her to 183 infamy when unwilling; though in early days he would have slain her without pity and without remorse for the same offense.

In making the following assertion, I do it not unaware that it may be stoutly challenged. With the exception, perhaps, of a few tribes in the northern part of the State, *I am thoroughly convinced that a great majority of the California Indians had no conception whatever of a Supreme Being.* True, 184 nearly all of them now speak of a Great Man, the Old Man Above, the Great One Above, and the like; but they have the word and nothing more. *Vox, et præterea nihil.* This is manifestly a modern graft upon their ideas, because this being takes no part or lot in their affairs; is never mentioned in the real and genuine aboriginal mythology or cosmogony; creates nothing, upholds nothing. They have heard of the white man's God, and some of them have taken enough interest to translate the word into their own language, as Po-koh', Lūsh, Sha, Ko-mūs', Kem'-mi Sal'-to, and the like; but with that their interest ceases. It is an idea not assimilated, and to become assimilated the whole of their ancient system of legends and theogony (if the word can be used where there are no gods) would have to be overthrown. By long acquaintance one may become so familiar with even a California Indian as to be able to penetrate his most secret ideas; yet when you ask him to give some account of this being he can tell nothing, because he knows nothing. "He is the Big Man Above"; that is 185 the extent of his knowledge. But ask him to tell you about the creation of the world, of man, of fire, and of familiar objects, and his interest is aroused; instantly this fabulous being disappears, and the coyote comes forward. The coyote did everything, made everything. That is what his father told him, and his father's father told *him*. If this Great Man had any existence in early days, why does he not appear sometimes in the real aboriginal legends? It is no argument against this theory that the names for the Supreme Being above given are purely Indian words. There are pure Indian words in many languages for such terms as "wheat", "rye", "iron", "gun", "ox", "horse", and a hundred others which they never heard of until they saw Europeans. They are very quick to invent names for new objects.

Therefore I affirm without hesitation that there is no Indian equivalent for "God". There are numerous spirits, chiefly bad, some in human form, some dwelling in beasts and birds, having names which they generally refuse to reveal to mortals, and haunting chiefly the hills and forests, sometimes remaining in the Happy Western Land. Some of these spirits are those of wicked Indians returned to earth; others appear to be self-existent. There are great and potent spirits, bearing rule over many of their kind; and there are inferiors. All these spirits are to be propitiated, and their wrath averted. There is not one in a thousand from whom the Indians expect any active assistance; if they can only secure their non-interference all will go well. To the California Indians great Nature is kindly in her moods and workings, but these malign spirits constantly thwart her beneficent designs, and bring trouble upon her children. Nature was the Indian's God, the only God he knew; and the coyote was his minister.

In an article in the *Atlantic Monthly*, Prof. John Fiske says: "Dr. Brinton has shown that none of the American tribes had any conception of a devil. * * * * * Barbaric races, while believing in the existence of hurtful and malicious fiends, have not a sufficiently vivid sense of moral abnormity to form the conception of diabolism." If, by the devil, we are to understand a being the opposite and equal of God, this is true. Of course, the thin and meager imagination of the American savages was not equal to the creation of Milton's magnificent, imperial Satan, or Goethe's Mephistopheles, with his subtle intellect, his vast powers, his malignant mirth; but in so far as the Indian fiends or devils have the ability they are wholly as wicked as these. They are totally bad, they think only

evil; but they are weak, and undignified, and absurd; they are as much
beneath Satan as the "big Indians" who invent them are inferior in imagination to John Milton. The true test of a devil is in his usefulness; and the
Indians stand much more in awe of theirs than we do of ours.

In his admirable work, "Uncivilized Races of Men", Mr. J. G. Wood
makes the following remark: "I have already shown that we can introduce
no vice in which the savage is not profoundly versed, and feel sure that
the cause of extinction lies within the savage himself, and ought not to be
attributed to the white man who comes to take the place which the savage
has practically vacated." Of other savages I am not prepared to speak,
but of the California Indians this is untrue. They smoked tobacco only to
a very limited extent, never chewed it, and were never drunk, because they
had no artificial beverage except manzanita cider, and that in extremely
limited quantities unfermented for a brief season of the year. They had
the vice of gambling much more than we, but, as shown above, it had no
injurious effect on their health. Great and violent paroxysms of anger were
almost unknown; they made no such senseless use as we do of ice-water,
and of hot, heavy, and strongly-seasoned food. They had not even the
vice of gluttony, except after an enforced fast, which was seldom, because
their plain and simple food was easily procured and kept in stores. Licentiousness was universal, but mercenary prostitution was absolutely unknown; hence there were none of those appalling maladies which destroyed
so many thousands on their first acquaintance with Americans.

Next, as to the second part of his remark, that the white man "comes
to take the place which the savage has practically vacated." Let us see to
what extent the Indians had "vacated" California before the Americans
came. In Chapter V it was shown that there were sixty-seven and a half
Indians to the square mile for forty miles along the Lower Klamath in 1870.
Before the whites came doubtless there were one hundred, but we will take
the former figure. Let us suppose there were six thousand miles of streams
in the State yielding salmon; that would give a population of four hundred
and five thousand. In the early stages of my investigation I was led to
believe that wild oats furnished a very large source of supply, but have
abandoned that idea as erroneous. In all oak-forests, acorns yielded at

least four-sevenths of their subsistence, fish perhaps two-sevenths; on the treeless plains the proportion of fish was considerably larger, and various seeds contributed say one-seventh. There are far more acorns in the Sierra and the Coast Range than on the Klamath, and all the interior rivers yielded salmon nearly as abundantly as that river. I think three hundred thousand might be added to the above figure in consideration of the greater fertility of Central and Southern California; this would give seven hundred and five thousand Indians in the State.

Let us take certain limited areas. The pioneers estimate the aboriginal population of Round Valley, when they first visited it, all the way from five thousand to twenty thousand. One thousand white people in it would be considered a very fair population, if indeed it would not crowd it. Mr. Christy estimates that there were from three hundred to five hundred Indians in Coyote Valley near Ukiah; now there are eight white families there, and they think they have none too much elbow-room. General Bidwell states that in 1849 there were at least one thousand souls in the village of the Korusi (Colusa). A Mr. Robinson pointed out to me the site of a village on Van Dusen's Fork which he thought contained one thousand people in 1850. Several other instances might be adduced if necessary. I saw enough in Northern California to convince me that there is many a valley in that section which once contained more Indians than it will of whites for the next century. The natives drew their stores from wide forests all around and from the waters; the whites depend chiefly on the valley itself.

The very prevalence of the crime of infanticide points to an over-fruitfulness and an over-population.

That they were equal to Europeans in bread-winning strength nobody claims, for they lived largely on vegetable food, and that of a quality inferior to bread and beans. But as athletes they were superior, and they were a healthy, long-lived race. In trials of skill they used to shoot arrows a quarter of a mile, or drive them a half-inch into a green oak. I knew a herald on the Upper Sacramento to run about fifty miles between ten or eleven o'clock and sunrise in September; another in Long Valley, near Clear Lake, ran about twelve miles in a little over an hour. The strength of their lungs is shown by the fact that they would formerly remain under water twice as long as an American in diving for mussels. The extraordinary treatment their women undergo in childbirth at the hands of the midwives shows remarkable endurance. No American could dance as they do, all night for days together, sometimes for weeks. Their uniformly sweet breath and beautiful white teeth (so long as they continue to live in the aboriginal way) are evidences of good health. Smoked fish and jerked venison are eaten without further preparation, and there is a considerable amount of green stuff consumed raw in the spring; but four-fifths of their food is cooked and then eaten cold. An Indian is as irregular in his times of eating as a horse or an ox, which may have an injurious effect on his health or it may not If an Indian can keep free from disease he lasts a long time; but when diseases get hold of him he goes off pretty easy, for their medicines amount to nothing. Mr. J. J. Warner, in a communication to the Los Angeles *Star*, gives an account of an appalling pestilence which he calls "remittent fever", which desolated the Sacramento and San Joaquin Valleys in 1833, and reduced those great plains from a condition of remarkable populousness to one of almost utter silence and solitude. Their treatment in the shape of a hot-air bath, followed by a plunge into cold water, added to its fatality, until there was scarcely a human being left alive. But the plains were evidently soon repeopled from the healthier mountain dis-   188 tricts, for Captain Sutter and General Fremont, in their day, found tens of thousands there to fight or to feed. It is the testimony of the old pioneers that they were much subject to fevers and lung complaints even in primitive times, especially along the rivers. Being compelled to live near the streams to procure a supply of water, they were exposed to malarial influences. They sometimes threw up mounds for their villages to stand on, but these were rather for a defense against high water than against ma-   189 laria. The old Indians protest that the present melancholy prevalence of ophthalmia, like some other diseases, is due to American influences, and that in old times they had good eyes. All things taken together, I am well convinced that the California Indians were originally a fruitful and comparatively a healthy and long-lived race. Mr. Claude Cheney, who was among them as early as 1846, on Bear River, states that, although they were rather subject to summer fevers along that stream, large families of children were quite common. They sought as much as possible to avoid the unhealthy lowlands in the dry season by going up into the mountains.

But, after all, let no romantic reader be deceived, and long to escape from the hollow mockeries and the vain pomps and ambitions of civilization, and mingle in the free, wild, and untrammeled life of the savage. It is one of the greatest delusions that ever existed. Of all droning and dreary lives that ever the mind of man conceived this is the chief. To pass long hours in silence, so saturated with sleep that one can sleep no more, sitting and brushing off the flies! Savages are not more sociable than civilized men and women, but less; they talk very fast when some matter excites them, but for the most part they are vacuous, inane, and silent. Kindly Nature, what beneficence thou hast displayed in endowing the savage with the illimitable power of doing nothing, and of being happy in doing it! I lived nearly two years in sufficient proximity to them, and I give it as the result of my extended observations that they sleep, day and night together, from fourteen to sixteen hours out of the twenty-four. They lie down at night-fall, for they have no lights; and they seldom rise before the sun, in summer generally an hour or two after. During the day they are constantly drowsing. When on a march they frequently chatter a good deal, but when a halt is called they all drop on the ground, as if overcome by the heat, and sink into a torpid silence. They will lie in the shade for hours in the middle of the day, then slowly rouse up, commence chattering, and march until night-fall.

CHAPTER XXXVIII.

ABORIGINAL BOTANY.

As employed in this chapter, the word "botany" is somewhat loosely comprehensive, and is used for lack of a better. Under it are included all the forms of the vegetable world which the aborigines use for medicine, food, clothing, etc. Of course, savages have no systematic classification of botanical knowledge; there are no genera, no species. Every oak, pine, or grass has its separate name. The Indians never group individuals together, except occasionally by adding one of the words *cha, du, po'-po, kom, wai, bak* (tree, bush, grass, seed, root, leaf), or something of that sort. But it is not to be supposed that the Indian is a superficial observer; he takes careful note of the forms and qualities of everything that grows on the face of the earth. True, he ascribes marvellous and impossible qualities to some plants, generally those which do not grow in his neighborhood, but this does not blind him to their real properties.

And as his perception of individual differences is nice and minute, so his nomenclature is remarkably full. I assert without hesitation that an average intelligent Indian, even if not a shaman, (or medicine-man,) has at command a much greater catalogue of names than nine-tenths of Americans. Nothing escapes him; he has a name for everything, though he never cultivates any plants. And, indeed, his extensive knowledge is not especially to be wondered at, being taught him with severity. In times of great scarcity they are driven by the sore pangs of hunger to test everything that the soil produces, if perchance they may find something that will appease the gnawings of appetite. They therefore know the qualities of all herbs, shrubs, roots, leaves; whether they are poisonous or nutritive, whether purgative, astringent, sedative, or what not, or without any active principle. And they have often found out these things by bitter experience in their own

190

191

persons. It is surprising what a number of roots, leaves, berries, and nuts, the squaw will discover. She will go out in the spring with nothing but a fire-hardened stick, and in an hour she will pick a breakfast of green stuff, into which there may enter fifteen or twenty ingredients. Her eye will be arrested by a minute plant that will yield her only a bulbous root as large as a large pea, but which the American would have passed unnoticed. The women are generally best acquainted with the edible matters, while the men are the authority as to the medicines.

There are seventy-three vegetable substances mentioned in this chapter. I am indebted to the kindness of Prof. H. N. Bolander, who identified for me many plants that I was unable to determine. There are a few specimens which are so scarce nowadays, owing to the ravages of stock, or so difficult to find in flower, that it was impossible to give their scientific names.

192 I will take this occasion to say that there are many substances popularly called "Indian medicines" which are humbugs, and which have been fathered upon the Indians by patent-medicine men. Whatever is set down in this chapter has been learned from the aborigines themselves.

In regard to medicinal herbs and plants, their usages are peculiar and sometimes amusing. As the practice of medicine among them is a source of great profit and prestige, it is sought to be invested with mystery. The shamans are always crafty men, keen observers, reticent. An old doctor always clothes his art with a great deal of superstition, secrecy, and pompous solemnity. In answer to impertinent young questioners, he says his simples do not grow anywhere in that neighborhrod; he is obliged to purchase them from tribes living at a great distance. I knew an old doctor and his wife, both as full of guile and subtlety as an egg is of meat, who always arose at the dead of night, crept steathily out of camp and gathered their potent herbs, roots, etc., then returned before any one was stirring and concealed them.

The Indians referred to in this chapter are the Nishinam, of Bear River, and the flora is that of the extreme lower foot-hills of Placer County. Their general name for medicine is *wen'-neh*, which denotes "good", but they frequently use the word "medicine", even among themselves.

To begin with the oaks, the species which produces their favorite acorns is the *Quercus Gambelii;* Indian name, *Cha'-kau.* They generally select those trees which have a free, coarse bark and large acorns. About the middle of October the harvest begins, when the Indian, armed with a long, slender pole, ascends the tree and beats off the nuts. A tree which has been well whipped looks as if it had been scourged in a mighty hail-storm. The old men generally assist in carrying them home in their deep, conical baskets, and there the squaws' duties commence. Holding an acorn on a stone, she gives it a slight tap with a stone pestle, called *su'-neh,* to crack the shell, which she strips off rapidly. They are then dried and beaten to powder in small hollows on top of some great rock. The flour is soaked a *Fig. 42* few hours in a large hollow scooped in the sand, the water draining off and carrying away the bitterness; after which it is cooked into a kind of mush 193 in baskets by means of hot stones, or baked as bread in an underground oven. The acorn which stands second in favor is that of the burr-oak (*Q. lobata;* Indian, *lauh*). In Placer County this oak seems to be more properly *Q. Douglassii,* as its branchlets are erect and rigid. There is an oak which they call *shu'-heh,* which seems to be something like a cross between the white and burr oak, having very white and coarsely rimose bark, and glabrous, shining, deeply sinuate leaves. Professor Bolander pronounces this also *Q. Gambelii.* The live-oak is *ha'-ha; Q. Wislizenia, ham'-mut;* the black oak, (*Q. Sonomensis*) *ham'-chu.* The acorns of these last three are eaten only when they can procure no others. There is one other very small species called *chi'-pis,* growing in the mountains; but I cannot determine from their descriptions whether it is the chinquapin or the whortle-berry oak.

The nut-pine or silver-pine (*Pinus edulis*) is *toan, toan'-em cha.* It is a great favorite with them, the most useful tree they have, and they always regret to see an American cutting one down. The nuts are a choice article 194 of food; and, burned and beaten to powder, or crushed up raw and spread on in a plaster, they form their specific for a burn or a scald. The pitch and the mistletoe (*Arceuthobium*) which grows on this pine are very valuable, in their estimation, for coughs, colds, and rheumatism. They set them afire, making a dense smudge, and then the patient, wrapped in a blanket, squats over it or stands on all-fours over it, and works and shuffles his blanket, so as to make the smoke circulate all through it, and come in contact with every portion of his body. When an Indian has an arrow-wound, or wound or sore of any kind, he smears it with the pitch of this tree, and renews it when it wears off. In the spring, if food is scarce, they eat the buds on the ends of the limbs, the inner bark, and the core of the cone (*ta'-eh*), which is something like a cabbage-stalk when green. The cone-core and bunch-grass are boiled together for a hair-dye. They are as proud of their black hair as the Chinese; and when an old chief who is somewhat vain of his personal appearance, or one of the dandies of the tribe, finds his hair growing gray, he has his squaw boil up a decoction of this kind, and he sops his bleaching locks in it. The tar (*shin'-dak*), which is worn by widows in mourning, is made of hot pitch and burned acorns, powdered; it is removed by means of soap-root (*Chlorogalum pomeridianum*) and hot water.

Chip'-pa is the willow, the long twigs of which are used both for arrows and basket-making. In making an arrow the hunter employs a rude kind of turning-lathe, a couple of sticks held in the hand, between which the twig intended for the arrow is tightly clamped and twisted around, which rubs off the bark and the alburnum, and makes it round. The long straight shoots of the buckeye (*po'-loh, po'-lem du*) are used for the same purpose. For the woof in basket-making they employ the wood of the redbud (*Cercis occidentalis—pad'-dit*), which is split up with flints or the finger-nails into fine strings, used substantially as thread. The willow twig is passed round and round the basket, the butt of one lapping the tip of the other, while the redbud strings are sewn over the upper and under the lower.

Ko'-toh is the manzanita. Its berries are a favorite article of food, and are eaten raw, or pounded into flour in a basket, the seeds separated out, and the flour made into mush, or sacked and laid away for winter. They also make quite an agreeable article of cider from them, by soaking the flour in water several hours, and then draining it off.

Alder is *shu'-tum;* poison-oak is *chi'-tok.* They are less easily poisoned by the latter than Americans; their children handle it a great deal while little. They eat the leaves both as a preventive and as a cure for its effects, though it sometimes poisons them internally. The women use the leaves freely in cooking; they lay them over a pile of roots or a batch of acorn-

195

196

bread, then lay on hot stones and earth. The bright-red berries of the California holly (*Photinea arbutifolia*—*yo'-lus*) are eaten with relish; also the berries of the elder, *nok*, and wild grapes, *pi'-men*. They call a grape-vine a bush, *pi'-men-en du*.

Soap-root, *hauh*, is used for poisoning fish. They pound up the root fine, and mix it into pools where the fish and minnows have no way of escape, and at the same time stir up the bottom until the water becomes muddy. The minnows thrust their heads out of the water stupefied, and are easily scooped up. Buckeyes are used in the same manner. Soap-root is also used to heal and cleanse old sores, being heated and laid on hot. Both soap-root and buckeyes are eaten in times of great scarcity; they are roasted underground thirty-six hours or more to extract the poison.

For toothache the remedy is the root of the California buckthorn (*Frangula Californica*—*lu'-hum du*). It is heated as hot as can be borne, placed in the mouth against the offending member, and tightly gripped between the teeth. Several sorts of mints, *hi'-suh*, are used in a tea or decoction for colds or coughs. Ague is believed to be cured by a decoction of the little mullen (*Eremocarpus setigerus*—*ba'-dah*), which grows on black adobe land in autumn. Colic is treated with a tea made from a greenish-gray lichen (*Parmelia saxicola*—*wa'-hat-tak*), found growing on stones. For rheumatism they take the leaves and stems of a parasite vine (*Galium*—*shesh-em*) which grows up in the middle of the chaparral bush, heat or burn them, and clap them hot on the place.

Yellow dock, *hit'*, is a valuable specific in their pharmacopœia. In case of acute pain of any description the root is heated hot and pressed upon the spot. In the spring the leaf is eaten boiled for greens, together with clover and many other things.

Bunch-grass, *bu'-puh*, is the subject of superstition. They believe that the long, slender stalks of it, discharged as arrows from a little bow against a pregnant woman, will produce a miscarriage; also, that they will hasten the time of maturity in a maiden. There is another thing which they call *wo-ko'-mah*, probably wild parsnip, which they believe to be a deadly poison. It will produce nose-bleed, and the people who keep it in their houses will surely die. I will here state that I cannot discover that the

197

198

Indians ever used poisons to any considerable extent to rid themselves of enemies; if they did, it was the old shamans, and they keep the matter a secret. The Indians profess to stand in great and perpetual dread of being poisoned by one another; and no one will taste anything handed to him by one who is not a member of his family, unless the other tastes it first; but they imagine a hundred cases of poisoning where one actually occurs.

Of grasses, they eat the seed of the wild oat, (*tu'-tu-tem kom*), but very sparingly. Wild clover, *chi'-wi;* alfilerilla, *bat'-tis;* and a kind of grass growing in wet places (*Melica—holl*) are all eaten raw when young and tender, or boiled for greens.

There are two kinds of mushrooms which they consider edible. The one of which they are fondest is called *pūl'-kut,* and is a little round ball, from the size of a marble to that of a black walnut, found underground in chaparral and pine thickets. They eat it raw with great relish, or roast it in the ashes. Another kind is the *wa'-chuh,* which grows in the ordinary form, brown on the upper side, chocolate-colored and deeply ribbed underneath, and easily peeled. It is eaten boiled.

Higher up in the mountains they find a root looking somewhat like cork, a piece of which they sometimes wear suspended to their clothing as a charm. It is called *chūk'* or *cham'-pu.* Indians of other tribes in the State invest different species of *Angelica* with talismanic attributes.

Under the popular name of grass-nut there is included a large number of plants with a small, round, bulbous root, all of which, with one exception, the Indians eat with much satisfaction. They are generally pried out of the ground with a sharp stick and eaten raw on the spot; but sometimes the women collect a quantity in a basket and make a roast in the ashes, or boil them. Most of them are by no means disagreeable to the civilized taste. There is the beaver-tail grass-nut (*Cyclobothra—wal'-lik*), the turkey-pea (*Sanicula tuberosa—tu'-en*), the purple-flowered grass-nut (*Brodiæa congesta— o'-kau*); the tule grass-nut (*ko'-ah*), a small bulb, with a single, wiry, cylindrical stalk, growing in wet places, which I could not identify; the climbing grass-nut (*Brodiæa volubilis—oam'-pūm wai*), sometimes planted by Americans for ornaments; the little soap-root (*Chlorogalum divaricatum—poy'-um*); the wild garlic (*Allium—ku'-ih*); the eight-leafed garlic (*shal*), the five-leafed garlic (*in'-shal*), and the three-leafed garlic (*wuk'-wi*); the yellow-blossom grass-nut (*Calliproa lutea—us'-tuh*); the long-leafed grass-nut (*Brodiæa congesta*, although the Indians have a different name for it from that mentioned just above, namely, *yoang wai*); the white-flowered grass-nut (*Hesperoscordium lacteum—yo'-wak wai*); and the wild onion (*Allium cepa—chan*). There is one other grass-nut, with a black bulb (*Anticlea—hak'-kul*), which the Indians consider poison, although it probably contains no more poison than other members of the liliaceous family.

The list of greens which they eat in the spring is also quite extensive. Besides the grasses and the yellow dock above mentioned, there is the mask-flower (*Mimulus luteus—pu'-shum*); two species of the *Angelica* (*hen* and *oam'-shu*), which are difficult to determine; the California poppy (*Eschholtzia Californica—ta'-pu*), either boiled or roasted with hot stones, and then laid in water; the rock-lettuce (*Echeveris lanceolata—pit'-ti-tak*), eaten raw; the wild lettuce (*Claytonia perfoliata—yau*), and a species of *Sanicula* (*man'-ku*), the root of which, long and slightly tuberose, is also eaten. Of the wild lettuce a curious fact is to be noted. The Indians living in the mountains, about at the elevation of Auburn, gather it and lay it in quantities near the nests of certain large red ants, which have the habit of building conical heaps over their holes. After the ants have circulated all through it, they take it up, shake them off, and eat it with relish. They say the ants, in running over it, impart a sour taste to it, and make it as good as if it had vinegar on it. I never witnessed this done, but I have been told of it, at different times, by different Indians whom I have never known to deceive me.

Of seeds, they eat the following: A kind of coarse, wild grass (*Bromus virens—do'-doh*); a species of yellow-blooming, tarry-smelling weed (*Madaria—koam'-duk*), the seeds of which are as rich as butter; the yellow-blossom or crow-foot (*Ranunculus Californicus—tiss*), of which the seed is gathered by sweeping through it a long-handled basket or a gourd; a little weed which grows thick in ravines (*Blennosperma Californicum—poll*), gathered the same way; also a weed (*shi'-u*) with little white blossoms distributed all along the stalks, which are thickly covered with minute prickles—I know not what it is. All these seeds are generally parched a little, and then beaten to flour, and eaten without further cooking, or made into bread or mush. The dry, parched flour of the crow-foot seed has that peculiar, rich taste of parched corn.

There is an umbelliferous plant (*sho'-kum*), the root of which the Indians esteem very highly for food; more highly than any other, it being their nearest equivalent to potatoes. I know not if it is the true cammas; I think it is at least a species of it. It grows on rocky hill-sides, blossoms in June and July, has an extremely delicate, fringe-like leaf, and a root about an inch long and a quarter as thick, sweetish-pungent and agreeable to the taste. In Penn Valley, Nevada County, they gather large quantities of it.

They are acquainted with the *Yerba santa*, but attach no particular value to it.

There is a plant (*pūm*) growing on north hill-sides, with a broad leaf, and a long white root as thick as one's little finger, which is highly esteemed as a medicine for internal pain of any kind, while the top affords edible greens. The Indians could not find a specimen of it.

Around old camps and corrals there is found a wild tobacco (*pan*), which Prof. Asa Gray pronounces *Nicotiana quadrivalvis* and Professor Bolander *N. plumbaginifolia*. It is smoked alone or mixed with dried manzanita leaves (*Arctostaphylos glauca*), and has a pungent, peppery taste in the pipe which is not disagreeable. Mr. A. W. Chase, in a letter to the author, states the Klamaths cultivate it—the only instance of aboriginal cultivation known in California. I think the Indians never cultivated it more than this, that they scattered the seeds about camp and then took care not to injure the growing plants. I have even seen them growing finely on their earth-covered lodges. The pipe, *pan'-em-ku-lah*, is generally made of serpentine (or of wood nowadays), shaped like a cigar-holder, from four to six inches long, round, and with a bowl nearly an inch in diameter.

There are two plants used for textile purposes. One is a kind of tule-grass or small bulrush (*Juncus—dok'-kŭn*), which they hetcheled with flints or with their finger-nails, bleached, and wove into breechcloths. For strings, cords, and nets they used the inner bark of the lowland milkweed

200

201

Fig. 43

(*Asclepias—pu*). When it is dry the Indian takes both ends of a stalk in his hand and crushes it in his teeth, or else passes it over a stone while he gently taps it with another; then strips off the bark and twists it into strands, then into cords. The rock milkweed (*oam'-pu*) has a medicinal value; they use the root for the toothache the same way the root of the buckthorn is used.

It is necessary to state that most of the medicines above mentioned are of the class which the women are allowed to become somewhat acquainted with and to employ. There are several other substances which are more rare and valuable, or at least they deem them more valuable, and which the medicine-men alone know anything about. They are found far up in the mountains or in other localities, and may be called the medicines of commerce, having a tolerably well-settled value in shell-money. I regret that I was generally unable to secure sufficiently complete specimens to determine them. For instance, there is a root (*lü'-no*) which I should call seneca snakeroot, but of which I could secure only a little piece. A root as large as a pipestem and about four inches long is worth $1. A decoction of it is used for diarrhea, that scourge of aboriginal life, also for venereal diseases. There is a bush (*cha'-pum*) found in the mountains, with a very pale, tea-green bark and minute golden specks on the small limbs, which is probably California sassafras, and which is very highly esteemed for coughs and colds, a tea of the bark being given. Another root (*pal'-lik*)—spignet from its appearance—is made into a tea and drunk for diarrhea. This also is very valuable. There is still another root (*lit'-we*) found on the Truckee which is good for the dropsy.

Although it is not strictly germane to the topic, I may be permitted to state that the Indians have names for all the internal organs of the human body; and their ideas of their functions and of the operations of medicine are at least as respectable as those of the Chinese.

YOKUTS BOTANY.

I will subjoin here some brief notes on plants and flowers brought in by the Indians of Tule River Reservation for inspection by the surgeon of the reservation and myself:

Che'-lis, shepherd's purse; the seed highly esteemed for pinole, a very nutritious, farinaceous beverage which the Indians learned from the Mexicans to make.

Ke'-yet-sah (*Cruciferæ*), with reversed siliques. Seed used in making panada or mush.

Ta-kor'-nes (*Trifolium*), hairy clover; eaten raw.

Port'-râ (*Trifolium*), another species; eaten raw.

Wa-tra'-ko (*Escholtzia Californica*); not eaten here.

Lâ'-chun (*Compositæ*); seed used for pinole; highly esteemed.

Po-tal'-lu Kai'-u-in (*Castilleia*), painted cup. This is called by the Indians "the coyote's rectum", which is the translation of the above name.

Poh'-ke-ūts, alfilleria; not eaten here.

Kit-nü'-sil (*Yerba Santa*, Span.); a decoction used for fever and for bad blood.

Trai'-yu; early, onion-like flower; small bulb used for food.

Nat'-tin Te'-eh; lupine from the mountains; not used. Indian name means "rattlesnake teeth".

Lun'-kūh' (*Allium*), wild onion; eaten green.

Men-e'-ling-hüt (*Phacelia*), two kinds.

Wal'-laikh, a willow-like shrub; used for medicine for rheumatism or other pain; beaten up and spread in the couch to be slept on.

So'-gōn (*Nicotiana*), wild tobacco; dried and beaten up very fine, then wet and compressed together into large solid lumps. Also used as a medicine for a cut.

Tan'-naikh (*Datura meteloides*), jimson weed; the root pounded up is "good for anything" as medicine; good for a cut, a gunshot wound, a bruise, etc. A decoction of the root acts like opium. Their priests sometimes drink it for two days in succession in order to get fully under its influence and become prophetic. Sometimes they are killed by it, which the Indians consider as a proof that their bowels were in bad condition.

Li'-pits (*Yerba mansa*, Span.); root pounded up and soaked in water; the water drunk for a bad stomach.

Kin'-min (*Quercus lobata*); acorns a great food staple; but rather inferior to—

E'-sin (*Q. gambelii*); the white oak growing up in the mountains, whose acorns are the favorite.

Tsi'-tikh (*Quercus*); a small species, grows on rocky points near the plains; acorns little esteemed.

Tau'-a-chit (*Quercus*); round, small leaves, perhaps another species of white oak. The acorns are used.

Ail'-loh (*Scirpus validus?*); tule pollen used for food. This is beaten off on a cloth in large quantities and is made into pinole or mush. The bulbous root is also eaten.

Hau'-pun (*Fresnio*, Span.); a root highly esteemed as a purgative in certain internal diseases.

Tro'-kot (*Chlorogalum pomeridianum*), soap-root; fibre used for household brushes; root for washing; also as a healing and cleansing medicine.

Tsuk'-kus (*Sporobolus*); a kind of coarse grass, of which the stalks are used in making baskets.

Ṭa-ka'-tu (*Cercis?*); bark used in making baskets.

A kind of fern (*Pellea Brewerii*) used as a beverage, like tea. Indian name forgotten.

Al'-lit, a kind of salt, principally alum in a crude state, collected by these Indians as a seasoning for greens. They go in the morning, when the dew is on, to a low, alkaline piece of ground, and either pull up the grass and dissolve the salt off from it in water, or collect it by sweeping a stick through the grass and washing off the adhering salt.

Tin'-nikh, matting made from tule, used for beds and to sit on in gambling.

MISCELLANEOUS.

Che'-hin kin'-ku (*Angelica*); used by the Hūchnom for a cough-medicine.

Kin'-ku-halkh, a little root used by the same tribe as a blood-purifier.

Huh'-wal (acorn), kokh (manzanita), kin-kil-leh' (bunch-grass), lēp (tar-weed), ēsh (sunflower); all these are used by the Hūchnom to make bread (hu-teh').

Mu-hach'-a-ko-len (*Angelica*); a panacea and charm among the Hupâ.

An oak mistletoe (*Phoradendron*); smoked by the Chimariko as a substitute for tobacco. Indian name unknown.

ANIMAL FOODS.

The following articles are either eaten or used for medicine by the Nishinam of Placer County.

Nauh (*Helix Vancouverensis*), snail; used for food.

Nauh (*H. Columbiana*), snail; used for food.

Shek (*Saturnia Cæanothi*), caterpillar; used for food.

Shek (*Arctia*, two species), caterpillar; used for food.

Shil'-lah (*Hyborynchus Perspicuus*), a small minnow. Sometimes the Indian shaman, after sucking a patient for a long time, pretends to vomit up one of these minnows (which, of course, he had previously concealed in his mouth), pretending that it had somehow been introduced into the system and had been the source of all the trouble.

Hol'-lih, crickets; used for food, roasted. Formerly they were often roasted in large numbers by firing the woods.

Pan'-nak, grubs found in decayed oak-trees; used for food.

Laih (*Engystoma*), a small frog; used for food.

Sho'-lah, slugs; eaten for food.

Ok'-o-pe-peh (*Phrynosoma*), a horned toad; given internally for medicine in certain stomachic affections.

Pit'-chak (*Sceloporus bi-seriatus*), another toad; used as the above.

Shol'-lo-koi-koi (*Gerhonotus multi-carinatus*), a lizard; used for medicine.

Shol'-lo-koi-koi, another lizard; used as the above.

Kūt (*Sphinx Ludoviciana*), a horned black worm; used for food. The Indian name denotes "a buck", so called on account of the horn.

Tai'-a-mun (*Coronella balteata*), a ring-snake; used by the Nishinam for medicine; eaten by the Washo of Nevada.

Earth-worms (*Lumbricus*), Indian name unknown to me; eaten in soup. The Nakum of Big Meadows dance and stamp violently, chanting all the while, to bring these worms to the surface.

Koy-o'-ta (*Onodonta*), a clam found in Owen's River, and in many other parts of California; eaten boiled.

No'-ko (*Mytilus edulis*), a clam; eaten by the Gallinomero of Russian   202
River Valley.

A clam (*Saxidomus Nuttallii*); eaten by the Indians of Eel River Valley.

Sal-i'-ki (*Acmea mitra*); a shell used by the Pit River and other tribes
in the ornamentation of women's dresses.

Hau-min'-kēt, dried whalebone, found on the coast; used by the
Hūchnom as an antidote for dyspepsia.

Cham'-bau (*Ortyx Californicus*). After eating the flesh of this bird,
roasted, the Nishinam dry the skins, and preserve them as a dainty for use
in case of sickness.

En'-neh, *grasshoppers;* eaten by the Konkau. They catch them with
nets, or by driving them into pits; then roast them and reduce them to
powder for preservation.

The skunk (*Mephitis*) is eaten by the Nishinam, when properly caught
and dressed.

CHAPTER XXXIX.

SUPPLEMENTARY FACTS.

[By an oversight the facts contained in this chapter were not prepared in time for insertion in the body of the report.]

I.—THE PRE-HISTORICS OF CALIFORNIA.

The fact of the almost total lack of ceramic remains, and the character of the relics found in the Alameda and other shell-mounds, show that the present race must either have supplanted or descended from one which was little more advanced than themselves. The few and simple stone implements used by the California Indians resemble, in their main purpose and design, those of the extinct races exhumed in the shell-mounds, only they are conspicuously ruder and simpler. Take the stone mortars, for instance. The pre-historical mortar is carefully dressed on the outside, and has three general shapes: either flattish and round, or shaped like a duck's egg with the bowl on the side, or else with the bowl in the large end and the small end inserted into the ground, or cylindrical with the bowl in the end. But the Indian now takes a small bowlder of trap or greenstone and beats out a hollow in it, leaving the outside rough. Whenever one is seen in possession of a mortar dressed on the outside he will acknowledge that he did not make it, but found it; in other words, it is pre-historical. The pre-historics used handsomely-dressed pestles, sometimes embellished with rings; but the squaw nowadays simply picks up a long, slender cobble from the brook.

The pre-historics of California carved out long, heavy knives, or swords, of obsidian or jasper, which were probably kept as family heir-looms from generation to generation, to be paraded as jewelry or borne aloft as a sort of mace on certain solemn occasions. The Indians of to-day have the same articles and use them for the same purpose; but their inferiority to

203

Fig. 44

432

their predecessors shows forth in the fact that they no longer manufacture them, but confine their ambition to keeping them in the family.

The pre-historics made out of sandstone or other soft stones a small and almost perfect sphere as an acorn-sheller; but the squaw nowadays simply selects for this purpose a smooth cobble from the creek-bed.

In the collection of Mr. A. W. Chase, of the United States Coast-Survey, there are spindle-whorls of stone, some of them found in mounds raised by extinct tribes and others found among the Klamath River Indians and the Noamlakki in gravel-mining claims. The Indians of this day use no such implement for any purpose whatever. Near Freestone, Sonoma County, I saw in possession of the finder what was probably a spindle-whorl of pottery; the only instance of the kind I know of.

In regard to tobacco-pipes the deterioration is not so manifest, for I have seen serpentine pipes of as handsome workmanship as any obtained from the mounds, though even these may be old heir-looms. But I still think there is deterioration shown in the fact that the Indians nowadays use so many wooden pipes of the rudest construction; though we have no means of showing that their ancestors did not use equally poor ones, since their wooden pipes, if they had any, have perished.

Then, again, as to the shell-mounds themselves. I am of the opinion that they are merely the accumulations of a race of men who dived for clams, as the Wintūn of the Upper Sacramento do to this day, to a limited extent. In other words, the Wintūn and other tribes are descended from a people who were more energetic and industrious than themselves.

Langsdorff and La Perouse both mention that they saw many Indians with magnificent beards, but now they are almost totally destitute of beards. Whether the ever-increasing drought and desiccation of the Pacific Coast, which have swept away the ancient forests, have also destroyed the beards of the aborigines, is a question I am not competent to determine

The legends connected with the Geysers make mention of the fact that idolatry existed among the California pre-historic tribes, while if those of to-day have any worship at all, it is fetichism. Fetichism is lower than idolatry. Regarding this subject of idol-worship, Mr. Chase, in a letter to the author, says: "That such has existed among tribes farther northward

there can be no doubt. For instance, there is a curious relic on the Columbia in the shape of a stone idol with three human faces, or, I should say, three attempts at representing human faces in stone.   *   *   *
It is now used for a hitching-post by a settler. I have never seen it myself, but give the facts on the authority of an officer of our service, who both saw and sketched it".

There are two legends, noted in place, one among the Karok and one among the Palligawonap, which, in my opinion, are a corrupted version of some old ethnic myth, and therefore point to a descent from tribes superior to the present.

I do not forget that the Indians, almost with one accord, attribute these superior stone implements to a race older and other than their own. There is also a Nishinam legend, which cannot be very well explained except on the supposition of a reference to an earli r race, from whom their forefathers suffered grewsome damage. On the   r hand, they all insist that their progenitors were created from the soi'   re they now live (to take all their accounts, there must have been at lea a hundred of these "special creations" in California), so that their legends are not consistent.

The theory of degeneration above advanced is quite in accord with the climatic changes and the deforestation which have taken place on this coast even within the historical period. We know, from the statements of Viscayno and other early Spanish explorers, that extensive forests were flourishing near San Diego and Monterey three hundred years ago, where now there are none. Viscayno, as quoted by Cronise, says the natives of Santa Catalina Island had large wooden canoes, capable of sea-voyages, whereas that island is now almost treeless. Fossil remains have been discovered in Southern California and Arizona which indicate that there were once heavy forests where now are barren wind-swept plains. Ruins of great walled cities and large systems of irrigating ditches in Arizona and New Mexico, on the Gila, Little Colorado, De Chaco, San Juan, and other streams, plainly show that these regions once contained an agricultural population, who were ultimately driven out by the ever-increasing drought and the failure of the streams. The great Sequoias, on the high Sierra, may perhaps be the last lingerers of a gigantic race of forest trees, which the changed climatic conditions of California have destroyed from the plains.

We know that the deforestation of Babylonia, Assyria, Palestine, and Greece was accompanied by a corresponding deterioration in the inhabitants, and it may have been also largely the cause of it.

While there is nothing to show that the present race of California Indians are descended from an agricultural people like the New Mexican Pueblos, there is much to show that their predecessors were superior to them, and that their predecessors were also their ancestors. The California Indians are simply a poor copy of the people whom we usually call prehistorics; but the copy follows the original so closely, that there can be little doubt that it is a copy made by transmission.

II.—ATHABASCAN VS. CALIFORNIAN.

1 wish to tabulate here some facts which show more plainly than has been done in the Report that California has witnessed a great invasion from the north before the historical period.

1. Let us start in Rogue River Valley, Oregon, and journey through Yreka and across the spurs of Mount Shasta down into the head of the great Sacramento Valley. North of Mount Shasta the languages are conspicuously harsh, often guttural, and abounding in such difficult consonantal combinations as ks, tsk, ps, sk, etc., as in the following words from the Shastika and Modok: *Ksup, tsi'-sup, ska'-gis, nis-wat'-ska, sna-wat'-ska* (five, father, nine, maṇ, woman). But south of this mountain the languages are largely vocalic, harmonious, and musical. The transition in crossing the Mount Shasta watershed is too abrupt to be explained by the gradual softening of the climate. The change is as sudden as it is when the traveler goes over the Splügen Pass from the rugged and knaggy German of Chur to the silvery accents of Milan.

2. The deep, circular cellar (not a cellar proper, but part of the dwelling) which is found in the lodges north of Mount Shasta and on the Klamath and Trinity indicates a long residence of the makers' ancestors in a rigorous climate. Directly you come south of the line above-mentioned, this subterranean feature ceases quite abruptly, the wigwam being built on

the surface, with only a hollow scooped out sufficiently to bank out the rain in a storm. This change, too, is quite too sudden to be explained by the greater warmth of the climate. On the Klamath and north of it the sudatory, or sweat-house, is wholly underground, but south of it everywhere it is almost always above, though covered with a layer of earth. The climate on the Klamath west of the mountains is very little colder than that on the Upper Sacramento, and not so cold as that on the Upper Trinity.

3. Among the Indians north of Mount Shasta, including several tribes within California, a majority of the shamans, or physicians, are women; but south they are almost wholly excluded from the practice of medicine.

4. These tribes north of the line, and more especially the Oregon Indians, are very fond of horses; while the true California Indian does not seek to accumulate wealth in horses, but prefers shells and makes all his bargains in that medium, and has little to do with the noble brute until you go far enough south to find a touch of Spanish blood in his veins.

III.—VARIETIES OF LODGES.

Perhaps the reader will not have noticed the large variety of styles employed by the California Indians in building their dwellings according to the requirements of the climate or the material most convenient. (1) In the raw and foggy climate of the northwestern portions of the State we find the deep, warm pit in the earth, surmounted by a house shaped something like our own, and firmly constructed of well-hewn redwood puncheons or poles. (2) In the snow-belt, both of the Coast Range and the Sierra, the roof must necessarily be much sharper than on the lowlands; hence roof and frame become united in a conical shape, the material being poles or enormous slabs of bark, with an open side toward the north or east, in front of which is the bivouac-fire, thus keeping the lodge free from smoke. (3) In the very highest regions of the Sierra, where the snow falls to such an enormous depth that the fire would be blotted out and the whole open side snowed up, the dwelling retains substantially the same form and materials, but the fire is taken into the middle of it, and one side of it (generally the east one) slopes down more nearly horizontal than the other, and terminates in a covered way about three feet high and twice as long. (4) In

Russian River and other warm coast valleys prevails the large round or oblong structure of willow poles covered with hay. This is sufficiently warm for the locality, is easily and quickly made, and easily replaced when an old one is burned to destroy the vermin. (5) On Clear Lake was found a singular variety of lodge; one with four perpendicular walls made by planting willow poles in the ground and lashing others to them horizontally, leaving a great number of small square interstices. Whether intentionally or not, these are exceedingly convenient for the insertion of fish for sun-drying. The roof is flat, made of poles covered with thatch. (6) On the great woodless plains of the Sacramento and San Joaquin the savage naturally had recourse to earth for a material. The round, dome-shaped, earth-covered lodge is considered the characteristic one of California; and probably two-thirds of its immense aboriginal population lived in dwellings of this description. The door-way is sometimes directly on top, sometimes on the ground at one side. I have never been able to ascertain whether the amount of rain-fall of any given locality had any influence in determining the place for the door. (7) In the hot and almost rainless Kern and Tulare Valleys occurs the dwelling made of so frail a material as tule.

IV.—A KONKAU ANNIVERSARY.

The dance for the dead (*tsi'-pi ka-mi'-ni*, "the weeping dance") corresponds somewhat to All-Souls' Day. It always occurs about the last of August, beginning in the evening and lasting until daybreak. They bring together a great quantity of food, clothing, baskets, and whatever other things they believe the dead require in the other world. Everything is bought or made new for the occasion; the food is fresh and good, the clothing is newly woven and fine, the ornaments are the best they can procure. These are hung on a semicircle of boughs or small trees, cut and set in the ground leafless; the smaller and lighter articles at the top, twelve or fifteen feet high, and the larger toward the bottom or lying on the ground. In the center burns a great fire, and hard by are the graves. On the opposite side of the fire from the offerings there is a screen made of bushes with blankets hung over them to reflect the light of the fire brilliantly on the offerings, which glitter like a row of Christmas trees   They seat

204

themselves on the graves, men and squaws together, as the twilight closes in around them, and begin a mournful wailing, crying, and ululation for the dead of the year. After a time they rise and form a circle around the fire, between it and the offerings, and commence a dance accompanied by that hoarse, deathly rattle of the Indian chant, which sounds so eldritch and so terrible to the civilized ear. Heavily the dancing and the singing go on from hour to hour, and now and then a few pounds of provisions, a string of shell-money, or some small article is taken down from the espaliers and cast into the flames. All through the night the funereal dance goes on without cessation; wilder and more frantic grows the chanting; swifter becomes the motion of the dancers, and faster and faster the offerings are hurled upon the blazing heap. The savage transports wax amain. With frenzied yells and whoops they leap in the flickering firelight like demons—a terrible spectacle. Now some squaw, if not restrained, would fling herself headlong into the burning mass. Another one will lie down and calmly sleep amid the extraordinary commotion for two hours, then arise and join as wildly as before in the frightful orgies. But still the espaliers are not emptied, and as the morning stars grow dim and daybreak is close at hand, with one frantic rush, yelling, they seize down the residue of the clothing (the clothing is mostly reserved until near morning) and whirl it into the flames, lest the first gray streak of dawn should appear before the year-long hunger of the ghosts is appeased.

There is another feature of this anniversary which is remarkable. I do not know as they determine the time for it by any savage ephemeris, but its occurrence marks their New Year's Day. It is therefore seized upon as a proper occasion for settling their accounts, wiping out all old debts, and making a clear ledger for the coming year. So, amid all these ululations, and the burning and fizzing of woolens and dried meat, those Indians who are not presently engaged in the dance may be seen squatted all around the fire in twos, busily reckoning their accounts on their fingers, tying and untying their strings of shell-money, handing over and receiving their shell-beads and other valuables, etc. On this eventful night, too, are made many marriage contracts for the ensuing year.

EDITOR'S NOTES

Page	Note Number	
19	1	Modok, or as it is usually spelled, Modoc, means "south." Both the Modoc and their linguistic neighbors to the north, the Klamath, called themselves Maklaks, "people."
20	2	No evidence exists that there are different racial odors. This statement probably derives from the body of American folk belief invented to justify the racism which has for so long been a part of American thought and action.
21	3	It is regrettable that Powers does not spell out the reasons for the abundant supply of *allikochick*. With population reduction there may have been more old shell money to go around, or perhaps the supply was increased by imports through white traders. See R. F. Heizer, "Counterfeiters and Shell Currency Manipulators Among the California Indians," *Journal of California Anthropology* 2 (1975): 108-110.
21	4	The author is describing the legalized payment of blood money. For further details see A. L. Kroeber, *Handbook of Indians of California*, Bureau of American Ethnology, Bulletin 78 (1925): chap. 2. (This work is cited hereafter as *Handbook*.)
22	5	For details of the institution of bride purchase and social status of the married couple, see Kroeber, *Handbook*, pp. 28-32.
23	6	This description is valid, and is generally true for most California tribes. For details see N. C. Willoughby, *Division of Labor Among the California Indians*, University of California Archaeological Survey, Report No. 60 (1963), pp. 1-80.
24	7	The author returns to the matter of the belief in a supreme deity on p. 413. This subject is treated in more detail by E. M. Loeb, "The Creator Concept Among the Indians of North Central California," *American Anthropologist* 28 (1926):467-493.

439

Page	Note Number	
25	8	The sacred character of collecting wood for the sweathouse was first noted by George Gibbs in 1851. It is also discussed by Kroeber, *Handbook*, pp. 41, 81.
26	9	This is a description of the curing shaman, always a woman. For further details see Kroeber, *Handbook*, pp. 63-68.
30	10	This account is of the priest who reenacts the sacred myth before the public dance can be held. For the myth-formulas, see A. L. Kroeber and E. W. Gifford, *World Renewal: A Cult System of Native Northern California*, Anthropological Records 21: 1 (1949).
31	11	Sexual license at the conclusion of a ceremony has been noted for the following tribes: Shasta, Maidu, Yurok, Karok, Wappo, Owens Valley Paiute, Pomo, Yuki and Juaneno.
32	12	Rather than being a "facetious excuse," this is one of many ritual beliefs about salmon, and Powers is reporting accurately the reason why the materials for the spearing booths are collected from the mountains each year. See Kroeber and Gifford, cited in note 10; and S. Swezey, *The Energetics of Subsistence-Assurrance Ritual in Native California*, Archaeological Research Facility, Contribution No. 23 (1975), pp. 1-46.
33	13	Since the picket fence enclosing graves was observed widely in northwestern California in 1849-1851, it is very unlikely that this is a feature learned from whites. See J. G. Bruff, *Gold Rush: the Journals, Drawings, and Other Papers of J. G. Bruff*, G. R. Read and R. Gaines, eds. (New York: Columbia University Press, 1949).
42	14	This "revelation" is a reference to the messianic Ghost Dance which originated among the Paviotso at Walker Lake, Nevada, and spread westward into California. See C. DuBois, *The 1870 Ghost Dance*, Anthropological Records 3:1 (1939).
44	15	The Yurok language has been studied and analyzed by R. H. Robins, *The Yurok Language*, University of California Publications in Linguistics 15 (1958).
49	16	Fishing practices and equipment are fully described in A. L. Kroeber and S. A. Barrett, *Fishing Among the Indians of Northwestern California*, Anthropological Records 21:1 (1960).

Page	Note Number	
57	17	The White Deerskin Dance is described by Kroeber, *Handbook*, chap. 3.
58	18	These sacred places are described by P. E. Goddard, "Wayside Shrines in Northwestern California," *American Anthropologist* 15 (1913):702-703.
59	19	For a fuller review of Yurok villages and population see Kroeber, *Handbook*, pp. 16-19. M. A. Baumhoff, *Ecological Determinants of Aboriginal California Populations*, University of California Publications in American Archaeology and Ethnology 49:2 (1963) deals with the relationship of native numbers in terms of "fish miles" of stream. (This series is cited hereafter as UCPAAE.)
66	20	A dead whale washed up on the beach was a welcome addition to the larder, and the coastal Yurok and Tolowa had strict regulations on who owned section of beach on which a whale might be thrown. See Kroeber and Barrett, cited in note 16, pp. 122-126.
67	21	The author refers here to the importance of possessing wealth in securing not only social status but also influence. Chiefs as such were not an institution in northwestern California. It was rich men who substituted for such civil officials.
69	22	This very large canoe is discussed by R. A. Gould, "Seagoing Canoes Among the Indians of Northwestern California," *Ethnohistory* 15 (1968):11-12. Despite Gould's proposal that canoes of this size were made in pre-white days, I am inclined to agree with Kroeber (*Handbook*, pp. 126-127) that they were made in response to the opportunity for carrying freight for the Americans to the ports at Crescent City and Eureka.
73	23	Hupa culture, territory, and towns are described by P. E. Goddard, *Life and Culture of the Hupa*, UCPAAE 1:1 (1903).
74	24	On native warfare in northwestern California see Kroeber, *Handbook*, pp. 49-52; Goddard, cited in note 23, pp. 62-63.
78	25	For a description of this Hupa dance see W. R. Goldschmidt and H. E. Driver, *The Hupa White Deerskin Dance; UCPAAE* 35:8 (1940).
79	26	Goddard, cited in note 23, discusses and illustrates these wealth items.

comes from the Hupa word meaning "distant" or "far off." Their land was the drainage of Yager Creek, Van Dusen Fork and Larrabee Creek, and the upper reaches of Mad River. See Baumhoff, cited in note 33, for their territory.

126   38   For the Yuki subgroups and culture see Kroeber, *Handbook*, chaps. 10-12, and G. M. Foster, *A Summary of Yuki Culture*, Anthropological Records 5:3 (1944).

127   39   The Yuki physical type, characterized by a very long and narrow head, broad nose and short stature is the most unusual of all Native Californians. See E. W. Gifford, "Californian Indian Physical Types," *Natural History* 26 (1926):50-60 [reprinted in R. F. Heizer and M. A. Whipple, eds., *The California Indians: a Sourcebook* (Berkeley: University of California Press, 1971), pp. 97-104)].

129   40   Omens of this sort were widely heeded among California Indians. The external world was thought to be full of malevolent spirits, and one avoided sickness or death or bad luck by recognizing omens and taking corrective measures.

132   41   Powers is noting the presence of male homosexuals. They are reported from nearly all tribes, but especially the Chumash and Mohave. The strong moral disapprobation of such individuals in our culture, which Powers reflects, was not held in the native societies.

133   42   The Yuki creator, Taikomol, is discussed by Kroeber, *Handbook*, chap. 12. See also A. L. Kroeber, "Yuki Myths," *Anthropos* 27 (1932):905-939.

133   43   Round Valley, the center of Yuki territory, was until 1850 quite beyond the zone of Spanish-Mexican influence. Corn-growing was introduced to the area with the establishment of the Nome Lackee Reservation in 1854.

139   44   The Huchnom are a major division of the Yuki.

140   45   It is not clear why the Pomo mixed the red clay in their acorn bread. Many ethnographers report the fact and give reasons such as improved taste, darker color, or better storability. Potter Valley is in Pomo territory.

145   46   For additional coyote tales see Kroeber, cited in note 42.

146   47   Pomo language classification is a complex subject. The first modern attempt at dialect differentiations was S. A.

Page	Note Number	
		Barrett, *The Ethnogeography of the Pomo and Neighboring Indians,* UCPAAE 40:2(1943). Barrett clarifies the problem of how many tribelet-dialect groups there were among the Pomo. R. Oswalt, "The Internal Relationships of the Pomo Family of Languages," *XXXV Congreso Internacional de Americanistas, Mexico, 1962* (1964): 413-421, provides the latest and most detailed statement on Pomo languages and their history.
147	48	Powers is correct: the Kastel Pomo are classed as Athabascan-speaking Wailaki.
150	49	Author is not correct. The so-called Kato Pomo are Athabascan-speaking and not Pomo. See P. E. Goddard, "The Kato Pomo not Pomo," *American Anthropologist 5 (1903):375-376.*
150	50	The "toxical principle" in buckeye nuts is prussic acid, which is readily volatilized by heat—usually provided in an earth oven such as described here.
151	51	This is a form of shinny. For a more detailed description see E. M. Loeb, *Pomo Folkways,* UCPAAE 19:2 (1926), pp. 217-218.
152	52	Both the Spanish missionaries and the Americans disapproved of cremation, though on different grounds. Many tribes changed from disposal of the dead by cremation to primary earth burial in response to this disapprobation by whites.
153	53	Studies of native education and child training are rare, but all support Powers' observation of leniency and lack of physical chastisement. Compare with W. J. Wallace, "Infancy and Childhood—a Study in Primitive Education," *Educational Administration and Supervision* (January, 1947): 13-25; G. A. Pettit, *Primitive Education in North America,* UCPAAE 43:1 (1946).
153	54	A good illustration of the intimate knowledge of tribal territory is in T. T. Waterman, *Yurok Geography,* UCPAAE 16:5 (1920).
154	55	No general study of native personal names has been made. For the Pomo see E. M. Loeb, cited in note 51, pp. 257-269. For Yokuts see A. L. Kroeber, "Yokuts Names," *Journal of American Folklore* 19 (1906):142-143.

Page	Note Number
155	56

Readers interested in identifying the Pomo tribelets listed here by Powers can consult S. A. Barrett, cited in note 47, and Kroeber, *Handbook*, pp. 973-995.

156   57   Despite this reputed Indian testimony on the great antiquity of wild oats *(Avena fatua, A. barbata)* in Pomo land, the several Pomo languages use the Spanish word "semilla" for this plant—a clear proof of its recent introduction.

157   58   Generally throughout California Indian societies the "peace chief" and "war chief" were different persons. Peace chiefs did not engage in battle but remained aloof so that they could arrange a truce, settlement, and peace. See S. R. James and S. Graziani, *California Indian Warfare*, University of California Archaeological Research Facility, Contribution No. 23 (1975), pp. 47-109.

158   59   This is an example of Powers' exaggeration. If the Pomo did have such loose morals it is more likely to have been one result of the degradation they suffered through preemption of their land and imposition of American rule. Some light is thrown on Pomo sexual attitudes in E. Colson, *Autobiographies of Three Pomo Women* (Berkeley: Archaeological Research Facility, 1974).

158   60   This male secret society did terrorize women, but this was not its chief purpose. See E. M. Loeb, *The Western Kuksu Cult*, UCPAAE 33:1 (1932).

159   61   These houses are described by S. A. Barrett, "Pomo Buildings," in *Seven Early Accounts of the Pomo Indians and Their Culture* (Berkeley: Archaeological Research Facility, 1975), pp. 37-63.

161   62   See note 7.

161   63   Belief in transmigration of souls into animals is widespread in California Indian cultures. Usually good souls are transformed into benevolent animals and bad ones into dangerous ones. See C. H. Merriam, "Transmigration in California," *Journal of American Folklore* 22 (1909): 433-434.

169   64   The arrangement of houses in rows, thus producing "streets," seems unusual, though such village layouts are reported for the Yokuts and the Chumash, and some

Yurok towns approach rows of houses (see T. T. Water-
man, *Yurok Geography*, UCPAAE 16:5 [1920]). This computation of original population based on archaeological
evidence is the first ever made in California. More recently
this method was used to estimate populations of tribes in
prehistoric times. See S. F. Cook and R. F. Heizer, "Relationships Among Houses, Settlement Areas, and Population in Aboriginal California," in *Settlement Archaeology*, ed. K. C. Chang (Palo Alto: National Press Books,
1968), pp. 79-116].

169   65   Loeb (cited in note 51, p. 246) reports "it does not appear
likely that the Pomo had any conception of child begetting
by the process of nature alone." He describes a series of
magical means to generate pregnancy.

172   66   The Watermelon Dance is presumably an adaptation or
transference of native ritual to an introduced food plant.
See note 43.

174   67   The Gallinomero are Southern Pomo. Kroeber (*Handbook*, p. 226) accepts Powers' suggestion that the label
from a chief with a Spanish name, Gallina.

175   68   Large multi-family houses are also reported for the
Chumash and the Yokuts.

175   69   This may have been how native existence appeared to
Powers in 1871, but it does not square with descriptions we
have of the aboriginal way of life. Under American domi-
nation there was not very much of the old busy life of hunting and collecting and carrying on the multitude of tasks
in a functioning society. Powers is describing the way of
life of a decimated, dispirited, and culturally excluded
remnant of a once larger and independent Native
California society.

178   70   Infanticide as a means of population control is reported
elsewhere for the Pomo. See B. Aginsky, "Population
Control Among the Shanel (Pomo) Tribe," *American
Sociological Review* 4 (1939):209-216.

178   71   The Pomo did fight, both among themselves on a tribelet-
to tribelet basis, and with other tribes that surrounded
them. See James and Graziani, cited in note 58; Kroeber,
Handbook, pp. 235-236; Loeb, cited in note 51, pp. 200-
211.

179   72   I have not found this dance described by the later ethnographers.

Page	Note Number	
181	73	Compare with note 57.

187   74

These baskets covered with brightly colored feathers represent the high point in California Indian basketmaking. See S. A. Barrett, *Pomo Indian Basketry*, UCPAAE 7:3 (1908), pp. 141-145; and F. G. Woodcock, "The Sun Basket," *Western Field* (December, 1907):339-341.

195   75

Author is referring to the Coast Miwok tribe. While many were missionized, pockets of survivors existed in Powers' time on the shores of Tomales and Bodega Bay. They are of some historical interest in being the tribe among whom Francis Drake summered in 1579. See R. F. Heizer, *Elizabethan California* (Ramona: Ballena Press, 1975).

197   76

Powers recognized one of the most interesting questions on California Indian ancient history. The Yuki, by reason of their distinctive language and physical type, were proposed by Kroeber (*Handbook*, p. 159) as "coming nearer, so far as can be judged at present, to being autochthonous Californians than any of the other modern natives of the State"—i.e. being the most ancient group still surviving. Opinions differ on this matter. For further discussion see R. F. Heizer, ed., *Archaeology of the Napa Region*, Anthropological Records 12:6 (1953), pp. 277-281.

205   77

There may be some connection between this imported style of dance house and the one used in the Down Ceremony described by Loeb (cited in note 51, pp. 387-391) as introduced from the east and performed in "a specially built earth-covered dancing house."

206   78

Powers is anticipating lexicostatistics, a method for calculating the time required for linguistic differentiation. See R. L. Oswalt, "The Internal Relationships of the Pomo Languages," *Actas y Memorias del XXXV Congreso Internacional de Americanistas, Mexico, 1962*, vol. 2 (1964): 413-428.

209   79

It may or may not be coincidence that just at this time the first Ghost Dance was being disseminated in northern California. See C. DuBois, *The 1870 Ghost Dance*, Anthropological Records 3:1 (1952).

214   80

Makhelchel in the Wintun name for the Southeastern or Lower Lake Pomo.

Page	Note Number	

216   81   This is the island and its village named koi. A. L. Kroeber, *The Patwin and Their Neighbors*, UCPAAE 29:4 (1932), gives a plan of the abandoned village in 1923.

219   82   The Patwin are treated in detail by Kroeber, cited in note 81. A map showing tribelet areas is contained in this work. C. H. Merriam, *Ethnographic Notes on California Indian Tribes*, University of California Archaeological Survey, Report No. 68, Part III (1967), pp. 257-281, has a detailed tribelet area map together with long lists of local groups and villages.

226   83   According to the tribe, this is a myth told about valleys which were filled with water in ancient times. A similar story is recounted about San Francisco Bay: it was originally a freshwater lake and became a saltwater bay after a great earthquake opened up the Golden Gate. The first published version of this tale known to me is in the *Report of the United States Exploring Expedition of 1839-42 Under Command of Lt. Charles Wilkes*. Powers is apparently quoting an informant from the village of Liwai near Winters. Writing in 1855, George Yount, *Chronicles of the West* (Denver: Old West Publishing Co., 1966), p. 163, gives this as an Indian account, as does Bayard Taylor, *Eldorado* (New York: Alfred A. Knopf, 1949), p. 13. Taylor apparently heard this story in 1849 and says it is an "Indian tradition of comparatively modern origin." J. W. Revere, *Naval Duty in California* (Oakland: Biobooks, 1947—first published in 1849), pp. 41-42, attributes the story to Costanoan Indians at Yerba Buena (i.e., San Francisco). Alexander S. Taylor in the *California Farmer* (a weekly newspaper) of December 7, 1860, and June 7, 1861, repeats it; and an author titling himself only H. B. D., in "Tradition of the California Indians," *Hesperian Magazine* 3 (1859): 326, tells the tale, which he says he got "from the lips of one of our most venerable pioneers."

234   84   Wintun salmon fishing is described by B. B. Redding, "Wintun Salmon Taking," *The Californian* (November 1881):242-245.

235   85   Girls' puberty rites are summarized in H. E. Driver, *Girls' Puberty Rites in Western North America*, Anthropological Records 6:2 (1941).

Page	Note Number	

243   86

For a later estimate of Shasta territory and villages see R. F. Heizer and T. R. Hester, *Shasta Villages and Territory*, Archaeological Research Facility, Contribution No. 9 (1970), pp. 119-158. The Shasta were studied early in the century by R. B. Dixon, "The Shasta," *Bulletin, American Museum of Natural History* 17 (1907):381-498, and most recently by C. Holt, *Shasta Ethnography*, Anthropological Records 3:4 (1946).

247   87

Redick McKee was one of the three federal treaty commissioners appointed by President Fillmore in 1851 to enter into treaties with the California Indians. Two detailed journals of McKee's treaty-making expedition to northern California exist, but in these there is no mention of this incident. Perhaps McKee did give Tolo the shirt off his back, but it is also possible that the story is pure fabrication.

248   88

For military reports on federal troop action against the Shasta in this period, see R. F. Heizer, *The Destruction of California Indians* (Salt Lake City: Peregrine-Smith, 1974), pp. 53-64.

250   89

It is reported for nearly all California tribes that persons dying far from home, on a war or trading expedition for example, would be cremated so the ashes could be returned to the natal village for burial. This is one of the most eloquent pieces of evidence of the deep attachment Native Californians had to their land, and of their desire for permanent occupation of this ground.

251   90

The extinction of the American horse occurred in the Pleistocene period. It is inconceivable that any Indian recollection of this phenomenon, even in myth, would have been preserved for 10,000 or more years.

253   91

For a statewide survey of face and body painting practices see J. Sherwin, *Face and Body Painting Practices Among California Indians*, Univeristy of California Archaeological Survey, Report No. 68 (1963): pp.81-140.

253   92

Canby and Thomas were trying to arrange peace with the Modocs and were killed during the negotiating session. This set off the Modoc War. See note 98.

254   93

There is a good deal of evidence that Modoc did make raids on the Achomawi and Atsugewi (Pit Rivers) to capture people whom they sold to the Oregon Klamath—who in turn took them to the great Indian market at The Dalles on the Columbia River.

255	95	Wokus (or Wocas) is a water lily. Its gathering and preparation are described in detail by F. V. Coville, "Wokas, a Primitive Food of the Klamath Indians," *Report of the U.S. National Museum for 1902* (1904): 727-739. Modoc material and social culture are described by V. F. Ray, *Primitive Pragmatists* (Seattle: University of Washington Press, 1963).
257	96	Artificial head deformation seems to have been practiced in California only by the Modoc. The custom is common further north along the Columbia River, especially among the Chinook tribe. It is assumed that the adoption of this trait is fairly recent rather than ancient, but only archaeology (not yet done) can answer the question.
260	97	This is clearly referring to the 1870 Ghost Dance which spread from Walker Lake, Nevada, where it originated. See C. DuBois, in note 79. Whether or not the Ghost Dance, which was anti-white in tone, was a causative factor in the Modoc War is uncertain.
261	98	Much has been written about the Modoc War. The most recent, and best, book on the subject is Richard Dillon, *Burnt Out Fires: California's Modoc War* (Englewood Cliffs: Prentice-Hall, 1973). Not all of Powers' opinions are supported by Dillon.
267	99	On native groups and their territories see F. Kniffen, *Achomawi Geography*, UCPAAE 23:5 (1928); C. Hart Merriam, "The Classification and Distribution of the Pit River Indian Tribes," *Smithsonian Institution Miscellaneous Collections* 78 (1927):1-52. Achomawi ethnohistory is summarized by E. Wheeler-Voegelin, "Pitt River Indians of California," *California Indians III* (New York: Garland Publishing Co., 1974).
268	100	Powers describes this country in "A Pony Ride on Pitt River," *Overland Monthly* 13 (1874):342-351.
271	101	One wonders what Powers would say about this aspect of American society today if he were still alive.

Page	Note Number	
272	102	Such a tale might have a factual basis in a recent, though pre-white, eruption. This myth is reminiscent of the Yokuts story of how the Sierra Nevadas and Coast Ranges were made, as detailed later in this volume (pp. 383-384).
275	103	The Nozi are better known as the Yana. It was from the southern dialect group, the Yahi, that the famous Ishi came. Yana culture is described by E. Sapir and L. Spier, *Notes on the Culture of the Yana*, Anthropological Records 3:3 (1943).
277	104	Powers should have known that the story was of no importance. There is no similarity between the Nozi (Yana) numbers and those of King Philip's tribe, the Wampanoag.
277	105	The Kombo are the Yahi (see note 103). The great mystery about them is probably due to the fact that they were a shy and small remnant. That the Yahi were not out-of-the-ordinary Native Californians is amply proved by the ethnographical data recorded from the last survivor, Ishi.
280	106	While it is true that the Yahi did use such a deerhead decoy, so did most other California tribes. An actual specimen from this tribe is illustrated in Kroeber, *Handbook* (Fig. 31) and is preserved in the Lowie Museum of Anthropology, University of California, Berkeley.
282	107	There is an abundance of ethnological recording on the Maidu, one of the largest and most widespread of the Sierran tribes. See R. B. Dixon, *The Northern Maidu*, Bulletin, American Museum of Natural History 17, no. 107 (1905), pp. 110-346; R. L. Beals, *Ethnology of the Nisenan*, UCPAAE 31:6 (1933).
284	108	For a survey of the reasons why native villages in California were abandoned see R. F. Heizer, "Village Shifts and Tribal Spreads in California Prehistory," *Southwest Museum Masterkey* 30 (1962):60-67.
285	109	The author is describing Indian life in the early seventies not more than twenty years after the onslaught of the Gold Rush. Populations were much reduced and much of their old territory was either laid to waste or kept from them. Their old way of life, the salmon, and deer were mostly gone. Really, all there was to do was try to survive, lie low, "drowse and mope" until death released them.

Page	Note Number	
285	110	This kind of duck net was used over most of Central California in aboriginal times. Duck decoys were also used generally in Central California.
285	111	Maidu ceremonies are detailed by Dixon (cited in note 107); E. M. Loeb, *The Eastern Kuksu Cult,* UCPAAE 33:2 (1933); and Kroeber, (cited in note 81).
288	112	For more of such tales see R. B. Dixon, *Maidu Myths,* Bulletin, American Museum of Natural History 17, no. 112 (1902), pp. 33-118.
306	113	In the 1860s and '70s many Maidu were taken from the Sierra region across the Sacramento Valley and placed under custody on Round Valley Reservation in Mendocino County. These reservations, which Kroeber described as little more than bull pens, were actually like concentration camps. With little or no care Indians died in them in great numbers. If they tried to escape they were tracked down by the soldiers in the military detachment assigned to each reservation. J. Ross Browne, "The Coast Rangers, II: The Indian Reservations," *Harper's Magazine* 23 (1861) :306-316, gives a true picture of what life in these places was like for the inmates.
311	114	Clowns or comic performers are known in many American Indian societies. They perform all sorts of outrageous and insulting acts which amuse the spectators at an otherwise serious and sacred performance. See J. H. Steward, "The Ceremonial Buffoon of the American Indian," *Papers of the Michigan Academy of Science, Arts and Letters* 14 (1931): 187-207.
313	115	The Nishenam (or as they are now called, Nisenan) are the southernmost Maidu. Their culture is described by Beals (cited in note 107) and A. L. Kroeber, *The Valley Nisenan,* UCPAAE 24:4 (1929).
316	116	Malaria was introduced by Hudson Bay Company trappers in the early 1830s. It struck hard for a few years at the tribes of the Sacramento and San Joaquin Valleys and then apparently subsided to a low level. See S. F. Cook, *The Epidemic of 1830-1833 in California and Oregon,* UCPAAE 43:3 (1955).
319	117	See note 89.
322	118	No record of this has been preserved in the ethnographic accounts. If true, it may have been an abortive effort at

organizing resistance to the whites. Surely Indians must have dreamed of organizing against the people who had taken their lands, but they must have realized they would have had little hope of success.

323   119   Here is an eyewitness description of how Sutter fed his Indian help at Sutter's Fort in 1846: "The Capt. [Sutter] keeps 600 or 800 Indians in a complete state of Slavery and I had the mortification of seeing them dine. I may give a short description. 10 or 15 Troughs 3 or 4 feet long were brought out of the cook room and seated in the Broiling sun all the labourers grate and small ran to the troughs like so many pigs and feed themselves with their hands as long as the troughs contain even a moisture." (J. Clyman, *James Clyman, American Frontiersman, 1792-1881* (San Francisco: California Historical Society, 1928) pp. 173-174.)

325   120   The Yokuts to the south also held a rattlesnake dance for the same purpose. See Kroeber, *Handbook*, pp. 504-506.

329   121   The Maidu Annual Mourning Ceremony where male and female images and property were offered in honor of those who died in the preceding year is vividly described by Dixon (cited in note 107).

333   122   California Indian games for gambling and sport are summarized in Kroeber, *Handbook*, pp. 846-850.

334   123   Ventriloquism as a device for impressing the audience is reported elsewhere for shamanistic performances in California.

335   124   Here, and elsewhere in this book, we hear reports of U.S. specie as well as native artifacts used as currency. Probably the shaman accepted the twenty arrows because he could peddle them to white collectors for $15.00.

336   125   See note 3.

337   126   R. E. C. Stearns was a serious student of this subject. See his "Ethnoconchology," *Report of the U.S. National Museum for 1887* (1889):297-334, and "Shell Money," *American Naturalist* 3 (1869):1-5. The "ul-lo" or "aulo" is the abalone with its irridescent shell.

338   127   The "kolkol" is a white chalk-like mineral (magnesite) which assumes a salmon color when it is roasted in ashes. The Pomo had great deposits of this in their territory and seem to have been the main manufacturers and purveyors

Page	Note Number	
		of this valuable item, often referred to as "Indian gold" in Central California.
341	128	This is one of the most common myths among native Californians—that of the origin of death. In the beginning, as in Genesis, the world was perfect and life was eternal. But there followed the institution of death, so that all men must die rather than live forever. This is somewhat different from original sin, but philosophically it is the same.
343	129	Nearly every California Indian tribe whose myths have been recorded tells a variant of the story of how fire was secured in ancient times for the benefit of man.
344	130	Apparently, in later prehistoric times, the shaping of bowl mortars was given up—perhaps because the hopper mortar (described and depicted in this volume) or the bedrock mortar was simpler or more efficient to use. The abundance of ancient stone portable mortars, whose manufacture was a mystery to the Indians who found (and used) them gave rise to the mythological origin of these antiquities. See Dixon, cited in note 107.
352	131	Powers seems to have been correct: the California Indians never did form a coalition or confederacy of tribes to fight their oppressors—either under the regime of the Franciscan missions from 1769 to 1834, or under the Mexicans from 1821 to 1846, or under the Americans from 1846 on. The probable reason is their long history of territoriality and independence—a way of life which had become so ingrained that they seem to have been incapable of surmounting their feelings of suspicion about neighbors.
353	132	Old Sam may have been a person who believed that survival lay in accommodation and not conflict. If so, he may have advocated abandoning unusual practices which the dominant whites interpreted as savage or uncivilized.
353	133	Taipoksi may have been thinking along the same lines as Old Sam (note 132), except he realized that accommodation meant playing the white man's game by collecting gold and selling it for the items of "civilized luxury." What we see here is one facet of the acculturation process— the accommodation which the Indians absolutely had to make in order to survive. Many remnant groups retreated to

Page	Note Number	

areas where whites would not go because there was nothing there they wanted, and thus survived by eking out a miserable existence gathering acorns, fishing, collecting seeds and hunting.

355   134   Powers' phrase "where they will not be disturbed by intruders" is probably significant. Even as late as the 1870s whites were likely to be disturbed by large gatherings of Indians because the memory of hostilities remained. For the oppressed Indians the opportunity to have a good time must have been an occasion of retrospection, release, and pure enjoyment—a truly nostalgic experience of living the way they did before the whites arrived to take their lands and decimate their people. It is nice to believe that Powers was correct in describing these occasions as "a world of riotous enjoyment the California Indians will compress into a week."

355   135   See Driver, cited in note 85.

357   136   This appears to be direct Indian testimony to a geological phenomenon happening within the memory of a living Indian.

358   137   We must not ignore the fact that evaluations of "impurity" or "dirt" depend to no small degree on the social attitudes of the individual making judgments or those of his society as a whole.

361   138   C. Hart Merriam, "Indian Village and Camp Sites in Yosemite Valley," *Sierra Club Bulletin* 10 (1917):202-209, provides a thorough review of the names and locations of these sites.

362   139   Place names of Indian origin in California have never been collected and published in their entirety. A. L. Kroeber, *California Place Names of Indian Origin*, UCPAAE 12:2 (1916), offers a substantial contribution (see also Kroeber, *Handbook*, chap. 58). E. R. Gudde, *California Place Names*, (Berkeley: University of California Press, 1949— and later editions), incorporates these and adds more names.

365   140   See note 138.

366   141   Other Yosemite Miwok myths have been recorded. See, for example, E. W. Gifford, *Miwok Myths*, UCPAAE 12:8 (1917).

Page	Note Number	
383	151	Compare with reference cited in note 18. Kroeber (*Handbook*, p. 499) says that Yaudanchi and Yauelmani Yokuts cremated the body of a man dying far from home and brought his ashes back—a practice widely reported in California. (See note 89.)
384	152	This is an example of the "sand maps" which Indians in the Far West are reported to have drawn. See R. F. Heizer, *Aboriginal California and Great Basin Cartography*, University of California Archaeological Survey, Report No. 41 (1958), pp. 1-9.
384	153	This is the Annual Mourning Ceremony known generally in Southern California and in the Sierra Nevada region. Kroeber (*Handbook*, pp. 499-501) and Gayton (both references cited in note 144) also give detailed accounts of this ritual.
387	154	The tobacco, a wild variety (*Nicotiana sp*), was pulverized, mixed with lime, and swallowed to cause vomiting, an act of purification. For details see Gayton (both references cited in note 144) and E. Voegelin, *Tubatulabal Ethnography*, Anthropological Records 2:1 (1938), pp. 36-38.
391	155	Kroeber (*Handbook*, pp. 478-479) shows that the supposed survivor was a Yauelmani or Hometwoli Yokuts who had earlier been in a mission where he had learned some of the Salinan tongue. The numerals given by Powers are Salinan in origin but converted to Yokuts puns. The man used to reel off this list of word to amuse his friends. It seems to be a genuine example of Indian humor.
393	156	Kroeber (*Handbook*, chap. 32 and plate 47) identifies and shows the location of these groups. See also Gayton (cited in note 144, map 1); and F. F. Latta, *Handbook of Yokuts Indians* (Bakersfield: Kern County Museum, 1949). The Palligawonap are a subdivision of the tribe called Tubatulabal. (See Voegelin, cited in note 54, p. 9.)
393	157	This may be a recollection of the malaria epidemic of the early 1830s. See note 116.
394	158	The suggestion of territorial invasion is probably the first such for California based on archaeological evidence.
394	159	These tule canoes ("balsas") are described by Latta (cited in note 156) and Kroeber (*Handbook*, p. 531). For a general survey of native Californian watercraft see R. F. Heizer

and W. C. Massey, "Aboriginal Navigation Off the Coasts of Upper and Baja California," *Bureau of American Ethnology Bulletin* 151 (1953): 285-312.

395   160   This seems a fair match for *Genesis.*

395   161   An etiological belief connected with astronomical observations of a simple order.

395   162   Many Yokuts and neighboring Western Mono (Monache) myths are presented by A. Gayton and S. Newman, *Yokuts and Western Mono Myths,* Anthropological Records 5 (1940), p. 1.

397   163   In general Powers is correct. See A. L. Kroeber, cited in note 142.

398   164   This is probably a ritual connected with the totemic moiety system. For details see E. W. Gifford, *Miwok Moieties,* UCPAAE 12:4 (1916); A. H. Gayton, "Yokuts and Western Mono Social Organization," *American Anthropologist* 47 (1945):409-426.

398   165   This is the forerunner of the Save the Redwoods League. Unfortunately, neither seems to have been effective in preserving these unique trees *(Sequoia).*

399   166   For Tahichapannah read Tehachapi. See Kroeber, *Handbook,* p. 602.

400   167   This brief and eloquent statement by Powers is the truth. For supporting evidence see S. F. Cook, *The Conflict Between the California Indians and White Civilization: I, The American Invasion,* University of California Publications in Ibero-Americana 23 (1943); R. F. Heizer, *They Were Only Diggers.* Ballena Press Publications in Archaeology, Ethnology and History, No. 1 (1974); R. F. Heizer, *The Destruction of California Indians* (Salt Lake City: Peregrine-Smith, 1974).

401   169   It is a fact that most Native Californians listed in a census of landless Indians taken seventy years ago by C. E. Kelsey [*Census of Non-Reservation California Indians, 1905-1906,* (Berkeley: Archaeological Research Facility, 1971)] have Anglo-American names. Whether all of the family names thus assumed were from "prominent" pioneers is doubtful, if only on the grounds that there were not that many prominent persons.

Page	Note Number	
401	170	On the meaning and source of names of California tribes see R. F. Heizer, *Languages, Territories and Names of California Indian Tribes* (Berkeley: University of California Press, 1966). Kroeber, (*Handbook*, check list on pp. 973-975) also provides this information.
402	171	This statement should not require refutation, but at the same time it cannot be ignored. It is either a bit of Powers' literary exuberance or very bad science—perhaps both.
402	172	On the physical characteristics of California Indians see E. W. Gifford, *Californian Anthropometry*, UCPAAE 22:2 (1926); Gifford, "Californian Indian Types," *Natural History* 26 (1926): 50-60; and F. Boas, *Anthropometry of Central California*, Bulletin, American Museum of Natural History 17 (1905) pp. 347-380. Data on physical strength is analyzed by R. F. Heizer and C. Treanor, *Observations on Physical Strength of Some Western Indians and "Old American" Whites*, Archaeological Research Facility, Contribution No. 22 (1974), pp. 47-57.
404	173	See source cited in note 58.
404	174	Whether it was the "best blood of the nation" that came to California in the Gold Rush is very much to be doubted. G. F. Parson, *The Life and Adventures of James W. Marshall* (Sacramento: Marshall and Burke, 1870) gives the following assessment in the biography of the man who discovered gold on January 24, 1848 at Coloma: "Take a sprinkling of sober-eyed, earnest, shrewd, energetic, New-England-business-men; mingle with them a number of rollicking sailors, a dark band of Australian convicts and cut-throats, a dash of Mexican and frontier desperadoes, a group of hardy backwoodsmen, some professional gamblers, whiskey-dealers, general swindlers . . . and having thrown in a promiscuous crowd of broken-down merchants, disappointed lovers, black sheep, unfledged dry-goods clerks, professional miners from all parts of the world, and Adullamites generally, stir up the mixture, season strongly with gold-fever, bad liquors, faro, monte, rouge-et-noir, quarrels, oaths, pistols, knives, dancing, and digging, and you have something approximating California society in early days."

And Hugo Reid, one of the 1849 California Constitutional delegates wrote: "Don't go to the mines on any account. They are loaded to the muzzle with vagabonds from every quarter of the globe, scoundrels from nowhere, rascals from Oregon, pickpockets from New York, accomplished gentlemen from Europe, interlopers from Lima and Chile, Mexican thieves, gamblers of no particular spot, and assassins manufactured in Hell for the express purpose of converting highways and byways into theaters of blood; then, last but not least, Judge Lynch with his thousand arms, thousand sightless eyes, and five-hundred lying tongues."

405	175	For an account of fighting among some of these chiefs and the Mexicans in the area north of San Francisco Bay see M. L. Lothrop, "The Indian Campaigns of General M. G. Vallejo," *Quarterly of the Society of California Pioneers* 9 (1932):161-205.
406	176	For a statewide survey see N. C. Willoughby, cited in note 6.
406	177	Powers is correct in pointing out that confederations or political alliances did not exist in Native Californian societies. Independent tribal units were the rule, and without strong leaders and the impulse or need to create a State, "powerful federative governments" did not develop. Although there was some intertribal fighting, and some groups were traditionally unfriendly, large scale warfare was unknown. By and large the California Indians were peaceable people, and it could be argued that they realized it was better to live in that manner than in a world of fear and alarm and fighting. See note 131.
408	178	Native Californian songs are often quite evocative poetry, even though not composed as such. Powers himself gives some examples in this book. See also D. Demetracopoulou, "Wintu Songs," *Anthropos* 30 (1935): 483-494.
410	179	Powers ignores the fact, in criticizing the Indians as "great thieves" that the Americans stole the Indian's land—took it by force and without compensation.
411	180	It should be remembered that the American was armed and more than ready to shoot down any Indian who might

challenge him, even as late as the 1870s when Powers wrote this. The main slaughter of California Indians was by now largely over, but between 1848 and 1870 from 50,000 to 70,000 Indians were killed in the state. (See references cited in note 167.) The demographic history of the California Indians is summarized in S. F. Cook, *California Indian Population, 1770-1970* (Berkeley: University of California Press, 1976).

411   181   If Powers were alive in 1976 and watched television or read the daily newspapers he might have been less scandalized by the incident he recites here.

412   182   Powers is reflecting American morality of the 1870s. Again, he could scarcely have penned these lines a century later.

413   183   Surely there was some Indian prostitution, but it was probably less a question of morality than one of somehow getting enough money to stay alive.

413   184   See note 7.

413   185   There are various creation myths. See A. Gayton, "Areal Affiliations of California Folktales," *American Anthropologist* 37 (1935):582-599. E. W. Gifford and G. H. Block, *California Indian Nights Entertainment* (Glendale: Arthur H. Clark, 1930).

416   186   Powers, in a similar calculation, came up with a total population figure of 1,520,000. ["The Northern California Indians, No. V (The Yuki)," *Overland Monthly* 9 (1872): 305-313] J. W. Powell, who arranged for the publication of the present volume, thought the figure of one-and-a-half million California Indians was far too high, and presumably at his urging Powers reduced that estimate to 705,000 as given here. Powell wanted an even smaller number, but Powers flatly refused to reduce it further. On November 3, 1876, Powers wrote to Powell as follows: "I have waded too many rivers and climbed too many mountains to abate one jot of my opinions or beliefs for any carpet-knight who wields a compiling-pen in the office of the __ or __ [sic]. If any critic, sitting in his comfortable parlor in New York, and reading about the sparse aboriginal populations of the cold forests of the Atlantic States, can overthrow any of my

conclusions with a dash of his pen, what is the use of the book at all?" S. F. Cook (cited in note 180) concludes that when the Spanish first settled in 1769 there were from 300,000 to 350,000 Indians in the State of California.

416   187   More data on physical strength and endurance are given in Heizer and Treanor, cited in note 172.

417   188   See reference note in 116 for details of the malaria pandemic of the early 1830s. This disease may have completely eradicated some tribelets, and vacant territories might then have been occupied by other groups. Though no record of such territorial shifts was ever made, either by on-the-spot observers or by later ethnographers, this theory could account for some of the tribal boundary lines recorded by ethnographers—lines which may have looked rather different in the decades preceding the epidemic.

417   189   Many long-occupied village sites are in the form of mounds, sometimes very massive and rising to heights of twenty feet. None of the excavations made in these has produced any evidence that they were artificially built; but rather, they seem to be the result of gradual accumulation of refuse.

419   190   On the contrary, there are highly detailed systems of native classification of plants and animals. Only recently, with the development of what is termed "ethnoscience," have these systems become recognized. The details of folk classification among California Indians was never investigated, and it is now too late to attempt it because the knowledge is lost. See B. Berlin, D. E. Breedlove and P. H. Raven, "General Principles of Classification Nomenclature in Folk Biology," *American Anthropologist* 73 (1973):214-242.

419   191   Powers is absolutely correct in saying this. C. Hart Merriam, a most competent naturalist with an interest in California Indians, recorded between 1901 and 1935 the native names of several hundred plants and animals from over fifty tribes. It is most impressive to see in these how many plant and animal names were provided by a single person. Such knowledge seems to have been the rule rather than the exception.

420   192   The information in this chapter is the earliest published
body of native California ethnobotanical knowledge—
another first for Powers.

421   193   This is a brief description of the acorn preparation process.
A survey article covering the variations of acorn processing
in California is E. W. Gifford, "California Balanophgy,"
Essays in Anthropology Presented to A. L. Kroeber (Berkeley: University of California Press, 1936), pp. 87-98.

421   194   California Indians were fairly strict conservationists of
plants and animals, because their survival depended on
these being available. See R. F. Heizer, "Primitive Man as
an Ecological Factor," *Kroeber Anthropological Society
Papers* No. 13 (1956):1-31.

422   195   For more details see R. E. Merrill, *Plants Used in Basketry
by the California Indians,* UCPAAE 20 (1923), pp. 215-242.

422   196   Considerable inquiry was made of Indians about whether
they were immune to poison oak and what remedies they
had for its unpleasant effects. It seems that Indians were
just as susceptible as whites, and they knew of no effective
remedy to relieve the itching.

423   197   See R. F. Heizer, "The Use of Plants for Fish-poisoning by
the California Indians," *Leaflets in Western Botany* 3
(1941):43-44.

423   198   Soaproot *(Chlorogalum pomeridianum)* contains a poisonous saponin. This principle can be removed by leach-
ing or application of heat as in an earth oven. Buckeyes
(Aesculus californicus) contain prussic acid, which can be
removed in the same ways. After removal of these consti-
tuents both are nutritious foods.

424   199   There is much written about poisoners and poisoning.
Most, perhaps all, is ritual or magical poisoning. For
details see L. S. Freeland, *Pomo Doctors and Poisoners,*
UCPAAE 20 (1923); pp. 57-73; E. Colson, *Autobiographies
of Three Pomo Women,* (Berkeley: Archaeological Research Facility, 1974).

426   200   Tobacco species used and tobacco-taking practices are
summarized in A. L. Kroeber, *Salt, Dogs, and Tobacco,*
Anthropological Records 6:1 (1941).

Page	Note Number	
426	201	A richly detailed account of tobacco growing and uses in one Klamath River tribe is J. P. Harrington, *Tobacco Among the Karuk Indians,* Bureau of American Ethnology, Bulletin 94 (1932).
431	202	*Mytilus* is the ocean mussel, not a clam.
432	203	We might call this Powers' "degeneration theory"— unfounded but of interest in being one of the earliest attempts to treat the subject of California archaeology. It is quite true that in some parts of the state the shaped globular stone mortar had been given up by the time of European discovery, and the flat hopper-mortar came to replace it. The latter may be simpler to make—though equally efficient—but it can scarcely be called "degenerated."
437	204	This is the Annual Mourning Ceremony once again. (See note 153.)

INDEX

INDEX

Printed in the United States
35784LVS00003B/31-51